THE FENIANS

The Fenians

Irish Rebellion in the North Atlantic World, 1858–1876

Patrick Steward and Bryan McGovern

THE UNIVERSITY OF TENNESSEE PRESS / KNOXVILLE

ubp

The paper in this book meets the requirements of American National Standards Institute / National Information Standards Organization specification Z39.48-1992 (Permanence of Paper). It contains 30 percent post-consumer waste and is certified by the Forest Stewardship Council.

Library of Congress Cataloging-in-Publication Data

Steward, Patrick.
The Fenians: Irish rebellion in the North Atlantic world, 1858–1876 / Patrick Steward and Bryan McGovern. — 1st ed.
          p. cm.
Originally presented as the authors' thesis under title: Erin's Hope.
Includes bibliographical references and index.
ISBN 978-1-57233-919-4 (hardcover) — ISBN 1-57233-919-5 (hardcover)
  1. Fenians—History.
  2. Ireland—History—1837–1901.
  3. Nationalism—Ireland—History—19th century.
  4. Irish Americans—Politics and government—19th century.
  I. McGovern, Bryan P.
  II. Title.

DA954.S74 2013
941.5081—dc23
                    2012026780

CONTENTS

ILLUSTRATIONS

ACKNOWLEDGMENTS

The authors express their gratitude to several individuals who played critical roles in the publication of *The Fenians*. This work began as a master's thesis entitled *Green Americans* and evolved into a dissertation called *Erin's Hope* before it was presented to the University of Tennessee Press in its current format. *Green Americans* would not be somewhere in the Tisch Library stacks at Tufts University today without tremendous guidance from Professor John Brooke, now of The Ohio State University. *Erin's Hope*, likewise, would have never been microfilmed for inclusion in the University of Michigan's dissertation repository without three years of vigilant critique by Professor Kerby Miller. Professor Miller served as graduate advisor to both authors when they were PhD students at the University of Missouri. His influence is evident throughout this work and throughout Bryan McGovern's previous publication, *John Mitchell: Irish Nationalist, Southern Secessionist*.

The initial research for this book began before the advent of email and internet archive catalogs. Accordingly, content for *Green Americans* was largely collected through interlibrary loan and phone calls to friends in distant cities who generously offered to photocopy and mail noncirculating sources to Patrick. Patrick is particularly grateful to the following individuals: William Amberg, Tim Bromelkamp, James Caparas, Randy Ebertowski, Cheto Navarro, and Patrick Montgomery. Patrick also re-extends his thanks to everyone who provided assistance during the writing of *Erin's Hope*: Patrick Brennan, R. V. Comerford, Richard Robbins, Catherine Steward, Connie Steward, the late Jack Steward, and Lauren Zadnik (now Lauren Kessinger). In particular, Patrick deeply appreciates the tireless editing efforts of his father, John Steward.

Patrick dedicates this work to his wife, Patricia, and to his daughter, Kayleigh. Kayleigh was born shortly before *The Fenians* was approved for publication and

Patrick wrote these acknowledgements on his laptop while four-month-old Kayleigh was on his shoulder with a mild case of the hiccups.

Bryan would like to dedicate this book to his wife, Janet, and his two sons, Brennon and Padraig. He would also like to thank his good friend and coauthor for allowing him the opportunity to work with him in revising his excellent dissertation for publication.

INTRODUCTION

The history of Irish physical-force republicanism—the desire for complete separation from Great Britain and the willingness to use violence to achieve it—is as old as the late eighteenth century, when the United Irishmen rebelled against British imperialism. Led mostly by middle-class Protestants, but supported by Catholic groups like the Defenders, the rebellion began in 1798 in what is now Northern Ireland, and eventually spread to the southeast and the far west. The United Irishmen failed due to a lack of coordination, and their cause was further hindered by the rebellion in Wexford descending into sectarianism. The republican tradition of the United Irishmen continued throughout the nineteenth and twentieth centuries, as Irish republicans took up arms against Great Britain in 1848, 1867, 1916, and 1919. The 1919 rebellion led to the creation of the semi-autonomous Irish Free State, but in 1921 Great Britain partitioned six mostly Protestant counties in Ulster, thus creating Northern Ireland. The new state remained part of the United Kingdom, and its leaders denied the Catholic population in Northern Ireland certain rights and privileges.

Since the 1960s, this form of republicanism, associated with militant organizations such as the Provisional Irish Republican Army and its various splinter groups, which are made up almost solely of Catholics, persists in its aspiration to drive the British out of Northern Ireland. The violence perpetuated by all sides (republicans, Orange Loyalists, and British officials) during the Troubles has been devastating, as the weaponry has become more sophisticated and the violence more random. Most Americans, even those unfamiliar with Irish history and politics, are aware of the recent history of the terroristic bombings by the IRA. Americans, however, are less familiar with the role that Irish Americans have played in supporting the IRA with money and weapons. Although the Good

Friday Agreement of 1998 brought a plan for peace to Northern Ireland, violence continues to plague Northern Ireland, especially during marching season in the summer when loyalists, to demonstrate their supposed superiority, march through Catholic neighborhoods. Physical-force republicanism has wrought terrible destruction, indeed; but Irish republicanism has been a response to British colonial oppression. To better understand its origins, we need to better understand its history. One such antecedent was the Irish Republican Brotherhood, also known as the Fenians.

In July of 1848, a group of middle-class intellectuals started a revolution to overthrow British rule in Ireland. As famine devastated the country, a number of well-educated, prosperous gentlemen, who had earlier formed the cultural nationalist organization known as Young Ireland in order to support Daniel O'Connell's peaceful call for repeal of the Act of Union, had come to the conclusion that physical force was necessary to save Ireland. O'Connell, known as "The Liberator" for his role in winning Catholic Emancipation in 1829, had opposed the Act of Union, which made Ireland part of the United Kingdom. Young Irelanders, however, became disenchanted with O'Connell's passive form of constitutional nationalism and his assertion that Ireland should abide by the British constitution while opposing English colonization. After O'Connell's death in 1847, and as the Famine grew worse, many Young Irelanders came to agree with John Mitchel that revolution was the only solution to Ireland's woes. Led by the landed Protestant William Smith O'Brien, the group made an infamous stand at Widow McCormick's farmhouse in Ballingarry, County Tipperary. The revolution was a dismal failure, and most of its leaders were soon arrested. Two of the men who took part that day, James Stephens and John O'Mahony, escaped arrest and made their way to Paris.

While in Paris, the two expatriate rebels conspired to create a more popular and formidable organization, and in 1858, Stephens and O'Mahony, who had subsequently made his way to America, respectively created the Irish Republican Brotherhood in Ireland and the Fenian Brotherhood in the United States. The Fenians, as members of this transatlantic society came to be known, were radical republicans who called for Irish independence from British imperialism as a means to resolve the island's political and social afflictions. Imbued with violent rhetoric that emanated from survivors of the Great Famine, Fenians insisted that physical force was the only way to eradicate British tyranny and oppression. The organization grew stronger, particularly in the United States after the Civil War, as thousands of Irish Americans believed that their martial skills could be effectively utilized to establish an independent Irish nation. The growth of the organization, mostly led by Irish Americans, would eventually culminate in three separate invasions of Canada from the United States, as well as a formidable but failed uprising in Ireland in 1867.

In order to understand Fenianism, we must first examine the beliefs of the group known as Young Ireland, how Fenianism descended from the cultural and intellectual movement of the 1840s, and how it was both similar and different. Stephens and O'Mahony first demonstrated their nationalist tendencies by partaking in the rebellion of 1848, as both men were attracted to the radical teachings of John Mitchel, an Ulster Presbyterian who called for military and social revolution as a means of expunging both British tyranny and the landlord class from Ireland. Although the patrician O'Brien steered the organization toward rebellion by the summer of 1848, Young Ireland had been a mostly middle-class bourgeois intellectual movement that promoted the Gaelic culture and more conservative and constitutional forms of nationalism. Young Ireland leaders, like Charles Gavan Duffy, opposed Mitchel's extremism at every turn, and revolution only became a gentlemanly last gasp after British repression threatened to destroy the group's leadership.

In many ways, Fenianism was a response to the inherent conservatism of Young Ireland's leadership. Stephens, O'Mahony, and the rest of the leadership advocated transatlantic cooperation, secret conspiracy, and physical rebellion to create an independent democratic republic in Ireland. Unlike the ecumenical Young Irelanders, which included both Protestants and Catholics, the IRB was mostly Catholic. The members tended to be lower-middle-class as opposed to educated intellectuals, and its base was focused more on Irish independence and social mobility than on cultural and intellectual pursuits.

The Fenians have often been ridiculed as hopeless fanatics who held irrational romantic notions of achieving the impossible: independence from the strongest military power in the world. Some historians have considered them dangerous terrorists, capable of mayhem and murder; other historians have accused the Fenians of using the organization as a networking society to help them achieve prosperity, status, and camaraderie in an ever-changing world. Given that many of these Fenians were immigrants, it easy to assume that the group offered stability and comfort in an alien world. But, if one looks at the rhetoric and the actions of many Fenians, one may clearly see that their reasons for joining were far more complex—and their chances of success far less hopeless—than many historians have maintained. Furthermore, while undoubtedly there was a social aspect to joining the organization, there also existed a legitimate desire to fight for Irish independence.

The Famine, more than any event, can explain why a number of Irishmen and women embraced Fenianism. The psychological scars borne by survivors of what the Irish called the *an Gorta Mór*, or the Great Hunger, imbued the Irish people with a disdain for British imperialism. Some Irish writers, like John Mitchel, went so far as to assert that the British government purposefully utilized the potato blight to implement policies of genocide and forced emigration to eradicate the Irish people from their land. Although it affected the growth of the agrarian middle class in Ireland, the Famine also resulted in over a million deaths, along with another million and a half who emigrated. These famine emigrants, particularly those who landed in the United States, held a particular contempt for the British government because many had not only lost friends and family to hunger and disease, but they had also held the political leaders in London responsible for their forced exile from their homeland.

Irish Americans latched particularly on to the genocide thesis and the exile motif and, in an environment of relative political freedom in the United States, made up the lion's share of the militaristic organization. While severe British law and government espionage in Ireland precluded effective militarization there, American laws were more liberal, allowing Irish nationalist groups to train for rebellion back home. Antebellum nationalist groups like the Irishmen's Civil and Military Republican Union and the Emmet Monument Association attempted to foment revolution in Ireland long before the creation of the IRB. These organizations were social as well as militaristic, but they were not much of a threat to British suzerainty. The Civil War, however, provided Irishmen the training and expertise they needed to cause potential havoc.

It is also important to understand Fenian ideology within the context of nationalist sentiment throughout the Western world during the mid-nineteenth century. The rise of romanticism and state governmental structures led to the establishment of various nationalist movements in France, Italy, Germany, and the United States. Young Ireland fashioned itself as an Irish version of a similar movement of lawyers and journalists in Italy and France; indeed, the 1848 summer rebellion in County Tipperary attempted to mimic the French revolution that had taken place earlier that spring. This global expansion of nationalist movements resulted from the rise of industrialism and the creation of modern states, often taking on more violent and racial connotations, which eventually led to the use of civilian or paramilitary force. In the United States, the escalation of Southern nationalism during the 1850s and 1860s, which led to secession by the Confederate states, and the increase of nationalist fervor in the North demonstrated that two variants of nationalist sentiment could coincide until force became inevitable. The same was true in Ireland during the nineteenth century as nationalists and unionists clashed over the future of Ireland. Fenianism would become associated with Irish nationalism throughout the late nineteenth and twentieth centuries, particularly a Catholic form of Irish nationalism, and its genesis would precede nationalist groups like the Irish Republican Army.

Still, in order to generate the money and weapons necessary for success, Irish Fenians needed to rely on their American cousins. Irish historian Sean Cronin has asserted that the Fenian movement, despite its transatlantic genesis, "was a product of the Irish in America." Whereas previous Irish nationalist movements had typically reflected and looked to a French political model for inspiration, the Fenians imitated the American form of republicanism, based on more conservative and less ideological notions of free-market capitalism and democratic ideals. The Fenian leadership in the United States viewed itself as a government in exile that would assume control of Irish politics after a successful revolution to root out the British government, which they viewed as the source of Irish economic, political, and social problems. The Fenians were made up mostly of Catholics but could never be considered a Catholic movement, because many of its leaders were anticlerical and called for the separation of church and state in Ireland, similar to the United States.[1]

Fenianism needed to be centered overseas because it could not operate within the constructs of British imperialist structures in Ireland. The British government passed laws preventing the freedom of speech and assembly in Ireland, and its desire to destroy Fenianism provided British authorities with the wherewithal to use whatever mechanisms necessary. The fact that Fenianism never became as prevalent within the Irish expatriate community in England perhaps demonstrates the ability of the British government to resist it; still, Fenianism became popular in other Irish communities throughout the world, including Australia. However, Fenianism became especially strong in the United States, where militant Irish nationalists leaders took advantage of American laws and the American political system. Still, despite a relatively lenient social and political environment in the United States, Fenians became overly reliant on governmental promises that were never kept.

Fenianism represented what Matthew Frye Jacobson has termed "the diasporic imagination." Although the Fenian organization may have been American in nature with American-like goals, Fenians felt a deep allegiance to Ireland, mostly due to an Irish American "political culture based on ideas of injury and displacement."[2] Nineteenth-century Irish immigrants embraced an exile motif that configured them as victims of British tyranny and, in more extreme arguments, as survivors of British genocide, which had forced them to emigrate from their homeland. Fenians believed that the only resolution to such British tyranny was independence through military strength. They came to realize that the British government, which had attempted to appease nationalists throughout the eighteenth and nineteenth centuries with piecemeal reforms that were often insufficient, would only abdicate control of Ireland via force.

We must also consider the impact of the American environment on Irish American Fenianism. Expatriates faced a hostile nativist population in the United States, and Irish nationalism provided them a chance to assert their ethnic identity while demonstrating their republican bona fides, and to demonstrate that Irish Catholic stereotypes were erroneous and unfair. As Thomas Brown argues, nationalism became an avenue for achievement and acceptance in American society.[3] Fenianism provided Irish Americans the ability to fight for independence back home while asserting their independence from the Catholic clergy and monarchical governments.

There is little doubt that a lack of effective leadership and internal division also damaged Fenian hopes in the 1860s, but British intrigue and harsh laws responding to Fenian activities, along with the duplicity of the American government, were just as harmful. The Fenian invasions of Canada, partially prompted by the alleged agreement by the United States government to remain neutral in the event of a cross-border raid, was halted when the police arrested a number of the invading Fenians. Irish nationalists believed they had struck an agreement with Secretary of State William Seward and President Andrew Johnson, who during a midterm election year were vying for the Irish vote. The Fenians soon discovered that they had been betrayed by the president and his administration.

Several other factors prevented the intercontinental, Irish nationalist Fenian movement from attracting enough public support to secure Irish independence from Great Britain during the mid-nineteenth century. Ineffective leadership, ecclesiastical opposition, and the protracted resolution of the American Civil War contributed to the containment of Irish patriotic expression throughout the North Atlantic World at a time that was otherwise conducive to political change in Ireland. Grandiose visions of a Fenian-led Irish republic never materialized, moreover, because the socioeconomic interests of the global Irish community evolved during the 1860s. Ardent Fenians consequently experienced far more setbacks than successes. Three Fenian military forays into British-held Canada were easily repulsed during the spring of 1866. Setbacks a year later included an island-wide, IRB-led rebellion that was quashed in less than a day and the haphazard voyage of the *Erin's Hope*, a touted Fenian vessel that failed to deliver a substantial cargo of American weapons to Irish insurgents. Thousands of Irish men and women participated in innocuous republican activities such as public lectures, picnics, and protest marches when Fenianism was at the height of its popularity. Relatively few of their compatriots, however, ever became true rebels.

Why the aforementioned reasons encouraged the people of Ireland and Irish expatriates to qualify their interest in the international Fenian movement is the primary focus of this study. Both of the Brotherhoods and their respective female auxiliaries could have jointly generated greater opposition to longstanding British control over Ireland. Anglophobia was prevalent throughout the mid-nineteenth century. A cyclical Irish economy continued to encourage rebellion by raising collective social expectations one moment and dashing them the next. Immigrants who had fled to the United States and Great Britain during the Great Potato Famine resented perceived and actual social inequity in Ireland because resettlement abroad did not guarantee a higher standard of living. Irish émigrés also widely hoped that their nation would be independent one day because they were routinely confronted by ethnic discrimination in their adopted homelands. The contemporary stature of the Fenian movement, nevertheless, declined even faster than it originally rose.

The failure of Fenianism is additionally intriguing because it had relatively broad sociocultural appeal. The typical Fenian was a literate, semiskilled laborer with aspirations for social advancement. IRB co-founder James Stephens was a well-educated, mathematically inclined son of a dyer. His cohort, John O'Mahony, was a descendent of a prosperous leaseholder.[4] A disproportionate number of Fenians had ancestral ties to southern Ireland, but men and women from all of Ireland's thirty-two counties embraced the movement. Some influential members of the organization, furthermore, were either Protestant or, as in the case of Stephens and his confidante, Thomas Clark Luby, were raised in interfaith families.

Fenians tended to attract Irish and Irish Americans from the province of Munster in the southwestern part of Ireland, an area of the country significantly affected by modernization during the nineteenth century. Munster, which includes the cities of Waterford, Cork, and Limerick, was profoundly anglicized and connected to the market economy. Modernization also indirectly shaped the lives of the people in the Munster countryside, as many during the Famine migrated to nearby towns looking for work. Direct exposure to sweeping economic changes and British bureaucracy seemed to motivate restless young men and women to embrace radical nationalism, whether in Ireland or in the United States.

The lack of more fervent Irish nationalist expression throughout the transatlantic world during the mid-nineteenth century has added credence to a contemporary premise that Fenianism was as much a recreational diversion for individuals with a keen sense of adventure as it was a subversive endeavor, but this should not detract from the sincerity and optimism of those involved. Professor R. V. Comerford and other modern-day historians have noted that leisure pursuits such as sporting events and gambling were often intermixed with IRB activities. Thousands of predominately single maids and female factory workers supported the Irish nationalist cause by organizing and attending fundraisers throughout the United States under the auspices of the North American–based Fenian Sisterhood. While expatriate Fenians were among the first immigrants who collectively participated in a transnational social movement, many individuals recognized that their support for Irish freedom advanced their political and professional careers in America. As William D'Arcy detailed in his seminal 1947 study of the Fenian movement, some of the most prominent Irish American members of the Brotherhood were celebrated Union officers and future United States congressmen.

Canadian historians such as Hereward Senior have offered an alternative assessment of the Fenians by primarily highlighting Irish nationalist military activity that occurred after the culmination of the American Civil War. Although respective Brotherhood invasions of New Brunswick, Ontario, and Quebec were relatively bloodless, they encouraged all of the then-autonomous Canadian provinces to enhance their domestic security by forming a unified colonial government under the 1867 Constitution Act. Fenian terrorists equally disquieted English society. Prison rescues, bombings, and the assassination of government officials reinforced stereotypical Victorian perceptions of the Irish as cowardly ignorant, ape-like thugs. However, these activities also forced British parliamentary leaders to offer socioeconomic concessions to the Irish people. This study uniquely blends Comferford's, D'Arcy's, and Senior's portrayal of the Fenians by suggesting that the movement primarily appealed to men in search of an adventurous way to enhance their economic prospects and to prove their manhood. But, more importantly, it gave them an outlet to express their anti-British sentiment, through the threat of physical force.

1

THE FOUNDATIONS OF FENIANISM

The 1858 creation of the Irish Republican Brotherhood (IRB) in Ireland and of the Fenian Brotherhood in the United States did not occur in a vacuum. The historical precedent set by nationalist groups like the United Irishmen in the late eighteenth century and Young Ireland in the mid-nineteenth century set the grounds upon which Fenianism was founded and operated. The modernization of state governmental structures, including the rise of democracy, industrialization, urbanization, and globalization, led to the establishment of various nationalist organizations in the Western world. That Ireland was occupied and governed by the most contemporary of these states ensured that modernization would affect Ireland. That many of its people made their way to the United States, perhaps the second most contemporary nation, would explain the appeal of nationalist organizations to Irish Americans. More importantly, the IRB and the Fenian Brotherhood, founded by James Stephens and John O'Mahony, respectively, were manifestations of real historical grievances, and the two men used perceived injustices to galvanize average Irish men and women.

Despite the efforts of Stephens and O'Mahony, the IRB and the Fenian Brotherhood remained virtually inconsequential entities during the first three years of their existence; however, they started to threaten British national security by the beginning of the American Civil War. Stephens and O'Mahony had minimal early success recruiting supporters after they founded their respective organizations in the spring of 1858. In time, however, predominately lower-middle-class Irish nationalists started forming secret IRB cells throughout Ireland and the United States. Irish Americans from impoverished backgrounds who had secured a limited degree of financial stability were ideal Fenian recruits. Hoping to join the middle class, they subconsciously cited unjust British rule over Ireland as the reason why they had not readily acquired a higher standard of living. Fighting under the Fenian banner for an independent Irish republic, in their estimation, would help them obtain a better life in their new home.

The IRB and the Fenian Brotherhood might never have been established if British government leaders had provided sufficient public relief to Irish victims of the Great Famine. Almost exclusively dependent on one crop for nourishment and income after the seventeenth century, the population of Ireland was reduced by one-fourth after the parasitic microbe *Phytopthora infestans* ravaged Irish potato fields for four years, beginning in 1845. Potato blights had led to relatively brief food shortages in Ireland on many prior occasions, and *Phytopthora infestans* had surfaced in the United States and Belgium earlier in the decade. However, in Ireland, four years of abnormally moist weather encouraged the devastating fungus to proliferate. British prime minister Robert Peel, the leader of the paternalistic Conservative Party, authorized government subsidization of public works projects as well as the purchase of American corn meal to supplement soup kitchens funded by the Quakers and other private charities. Yet peasants often had to leave their land in search of food when affluent landowners either ignored—or could not fulfill—their legally mandated responsibility to underwrite road grading, wetland drainage, and other labor-intensive projects near their property during times of economic crisis.[1] Many malnourished Irish men and women, moreover, were unfamiliar with corn and did not know how to grind grain products properly. As a result, some of the peasants became ill from consuming raw corn. As potato crops continued to fail, many wealthy farmers heartlessly increased the size of their pastures in order to raise animals at a time when greater staple food production was more imperative. Thousands of penniless cottiers consumed seed potatoes that had been originally earmarked for the next planting season and eventually resorted to eating grass.

The ascendancy of the Whig Party in July 1846 would only exacerbate the situation in Ireland, leading many Irish nationalists to espouse that the British had perpetrated genocide to depopulate Ireland. As a proponent of laissez-faire economics, the new prime minister, Lord John Russell, refused to place price controls on Irish commodities. Hibernian farmers thus freely sold locally produced grain and livestock on the open market during the latter stages of the Famine, while thousands of evicted tenants starved to death as they squatted along public carriageways and other makeshift places of refuge. Typhus, cholera, and other illnesses subsequently became nineteenth-century Irish equivalents of the Plague. About one million people ultimately perished, as communicable diseases spread through dense population clusters. Among the victims, poor women and children were particularly vulnerable to disease and starvation. One million slightly more fortunate people emigrated to Britain and North America, often in desperate attempts to escape almost certain death. Perceiving themselves as involuntary exiles, the men and women who were a part of the Famine Diaspora would long attribute their plight to British colonial domination of their homeland, even though many environmental and demographic factors had greatly intensified the calamity.

Anti-English sentiment became a transnationalist phenomenon wherever Irish immigrants settled, including Great Britain, where Fenianism flourished in reaction to the xenophobia and poverty with which Famine refugees had to contend in their adopted communities. English, Scottish, and Welsh laborers frequently harassed recent Irish immigrants, who were willing to toil for less-than-prevailing local wages. Picks and axes were wielded as weapons at Gorebridge and other massive civil engineering project sites, where unskilled Irish and Scottish navies often sparred alongside railbeds when temporary job contracts were announced. Religious riots, including a violent pre-1852 election fracas in Stockport, frequently occurred in working-class communities.[2] Lower-class expatriates in Liverpool were responsible for half of all reported assaults and public disturbances, even though they composed only 25 percent of the local population.[3] Displaced Irish immigrants were also proportionally over-represented in English penitentiaries.[4] Other Irishmen vented resettlement frustrations by frequenting establishments that catered to despondent Famine refugees. In the Welsh mining center of Merthyr Tydfil, Irishmen gathered at a barroom that was appropriately called the "Exile of Erin" a decade before the Fenian movement surfaced in their community.[5] In time, similar taverns would become Fenian meeting sites in many communities throughout the British Isles.[6]

Famine immigrants who sought economic refuge in North America remained equally resentful of the British government. Ocean travel was expensive and dangerous in the mid-nineteenth century. Most peasants pawned their few heirlooms and pooled their financial resources to afford one of the costliest expenditures they would likely ever make. Some lucky tenants, however, received financial assistance from landlords who were either magnanimous or simply interested in removing their leaseholders so they could regain full title to their rental property.[7] Good-byes among family members were typically hurried affairs. Destitution and widespread fear of communicable diseases inhibited large numbers of friends and families from hosting the traditional convivial "wake" for departing emigrants. Nine percent of Famine immigrants destined for the Western hemisphere perished while onboard ship. Mortality rates for those en route to Canada were even higher, as crossing subarctic waters in often harsh weather was particularly dangerous. In addition to storms, shipboard diseases endangered all men and women who traveled to the New World in vessels that were, appropriately, dubbed "coffin ships." Sea captains often swindled sick and hungry passengers by prolonging their voyages in safe waters so that immigrants, who were required to bring their own food and water onboard, would run out of personal provisions and be obliged to purchase overpriced supplies stowed in private ship holds.[8] Hucksters and confidence men also victimized many Irish immigrants the moment they stepped onto the wharves of New York, New Orleans, and lesser-utilized immigrant *entrepôts*.[9] Weary and exploited, Irish immigrants to America would long blame their miserable voyage to the New World on the British.

Widespread resentment of the British government's official response to the Famine encouraged precursor organizations of the IRB and the Fenian Brotherhood to test the feasibility of a transatlantic Irish nationalist movement. Many members of the intellectual-led Young Ireland movement exchanged their pens for swords when the height of the Famine occurred—at roughly the same time that French republicans surprisingly overthrew the unpopular French Orléanist monarch Louis-Philippe. Yet Young Ireland leaders proved that they had been more effectual writing Anglophobic diatribes in the popular Irish nationalist newspaper, *The Nation*, than orchestrating subversive activities. A Young Ireland emissary named Thomas Francis Meagher was arrested in Ireland and transported to Australia after being convicted of treason for attempting to secure support from the Irish Republican Union (IRU), a Manhattan-based militant nationalist group predominately comprised of Irish-born veterans of the recently concluded Mexican-American War.[10] Although the Fenian Brotherhood would have somewhat greater success shuttling men and money across the Atlantic two decades later, unsuccessful efforts by Young Ireland to single-handedly engage British forces foreshadowed many of the logistical problems that the IRB would confront in the mid-1860s.

Young Ireland's efforts on the battlefield were significantly more fraught with failure. The head of the movement, William Smith O'Brien, lacked military experience as well as peasant and ecclesiastical support when the July 1848 suspension of habeas corpus laws throughout Ireland—which led to the arrest and imprisonment of many prominent nationalists—forced him to either mobilize his few hundred devoted supporters before the approaching harvest or flee to France.[11] With such a sparse army, the aristocratic O'Brien and other Young Ireland commanders should have resorted to guerrilla tactics. They instead fought conventionally, adhering to romantic notions of gentlemanly honor. In one famous example, O'Brien exhibited his love of pomp and circumstance by temporarily withdrawing his men from the village of Mullinahone when the local police barracks commander revealed that he could not surrender his garrison without professional disgrace unless the insurgents briefly retreated and returned with a larger force. Predictably, the officer and his subordinate constables absconded with their weapons and ammunition the moment after O'Brien and his followers acceded to this request. Young Ireland's preference for chivalry instead of combat was again evident two days later, when another educated nationalist leader, named John Blake Dillon, allowed a British regiment of well-armed Irish Hussars to pass freely through the barricaded Tipperary coal-mining village of Killenaule on condition that warrants would not be issued to his men. Twenty-four-year-old James Stephens was subsequently incensed when he was ordered to escort an officer's horse through the town. Skeptical of his commander's actions, the O'Brien aide-de-camp and future IRB leader concluded that gallantry and decorum would do nothing to end British control over an island that had four times as many constables per capita than France, the largest police state on the European continent.[12]

O'Brien's persistence about respecting personal property and the safety of civilians virtually ensured that a successor Irish nationalist movement would emphasize brute military force over martial decorum. Having cornered a detachment of forty-six police officers inside a Ballingarry farmhouse on July 30, Stephens's fellow Killenaule standoff participant, Terence Bellew MacManus, and several other Young Irelanders started a fire next to the inadequately defended rear entrance of the residence, hoping that the rising smoke and flames from the burning hay would force the constables to yield. However, O'Brien ordered his men to extinguish the conflagration when the owner of the residence feared that her five young children were inside the threatened home.[13] Courteously, O'Brien approached the house to announce that none of the occupants would be harmed if they vacated the Widow McCormack's property immediately. Whether such diplomacy would have proved effective will never be known, because rowdy spectators gathered nearby began throwing stones while O'Brien was negotiating with the constables. Suspecting an attack, the entrapped policemen returned fire. A gunfight ensued, but lacking sufficient ammunition, the Young Irelanders retreated before police reinforcements arrived. Later in the day, bullets struck Stephens in each one of his legs when he and several other retreating men were accosted by a police patrol. Hoping to avoid further bloodshed, O'Brien demonstrated that he was of the same political bent as the legendary, but largely pacifist, Irish nationalist statesman Daniel O'Connell, when he decided at a makeshift conference that night outside Ballingary to disperse all their men.[14]

Young Ireland's determination to fight a gentleman's war destroyed its good standing with radical Irish nationalists throughout the Western world. O'Brien had always opposed the more radical tenets of his imprisoned colleague John

Mitchel who, until his dubious arrest and sentence to transportation in May that eventually landed him in Van Diemen's Land (Tasmania), had advocated guerilla warfare against the British.[15] Irish American nationalists, who tended to embrace more radical measures than many of their allies back home, became especially disenchanted. Thus, war funds collected by prosperous Irishmen in Memphis a month after the Ballingarry altercation were never forwarded to Ireland, and many members of the IRU decided that the best way to prepare for the next potential Irish revolution was to join one of the predominately expatriate New York state militia regiments.[16]

Stephens's involvement with the Young Ireland insurrection was also significant because it placed him in personal contact with other future Fenian leaders. Stephens took a liking to O'Mahony when the two men first met at an impromptu Young Ireland war council the night before the Ballingarry fiasco, because his future comrade implored his fellow insurgents to remain on a war footing. Reconnoitering farther west, in O'Mahony's opinion, would have united the Young Irelanders with Munster peasants who sympathized with their objectives. In reality, O'Mahony was only able to orchestrate a few insignificant attacks over the following week, before desertions and aggressive British countermeasures completely thwarted his efforts to reinvigorate the rebellion.[17] Stephens also solidified his relationship with early Fenian leader Michael Doheny during a flight into exile that included a narrow escape from a lynch mob and a three-day convalescence in the home of a romantic interest.[18] Stephens ultimately escaped to France on his own, several weeks after family members conducted a mock funeral for him in his hometown; O'Mahony arrived on the European continent shortly thereafter.

Stephens and O'Mahony reaffirmed their opposition to chivalrous warfare and acquired valuable insights from continental European revolutionary leaders during their extended sojourn in Paris. Nonetheless, they failed to develop a strategic plan that would enable them to avoid many of the failures which the Young Irelanders had made during the summer of 1848. O'Brien had mistakenly assumed that starving peasants would instinctively follow middle-class idealists who lionized Rousseau's social contract and Johann Herder's promotion of the nation over the individual. Stephens, however, would later lead several recruiting initiatives through the Irish countryside, where political activism was limited. Venerable secret vigilante groups known by a variety of names, including Ribbonmen and Whiteboys, had long intimidated government-backed landlords, who often exploited their leaseholders, by damaging property and mutilating livestock. However, once Stephens established the IRB, members of these organizations would be hesitant to sanction an open rebellion owing to fear of landlord and government reprisal. As a result, the Fenian movement, like its Young Ireland antecedent, would never truly represent the political will of the Irish people. Stephens and O'Mahony would also fail to devise a method to prevent Irish Catholic Church leaders from censuring the Fenian movement in the same manner that many influential bishops and curates had condemned forerunner nationalist organizations. Neither exile ever devised a comprehensive method to counter ecclesiastical opposition to his initiatives, even though almost all members of the Irish clergy had claimed that O'Brien and his cohorts were godless emulators of the Italian revolutionary Giuseppe Mazzini and other anti-Papist insurrectionists. New York archbishop John Hughes had donated five hundred dollars to the Young Irelanders for "shields, not swords," as he put it, but the majority of his clerical colleagues believed that the "Men of '48" would have sundered the moral fiber of the Irish nation if they had actually acquired power.[19]

Similar to the Young Irelanders, Stephens and O'Mahony were intellectual nationalists, and their credibility as revolutionary leaders would eventually be compromised by their minimal exposure to combat. Other than manning anti-Orléanist barricades during an ephemeral Parisian insurrection, both men remained battlefield tyros. Even though they fraternized with French, Italian, and Polish nationalist conspirators in sidewalk cafes and humble garrets, they devoted much of their time to sustaining themselves with intermittent employment. O'Mahony worked as a Gaelic language instructor, while the multilingual Stephens earned money as a tabloid journalist, tutor, and—most notably—as the French language translator of Charles Dickens's subtly anti-American novel, *Martin Chuzzlewit*. Because their literary and pedagogical skills commanded only modest commissions, at one time the two future Irish nationalist leaders had to reside in a shabby dwelling that was meagerly furnished with backless stools and straw bedding.[20]

Despite the obvious limitations of Stephens and O'Mahony to lead a successful transatlantic republican movement, Irish nationalists in the Atlantic world were so vehemently anti-British—especially after the Great Famine—that independence via revolution remained a possibility. Many Catholic Irish Americans had embraced the Protestant John Mitchel's assertion that the British government had used the Famine to further its colonization of Ireland. Mitchel promulgated the thesis that Britain's lack of assistance to a fellow member of the United Kingdom had resulted in deaths upwards of one million people, and thus constituted genocide. At the very least, many expatriates accepted the notion that massive emigration implied a desire by the British and Protestant Ascendancy to remove Irish peasants from the lands so that landlords could convert their farms to the more profitable methods of grazing.[21]

A future IRB and Fenian Brotherhood strategy to secure foreign military aid was also rooted in history. Stephens and O'Mahony both knew that the French government had offered the United Irish revolutionary movement assistance during its failed Irish uprising in 1798. Originally established as a gentleman's debate club, the United Irishmen evolved into a subversive movement comprised of men who wanted the British government to continue a recent precedent of offering substantial political concessions to Irish elites. English leaders had prevented an insurrection from occurring in Ireland at the height of the American Revolution by granting significant legislative autonomy to the Irish Parliament, but ardent United Irishmen insisted on outright devolution in the 1790s. To achieve this objective, Theobald Wolfe Tone and other leading United Irishmen signed a pact with the quasi-dictatorial French Directory, which led to a substantial invasion initiative in December 1796. Led by the highly regarded French general Lazare Hoche, fourteen thousand members of the Grande Armée were transported across the outer English Channel to southwest Ireland, but fierce winds prevented an invasion force from landing on the beaches that ringed Bantry Bay. When another invasion attempt was delayed by Napoleon's unremitting effort to augment and consolidate territorial acquisitions on the European continent, United Irish operatives began to link their organization with a secret Catholic society called the Defenders.

The tenuous nature of the United Irish/Defender coalition foreshadowed the inability of the Fenians to receive greater ecumenical Irish nationalist support. Although they were ardent supporters of greater Irish political autonomy, the Ulster-based Defenders were primarily concerned with protecting themselves from land-hungry Protestants. The two partners, therefore, repeatedly attempted to dominate one another.[22] Mutual suspicion facilitated the prompt defeat of Irish forces when they rebelled throughout the island in 1798 and presaged greater socioeconomic stratification between mid-nineteenth-century Irish nationalists and their politically apathetic fellow countrymen. Most Fenians, nevertheless, deeply admired Tone and another Protestant United Irishman named Robert Emmet. Bitterly opposed to the corrupt postrevolution dissolution of the Irish Parliament in 1801, Emmet had emulated an older brother (who later became a New York State attorney general) by leading an unsuccessful one-day revolt two years after the Act of Union definitively re-established British suzerainty over Ireland. Captured in the Wicklow Mountains shortly after he failed to turn a violent Dublin street demonstration into a nationwide insurrection, Emmet remained passionately devoted to Irish independence when he was executed on September 20, 1803.

In addition to esteeming antecedent Irish nationalists, Stephens and O'Mahony admired contemporaries who had unsuccessfully fought for Irish independence. James Finton Lalor and John O'Leary were later held in high regard by the Fenians because they and two hundred of their supporters had attacked a police barracks in the small County Waterford village of Cappoquin while Queen Victoria was visiting Cork and Dublin in August 1849. Although it was unsuccessful, this effort stood in stark contrast to the tepid nationalist initiatives of former O'Connell disciples, who had concurrently formed the mainstream Independent Irish Party (IIP) and an affiliate organization called the Irish Tenant League (ITL). At roughly the same time that Lalor and O'Leary had risked death and imprisonment for Irish freedom, two IIP leaders named John Sadlier and William Keogh had accepted ministerial appointments in a Whig government led by Lord Aberdeen.

Mitchel shared Stephens and O'Mahony's belief that an Irish nationalist revolution could be successful in the early 1850s on condition that its supporters received significant backing from a superpower ally such as France. An unjustly convicted nationalist subversive, Mitchel escaped from Tasmania in August 1853 and arrived in New York three months later to reconstitute the remnants of the IRU as a new organization called the Irishmen's Civil and Military Republican Union (ICMRU). A precursor to the Fenian Brotherhood, ICMRU united middle-aged benefactors with younger men who would serve in an Irish army of liberation. Mitchel optimistically envisioned the ICMRU at the time of its founding on April 13, 1854, as an affiliate of the Russian Army. With the majority of British military forces deployed in the Crimea at the time, Ireland was vulnerable to internal political strife, and Canada was susceptible to an expatriate-led invasion. All the organization needed was weapons and money from Czar Nicholas I; however, the Romanov monarch never offered any assistance to the ICMRU. The Russian ambassador in Washington noted that fellow members of his government could not assist Mitchel even if they wanted to, because the British and French navies had blockaded the Black and Baltic Seas.[23] Limited nationalist sentiment within the greater expatriate community was more disappointing. Forty thousand dollars in pledges, a series of lectures, and a modest public demonstration in Montreal were not enough to recruit and outfit a significant number of Irish filibusterers.[24] The ICMRU and an affiliated women's auxiliary were thus short-lived. Having incensed the Irish American community by becoming an outspoken editorial critic of Archbishop John Hughes and of Catholic priests who, he believed, had helped quash the Young Ireland movement, Mitchel ceased publication of his Manhattan newspaper and relocated his entire family to the rugged foothills of eastern Tennessee. Prophetically, in an 1855 missive, the polemicist-turned-gentleman-farmer reiterated his long-held belief that, in the absence of an alliance with an international superpower, a new Irish revolutionary organization would be "(as they always have been) a scene of personal jealousies & factions, an occasion for misappropriating money, a machinery that will be worked by American politicians, and a source of disgust and disappointment to our impatient people."[25]

John O'Mahony remained optimistic about the chances for revolutionary success and was neither disheartened by Russian refusals to assist the Irish Republican Union nor discouraged that expatriates expressed greater respect for Catholic Church prelates than for nationalist ideologues such as Mitchel. Having originally left Paris in late 1853 to assist IRU efforts in New York—at the same time Stephens was returning to Ireland by way of England—the future Fenian leader teamed with Michael Doheny to establish a new paramilitary organization called the Emmet Monument Association (EMA), eleven months after the demise of the ICMRU. The EMA, whose name derived from Robert Emmet's 1803 gallows plea to have no epitaph written on his tombstone until Ireland was free, had its unmarried members drill every week and remain perpetually obliged to report for active duty without hesitation and on short notice. For their part, family men were invited to join an EMA auxiliary organization. As the leaders of two interdependent societies, O'Mahony and Doheny published a newspaper entitled *The Honest Truth* and unsuccessfully resumed petitioning for Russian military assistance. A fellow Young Irelander who had become a successful lawyer after immigrating to the United States, Doheny assumed that Famine immigrants would remain involved in Irish nationalist affairs as they began to acquire modest disposable incomes and a limited amount of free time. Despite the arduousness of Irish immigrant life and the prevalence of nativist sentiment, Doheny believed that life in the United States augured well for a new Hibernian independence movement. Expatriate artisans earned up to three times the salary they could command in Ireland; there was little evidence, however, of a trickle-down effect that benefited unskilled laborers. Manufacturing and commercial revenue lined the pockets of the rich rather than those of the immigrant working class. Government-owned land may have been plentiful, but few Irishmen could afford to pay $1.25 an acre, let alone meet the cost of agricultural supplies and transportation expenses to minimally accessible regions of the American frontier.[26]

Doheny's premises were further substantiated by often-deplorable expatriate living conditions at the time the ICMRU was replaced by the EMA. New housing lagged behind skyrocketing population growth in the mid-nineteenth century. Typical Irish immigrant families saved money by leasing one room in a subdivided old mansion or a converted warehouse. The less fortunate hastily built shanties in alleyways or in the backyards of former middle- and upper-class townhomes. In one extreme example, thirty-nine people lived in a small subterranean abode in the Fort Hill section of Boston.[27] Land was more plentiful in

Philadelphia, but the predominately Irish Port Richmond neighborhood was still crowded, with an average 10.42 inhabitants per dwelling.[28] Virtually all these lodgings were unfit for habitation. Running water was a luxury, and few tenements adequately protected occupants from the elements. In 1850, an estimated twenty-nine thousand Irishmen lived in Lower Manhattan cellars that generally maintained a constant comfortable air temperature but were often flooded with fetid water when heavy rain overburdened primitive municipal sewer systems.

Most Irish Americans lived in squalor, and the configuration of Irish American enclave communities exacerbated conditions for Famine refugees already suffering in their adopted homeland. Few expatriates who worked in slaughterhouses and gasworks could afford commuting expenses or tolerate an extended walk back to their homes after a long day on their feet. Consequently, they often lived in proximity to their stench-ridden places of employment.[29] Noisome odors also emanated from poorly ventilated residences as well as from indoor and outdoor privies. Densely populated immigrant enclaves became perfect breeding grounds for typhus, cholera, and other communicable diseases that had spread throughout Ireland during the Great Famine. As Irish immigration helped increase the United States Catholic population over 130 percent between 1850 and 1860, Irish neighborhoods led the nation in infant mortality, while the median life span of an adult Irish immigrant was only fourteen years from date of arrival in North America.[30]

Although most Irish American nationalists did not reside in émigré ghettos, they inferred that social conditions in the United States would impel their poorer countrymen to support an Irish republic. And, indeed, the desire of middle-class expatriates to establish an independent Ireland was usually based on a presumption that involuntary exile was the overall cause of expatriate social problems; however, conditions in the new land also resulted in greater instability, as expatriates fatalistically accustomed to natural disasters and discrimination had tremendous difficulty adapting to the prevailing social optimism in antebellum America. In 1856, two-thirds of the emotionally disturbed inmates at the Philadelphia State Hospital and half the patients at New York City's Blackwell Island Lunatic Asylum were Irish.[31] Other émigrés resorted to crime and composed large percentages of the general prison population. Irish men and women, typically guilty of larceny, were among the largest ethnic groups in Pennsylvania's Moyamensing Penitentiary a decade after the Great Famine.[32] Criminal statistics were similar in the South. Immigrants who could not depend on the support of the church and benevolent societies often resorted to begging. Indigent Irish mothers often allowed street mendicants to cradle their babies in public in exchange for a percentage of any spare change the cadger may receive. On the streets of immigrant enclaves, omnipresent pawnshops were a powerful symbol of desperation and high crime rates. Equally ubiquitous taverns confirmed that many Irishmen had lost hope of social mobility and succumbed to alcoholism. Several Irish grogeries in Philadelphia were no more than tawdry, barely furnished halls euphemistically named after affluent Americans, such as John Jacob Astor and Stephen Girard. The "Break of Day House," however, was a more appropriately named antebellum Irish American tavern.[33] The patrons of these establishments—like expatriates who were confined to asylums and prisons—were not ideal nationalists. Their plight and behavior, however, eventually inspired thousands of more reputable immigrants to become Fenians and fight for Irish freedom.

The EMA and other Irish nationalist-oriented entities that later evolved into the Fenian Brotherhood also organized in reaction to longstanding anti-Irish sentiment in the United States and Canada. Affluent, class-conscious Congregationalists, Episcopalians, and Unitarians had long accused Irish émigrés of causing rising social problems and of abetting the emergence of unrefined "new money" capitalists who made their fortunes by paying low wages to immigrant labor. In the mid-nineteenth century, the inventor of the telegraph, Samuel Morse, wrote two books linking the Vatican and Catholic European monarchs to a host of nefarious activities, including subversive Papal efforts to usurp control of the United States government. Noted abolitionist preacher Lyman Beecher believed Irish Catholics were unworthy of American citizenship because they were undereducated.[34] Anti-Catholic propaganda imported from England, and the 1836 publication of a mendacious book entitled *Awful Disclosures of the Hotel Dieu Nunnery of Montreal,* further heightened nativist sentiment throughout the nation. In the supposed exposé, a female Protestant convert to Catholicism discovers, upon her initiation into a French Canadian religious order, that sisters unwilling to have sex with priests were executed. The children of these illicit relations, according to the author, were baptized and then thrown into a pit to die.

Labor and religious tensions also provoked expatriate nationalist sentiment in the United States. About thirty-five major anti-Irish riots occurred in Saint Louis, New Orleans, Cincinnati, and other cities between 1830 and 1850, as immigrants lowered wages in industries already revolutionized by modern production technology that required less manpower. The August 1834 burning of a Charlestown, Massachusetts convent was one of the most notorious acts of religious violence in American history. Intra-working-class disturbances in the Kensington and Southwark section of Philadelphia a decade later led pundits to rename the Pennsylvania metropolis the "City of Brotherly Hate" and "The Murderous City."[35] As Famine immigrants fled to America thereafter, Catholic churches were vandalized in several urban centers and discriminatory anti-

Irish hiring practices began to proliferate in the American workplace. Outside the United States, religious conflicts that had originated decades earlier in Ulster sparked riots in Ontario and other sections of Canada, as Protestant members of the Orange Order were known to fight with Irish Catholics on days of historical or religious significance.

Irish Catholic immigrants who harassed German émigrés and fought among themselves further convinced Protestant nativists that they were racially superior to people of Celtic lineage. Young expatriates in Manhattan often jeered at German mourners during graveside funeral services in what was then the only Catholic cemetery in the entire city.[36] Irish internecine conflicts, likewise, were collectively embarrassing, but violent disturbances were usually incidental. In the fall of 1846, for example, immigrants from the Irish provinces of Ulster and Connaught who resided in Worcester, Massachusetts established a secret organization called the Shamrock Society that may have been modeled after similarly named associations that strove to ensure the employment of their members. In principle, the objectives of the fraternity appeared rather innocuous. Supporters pledged to "help and defend members against real or imaginary wrongs or insults inflicted on or offered to any members, and to revenge each others' wrongs on every favorable occasion."[37] The local clergy, however, believed the group was a threat to the established social order.

After becoming aware of the organization's existence within his own congregation, Father Matthew W. Gibson demanded that the leader of the Shamrocks publicly renounce his actions during a Sunday mass. The parishioner obeyed, but the next year a successor group called the Shamrock Benevolent Society surfaced with the same objectives. This new organization provoked the church as well as immigrants of Munster and Leinster heritage. Gang fights and individual melees became common between the northern Irish Shamrocks and the immigrants from the southern half of the island whom they had shunned. The priest who condemned the society, meanwhile, had to have his rectory protected by a deputy sheriff two days after a placard reading "Saxon tyrant" was placed on his doorstep. A petition to have Gibson transferred was rejected by his superior, Bishop John Bernard Fitzpatrick of Boston, shortly thereafter. The group dissolved when its president and his brother-in-law were accused of embezzling, but nativists could argue that their anti-Irish attitudes had been further legitimized. Catholic Church leaders had foreshadowed their eventual opposition to the Fenian movement, moreover, by suppressing an outbreak of insubordinate activity under their purview.

Irish republican expression throughout the United States was exacerbated by nationwide attempts to curtail rising expatriate participation in American government. Rich and poor Protestants jointly supported the vehemently anti-Catholic

Supreme Order of the Star Spangled Banner to prevent Irish and German immigrants from obtaining substantial socioeconomic clout during the mid-1850s. More commonly known as the American Republican Party, or the Know-Nothings, members of the Order temporarily dominated elected governments throughout the United States. Massachusetts governor Henry Gardner and majority party politicians in the Commonwealth House and Senate attempted to constitutionally prohibit newly arrived Catholic Europeans from voting or serving in state government until they had been in the nation for fourteen years.[38] American Party governors in Kentucky and Maryland were among many nativist politicians who likewise sponsored and supported the passage of unconstitutional anti-Irish laws, such as immigrant suffrage literacy tests. Farther west, in Chicago, a Know-Nothing-controlled city council emulated other attempts to bar immigrant Catholics from public offices and employment by requiring all policemen to be native born.[39] To the benefit of the Irish American community, the apex of Know-Nothing political power was brief. Wracked by an internecine debate over slavery, the American Party collapsed in 1856, and many laws passed by its supporters were repealed in due course. Hibernophobia continued to abound, however, in countless American communities. Banned Irish civilian militia regiments—including a Boston unit that had maintained public order in June 1854 when a riotous crowd obstructed the extradition of an escaped slave to the South—were not allowed to return to full strength in Massachusetts, Connecticut, and Ohio until the Civil War.

Expatriate Anglophobia was fostered by Protestant tendencies to associate Irish émigrés with African Americans.[40] In common parlance, expatriates were "niggers turned inside out," while rural whites sometimes referred to blacks as "smoked Irish." Particularly destitute Irish Americans were often deemed members of an under-class even lower than slaves. Bonded labor was an enormous investment, and Southern planters usually refused to allow their chattel to perform hazardous work. As in the North, where three thousand Irish laborers replaced Protestant navies who refused to work on the Erie Canal during a malaria outbreak, engineering projects below the Mason-Dixon line were often completed by poor white Hibernians. These hiring practices reinforced the notion that Irishmen were expendable laborers rather than citizens who contributed to the success and prosperity of their communities. Irish American men repeatedly complained of "white slavery" and the "slavery of wages," in part because a healthy adult male slave often sold for over one thousand dollars at auction, whereas Irish workers earned $965 a year on average in 1860. Free Irish men, in simple economic terms, were valued less than typical Protestant laborers (whose average income was $1,555) and black slaves, who were considered by racial theorists and their adherents to be anthropologically inferior to whites.[41]

Before the advent of a formidable expatriate nationalist movement,[42] socio-economically immobile émigrés who performed what was then often called "nigger work" channeled many of their frustrations toward African Americans. Gang fights routinely erupted in East and Gulf Coast dockyards, as racially divided teamsters and stevedores hustled for work. Intense, but nonviolent, competition was similarly evident in the female-dominated domestic service industry.[43]

Antebellum expatriate social mobility was ultimately a double-edged sword for the Irish nationalist movement. Émigrés who advanced into the middle class usually became acculturated Americans who increasingly eschewed their former dreams of returning to Ireland with enough money to purchase a farm or a small business. Irish nationalist expression would have been almost nonexistent, however, if poor Irish immigrants had not obtained a modestly higher standard of living and some form of education during early adulthood.[44] Nationalist expression was relatively uncommon within destitute enclave communities, because men and women who were always struggling to survive had little time to be politically active. Patrick Henry O'Rorke became a Fenian after being raised in a poor but upwardly mobile family and then graduating as the second Irish-born appointee to the United States Military Academy.[45] The best nationalists thus resembled the somewhat successful Irish Americans analyzed by Stephen Thernstrom in his seminal study of mid-nineteenth century Newburyport, Massachusetts. In 1851, typical Fenians were among the roughly 60 percent of all Irish Americans between the ages of twelve and forty who could read and write.[46]

In light of modest expatriate social mobility in the mid-nineteenth century, the Fenian movement—to both its benefit and its detriment—would emerge at a time when many Irish fraternal organizations and mutual aid societies initially became popular. Members of the Saint Louis–based Missouri Hibernian Relief Society bridged homeland and ethnic enclave cultures by working to relieve social stress in Ireland and underwriting immigration expenses.[47] By assisting new émigrés, Relief Society members and their counterparts in other cities remained cognizant of social and political events back in Ireland.[48] By the 1860s, members of similar organizations would routinely participate in Fenian activities, such as picnics and parades. Yet, the existence of other organizations also hindered the growth of the Brotherhood. With so many societies open to membership, Brotherhood leaders had less opportunity to recruit men in search of a leisure diversion who could later be exposed to Fenian political doctrine. In general, expatriates who had mostly acculturated to American society found fraternity and camaraderie by joining benevolent organizations that were chartered to enhance the overall quality of émigré life. For example, the Shamrock Building and Loan Association in Philadelphia resembled a myriad of groups throughout the United States that underwrote immigrant housing costs. Other middle-class organizations were oriented toward individual improvement. Father Mathew Temperance societies, for example, were widely popular in Ireland and America mostly because the organization promoted economic and spiritual self-improvement.

Post-Famine efforts to expand the American Catholic Church further inhibited the influence of the Fenian movement. Ecclesiastical leaders supervised a massive spiritual expansion into Irish immigrant daily life during the mid-nineteenth century. Sunday mass had been a standing-room-only affair in many urban centers in the 1840s merely because there were not enough facilities or priests to accommodate immigrants who actively practiced their faith. By the 1860s, however, Catholic bishops around the country had received enough lay financial assistance to enhance diocesan services significantly. By 1850, every parish in Philadelphia had a free parochial school, and thirteen new churches were built throughout the city over the following twenty years.[49] Expansion in New York City was even more significant. Twenty-three new parish churches were consecrated, while seminarians began matriculating at the newly established Saint John's College in the Bronx.[50] Organizational growth of this magnitude in the then-four-borough city and in other metropolitan areas would not have been possible without the assistance of European-based religious orders. Including the Christian Brothers and the Sisters of Mercy, clerics and monks from the Old World led a vigorous movement to develop Catholic institutions in the United States. As a specific example, the Sisters of Charity responded to a nationwide cholera pandemic in 1849 by founding Saint Vincent's hospital in Greenwich Village, while the Sisters of Saint Joseph dedicated a similar facility to their spiritual patron in Philadelphia.[51] In schools and other learning environments that maintained traditional Old World values, the Church could propagate its own brand of anti-British sentiment.

O'Mahony and Doheny did not have the resources to suppress a devastating internal conflict within the Emmet Monument Association at the same time that expatriate benevolent societies and the Catholic Church were encouraging expatriate assimilation into American life. With their personal integrity damaged by rivals who had defected from the EMA and formed a competing nationalist organization that also appealed to young expatriate males, O'Mahony and Doheny suspended their subversive activities not long after one of their emissaries, Joseph Denieffe met with James Stephens in Dublin during the summer of 1855 and failed to arouse interest in a transatlantic nationalist movement in Ireland.[52] Having accused many prominent Irish Americans of being fence-sitting "Yankee-doodle tinsel patriots," O'Mahony resumed his writing career and briefly contemplated chartering an Irish colony in the Midwest.[53] Because EMA membership had peaked at roughly two thousand, O'Mahony remained largely unknown outside the Manhattan expatriate community.[54] Within a decade, however, the future nationalist leader would be popular enough to be photographed by the renowned Civil War photographer Matthew Brady.[55] In the interim, the only armed expatriates in the United States were members of the New York state militia. Although they had not been forced to disband at the apogee of the Know-Nothing movement because Irish Americans had already obtained some influence among state government officials in Albany, most expatriate soldiers did little more than perform ceremonial drills on public holidays for the next five years.[56] In accordance with predictions by Mitchel, Irish Americans were unable to instigate a rebellion three thousand miles away in Ireland without assistance from a powerful British rival, such as France. In general, the Irish immigrant's capability to overcome the adverse experience of resettling overseas would prove to be a greater impediment when the Fenian Brotherhood was established three years later.

Despite the relatively prosperous post-Famine conditions in Ireland, James Stephens was optimistic about the possibility of an imminent Irish revolution a year after he met with Denieffe. While canvassing Munster and Leinster over the course of several months to gauge potential popular support for another Irish nationalist movement, the one-time Waterford and Limerick Railway civil engineer found little evidence of antigovernment unrest.[57] When they respectively met the returned Parisian exile in their Dublin and County Limerick residences, former Young Irelanders John Dillon and William Smith O'Brien both refused to endorse a new militant movement. Equally disheartening to Stephens was a widespread lack of social activism among the rural Irish population. Peasants generally disliked the British government, but they limited their civic activism to local matters. Public awareness of national issues was lacking, even though improved transportation networks had enhanced intra-island trade and communication. Political knowledge in the countryside was largely rooted in hyperbolic Celtic folklore that hedge schoolmasters and itinerant raconteurs told to the young and old alike.[58] Perhaps in exaggeration, Michael Doheny wrote in an account of his 1848 escape to France that he and Stephens had trekked through areas of County Cork and County Kerry where no one had ever heard a speech by Daniel O'Connell or read a copy of *The Nation*.[59] Another Fenian native from County Galway likewise noted years later that in his youth most locals knew nothing of Irish history. Stephens and his early colleagues were thus intellectually distanced from potential supporters. Few peasants had developed nationalist sentiments by reading Sir Walter Scott's *Ivanhoe*, the romantic works of William Wordsworth and Walter Savage Landor, or other notable English literature titles that Stephens enjoyed.[60]

Besides the relative political naïveté of Irish peasants, Stephens's failure to cultivate a rural constituency in the late 1850s was arguably attributable to the absence of a detailed IRB reform agenda that would have enticed potential supporters who generally believed in folkloric prophecies of forthcoming Irish independence. Other than terminating the British government's control over Ireland, the objectives of the IRB were nebulous. Fenianism was not portrayed as a revolt against oppressive taxation, legislative representation, or even ubiquitous bureaucratic discrimination against Catholics.[61] Stephens revealed his desire to recruit schoolmasters, medical students, and other educated people by touting classical republican notions of resisting tyranny and fortifying personal integrity[62]; yet the thousands of marginally educated Irish Catholics possessed little appreciation for such ideological nuances. Like many of their Defender antecedents, a sizable percentage of the Irish population believed its own participation in a militant organization was unnecessary because the sixth-century monastic leader Saint Columbkille had prophesized that God would unilaterally expel all foreign oppressors from Ireland at some point in the future.[63] Only through perseverance did Stephens eventually acquire some notoriety under the Gaelic nom de guerre, *an Seabhach Siúbhalach*. The adopted nickname, which was often phonetically translated into English as "Mister Shooks," but actually meant "the Wandering Hawk," provided Stephens with a rebellious aura similar to those of agrarian vigilantes who claimed to be led by a fictitious individual variously known as "Captain Moonlight" and "Captain Rock."

The dispiriting dearth of nationalist sentiment in the Irish countryside did not dissuade O'Mahony and his expatriate colleagues from attempting to rekindle Irish nationalist expression. Completing an extensively annotated English version of Father Geoffrey Keating's seventeenth-century Gaelic masterpiece, *Foras Feasa ar Éirinn*, left O'Mahony so exhausted that he took temporary refuge in an asylum. At the same time, however, translating the 750-page, pro-Catholic, protonationalist history of pre-Norman Ireland had renewed O'Mahony's desire to establish a true transatlantic republican movement.[64] Accordingly, the former Tipperary estate owner met with Doheny, Thomas Kelly (another nationalist soon to be well known), and one other person to draft a revised secret plan that was subsequently hand-delivered to Stephens. Soon thereafter, the former Young Irelander accepted O'Mahony's invitation to lead a new militant organization, with certain stipulations. In addition to being recognized as a provisional dictator, the upstart nationalist leader insisted that American supporters underwrite his recruiting endeavors. In January 1858, O'Mahony and his colleagues were instructed, in a letter delivered by their former EMA compatriot Joseph Denieffe, to start remitting £80 to £100 a month to IRB operatives.

At pegged exchange rates of five American dollars to one British pound, this stipend was a substantial sum because per capita personal income had decreased since the Panic of 1857. Two decade-old precedents suggested, however, that politically active expatriates would support IRB initiatives. Memphis expatriate community leaders had raised money for the Young Ireland movement, and an MP from Meath had noted in an 1848 House of Commons speech that he had recently met a departing Irish immigrant who was fully confident that his sons would one day return to Ireland "with rifles on their shoulders."[65] Stateside Famine relief efforts had been substantial during the 1840s. Political leaders, such as Vice President George Mifflin Dallas and Massachusetts senator Daniel Webster, had launched nonpartisan and ecumenical charitable campaigns that included a remarkably successful Boston initiative led by the celebrated poet John Greenleaf Whittier.[66] Philadelphia mayor John Swift and Eastern Pennsylvania Quakers similarly collected clothing and monetary donations worth $75,000, while Catholics and Episcopalians throughout the rest of the state remitted nine thousand dollars to Irish charities.[67]

Although he was finally able to provide Stephens with an initial subvention by the following March, O'Mahony was unable to fulfill his colleague's additional request to dispatch a five hundred-man army across the Atlantic.[68] Stephens had hoped that a large expatriate force would be promptly mustered and dispatched to England, where they could skirt restrictive Irish gun laws by purchasing arms at their own expense and then proceed to Ireland. No formal Irish nationalist organization existed in the United States at the time, so the prospects of securing greater expatriate support was initially slim. The IRB was thus officially christened under inauspicious circumstances hours after Denieffe returned to Dublin with O'Mahony's first remittance on Saint Patrick's Day. Gathering, according to various accounts, either in Stephens's lodgings or at a nearby lumberyard owned by a former Young Irelander, the charter members of the organization launched the new republican movement by reciting an affirmation that was remarkably similar to an indoctrination pledge used by Italian Mazzinists in the early 1830s.

The two authors of the first IRB oath, Thomas Clark Luby and Stephens, quickly attempted to expand their newly chartered organization by embarking upon another series of recruiting tours throughout southern Ireland. As in his previous investigative jaunts around the Irish countryside, Stephens discovered that even though agrarian disturbances would briefly surface in his native County Kilkenny during the upcoming summer, most of the people he and Luby encountered were politically complacent. A noteworthy exception included the approximately one hundred members of the Phoenix National and Literary Society. Superficially disguised as a collegial debate club, the Skibbereen-based fraternal organization was actually a poorly equipped and undertrained nationalist militia led by a twenty-seven-year-old grocer named Jeremiah O'Donovan Rossa. Upon developing a rapport with Stephens, Rossa agreed to incorporate his organization into the then-miniscule IRB and help recruit new members in Munster. The conclusion of this alliance was Stephens's first real success as a nationalist leader, but it proved ephemeral when British authorities arrested Rossa and many of his colleagues six months later.[69] The IRB was thus little more than a cadre of militants when Stephens made his first of several visits to the United States during the fall of 1858. Nevertheless, the Phoenix Society/IRB merger suggested that men of modest but not destitute means, such as farmers, journeymen, and artisans, would eventually support the Irish republican movement.

In an effort to protect his small but slowly increasing number of fellow conspirators from government spies, Stephens modeled the IRB after radical organizations that had surfaced on the European continent in the 1820s. Hierarchical command networks previously developed by the French Blanquists and the Italian Carbonari were utilized to inhibit contact among members and to prevent turncoats from compromising what Stephens confidently believed would eventually become a nationwide movement. Optimistically, the chief organizer or chief executive of the Irish republic, as Stephens was often interchangeably known, envisioned each of Ireland's four provinces being administered by a deputy who would report directly to the IRB headquarters staff. Personnel below the executive level were to be divided into small, insulated groups called "circles." In principle, each circle was to be the size of a military regiment and led by the equivalent of a colonel, called a "center." A center held the rank of "A," while subordinate captains were "Bs." Sergeants and privates with respective "C" and "D" ratings composed the bottom of the clandestine pyramid. Regardless of merit, vacant offices were to be immediately filled by the next highest-ranking officer.[70] In the further interest of security, a private, or "D," was only supposed to know the identity of the eight other people in his own unit; his sergeant would collaborate with his men, seven other "Cs" and one "B." Likewise, a captain was to limit his contact to seven sergeants, his fellow captains, and his center. Fenian cells were never impenetrable, however, and they inadvertently fostered suspicion among its members.[71] The members of one nine-man cell usually interacted with other IRB men who resided in the same local area because drilling such a small number of men at any one time was inefficient and impractical. Maintaining secrecy, moreover, required diligence, and members of many IRB circles were either too lazy or unwilling to self-impose stringent security safeguards.

Stephens's obsession with security explains his early reluctance to openly disseminate his ill-defined IRB political agenda. Anecdotal and extant historical evidence suggests that the former Young Irelander shared O'Mahony's reported desire to "confiscate the land of Ireland" and equitably redistribute it amongst the

Irish population.[72] He also originally favored the construction of a large Irish navy and tepid social reforms, such as the establishment of a national university. His admiration for centralized power was evident in his proposal to provide an Irish president with life-tenure and the power to control deliberations within an exclusive, 150-member senate. Stephens also once proposed that a ceremonial Irish throne be offered to the talented French general of Irish descent, Marie Edmé Patrice Maurice de MacMahon, in an apparent attempt to enhance the possibility of a Franco-Fenian alliance.[73] Yet, more substantial calls for reform were never forthcoming from the IRB leader because Stephens believed that political independence was the only issue that would unite Irish men and women of disparate economic and religious backgrounds.[74]

Stephens was averse to publicly expressing his personal agenda for a variety of reasons. In addition to security concerns, Stephens believed that recent precedents had demonstrated that licit nationalist activities were of limited value. The English Chartists had been summarily ignored or repressed by the British government for several years. An 1860 petition for a plebiscite on the resumption of autonomous Irish government, moreover, had achieved nothing after garnering signatures from four hundred thousand people.[75] Stephens may also have decided that it was better to keep his goals undisclosed, because he questioned the then-fashionable utilitarian premise that government programs should be designed to benefit as many people as possible.[76] In the absence of a clear agenda, it is fitting that the "R" in IRB was widely believed to represent the word "revolutionary," rather than "republican," in the early years of the movement. More significantly, face-to-face recruiting would never garner enough Irish manpower to defeat British military forces fighting close to home.

At the time Stephens arrived in the United States after meeting with O'Donovan Rossa, expatriate indifference to militant republicanism was as widespread among Irish American community leaders as within the Irish peasant population. Immigrants who had been incessantly exploited by the inequities of Irish society continued to express defeatist sentiments in the New World. Assuming that they would always be exploited whether they fought for empowerment or not, many émigrés resigned themselves to the inherent injustices of mid-nineteenth-century America. The formal appointment of John O'Mahony as leader of a North American IRB auxiliary was largely ignored. Pro-Irish Democratic Party leaders tacitly sanctioned the movement by allowing the forty charter members of the organization to conduct their first meeting at Tammany Hall, but Fenianism failed to attract much interest in the months that immediately followed.[77] Stephens's subsequent swing through New England included a Boston encounter with several disingenuous drunks and eight dollars in net contributions once all his expenses were paid.[78] Of the limited publicity Stephens and O'Mahony received, most was negative. An attempt to disguise their early stateside fund-raising efforts as a "Fair Trial Fund" campaign to offset the legal fees of Phoenix Society members who had been indicted for sedition was exposed by an expatriate journalist and openly criticized in the Irish American press.

Stephens's continued failure to secure personal endorsements from influential Young Ireland veterans was more damaging than the Fenians' dubious financial activities. Thomas Francis Meagher had become such a celebrity after escaping from Tasmania that he was able to arrange an impromptu meeting between Stephens and President James Buchanan at the White House. Despite the initial courtesies he extended to the aspiring nationalist leader, Meagher eventually distanced himself from Stephens because he surmised that an Irish revolution had no present chance of success.[79] Likewise, John Mitchel first received Stephens favorably when the IRB leader paid an unannounced visit to the British felon's home just outside Knoxville in October. On receiving a letter from John Dillon that criticized Stephens, however, Mitchel concluded that the once-brash Young Irelander was a charlatan who lacked both the requisite skills and the strategic vision to lead Irish nationalists to victory. Mitchel did not believe Stephens's claim that he had fifteen thousand men armed and ready for battle in Ireland.[80] His appraisal proved prophetic, as Stephens would eventually spend considerable time chastising O'Mahony when he should have been plotting a credible insurrection.

Stephens's efforts to woo influential French military and political leaders into a Franco-Fenian alliance were equally unfruitful when he returned to Paris at the end of 1858. The IRB's presentation of a commemorative sword to Patrice MacMahon earned a sincere display of appreciation from the Gallic military leader, but the Irish descendent wisely declined to endorse IRB endeavors at a time of cross-Channel détente. French emperor Napoleon III was a lifelong Anglophile and the two powers had united against Russia in the Crimea and Far East.[81] Notwithstanding competitive French and British efforts to build the largest navy in the world, centuries of Anglo-Franco hostilities were drawing to a close. In an age of increasing *détente*, Stephens would have been more successful if he had not acted as a borderline megalomaniac.[82] Rather than accepting responsibility for his disappointing early efforts as a nationalist leader, Stephens wrote in a private diary at the time that all his detractors were unquestionably "false to Ireland."[83] Yet Stephens himself betrayed his own conflicted feelings toward his homeland by remaining in France until the end of 1860.

Bad publicity and disappointing recruiting results prompted O'Mahony to rechristen his organization the "Fenian Brotherhood" after the "Fair Trial Fund" debacle subsided and Stephens arrived in France. "Fenian" was not a new term;

it had surfaced in the late eighteenth century as the modern anglicized name of a legendary band of Irish soldiers called the Fianna.[84] According to Middle Age transcriptions of pagan-era folklore, a powerful second- or third-century king named Conn had instructed the superhuman warrior Fionn MacCumheill to attend the great fairs of Tara, Uisnech, and Taillte to recruit an army of skilled warriors who would protect Ireland from foreign invasion. Fionn, whose abilities may have been based on the embellished exploits of an actual man, was blessed with incredible fighting prowess and, like the Greek god Hercules, could predict the future by chewing his thumb.

Prospective members of the Fenian movement who had been schooled in Irish myths may have been attracted to the Brotherhood because they knew that Fionn's henchmen had been long portrayed as exceptional people. All Fianna candidates were required to memorize twelve books of poetry then complete several extraordinary physical challenges before taking oaths that enabled their admission into one of three one thousand–man battalions. Among their many honor-bound obligations, members of the Fianna promised that they would aid strangers, take no cattle by coercion, marry women of virtue, and retreat only when outnumbered nine to one. They also pledged never to betray Ireland, even if they were offered "the whole of the world or the country of everlasting youth."[85] Unlike the prophecies of Saint Columbkille, moreover, several sagas suggested that the Fianna had been sleeping for centuries in the Irish mountains and would remobilize if called upon to fight an overbearing adversary. In light of subsequent tensions between the Brotherhood and the Catholic church, it is an interesting coincidence that some of the Fianna sagas were also anti-Christian. In one tale, Saint Patrick condemns the renowned combatants to eternal damnation; in response, the men of the Fianna retort, "It is better to be in hell with Fionn than in heaven with pale and flimsy angels."[86]

The organizational title "Fenian Brotherhood," however, falsely suggested that Stephens and O'Mahony's fledgling republican movement was linked to a Gaelic linguistic revival. The rapidly dying Gaelic language was of little relevance to the IRB and its stateside auxiliary. One leading Fenian believed that O'Mahony anticipated a resurgent use of the Irish native tongue in an independent Ireland, and some republicans occasionally called for bilingual education. Nonetheless, restoration of the Celtic tongue was not a Fenian priority. O'Mahony was a founder of a New York City Gaelic society, but *The Phoenix*, an antebellum Fenian newspaper that he had established, limited its use of the Irish language to translated lists of geographic place-names.[87] Gaelic sporadically appeared in contemporary nationalist poems and ballads, but early Fenian leaders deduced that they needed to secure support from a heterogeneous population. Similar to the Young

Ireland leader, Thomas Davis, the Fenians generally believed that pervasive use of English would encourage Catholics, Dissenters, and Anglicans to unite against foreign rule.[88] The Fenians thus used the language of their enemies to broaden Irish awareness of many injustices that had occurred since twelfth-century Anglo-Norman invaders first arrived in Ireland.[89]

The Fenian Brotherhood differed from Davis's Young Ireland movement in that it was transatlantic, and because its American leaders espoused a degree of fealty to the United States government. Articles in *The Phoenix* frequently highlighted the extensive presence of Irish and American-themed decorations at Fenian balls, lectures, and, in particular, the 1860 New York City Saint Patrick's Day parade.[90] In theory, O'Mahony might have had greater success recruiting new members by emphasizing the many burdens of expatriate life or IRB land redistribution proposals. The obituary section of *The Phoenix* was called "Irish Deaths in America," suggesting that expatriates who died in the United States perished in exile. He also once wrote, "We owe this country no obligation; it has conferred no favor on us . . . we give the country more than we get."[91] Overall, his ideological position demonstrated that his greater love for Ireland did not prevent him from respecting American democratic principles. In the June 4, 1859, debut issue of his Manhattan-based newspaper, he wrote:

> *The Phoenix* shall inculcate upon all its Irish-American readers the
> duty of allegiance to the constitution of the United States whether
> they are citizens or not. This allegiance can never interfere either
> with the higher duties they owe to the land of their birth or with the
> love which should bind them to their parents, kindred and friends
> still in that bondage from which they themselves but yesterday fled
> hither.[92]

O'Mahony's advocacy of divided Irish American nationalist loyalty was controversial. R. A. Burchell notes that many members of the San Francisco Irish community never emphatically supported the Fenian movement because they believed its physical-force nationalist agenda hindered expatriate social mobility. Irish immigrants who had no intention of ever resettling in Ireland concentrated on improving their own communities and dismissed northern California members of the Brotherhood as nostalgic reactionaries.[93] Indeed, with the passage of time, more and more expatriates would feel the same way.

The divided patriotism of the early Fenian Brotherhood agenda was partly the result of rapid social change and Irish immigrant longing for acceptance in their adopted homeland. Cultural upheaval fostered a strong sense of personal liberty among expatriates who arguably would have been more devoted to Ireland if they had resided in a more authoritarian mid-nineteenth-century society. Population growth, territorial expansion, and varied opinions toward slavery dramatically altered the American political landscape in the decades immediately preceding the Civil War. Gold rushes and westward settlement promoted social and geographic mobility, thus contributing to the instability of the American government. At the same time, major political parties were being crippled by disunity. Delegates endured forty rounds of balloting at the 1852 Democratic National Convention before finally nominating the proslavery New Hampshire senator Franklin Pierce to be their presidential candidate. The rival Whig Party did not select Mexican War hero Winfield Scott until fifty-two separate floor votes winnowed the field of contestants to one compromise candidate. Pierce's victory occurred after many expatriate voters in New York tried to make Irish independence a major campaign issue.[94] In sum, Irish expatriate society was philosophically unsettled because New World society was volatile.

The leaders of the Fenian Brotherhood incorporated elements of representative democracy into their organization to attract recruits at a time of rising individualism. O'Mahony maintained almost absolute control over nationwide Brotherhood operations, but local Fenian leaders were usually selected by their peers. In the European tradition of deference to the wealthy, most Fenians who held the equivalent IRB rank of "B" or "C" were usually esteemed members of their respective communities; they were not authoritarian, however. Kevin Brady states that the local nationalist hierarchy in Philadelphia was primarily comprised of educated middle- and professional-class gentlemen, whereas the typical rank-and-file member most likely resided in Irish enclave ghettos, including Moyamensing, the Northern Liberties, and Port Richmond.[95] The demographic distribution of other Fenian circles was similar. Robert Peard had "accumulated significant property" and had been a member of a close-knit political debating society called the Erina Club before he became the leading Fenian in Milford, Massachusetts. He had also lived in the central Massachusetts mill town for twelve years and had been the colonel of a local Irish militia.[96] The original seven members of the Worcester Fenian circle executive board were also community leaders. Four "Outer Ring" councilors had been officers in the Worcester equivalent of Peard's militia. At least two others were actively involved in the temperance movement. Most of the men who eventually became prominent within the Worcester circle were born in southern Irish counties, and one was a County Kilkenny native. Whether their family ties to the comparatively prosperous Irish provinces of Leinster and Munster commanded status, or were merely a reflection of Famine-era migration patterns, is unclear. Two other people on the committee were native New

Englanders, and one had originally hailed from eastern Canada. The birthplace of the last member, James Lee, is unknown. The median age of the seven members with recorded birth dates was 29.3 years.[97] Significantly, this demographic data shows that Irish nationalist powerbrokers in Worcester were of roughly the same age and social background as high-ranking Fenians in New York City and prominent Irish American Civil War officers, who were primarily naturalized citizens in their thirties.

Regarding administration, O'Mahony and his deputies developed questionable auditing practices that had long-term repercussions, but they only classified sensitive documents and correspondence, apparently believing that their activities were protected under American law. Accustomed to police surveillance, John O'Leary was perplexed when he was welcomed to New York City in April 1859 by a militia brass band and was asked to address a curious crowd that had gathered outside his hotel in anticipation of seeing an influential Irish nationalist.[98] Such openness was also demonstrated within local circles. The twenty-two men who attended the charter meeting of the Worcester, Massachusetts circle two months after O'Leary's visit to New York decided that whether they operated in secret was at the discretion of O'Mahony.[99] Fenian activities were routinely reported in community newspapers. The effort to publicize Fenian activities may have been, in part, a reaction to the enduring prevalence of nativist sentiments throughout the United States. An 1859 letter to the central Massachusetts *Milford Journal* demonstrated that local Protestant landowners despised Irish Catholics even for fairly innocuous behavior:

> There are scattered, over town on the Sabbath, gangs of [Irish] men
> and boys, playing at ball, gunning, fishing, and so deporting them-
> selves, as to excite the disgust of decent citizens to say nothing of
> those who wish to see the day kept as holy time. And then, again,
> at this season of the year, their children—impudent and destructive,
> if not thievish—roam about the suburbs, breaking down walls and
> fences, tramping through mowing lots, intruding upon flower and
> vegetable gardens and robbing trees of fruit—in which operation
> the limbs are broken or otherwise much injured.[100]

Notably, fruit pilfering served as a catalyst for additional complaints against the Irish population in Milford. Over the following months, other town residents submitted letters to the editor complaining not only of Sunday orchard raids but also of Irish behavior in general. Two writers bemoaned an Irish penchant for rum, and one of them condemned both Irish Catholic and German immigrants by writing, "Wipe out this class alone, from our borders, and the aspect of society would immediately be improved."[101] Milford Protestants were hardly exceptional in despising the Irish. Yet these attitudes are remarkable because, less than two years after these publications in the town newspaper, seventy-eight members of the local expatriate community, who were most likely Fenians, enlisted in the Union army just days after the onset of the Civil War. In the face of prevailing prejudice, these men and other Famine-era immigrants would decide to defend the integrity of the United States Constitution while supporting a nascent transatlantic organization that had yet to attract a sizable constituency. Supported by several thousand Irishwomen, socially mobile expatriates and native Hibernians who had experienced poverty and discrimination would take up arms to defend their perceived civil rights and to advance the cause of Irish liberty.

2

THE FIGHTING IRISH

Contrary to early Fenian expectations that the Civil War would abet the Irish nationalist cause, Southern secession ultimately undermined Stephens and O'Mahony's efforts to expel the British from Ireland by expediting expatriate assimilation into American society. A de facto Anglo-Confederate alliance gave Irish American federal soldiers hope that Ireland and the United States could forge their own alliance and eventually drive the British out of Ireland. Although Famine-era émigrés were proportionally under-represented in both the Union and Confederate armies, the wartime military service of Fenians and other expatriates increasingly garnered the grudging respect of Yankee community leaders and plantation patriarchs, who had historically disparaged all Catholic immigrants.[1] Anti–Irish Catholic sentiment remained prevalent both within and outside the military during the War between the States, but decreasing nativist sentiment in the 1860s encouraged thousands of émigrés to limit their Irish patriotic expression to attending picnics and lectures. Because true Fenians remained a devoted minority within the transatlantic Irish community in 1865, O'Mahony's decision to consistently endorse the Union war effort was arguably counterproductive, as it promoted Irish acculturation and acceptance into American society.

After initially fearing that the outbreak of the Civil War would distract expatriates from their cause, Fenian leaders on both sides of the Atlantic concluded that Union or Confederate army military service would expose prospective Irish rebels to combat before proceeding to Ireland to engage the British Army. As Thomas Francis Meagher argued, "If only one in ten of us come back when this war is over, the military experience gained by that one will be of more service in a fight for Irish freedom than would that of the entire ten as they are now."² Rebel supporter John Mitchel echoed this sentiment by stating, "I think it highly desirable that young Irishmen should learn the art of war, somewhere, seeing that it is a transportable offence to learn it at home."³ The possibility that a substantial number of Irishmen would die fighting for the North or the South rather than for Ireland was largely discounted by these men and many others who first believed that the Civil War would be resolved in a matter of weeks. For a variety of ideological reasons that often had little to do with Irish politics, about one hundred and ninety thousand Hibernians would ultimately enlist in the Union and Confederate armies.

An Anglo-Confederate alliance had given hope to Irish American nationalists. Expatriate federal soldiers hoped that Ireland and the United States could forge their own alliance and eventually drive the British out of Ireland, while providing expatriates residing in the North with the opportunity to defend the United States Constitution and emulate Irishmen who had fought in foreign armies for the ostensible benefit of their homeland. Beginning with the 1691 exodus of defeated Irish officers known as Wild Geese, Hibernian soldiers had ventured to the European continent to engage in idealistic and self-serving combat against the English in the armies of Catholic monarchs. The Spanish Habsburg throne maintained a Regimento de Hibernia and a Regimento de Ultonia (Ulster) during the eighteenth century. Louis XV of France similarly subsidized an Irish Brigade that rallied from defeat to overrun Anglo-Dutch forces at the seminal 1745 Battle of Fontenoy in modern-day Belgium and was deployed to Savannah in the latter stages of the American Revolution.⁴ Although not always victorious, members of these brigades were widely admired. Devoted Fenians could take solace in knowing that even if they were to fail, tradition suggested that they would receive the admiration of the Irish populace. Dublin, Cork, and Ballyshannon natives had enthusiastically welcomed the defeated Papal Irish Brigade home from Risorgimento Italy in 1860.⁵

Early Fenian Brotherhood and overall Irish American support for the Union war effort was at odds with antebellum expatriate political attitudes that had compared the South to a subjugated Ireland. A Southern sympathizer before the war, Meagher echoed the sentiments of many fellow Irish Americans when he enunciated his reasons for raising a company of recruits who joined the New York 69th militia regiment:

> Looking at every aspect of the question, I do not see what better
> course I could take. Duty and patriotism alike prompt me to it. The
> Republic that is the mainstay of human freedom, the world over, that

gave us asylum and an honorable career is threatened with disrup-
tion. It is the duty of every liberty-loving citizen to prevent such a
calamity at all hazards. Above all, it is the duty of Irish citizens, who
aspire to establish a similar form of government in our native land.[6]

An October 1861 letter to Meagher from William Smith O'Brien suggests
that the political views of the new Union sympathizer may, when the war began,
have been at least partly based on personal ambitions. Thousands of expatriates
who resided in the North, however, believed that the freedoms and economic opportunities guaranteed by the United States Constitution had to be defended,
even if the Irish themselves had been frequently mistreated under American law.[7]
Southern military aggression, in the estimation of law-abiding members of the
immigrant community, was tantamount to treason, and Victorian-era masculinity
dictated that citizens of affronted nations defend their honor even if they once
shared the political sentiments of their new enemies.[8] Allied as members of the
Democratic Party, East Coast Irishmen and plantation patriarchs had commonly
espoused Jacksonian America values until suspicious Southern elites refused to
endorse Stephen Douglas's presidential campaign in 1860. Irishmen residing in
the North End of Boston nearly instigated a riot in April 1861, when a vessel from
Savannah flying rebel insignia arrived on a town wharf. The future highest-ranking
Fenian in the Union army, General Thomas A. Smyth, had similarly voted for
Southern Democrat John C. Breckinridge instead of Douglas six months earlier,
but he enlisted in the Union army as soon as Abraham Lincoln issued a public call
for seventy-five thousand volunteer soldiers.[9] An announcement placed in leading
Chicago newspapers nine days after the Confederate shelling of Fort Sumter was
similarly well received, impelling twelve hundred Illinois Irish residents to enlist
"For the Honor of the Old Land [and to] Rally for the defense of the New."[10]

New York state militia colonel Michael Corcoran was a more reserved Union
supporter than fellow Fenian Thomas Smyth. The first sworn American member of
the Fenian Brotherhood, Corcoran had gained national recognition four months
before the war when he was court-martialed for refusing to march the members
of his almost exclusively Irish regiment before the visiting the Prince of Wales.[11]
In admiration of his defiant decision, expatriates residing in Charleston, South
Carolina, sent the former Ribbonman a gold-laden palmetto walking stick and
organized a local festival in his honor.[12] Although the gift was highly symbolic—
Yankee abolitionist senator Charles Sumner had been beaten by a cane-wielding
South Carolina congressman in 1856 after condemning the South—Corcoran refused to be an apologist for slavery and states' rights once the war began.[13] Like-
wise, and contrary to assertions by skeptical *New York Times* journalists, the men

he led into federal service before he received an official pardon had no intention of defecting en masse to the Confederacy.[14]

Despite his fealty to the Stars and Stripes, Corcoran remained more wary of Irish participation in the Civil War than Meagher as recruiting stations were established in every Manhattan Irish neighborhood and six thousand expatriates applied to serve in an expanded one thousand–man 69th New York regiment.[15] During a public address at the beginning of the war, the Tammany Hall protégé advised members of the Fenian Brotherhood, "If you aren't already in the Army, stay out of it . . . reserve your lives for Ireland." Perhaps in light of traditional mistreatment of expatriate soldiers in the army or out of ethnic pride, he added, "but if you must enlist, join an Irish regiment."[16] Corcoran similarly dissuaded the middle-aged O'Mahony from joining an active duty regiment when he returned from an inspection tour of Ireland a month after the beginning of the war. "Irrespective of any other consideration," Corcoran wrote, "our Irish cause would grievously, if not fatally suffer by the withdrawal of your immediate services and supervision."[17] O'Mahony, therefore, initially limited his military activity to serving as the titular colonel of the Phoenix Zouaves, an all-Fenian Home Guard that had originally started drilling as a paramilitary unit sixteen months earlier, in preparation for a revolution in Ireland.[18] He hoped, as Corcoran predicted, "That our organization will derive considerable impetus and strength from the military enthusiasm prevailing here at present."[19]

Many Fenian expatriates among the many Irish Americans who joined the Union army were ideal paramilitaries. As an example, the 40th New York Regiment, also known as the Mozart Regiment, which included four companies from Massachusetts, demonstrates the desire of Fenians to eventually utilize their American military training to free Ireland. Seventy-eight suspected Fenian volunteers who enlisted in Milford, Massachusetts on June 11, 1861, were of a lower social status than the sixty-nine (presumably Protestant) members of the mill town community who had earlier mustered into the 40th New York Regiment. The seventy-eight volunteers were also predominately single, however, and thus were probably more mobile and receptive to a martial lifestyle. (see Table I). The members of a Fenian circle that enlisted en masse in the largely Irish Tenth Ohio Infantry, likewise, were generally in their early twenties.[20] James McKay Rorty spoke for Fenians who joined the Union army when he explained why he had enlisted in a letter to his disapproving father:

Apart from the motives of self interest, and the higher one of attachment to, and veneration for the Constitution, which urged me to defend it at all risks, there is another, and a deeper one still which weighed heavily with me, namely the hope that the military knowledge or skill which I may acquire might thereafter be turned to account in the sacred cause of my native land.[21]

Sharing Rorty's sentiments, many pragmatic Irishmen reasoned that they would gain greater acceptance from northern Protestants if they proved their mettle on the battlefield. Presumably, even the most skeptical nativist would have difficulty questioning the loyalty of Irish Americans who had risked injury and death for the preservation of the Union; of equal importance was that Rorty and other Fenians had enlisted to prepare for an eventual revolution in Ireland.

Age and Profession Distribution of Milford Union Army Enlistees (June 1861)		
	Irish-born	"Yankees"
Number in Sample	79	69
Average Age (years decimalized)	24.0	25.1
Unskilled	75 (94%)	44 (64%)
Artisan	1	14
Shopkeepers/Clerks	0	11
Unknown Profession	2	0

Because only the year of birth (and not the exact date) was included in the records of Milford recruits born in Ireland, the average age of the Irish volunteers was calculated on the assumption that their births were equally distributed throughout the year. If everyone in the sample group had celebrated his birthday on the date of his enlistment, the average age of the company would be 23.5 years old. In an alternative scenario (all non-native recruits born 364 days *after* the date they enlisted), the average Irish recruit—at 24.997 years old—would still be 37.5 days younger than his "Yankee" counterpart. It is also possible that all these figures, Irish and Yankee alike, are too high. Civil War–era teenagers were more likely to say they were older so they could enlist before they reached the minimum enrollment age of eighteen; conversely, middle-aged men often lied, claiming they were younger than they were. The estimated average age of Union army enlistees was 25.8 years.[22]

Additional analysis of the Milford Fenians who enlisted in the Union army reveals that "Yankee" recruits were more rooted in the community than the average Fenian. In the 1860 Census Index, 25.6 percent of Irish-born men who joined the Ninth Massachusetts Infantry on June 11, 1861, are listed as town residents; within this group, only one man possessed any property. Similar to the Union army average, 30 percent were temporarily separated from their wives when they reported for military service.[23] Of the Protestant townsmen who enlisted at the same time, 39.1% appeared in the census records compiled a year earlier, 51 percent was married, and one owned property. Irishmen in the sample had slightly more children, on average (2.3 to 2.0). Overall, however, these statistics imply that many of the Fenians who likely followed Captain Robert Peard into service were itinerants who had wandered from mill town to mill town in search of employment before wartime military service seemingly offered a monthly paycheck and other attractive benefits. (See Table II.)

Besides patriotic sentiment, the reason for the large number of Irish laborers in the Milford sample may have been because of mid-nineteenth-century workplace conditions in America rather than owing to a desire to obtain military training before a revolution in Ireland. Increasing technological innovations in shoemaking, textiles, and other industries monotonized factory work and destabilized demand for manual labor. The Union army and navy alternatively offered enlistees a guaranteed salary of thirteen dollars a month plus board at the beginning of the war. Paydays became notoriously irregular, and the dependents of many soldiers struggled to keep food on their tables as the war continued. Nonetheless, not having to worry about accommodation expenses was appealing, as rents had consumed a large portion of the $1.01 average daily national wage in 1860.[24] The camaraderie of outdoor life—despite frequent periods of inclement weather— may also have appealed to prospective recruits accustomed to stuffy air and dim light in their places of employment.

For a variety of reasons, more Irish Americans did not follow the Milford Fenians and other expatriates into the Union army, as Stephens and O'Mahony had hoped. Irresolute expatriates, who were unlikely to become militant Irish nationalists, feared death, dismemberment, and hanging as "savages," a fate that the

Property Ownership and Marital Status of Milford Union Army Enlistees included in 1860 Census Index, June 1861		
	Irish-born	"Yankees"
Number in Sample	20	27
Property Owners	1	1
Married Enlistees	6 (30%)	14.0 (51.9%)
Married Enlistees' Average Number of Children	2.3	2.0

Southern press promised captured Irish and German captives.[25] Many Irishmen also reasoned that only the foolhardy would join an army led by many Know-Nothing officers, who permitted their soldiers to desecrate Catholic churches and cemeteries.[26] Treatment of Catholic infantrymen had been reprehensible during the Mexican War, and many Irish Americans remembered the particularly inhumane hanging of several émigré soldiers who were captured after they defected from the U.S. Army and joined the famed *San Patricio* Brigade. More importantly, many immigrants assumed that the expansion of the army would tighten the labor market and boost wages, while Northern victory would lead to an inundation of free blacks from the South, who would work for lower pay.[27] As an example of the general expatriate indifference to military service that was damaging to the Union war effort and the Fenian movement alike, Boston resident Maurice Sexton pragmatically wrote in a November 1861 letter to his siblings in County Cork that he "would probably fight if conscripted but might instead return home if the Irish agricultural economy improved."[28]

Per capita expatriate enlistment during the Civil War was slightly higher in the South. Many of the approximately forty thousand Hibernians who enlisted in several designated Irish Brigades and other Confederate regiments were sympathetic to the Fenian movement because they believed the Rebel cause was an honorable defensive stand against imperial aggression.[29] Few Irish families in the South owned slaves, but expatriates often feared that vindictive Northerners were minions of the recently executed John Brown. If they were not resisted, these abolitionist sympathizers would presumably attempt to confiscate the meager land and possessions of poor Southerners as well as the vast soil-rich plantations owned by upper class patriarchs.[30] As proponents of Thomas Jefferson's literal interpretation of the United States Constitution, mid-nineteenth century Irish Southerners maintained a proud legacy of antigovernment defiance. In addition to the Regulators, a group of North Carolinians who had revolted against corrupt colonial officials preceding the American Revolution, eighteenth-century expatriates from Mecklenburg, North Carolina had issued a famous series of resolves on May 31, 1775, that nullified the authority of King George III and the British Parliament in favor of local government. In a similar spirit, Irishmen who belonged to Captain Joseph Kelly's Fifth Missouri Confederate infantry regiment composed two verses of a marching song expressing their belief that they were emulators of the United Irishmen rather than traitors to the American Union.

You call us rebels and traitors, but yourselves have thrown off that
name of late.

> You were called it by the English invaders at home in seventeen and
> ninety-eight.
> The name to us is not a new one, though 'tis one that never will
> degrade.
> Any true-hearted Hibernian in the ranks of Kelly's Irish Brigade
>
> Chorus
>
> You dare not call us invaders, 'tis but states rights and liberties we
> ask;
> And Missouri, we ever will defend her, no matter how hard be the
> task.
> Then let true Irishmen assemble; let the voice of Missouri be obeyed;
> And northern fanatics may tremble when they meet with Kelly's
> Irish Brigade.

Still others saw the war as little more than an opportunity to earn greater income. A meager ten dollar enlistment bounty drew several New Orleans Irish levee workers into the Confederate army shortly after the shelling of Fort Sumter, while several fellow expatriates with maritime seafaring skills joined the Rebel navy. Later, middle- and upper-class Irishmen in Southern port cities became war hawks because they stood to profit from running badly needed supplies through the Union naval blockade.[31] Altogether, Irish regiments were formed in eight of the eleven Confederate states.[32]

Economic self-interest was not limited to poor Irish Americans who enlisted in the Confederate army. Protestant County Cork native Patrick Royne Cleburne believed he had everything to lose if the North conquered the South. Embarrassed by failing a Trinity College medical school entrance examination, the Saint Patrick's Day–born Cleburne enlisted in a British infantry regiment three years before immigrating to Helena, Arkansas at the age of twenty-one. Having joined a local militia that was mobilized for active duty after the shelling of Fort Sumter, the prosperous Fenian-sympathizing attorney rose in rank from private to one of only two foreign-born Rebel brigadier generals. Indifferent to slavery—in 1863 he shocked the South by proposing to muster blacks into the Confederate army—Cleburne best expressed his reasons for fighting in a May 1861 letter to his brother in Kentucky:

I am with the South in life or in death, in victory or defeat. I never owned a Negro and care nothing for them, but these people have been my friends and have stood up for me on all occasions. In addition to this, I believe the North is about to wage a brutal and unholy war on a people who have done them no wrong, in violation of the government. They no longer acknowledge that all government derives its validity from the consent of the governed. They are about to invade our peaceful homes, destroy our property, and inaugurate a servile insurrection, murder our men and dishonor our women. We propose no invasion of the North, no attack on them, and only ask to be left alone. They cannot conquer us but would turn the wolf from their own door by letting this idle, brutal mob come here to be destroyed.

Joe [another Cleburne sibling] speaks of joining the Northern army. He says the stars and stripes must be held up, that Davis or Lincoln must be president, that all the laws must be enforced, the Government must be maintained, but there is not one argument, one reason in his letter. Let him ask himself why the free people of Arkansas should be robbed and murdered merely because they have determined to live under the laws of their own making. Let him ask himself what the North will do with Arkansas. If she conquered it, will she keep a standing army of 30,000 men here to maintain her conquest? We are not striving to become tyrannical invaders. Our army is for protection, Lincoln's to subjugate and enslave the whole Southern people and divide the property among his vulgar unprincipled mob.[33]

As evidenced by the closing sentences of this missive, Cleburne feared that a defeated South would become a subservient colony little different from Ireland.[34] Similar sentiments had surfaced in the 1830s among Irish immigrants in Texas when the Mexican government attempted to assert greater control over its northernmost province. Unmolested by bureaucrats based hundreds of miles to the south, the Irish of Refugio County originally enjoyed lucrative settlers' rights in a newly independent nation that extended preferred civil status to Catholics. Early calls for secession were ignored until Mexican general Antonio Lopez de Santa Ana actually marched toward San Antonio. In defense of personal property, many Irishmen fought at the Alamo and became the forefathers of the short-lived Texas Republic.[35]

This sentiment mirrored John Mitchel's assertions that the South and Ireland had much in common; that both were exploited colonies of imperialist industrial nations. In speeches in New Orleans and Mobile, Mitchel maintained that New York profiteers benefited from agricultural produce created in the South: "The Shipping is Northern, the revenue Northern, the profit of trade and manufactures, Northern. The political power is on the point of becoming Northern too." Mitchel hoped that the parallels he drew between the South and Ireland would lead to an alliance that might eventually gain economic and political independence from the United States and Great Britain, respectively.[36]

The large number of Irish Southerners who did not support the Confederate war effort were unlikely Fenian recruits because they were either apolitical or had a profound admiration for established government institutions.[37] At a time when the Lincoln administration was being compared to an imperialist British monarchy, Irish desire to defend the integrity of the United States Constitution actually surfaced in many Southern expatriate enclaves. Such respect for federal authority would presumably have been even more pervasive if the "warmongering abolitionist" president and his "Black Republican" cabinet secretaries had decided to contain rather than conquer the South in 1861.[38] Irishmen in New Orleans—like their counterparts in the 69th New York Militia—were widely accused of being loyal to the enemy at the beginning of the war.[39] Although the presence of former Rebel expatriates was ultimately less common in the Fenian movement, Irish militants likely benefited from Catholic immigrant respect for prevailing bureaucratic authority in the American South. Presumably, fewer Fenians in the Union army were killed before they had the opportunity to fight for Ireland because they faced fewer fellow Hibernian opponents on the battlefield.

Other indications that many potential Fenian recruits were more ideologically attached to the Union war effort than to the independence of their homeland surfaced when the first of several predominately Irish regiments was dispatched to the South. Thousands of enthusiastic well-wishers patiently waited along Broadway for several hours to view a behind-schedule parade in honor of the departing New York 69th State Militia Regiment. Hearty displays of émigré allegiance to the Union occurred when several fraternal organizations, including O'Mahony's Phoenix Zouaves and the Irish infantrymen themselves, belatedly appeared marching behind a large banner that read "Remember Fontenoy." A woman spontaneously volunteered to serve as a field nurse, and an elderly man offered to enlist as a substitute when one soldier in the ranks abided the pleas of his weeping spouse not to risk his life by going off to war. As more troops proceeded to an Annapolis-bound steamship, the aged gentleman's offer was politely declined and the soldier was allowed to stay with his family.[40] An equally festive reception occurred nine days later, when Washington, D.C. residents cheered the men of the 69th as they passed through the Capitol and established a temporary camp at Georgetown University. Countless well-wishers similarly lined Wabash Street when the Illinois Irish Brigade left Chicago on July 15.[41]

Poems and airs that were read and sung by expatriate soldiers from the North during the early stages of the war were additional indications that Irish Americans had not joined the Union army solely to obtain military training in preparation for a Fenian revolution. James DeMille borrows Gaelic phrases and words in his straightforward 1861 fighting anthem of the Irish Legion:

> Ye boys of the sod, to Columbia true,
> Come up, boys, and fight, for the Red White and Blue!
> Two countries we love, and two mottoes we'll share,
> And we'll join them in one, on the banners we bare:
> Erin mavourneen! Columbia agra!
> E pluribus unum! Erin go braugh!

The four-verse "Song of the Irish Brigade" places even greater emphasis on the Irish struggle for independence, while detailing the responsibilities and objectives of the regiment at hand. After half the lyrics exclusively address Irish politics, the closing stanza reminds the listener that the Union war effort is of the utmost priority:

> How we're pledged to free this land,
> So long the exile's resting place;
> To crush for aye a traitorous band,
> And wipe out treason's deep disgrace.
> Then let us pledge Columbia's cause,
> God prosper poor old Ireland too!
> We'll trample all the tyrant laws:
> Hurrah for the old land and the new.

More succinct, but in the same divided nationalist spirit, were two similar jingles that were written during the Civil War.

> Faithful here to flag and laws,
> And faithful to our sire-land,
> Fighting for the Union cause
> We learn to fight for Ireland.

When concord and peace to this land are restored,
And the union's established for ever,
Brave sons of Hibernia, oh, sheathe not the sword;—
You will then have a Union to sever.

Although artistically pedantic, these simple compositions defined a significant aspect of Irish American identity. When singing them in camps, on marches,
and along pickets, young Irishmen reminded themselves why they had enlisted to
fight in the current war and why they hoped that Ireland would one day become
an independent nation. These slogans, in other words, helped foster what political
theorist Benedict Anderson has dubbed an "imagined community." Fenians who
did not know one other and perhaps lived thousands of miles apart were unified
by a core set of beliefs that were not entirely rooted in historical fact but were
powerful enough to persuade people to risk life and limb. What the poems did
not reveal was that Irish American soldiers were more inclined to risk their lives
for the United States than for Ireland.[42]

In hindsight, it is remarkable that expatriate soldiers and civilians supported
the Union army with relative enthusiasm at the beginning of the Civil War given
that Irish enlisted men were widely reviled by nativist officers. Instances of anti-
Irish discrimination—that potentially could have been publicized to encourage
Fenian rather than American loyalties—were abundant. After secretly observing expatriate soldiers in training on a Boston Harbor island, a spy employed by
Massachusetts Republican governor John Andrew queried in May 1861, "What
would people think of Massachusetts when they saw such ignorant, vicious, and
vile men?"[43] One pedestrian observing the embarkation of the Ninth Massachusetts Infantry six weeks later commented wryly, "There goes a load of Irish rub-
bish out of the city."[44] Many complaints were petty. A Protestant officer in the
Ninth Massachusetts wrote to Governor Andrew in October 1861, "The state
flag has never been out on any parade review, nor line of battle. Since we have
been in Virginia it has always been supplanted by the Irish Ensign—thus insult-
ing the state."[45] Ironically, the embroidered motto on the regiment's battle flag—
"Thy sons by adoption, thy firm supporters and defenders from duty, affection and
choice"—was clearly patriotic and certainly not encouraging to Fenian leaders,
who assumed expatriates would return to Ireland after the Civil War was over.[46]

Warranted anti-Irish criticism was directed at a type of expatriate soldier
who would never be a good Fenian recruit. The Sixth New York Infantry was
largely comprised of expatriates who had worked in dog-fighting and rat-baiting
dens. Irishmen who belonged to the Eleventh New York Infantry broke into local taverns and charged their bar tabs to Jefferson Davis when they first arrived

in Washington, D.C.[47] However, most Irish Americans enlisted in multi-ethnic Yankee regiments, rather than in units such as the 69th New York, and the majority of these men behaved like typical soldiers.[48] Occasionally disrespectful to their superiors, most expatriate enlistees obeyed orders and fought bravely. The prewar Milford Fenian circle leader Robert Peard was described in an early war report, for example, as a cultured gentleman.[49] Many Irish soldiers in the Confederate army behaved in the same manner as their Union counterparts. Members of the Southern Irish Brigade ("A" Company, Sixth Louisiana Regiment) were so infamous for truculent behavior in camp that they frightened the Richmond civilians they had been assigned to protect.[50] Rudolf Coreth, an Austrian immigrant who had joined a Texas cavalry regiment, corroborated stories of Irish misbehavior in the Confederate army; letters to his family, dated November 1861, describe expatriate soldiers from Galveston as a dissolute gang of former dockworkers who could be controlled, "only by means of great strictness."[51] Men who would only obey under threat of court-martial were not likely to be effective Fenian paramilitaries.

During the early stages of the war, American Fenian leaders maintained close ties to the New York 69th in an effort to maintain the support of respectable pro-Republican Irish soldiers like Captain Peard. In addition to dispatching frequent letters to nationalist members of the regiment, John O'Mahony and a future president of the Fenian Brotherhood named John Savage both traveled to Arlington, Virginia to attend the dedication of an Irish Brigade defensive battery that had been completed two weeks ahead of schedule. Nonetheless, there were a variety of indications during the first summer of the war that many members of the 69th would probably never take up arms in an Irish struggle for independence. At a time when Archbishop Hughes and other Catholic Church leaders had started to condemn the Brotherhood as a dangerous organization, most off-duty soldiers displayed their strong respect for diocesan authority by attending daily mass on their own volition. Strong pro-American sentiment was evident when the regiment cheered vigorously after Meagher read the Declaration of Independence aloud during a Fourth of July ceremony. Discouraging discipline problems also surfaced. One militia company temporarily refused to participate in a work detail because its members had yet to be paid, two months after they had enlisted.[52] As the regiment was thus comprised of a variety of soldiers who were either unwilling or unattractive recruits, O'Mahony spent the remainder of the war striving to persuade more expatriate enlisted men to share James Rorty's published beliefs that Fenians were unequivocally loyal Union soldiers who loved Ireland more than America.[53]

The extent of Irish American commitment to the Union and to the Confederacy was particularly evident when the First Battle of Bull Run was fought under a blazing sun on July 21, 1861. Even though their ninety-day enlistments expired in less than forty-eight hours, members of the 69th aggressively engaged expatriate longshoremen who belonged to the Louisiana Zouaves. By fighting specifically against one another, Irishmen on both sides of the battlefield definitively demonstrated that their common fealty to Ireland had been eclipsed by the respective patriotic causes of the North and the South. Evidence of this divided sentiment once again surfaced seven weeks later, when expatriate residents of Charleston, South Carolina threw stones at a convoy of Union army Irish prisoners that included Michael Corcoran and other émigré soldiers who had been captured at what Southerners were then widely calling the Battle of Manassas. No one was seriously injured during the incident, but the ideological divisions that compromised Fenian efforts to unify expatriates on both sides of the Mason-Dixon Line under one common nationalist cause had become undeniable in the once universally oppressed immigrant community.[54] A celebrity among the Southern Irish community seven months earlier, Michael Corcoran was often ill treated as a POW. More fortunate were the Bull Run veterans who were warmly welcomed back to Manhattan on July 27. Similar to the excitement of its April departure, a local battery fired a sixty-nine-gun salute, and the Fenian Phoenix Brigade escorted its battle-tested kinsmen through Manhattan streets crowded with boisterous spectators.[55] Thirty-eight percent of the thirteen hundred expatriates who had fought in the first major battle of the Civil War immediately re-enlisted for three more years of military service in a newly constituted multistate unit called the Irish Brigade.[56] Union general William Tecumseh Sherman noted that unlike other one hundred–day enlistees, the men of the Irish Sixty Ninth would fight while members of other regiments were in a "state of mutiny" after the Battle of Bull Run.[57]

Extensive Irish American participation in a transatlantic funeral procession three months after the First Battle of Bull Run demonstrated that a portion of the expatriate community would support militant republican initiatives as long as Hibernian assimilation into American society was incomplete. Although Terence Bellew MacManus had died in relative obscurity on January 15, 1861, he was widely mourned throughout the United States and Ireland after a group of West Coast Fenians decided to have his remains removed from the local Lone Mountain Cemetery and have them re-interred in Ireland. MacManus had been largely apolitical and professionally unsuccessful after he had escaped from Australia in 1852 and resettled in San Francisco. He had also become an alcoholic, and his accidental death may have been caused by inebriation. Still, in an attempt to drum up support for the IRB, expatriate nationalist leaders assumed that MacManus could be cast as a republican martyr. Thousands of Bay Area Irish Americans thus initiated a protracted display of respect for the deceased revolutionary by lining San Francisco thoroughfares when his remains were escorted to a city wharf and placed onboard the southbound Pacific Coast packet *Uncle Sam* in mid-August.[58]

A month later, a more substantial tribute and parade followed, under the direction of Thomas Francis Meagher in New York. An honor guard was dispatched to the *Champion* so that the first groups of mourners could view the rosewood-lined iron casket before it was removed from the vessel that had transported the body through the Caribbean and the Atlantic after being carried across the Isthmus of Panama.[59] The coffin was thereafter placed inside the lavish Astor House Hotel for additional visitations. Archbishop Hughes also participated in the MacManus obsequies by serving as the celebrant of a requiem mass. Despite his rising suspicion that Fenianism was a threat to the temporal authority of the Catholic Church, Hughes bolstered the spirits of Irish nationalists in attendance by stating, "There are cases in which it is lawful to resist and overthrow tyrannical government."[60] On October 18, large crowds of Irish expatriates gathered on the same stretch of Broadway along which the 69th New York Militia had recently marched to pay its final respects. Thirty-two pallbearers and a cortege of Irish fraternal organization representatives culminated the American MacManus commemorations by conveying the already well-traveled coffin to a Munster-bound steamship.[61] Over the following month, Michael Doheny led an American delegation that was assigned to escort the body all the way to Dublin.

Similar commemorations were organized and equally well supported in Ireland, even though Stephens had to contend with many influential people who opposed his agenda and his authority. Bishop William Keane of Cloyne accommodated the Fenians by allowing local mourners to pay their respects to MacManus at a Queenstown church at the beginning of November. Maynooth seminarians attended a requiem for the deceased nationalist on November 3.[62] Bishop William Delany of Cork, however, prohibited any memorial service to be conducted within his diocese.[63] Stephens knew full well that the IRB was unprepared for revolution, so he took several precautionary measures after he heard a false rumor that Doheny and several accomplices would abscond with MacManus's body when the funeral procession reached Limerick Junction by rail. To prevent his American colleague from possibly using the corpse as a patriotic talisman, Stephens and some of his County Tipperary allies scrutinized local mourners when they gathered on the Limerick platform before the cortege train briefly stopped at the station. Then, leaving nothing to chance as the locomotive was fired for departure, Stephens deftly called on the assembled crowd to kneel and recite an *Our Father* and a *Hail Mary* for the deceased hero. In the midst of the docile and reverent on-lookers, pulling off any high jinx would have been most difficult. Whether or not Doheny had planned any heist,[64] the moment passed without incident.

Having averted a possible internal challenge to his authority, Stephens proceeded to contain influential nationalists and surviving MacManus family members who wanted the former Young Ireland priest Father John Kenyon to serve as the celebrant at a sedate final memorial service in Dublin. Such an indirect effort to stifle the burgeoning IRB was hardly surprising; William Smith O'Brien was in the midst of further distancing himself from Stephens, and John Mitchel had recently recommended that the IRB refrain from turning the MacManus burial into a public spectacle. Refusing to cooperate with fellow nationalists, Stephens took several measures to ensure that he would orchestrate a grand display of patriotic expression modeled after the large funeral James Finton Lalor received when he had died ten years earlier. At first, Stephens packed a committee that was empanelled to supervise MacManus tributes in the Irish capitol. He then skirted significant interference from Archbishop Paul Cullen by organizing a week-long vigil for his former comrade at the secular Mechanics' Institute.

Stephens capitalized on his victory over more conservative Irish nationalists by persuading thousands of Irish men and women to participate in a final MacManus cortege to Glasnevin cemetery. Posters distributed throughout Dublin implied that honoring the deceased Irish nationalist was a civic responsibility for all patriotic men and women. Large crowds responded by viewing the coffin while it was on public display and by following arm-banded marshals through Dublin during a parade that preceded the final burial of the remains. Led by a former British soldier who served as grand marshal, well-dressed small shopkeepers, tradesmen, and laborers marched through the city on a dreary mid-November Sunday in the company of lower-class male juveniles and politically active women.[65] Police detectives later suggested in filed reports that the overall age, dress, and demeanor of the mourners demonstrated that countless militant nationalists were present at the procession.

Overt signs of antigovernment defiance were limited during the MacManus funeral procession. All marchers briefly stopped and removed their hats in front of the spot where Robert Emmet had been executed in 1803. In addition, the crowd cheered each time the fiery Irish nationalist cleric Patrick Lavelle hinted at revolution during an otherwise terse and atypically temperate graveside homily. The thirty-five-year-old clergyman chastised the crowd for such outbursts, however, presumably because he knew that Archbishop Cullen had been reluctantly persuaded that MacManus was entitled to a Christian burial.[66] Concluded under torchlight, the MacManus funeral celebration was a great IRB victory that sustained transatlantic interest in the Fenian movement after Confederate army resiliency had quashed assumptions that combat-tested expatriates would soon arrive in Ireland to train republican volunteers. Philadelphia Fenians, for instance, publicly thanked the members of the American funeral delegation for their services after they returned to the East Coast.[67] Nonetheless, popular support for the IRB started to wane shortly thereafter. When Doheny died unexpectedly in early 1862, Stephens still could not afford a tombstone for the MacManus gravesite. Potential IRB recruits also began to heed Archbishop Hughes's advice to immigrate to American states that had remained in the Union.[68]

Depleted coffers may have only been a temporary problem for the IRB if an Anglo-American naval altercation at the time of the final MacManus funeral had fulfilled long-standing Fenian hopes for a transatlantic war. Having received word that two London-bound Confederate emissaries had boarded a British mail steamer in Havana on November 7, Captain Charles Wilkes, of the fifteen-gun sloop *U.S.S. San Jacinto,* intercepted the *R.M.S. Trent* in the Bahama Channel two days before the MacManus funeral by firing a pair of warning shots. After inspecting the English ship, Wilkes detained George Mason's grandson, James Murray Mason, John Slidell, and their respective private secretaries.[69] In an effort to protect the global reputation of the United Kingdom, British prime minister Lord Palmerston thereafter demanded that the two former United States senators and their assistants be released immediately because traveling between neutral ports did not violate international law. Although he feared that the Union army may soon be confronted by two formidable enemy powers, Abraham Lincoln refused to capitulate because he believed that Mason and Slidell were traitors who had been arrested while attempting to endanger American domestic security. A crafty diplomat who had formerly served as foreign office secretary, Palmerston retaliated by ordering eleven thousand British soldiers to join an influx of Canadian volunteers who had enlisted in local militias because of the crisis.[70] The Royal Navy was also placed on alert, and a substantial Union purchase of British saltpeter was suspended. Supported by a powerful English civic group called the Southern Aid Association as well as by rising political rivals Benjamin Disraeli and William Gladstone, Palmerston was confident enough to ponder whether victory in an intercontinental military conflict might guarantee long-term British geo-political supremacy.[71]

Fenians around the world expected that an imminent war between the United States and Great Britain would encourage the Lincoln administration to support Irish independence and potentially unite all Hibernians in a common cause.[72] Maurice Sexton expressed the following in the same letter about potential Union army conscription that he had written to his siblings in County Cork:

> If either the British or French governments provided military sup-
> port to the South, the whole population of the United States would
> rise up in arms . . . there would be a general stampede of both native
> and foreign rich & poor no distinctions, it would not be a war, aggra-
> vated as it is now by means of a few republican fanatics.[73]

If such social unity had arisen, as Sexton predicts here, Fenians and other nationalists could have feasibly acquired enough political leverage to assure that Irish independence would became a condition of any Anglo-American peace agreement.
At the same time, John Mitchel argued in a December 1861 letter to the *Cork
Examiner* that de facto British assistance to the South did not preclude a possible Fenian-Confederate alliance; however, most Irish nationalist leaders openly
expressed their support for the Union throughout the *Trent* Affair.[74] A Dublin
IRB demonstration against the Confederacy was followed by expatriate rallies in
several cities, including London and Philadelphia.[75]

Fenian sympathizers were disappointed when a bilateral desire to maintain over two decades of détente prevented the *Trent* debacle from escalating into
an Anglo-American war. As Christmas approached, Queen Victoria instructed
her terminally ill husband to initiate a dialogue between British and American
negotiators. Receptive to this deathbed diplomacy, President Lincoln authorized
the January release of the four *Trent* prisoners from a Boston fortress and sym-
bolically censured the widely popular Captain Wilkes for attacking a sovereign
vessel without provocation.[76] Because insurrection in Ireland was unlikely for the
immediate future, Fenian hopes of securing military and political assistance from
the United States government depended on the Union's capability to defeat a
Confederate government that still received significant support from Great Britain. Although not a Fenian, the editor and barrister P. J. Smyth wrote to William
Smith O'Brien:

> With America dismembered, there goes the last and only hope of
> Ireland. With the Union restored comes Irish freedom. Let the
> Union come out of this conflict intact and America may dictate . . .
> the independence of Ireland. . . . A solemn duty devolves then upon
> Ireland and Irishmen. The United States are fighting our battle.[77]

Left with little to do as long as the Civil War wore on, Stephens tended gar-
dens and riled his class-conscious colleagues by courting the beautiful daughter
of a Sandymount publican. O'Mahony, likewise, devoted less time to the Fenian

movement, as thousands of potential nationalist combatants became more devoted to either the Union or the Confederacy than to their subjugated homeland. Although the protracted Civil War would offer Fenian leaders an opportunity to retool their recruiting strategy, the MacManus funeral procession and other efforts to expand the transatlantic Irish nationalist movement were inconsequential after the *Trent* Affair was resolved and the so-called War between the States became a drawn-out struggle.

3

GREEN AMERICANS

Unmitigated Fenian Brotherhood support for the Union army became increasingly illogical as the Civil War progressed. All but relatively few expatriate soldiers and civilians were exploited and underappreciated in the early 1860s. O'Mahony and his colleagues would likely have had more success recruiting Irishmen who were frequently used as cannon fodder on the battlefield and as disposable employees in the workplace. Southern Irishmen who routinely fraternized across picket lines with fellow expatriates would also have been more inclined to establish Brotherhood chapters in their communities if Fenian leaders had called for Confederate independence. Although O'Mahony was opposed to slavery, expatriate civilians could have been recruited by aggravating their traditionally racist attitudes toward African Americans. The promulgation of the Emancipation Proclamation after the September 1862 Battle of Antietam precipitated a protracted period of Irish American angst in the North that endured through the outbreak of several antidraft riots and the restoration of peace at Appomattox Courthouse. But O'Mahony never compromised his integrity and morals by using racist diatribes to win expatriate support; to the contrary, he remained openly loyal to a nation that he had often subtly criticized in his prewar newspaper, the *Irish People*.

Widespread anti-Catholic discrimination in the Union and Confederate armies continued to surface as early assumptions of a prompt Northern or Southern victory proved unfounded. Largely unappreciated for their willingness to enlist, Irish American soldiers were routinely disparaged. Expatriate Union officer R. T. Farrell had written from Detroit in December 1861 that his commanding officer was "an inveterate Enemy of Catholicism."[1] T. C. Fitzgibbon of the Fourteenth Michigan similarly requested to be transferred to Colonel James A. Mulligan's Chicago Irish Brigade so that he could serve "amongst our own race and people," rather than for the "bigotedly Protestant" superiors he currently served.[2] Tenth Ohio drummer boy Daniel Finn recorded in his journal that Protestant members of a sister regiment had ransacked a Catholic Church in Summersville, Virginia.[3] New England troops later set a Jacksonville, Florida Catholic church on fire and converted a Savannah cemetery into a Union fortress despite vehement objections from the local bishop.[4] The early war correspondence of Robert Gould Shaw, the future commander of the celebrated 54th Massachusetts Colored Regiment, similarly revealed condescending Protestant attitudes toward Irish enlisted men. In a March 1862 letter to his parents, the Boston Brahmin boasted, "With the Irish left out, the other New England regiments are of as good material as the Thirteenth."[5] Almost as galling, many Protestant colonels, like their predecessors who had fought in the Mexican War two decades earlier, did not allow chaplains or visiting parish clergymen to provide pastoral guidance to their Irish troops. As a result, Catholic soldiers were often unable to confess their sins before risking their lives in battle.[6]

Nativist sentiment within the Union army had a significant impact on the expatriate civilian community in the North as well. Rising suspicions that Irish soldiers were deployed as human shields for Protestant infantrymen eventually incited an expatriate priest to accuse the Lincoln administration of prosecuting the war with the hope that "every Irishman [would] perish by rebel hands."[7] The August 1862 publication of a coward list in Davenport, Iowa, failed to shame certain expatriate civilians into enlisting, and the editor of a newspaper to the south in Keokuk commented:

> On account of the large number of our laboring classes, who have
> left the city and county for the army, our farmers and others needing
> help begin seriously to feel the want of hands at living prices. Many
> a "Patrick" who is cursing the administration and the war, but is sure
> to save his hide intact unless that abominable "dehraft" comes along
> is demanding and receiving better wages for his work than ever be-
> fore. That's the way it is ruining him.[8]

Scapegoating the Irish was an unwarranted affront that the Fenian leadership could have better exploited, even as countless men from other sociocultural backgrounds were reluctant to serve in the wartime military. The proportional difference between Irish and Protestant enlistments in the North was comparatively narrow. Civil War–era records from Concord, Massachusetts reveal that the number of Irishmen who donned Union blue uniforms only trailed Protestants by 9 percentage points (12 to 21 percent, respectively).[9] Because four out of five Protestants in a consummate Yankee New England community remained at home, the Irish were not exceptionally unpatriotic and were only somewhat distinct in demographic terms. Far more Irishmen joined the Union army than the IRB and the Fenian Brotherhood combined.

Hypothetically, Fenian Brotherhood membership would have skyrocketed if John O'Mahony had ignored his abolitionist beliefs and publicly denounced the Lincoln administration after the Emancipation Proclamation was provisionally announced in September 1862. Feeling that their bravery and courage was under-appreciated, expatriate soldiers and their fellow civilians concluded that expanding the earlier abolition of slavery from United States Territories to Rebel-occupied sections of the eleven Confederate states would be an affront to their Irish ethnic identity. Echoing widespread expatriate beliefs that slaves were protected under the Fifth Amendment as personal property, Irish Brigader William Pippey had informed a male relative two months earlier, "If anyone thinks that this army is fighting to free the Negro . . . they are terribly mistaken."[10] The announcement of the Proclamation also incited civilian unrest in a half-dozen cities.

Unwilling to compromise his moral and ideological principles, O'Mahony continued to belong to a segment of the expatriate population that was loyal to the Union and, presumably, better disposed to become postwar Fenian supporters. Dualistic patriotic expression continued to surface both in the military and on the home front in the months that followed the daring Irish Brigade assault on the Confederate-held "Bloody Lane" at Antietam. Members of Meagher's depleted forces sang the abolitionist air "John Brown's Body" as they marched out of Harper's Ferry to engage Confederate forces in nearby Charles Town, Virginia (now West Virginia) in October 1862.[11] "Almost the whole Irish population" of Philadelphia gathered at the city's Baltimore depot to welcome the paroled Confederate prisoner Michael Corcoran home from the South. Large crowds also assembled in Manhattan when the former militia commander returned to his adopted city to raise a new Irish Brigade sister battalion called the Corcoran Legion.[12]

Although it had the potential to bolster expatriate support for the Fenian movement, the Emancipation Proclamation also stunted the sociopolitical influence of Irish nationalist leaders because it further diminished the possibility of an Anglo-American war. Resolution of the *Trent* Affair notwithstanding, rumors had abounded in early 1862 that Royal Navy captains would liberate Confederate ports from Federal blockade to restore antebellum trade networks. Once the Lincoln administration mandated the manumission of bonded labor, however, British government officials risked becoming international pariahs if they aggressively supported the South. Opposing a country that was now officially in favor of freeing slaves in Rebel-held territory could easily be considered hypocritical because slavery had been abolished throughout the British Empire in 1838. Parliamentary leaders also recognized that there were several sensible economic reasons to remain neutral. Many English capitalists had substantial outstanding investments in the North, while stockpiles of Egyptian cotton negated the need for continued trade with Confederate plantation owners. English and Irish laborers in Yorkshire and Lancashire, moreover, remained largely sympathetic to the Union because it was a bastion of democracy and opportunity.[13] Liverpool shipbuilders continued to antagonize Americans in the North by supplying the Rebel navy with technologically advanced frigates, such as the formidable *CSS Alabama*, but the threat of a transatlantic war, to the dismay of the Irish nationalist community, was now an even remoter possibility.

Irish men and women throughout the North had adequate reason to assume that their wartime support of the Union was underappreciated in the months that preceded formal enactment of the Emancipation Proclamation. Lincoln's decision to relieve the popular Union army general George McClellan after the Battle of Antietam aroused lasting Irish animosity toward the Republican president. "Little Mac" had been respected for his reluctance to engage Rebel forces unless he had superior manpower. Expressing admiration for their former leader, Irish Brigade members dropped their regimental flags in protest when McClellan formally relinquished his command to Ambrose Burnside on November 10. Although the change in leadership had been intended as a measure to invigorate the Army of the Potomac, rather than as an affront to the expatriate community, Burnside's appointment inadvertently precipitated a pivotal event in Irish American history— one that arguably compromised the Fenian movement by exacerbating rising expatriate distaste for warfare. Initially emulating his predecessor's reputation for being cautious, Burnside stalled a late winter campaign into Virginia on the east side of the Rappahannock River, even though his men could have crossed shallow fords and captured the inadequately defended city of Fredericksburg. Although the town was of tremendous strategic importance, Burnside continued to keep his men in camp when Confederate regiments started reinforcing sections of the river port in early December. Convinced that an attack had become unfeasible, members of the Irish Brigade were later surprised to participate in a massive charge against Robert E. Lee's well-fortified position on a nearby hillside.

Successful Union capture of the Fredericksburg city center on December 11 was of little consequence after Confederate forces repaired to more formidable high ground defenses on the southwest outskirts of town. Meagher's men initially relished the opportunity to assault a Rebel position situated above a field belonging to a farmer who had donated much of his 1848 crop to Irish Famine relief.[14] In a gesture of ethnic unity, each soldier placed an evergreen sprig in his hat before the attack on December 13, and then attacked with a "half-laughing, half murderous look in [their] eye[s]." Immediately harried by a maelstrom of Confederate gunfire, the members of the brigade made six unsuccessful advances over the next several hours. During each engagement, they were repulsed by the men of two Southern Irish regiments, who had reportedly bemoaned having to kill fellow Hibernians. Fatalities were high throughout the day, but the expatriate Billy Yanks had been repeatedly buoyed to fight by a collective sense of pride. One brigade officer had rallied his men before an attack by yelling "Remember what they will say about us in Ireland."[15] Such determination garnered the respect of the Confederate forces holding the higher ground. When finally repulsed, rebel soldiers raised a cheer to honor the bravery of their foes. Confederate General A. P. Hill's alleged cuss, "That Damned Green Flag Again," appropriately became the title of a popular ballad. The brigade, like most of the other Union regiments that had advanced on Marye's Heights, suffered substantial casualties. In addition to the loss of fifty lives, three of the brigade's four colonels were among the 421 soldiers wounded in what had clearly been a suicide mission.

Postbattle displays of Hibernian fraternity deceptively suggested that Brotherhood leaders had not jeopardized the possible establishment of a sizable Fenian army by publicly supporting the Union war effort. A rebel soldier who had been a former member of Rossa's Phoenix Society sparked a demonstration of universal Irish fealty when Union forces retreated back across the Rappahannock by leading expatriates from both armies in singing T. D. Sullivan's nationalist anthem, "Ireland's Boys Hurrah."[16] Rebel and Yankee Fenians also clandestinely met in a picket-lined ravine after the two sides set up permanent winter quarters across from each other on the Rappahannock River to discuss how expatriate veterans from the North and the South might be able to attack British forces once the Civil War was over.[17] The enduring bilateral nationalist sentiment of many brigade members was encapsulated within the pages of the New York journal the *Irish-American*: "if [the expatriate] soldier fought as an American citizen, he also fought as an Irish exile."[18]

Although poignant, such displays of common Irish respect during the Fredericksburg campaign were not unprecedented and, more importantly, not guaranteed harbingers of success for the Fenian movement. Hours after defeating their Anglo-Dutch adversaries at Fontenoy on May 15, 1745, members of the French Irish Brigade had sung a tune entitled "St. Patrick's Day" to memorialize Hibernians

from both armies who had been killed on the battlefield that day. The fraternal bonds between Irish nationalists in the Union and Confederate armies
were strong, in other words, because they had existed for centuries. The Fenian
Brotherhood would never be able to capitalize on this legacy, however, because
the presence of dead Irishmen lying in the half-frozen Virginia countryside had
irreparably curbed expatriate enthusiasm for warfare. Many expatriates wanted
the Lincoln administration to sue for immediate peace; others became emphatically opposed to fighting another war in Ireland once the North finally defeated
the South. Persuading soldiers described after the Marye's Heights charge as "the
most dejected set of Irishmen you ever saw or heard of" to complete their tours
of duty and devote themselves to Fenianism had become unrealistic.[19] Dying in
defense of the Constitution, States' Rights, or an independent Ireland all seemed
worthless after two years of battlefield bloodshed, incessant subjection to stern
military discipline, and countless days in foul, insect-infested field camps.[20] As
one Yankee officer lamented after the Union army retreated from Fredericksburg,
"It will be a sad, sad, Christmas by many an Irish hearthstone in New York, Pennsylvania, and Massachusetts."[21]

Continued Fenian Brotherhood support for the Union was remarkable after
the Battle of Fredericksburg. While their potential and actual constituents complained of discrimination and perceived preferential government treatment of
African Americans, O'Mahony and others still expressed dualistic patriotic sentiments that barely distinguished a preferential love of Ireland. If any prominent
Irish nationalist leader had to account for substandard devotion to the Union at
the end of 1862, it was Thomas Meagher. The former Young Irelander would not
formally become a Fenian for another year, but it was already widely assumed that
he would eventually reassess his initial reservations about Stephens and lead an
expatriate expedition across the Atlantic. Meagher's less-than-admirable behavior
at Fredericksburg was thus a potential liability for the IRB. Blaming an ulcer-
ated leg for his inability to lead brigade charges up Marye's Heights, the man
who had earned the epitaph "of the sword" when he publicly denounced passive
resistance to British suzerainty over Ireland in the 1840s may have actually been
drunk when the assault began. Also, previous indications that he was an oppor-
tunist blossomed after the battle. Having witnessed the brigade assault before
he was shot in the jaw, William McSparron wrote to his niece in January, 1863
"all [Meagher] wants is a big [na]me, he Cares nothing for the men."[22] Maurice
Woulfe echoed a New York antiwar editor who wrote in a letter to his uncle nine
months after the battle that Meagher had "been the means of bringing thousands
of Irishmen to their graves."[23] In reference to the opinions of a sergeant he met in
Washington, Woulfe wrote, "[Meagher] was a gentleman and a Soldier but that

he wanted to gain too much praise he used not Spare his men at all."[24] Over time, the motivation behind the tactical decisions of other Fenian leaders would also be questioned. In the interim, however, O'Mahony and his colleagues remained devoted to the preservation of the United States Constitution and to the establishment of an Irish republic.

Formal enactment of the Emancipation Proclamation three weeks after Union troops retreated back across the Rappahannock River further tested expatriate loyalty to the Union war effort. Although the central provisions of the new law offered little or nothing to most African American slaves, collateral clauses attenuated marginal Irish social superiority over black men by allowing more freedmen and escaped slaves to join the Union army. Other than a few sailors who joined the Union Navy and several hundred soldiers who mustered into three colored regiments that had been formed a few months earlier, African American males had only been able to support the Northern war effort by working as underpaid laborers and valets. Often called "contrabands," these civilian employees were derided by the Irish throughout the war. Twelve-year-old Daniel Finn expressed a sense of superiority over black adults when he wrote in his journal that he and some fellow musicians in the predominately Irish and pro-Fenian Tenth Ohio Infantry had "sent our nigger [servant] home to his master with a letter stating we were no abolitionists."[25] In Irish estimations, mustering any more free blacks into the army devalued their collective sense of superior manhood and jeopardized their prospects of postwar upward social mobility. If black men were also afforded the opportunity to demonstrate patriotism and bravery, Irishmen would have to compete with even more veterans in the job market once one of the two warring armies surrendered.

Archbishop Hughes, who was at the forefront of a church that denounced many abolitionists as anti-Union revolutionaries, astutely assessed Irish American attitudes toward the Civil War after the Proclamation became official law; in his words: "[Catholics] are willing to fight to the death for the support of the Constitution, the government and the laws of the country. But if they are to fight for the abolition of slavery, then indeed, they will turn away in disgust from the discharge of what would otherwise be their patriotic duty."[26] Evidence of such lowered morale also appeared in a letter written by Andrew Sproule. Anti-slavery himself, the Protestant farmer originally from County Tyrone noted in January 1863 that other Irishmen in his regiment were in poor spirits as they dug a bypass channel along the Mississippi River. From his camp near the well-fortified Rebel-held city of Vicksburg, he wrote, "The boys is getting tired and the[y] are down on this Proclamasion of the Presidence the boys are aposed to freeing the neegro and that is the cry the[y] do n[ot] want the darkey free."[27] In frustration, other expatriates circulated accusations that African Americans were unfit for combat. Peter Welsh of the 28th Massachusetts wrote in a letter home to his wife:

> I see by later papers that the governor of Massachusetts has been au-theured to raise nigar regiments i hope he may suceed but [I] doubt it very much if they can raise a few thousand and send them out here i can assure you that whether they have the grit to go into battle or not ... they will have to go in or they will meet as hot a reception in their retreat as in their advance The feeling against nigars is intensly strong in this army as is plainly to be seen wherever and whenever they meet them They are looked upon as the principal cause of this war and this feeling is especially strong in the Irish regiments.[28]

Two editorials published on the same topic in the Boston Catholic establishment newspaper, the *Pilot,* also conveyed the perception that blacks were inferior to the Irish. In the July 20, 1861, issue, the editor of the journal, Patrick Donahoe, opined that "the white men of the free states do not wish to labor side by side with the Negro [and] not one volunteer in a hundred has gone forth to ... liber-ate slaves."[29] His comments two years later echoed these sentiments with overtly racist stereotypes:

> One Southern regiment of white men would put twenty regiments of them to flight in half an hour. Twenty thousand negroes on the march would be smelled ten miles distant. No scouts need ever be sent to discover such warriors. There is not an American living that should not blush at the plan of making such a race the defenders of national fame and power; and every American living, if he has any independent patriotism in his heart will cry it down.[30]

Some Irish soldiers grudgingly accepted black recruits either sincerely or in rec-ognition that for every black man in uniform, one more Irishman could remain in the civilian workplace.[31] Given that Meagher had delighted a crowd of specta-tors with antiblack remarks during an October 1861 Union recruiting rally at the Boston Music Hall, it is not surprising that greater amity did not flourish between the two minority communities overnight.[32] The Fenian Brotherhood did not fos-ter interracial cooperation either, as membership in their organization potentially offered Irish males an opportunity to demonstrate their virility in an all-white paramilitary organization.

Fenian leaders still refrained from capitalizing on persistent anti-Irish senti-ment within the Union army as the Civil War dragged into a third year. Institutionalized discrimination against Irish soldiers continued to surface after the Battle of Fredericksburg. After reprimanding two expatriate deserters, Colonel James McQuade reported to an investigative commission that "[Irishmen] needed to be handled as severely as justice will allow."[33] In another letter home, Rudolph Coreth wrote in February that Southern Hibernian soldiers were "animals" when fortified with alcohol.[34] Brotherhood reluctance to be more opposed to the war may have been based on the many instances of dualistic patriotic expression that occurred in various Union regiments. Close analysis of the use of the word "American" in letters written by two non-Irish officers who belonged to the Ninth Massachusetts Infantry suggests that expatriates in the regiment were not passionate Union supporters. G. B. White requested to be transferred into "some American Regiment," presumably because his Irish comrades, who included the aforementioned Fenians from Milford, did not meet his expectations as Union soldiers. In a similar complaint, a fellow New Englander wrote "an American is entirely out of place in an *Irish* [italics in the original] regiment."[35] Yet the opinions of these people were not universal; 155 members of the Ninth Massachusetts were absent without leave at one point in April 1863, but one Union general reinforced his belief that the Irish were the cleanest, most disciplined soldiers in the army by writing, "If tomorrow I wanted to win a reputation I would prefer Irish soldiers to any other."[36] The many Irishmen who dutifully fulfilled their responsibilities in uniform were thus the type of men that O'Mahony hoped to recruit upon the conclusion of the war.

The proliferation of enlistment incentives after the introduction of the Emancipation Proclamation complicated Fenian recruiting efforts. Most Northerners who accepted "bounties" to enlist were not ideal Irish nationalist warriors. Reluctant to fight, they waited until signing bonuses had become so high that the risk of accepting "blood wages" was offset by the guarantee of having enough seed money to buy a quality home or start a business if they survived the war. Honorably discharged expatriates with ready cash in their hands would more likely enjoy the comforts of postwar life than accept a commission in an increasingly mismanaged organization. Bounties also lured Irishmen westward across the Atlantic and into the Union army. Men who might have joined an IRB circle in the homeland received a deferred equivalent payment of ten years' wages in Ireland just by adding their name to an enlistment roll. Given that the Irish Brigade unofficially sponsored a Fenian circle that held Sunday night meetings renowned for the singing of nationalist songs and the consumption of whiskey punch, some of these immigrants may have became active expatriate nationalists.[37] Yet by the end of the war, lucrative signing bonuses left Irish in America and Ireland alike with thousands of new widows and orphaned children.[38]

The combination of wartime inflation and a modest industrial production slump in the North provided potential Fenian recruits with another incentive to ignore Corcoran's admonition to "save yourself for Ireland." The increasing cost of retail goods outpaced rising wages by roughly 20 percent in the depleted labor market—a discrepancy due in large part to the hiring of female and adolescent replacement workers. Union army disability benefits also appealed to potential Fenians, because few employers offered meaningful compensation when laborers were killed or maimed in the workplace. Irishmen burdened by debt or destitution furthermore recognized that enlistment under such terms could be an immediate cure-all for personal financial problems. Bounties that guaranteed annuity payments for services rendered could be traded like bearer bonds; thus many new recruits in immediate need of cash sold the rights to their deferred signing bonuses to speculators at a discount. Yet most Irishmen did not assess the hazards of wartime military service as an acceptable sacrifice for potential socioeconomic advancement in the future.

Continued instances of Irish fraternization across enemy lines sustained the possibility that Yankee and Rebel expatriates would jointly support the Fenian movement after the war. In addition to the impassioned singing of "Ireland's Boys Hurrah" after the Battle of Fredericksburg, sporadic gunfire often ceased when expatriate enlistees performed sentry duty. In the words of Irish Brigade historian David P. Conyngham, a "most friendly feeling" would arise when expatriate representatives from both armies stuck their muskets into the ground as a sign of truce and disobeyed orders by conversing and bartering with each other.[39] Such behavior was understandable, as many Irishmen in both armies were equally devoted to Irish independence. While Union soldiers sang the "Song of the Irish Brigade," a Confederate company from Vicksburg called the Sarsfield Southrons utilized the French Irish Brigade war cry, *Faugh a Ballagh* ("Clear the way"). Hibernians who belonged to a company of soldiers recruited in Mobile, Alabama were also potentially good Fenian recruits because they carried a double-layered flag that had rebel insignia on one side and Irish symbols on the other.[40]

The indissoluble fraternal link between Irishmen from the North and South continued to be noticeable during the middle stages of the Civil War. First generation Irish American James Sullivan—who had aided a wounded North Carolina rebel left in the forest two days after the Second Battle of Bull Run—was docked one month's salary in May 1863 after being caught trying to speak with some men in an enemy patrol.[41] At Gettysburg, twenty-one-year-old rebel Captain John Dooley recalled an encounter with a disenchanted Irishman from Lowell, Massachusetts who said that he had served with John Mitchel during the Young Ireland uprising, even though the nationalist firebrand had been arrested before the insurrection began, in July 1848:

A Yanko-Irish soldier told me he was from Lowell, Mass., and that he had been a soldier under John Mitchell in '48. Having heard that John M's three sons were in the Confederate army he wished to hear something about them. He seemed much pleased when he learned that I could give him so much information about the Mitchells. And then Cronin [a wounded Rebel soldier] and I began questioning him and asking him how it was possible for him who had in '48 fought or intended to fight for the same cause for which we were contending, how could he consistently turn his back on his principles and for the pitiful hire of a few dollars do all in his power to crush a brave people asserting their right to self government; and now that he was engaged in the cause of tyranny, fighting against honesty, Justice, and right, and moreover against those very gallant young men he was seeking to hear of, what, we asked, would Mr. Mitchell think of him?[42]

The Union soldier, who later offered a tent and two blankets to his native country-men, answered in tears that he had been coerced into enlisting. Dubious stories of cross-picket solidarity also abounded in both armies. In one example, Union and Confederate Irish soldiers reportedly refused to fire on one another during one of the many military engagements in and around the vicinity of Winchester, Virginia.[43]

False but prevailing assumptions that Irish males were inherently violent buttressed Fenian expectations that expatriate espousals of Irish nationalism would become more prevalent once the Civil War was over. The insubordinate behavior of expatriate soldiers reinforced a stereotype throughout the fractured United States that Irish Americans had enlisted in the Union or Confederate armies simply because they enjoyed a good fight.[44] The aforementioned James Sullivan was credited by his commanding officer as having "reckless Irish cour-age."[45] Interestingly, some Union Irishmen believed that they themselves were predisposed to fighting. As future Medal of Honor–recipient Felix Brannigan wrote while serving as a 79th New York Infantry private in 1862, "There is an elasticity in the Irish temperament which enables its possessor to boldly stare Fate in the face."[46] Notably, however, in all of the information contained in Civil War letters dispatched to Governor Andrew, the behavior of Massachusetts Irish soldiers remains indistinct; other ethnic and "American" regiments were equally criticized for their rough behavior.[47]

The Fenian Brotherhood aspired to recruit a formidable paramilitary army, and a putative Irish penchant for brutality within the mid-nineteenth century expatriate civilian community was encouraging. Boxing, which was illegal in many states and municipalities, was widely popular among the Irish. The eloquent Civil War diarist Mary Chestnut recorded in her memoirs that some affluent Southerners believed that the Irish had a natural inclination to resist authority. In June 1865, one of her acquaintances may have offered a vague hint of scalawag opportunism when he commented that he admired Yankees but had been a Confederate sympathizer because, "I was born a rebel--being an Irishman."[48] In truth, economics rather than heredity primarily fueled such acts of violence. Within the civilian workplace, Irish longshoremen and independent fire companies routinely used physical intimidation to secure temporary employment and service contracts. [49] A multitude of vicious Irish American street gangs included the Dead Rabbits of Lower Manhattan and Philadelphia's Schuylkill Rangers.

The outbreak of several antidraft riots in the midst of the Civil War reinforced the stereotype that Irishmen were exceptionally aggressive. The March 1863 Federal Enrollment Act instituted conscription provisions that exacerbated the misperception that military service was a poor man's burden.[50] Loopholes benefited the rich, and economically depressed communities were required to fulfill inordinately high enlistment quotas. A three hundred dollar exemption fee offended Irish laborers because it implied that a healthy adult male slave was worth more than a free Irish American male. Blacks, moreover, were not citizens under the law and could not be drafted. Accordingly, many Irishmen believed that the demise of an all-volunteer army was an abolitionist plot to eliminate the American Catholic population.[51]

The jovial atmosphere that prevailed when the first draft lottery was held in a New York City square on Saturday July 11 falsely suggested that Northern civilians had acquiesced to the prospect of nationwide conscription; instead, violence ensued after the names of 1,236 selected draftees were published in local papers two days later. Massive crowds began lynching African Americans and burning buildings. A heroic young Irishman and four associates helped 237 black children escape certain death after a wild crowd set their Negro orphanage on fire and yelled, "burn the niggers' nest."[52] Other protesters attacked Irish Protestant immigrants who belonged to the anti-Catholic Orange Order and a ten-year-old girl was killed after she beseeched several thugs to disperse.[53] Prominent Irish Catholic supporters of the Union were also subject to attack. Most noteworthy, influential Irish Brigade officer and draft supervisor Robert Nugent returned to Manhattan from Gettysburg to discover that his home had been vandalized. Although the unprecedented mayhem appeared to have erupted spontaneously, pervasive Irish antiblack sentiment had actually encouraged striking Irish stevedores to meet in waterfront grogeries before the draft to plot attacks against black scab laborers once the first conscripts were selected.[54] That such a small group of conspirators had been spontaneously joined by thousands of other men and women was, in part, attributable to a previous government decision to offset mounting defense spending by downsizing public relief programs that had predominately benefited destitute Irish men and women. Such behavior was not universal within the émigré community; indeed, Irish residents of the First, Fourteenth, and Fifteenth Wards made noted efforts to contain expatriate rioters.

When rioting continued into the latter half of the week, government officials called on Irish church and military leaders to quell the draft demonstrators. Thousands of soldiers, including Nugent, were reassigned from conducting patrols in central Pennsylvania to policing the streets of New York City. In a brief public address from the balcony of his Madison Avenue residence on July 17, Archbishop Hughes belatedly ordered the rioters to return to their homes.[55] O'Mahony remained inactive throughout the riots, even though he could have attempted to persuade rioters that an independent Ireland would be a better home for expatriates than America. Of particular interest, he could have noted that conscription laws were anti-Irish because they required resident aliens to leave the United States within sixty-five-days' notice if they did not want to become eligible for the draft. Yet the Fenian Brotherhood founder remained faithful to the Union as antiblack violence spread to Boston and other communities in the North. Confederate defeat was important to the Fenian hierarchy.[56] Attempting to foster Irish patriotic sentiment amongst hooligans who had instigated the deaths of over one hundred people and had caused an estimated 1.5 million dollars in property damage would thus have been a waste of limited Fenian resources.[57]

In an effort to curb rising Irish male emigration during the American Civil War, IRB leaders differed from their Fenian Brotherhood counterparts by increasingly opposing the Lincoln administration. Despite the risk, Irishmen were willing to enlist in the Union army in exchange for free passage to the United States. As émigrés remitted less money during the war, and a prolonged, inordinate rainfall decreased Irish agricultural production during the early 1860s, economic want inspired many young Irishmen to emigrate.[58] United States Consular offices throughout Ireland continued to receive letters from Irishmen offering to enlist. Congressional efforts to woo Irish immigrant recruits by offering guaranteed American citizenship in exchange for one year of military service also drew thousands of young Irishmen into the Union army. When Irish newspapers reported that the Union had arranged to underwrite transatlantic passenger fares to prospective recruits, Mark Mulligan wrote:

My Dear Sir—

I hope you will pardon my intrusion—it is the Solicitude of my Son who is an able-bodied young Man and is desirious of going out to join his Brother Christopher Mulligan in the U.S. Army and not having the means of paying his Passage he wishes to know if you could do any thing in the way of forwarding him to his Brother as he inclined to join that Honble Service as soon as he arrives there and as he is out of employment in the Alternative he will be under the necessity of joining the British Service.

I am Dear Sir Your Obt and Humble Servt Mark Mulligan[59]

American citizen and Mexican War veteran Thomas Conroy, likewise, informed United States diplomats three months later, "I am willing to fight And loose the last Drop of my Blood under the Stars and stripes once more if the American Consul will Do me the fevour [sic] to grant me a passage home onc more."[60] Little could be done to stop such men from leaving Ireland along with politically disinterested emigrants who were likely to join the Union army because civilian jobs paid little in the North and because maritime access to Southern ports were stymied by an ongoing Union naval blockade. Court testimony reveals that sixteen Irishmen, who had illegally enlisted in the United States Navy when the USS *Kearsarge* underwent repairs in Queenstown, would have been just as willing to become rebel sailors if they had been presented with the opportunity. Confederate emissaries, such as John Bannon, thus had little success discouraging Irish emigration during the war. Although William Smith O'Brien and John Martin had endorsed the purpose of Bannon's mission, peasants and lower-middle-class shop workers in search of employment largely ignored the Saint Louis Catholic curate.[61] As a result, Bannon failed to halt potential Fenian recruits from leaving Ireland. Thousands of socially conservative Irish men and women had little affinity for the relatively progressive Union. A substantial number of other Irish males freely emigrated during the war, however, because they needed work and had been raised in families that had been opposed to slavery ever since Daniel O'Connell had emerged as an ardent abolitionist.[62] Although some of these men would join the Fenian Brotherhood after they reached America, they would never be available to serve as frontline fighters in the IRB.

The introduction of a Dublin-based Fenian newspaper partly offset the negative impact that wartime immigration had on the IRB. Initially funded by money that Thomas Luby had raised during a trip to the United States, the *Irish People* became the primary ideological voice of the IRB the same month that the

USS Kearsarge landed in Cork. After the November 28 debut edition, each weekly issue contained news bulletins, discursive editorials, and well-written poetry that openly condemned British suzerainty over Ireland. Peasants and townspeople were repeatedly called on to use their alleged Irish fighting prowess to secure the establishment of an independent Ireland. Tepid street protests and public demonstrations, in the estimation of *Irish People* editors, would never rectify long-standing socioeconomic inequities or reunite an ethnic community that had yet to fully recover from the Famine. As a reward for military service, Irish patriots were led to believe that they could anticipate greater social equity, land reform, and a definitive separation between church and state. Fenian admiration for Thomas Carlyle was also evident in the paper, even though he occasionally derided the Irish nationalist movement.

Although operating at a loss, *Irish People* staff members established a solid customer base among the Irish at home and abroad. British officials noted that the paper was an "ably written" addition to an already competitive media market.[63] Expatriate soldiers in the Union army were among the many devoted Americans who enjoyed reading the paper's male- and female-written poetry and prose.[64] Fenian official J. W. O'Brien noted the heavy stateside demand for the paper when he requested in an open letter that copies be returned once they were read so that they could be redistributed to other circles.[65] Yet public dissemination of nationalist goals, and editorial predictions that Civil War veterans would "turn their eyes and hearts fondly towards the land of their birth" once peace was restored, readily attracted the attention of British government officials.[66] Saved from disappearing into anonymity, Stephens and his principal colleagues henceforward became suspected subversives whose published materials were later used as prosecutorial evidence during the trials of several Fenian suspects.

The launch of the *Irish People* was overshadowed by an internal leadership crisis within the Fenian Brotherhood. Midwest expatriates who were frustrated that the IRB had not conducted a single military operation since it was established five years earlier challenged O'Mahony's authority in the fall of 1863 by calling for greater control over the management of the stateside Brotherhood and for a substantial modification of Fenian military strategy. Although he had espoused the merits of representative government on many occasions, the former Munster estate owner always believed that he had a mandate to abet republican initiatives in Ireland. Rival expatriate nationalists ultimately won concessions from O'Mahony, therefore, by coercing him into either democratizing the Brotherhood during a proposed national Fenian convention or risk appearing to be a hypocritical tyrant. Most of the eighty-two delegates who traveled to Chicago to attend the four-day Fenian convention in early November were civilians who represented circles in twelve states and the District of Columbia. A handful of other attendees were Union military officers whose army-authorized presence suggested that the United States government endorsed the Brotherhood's objectives. O'Mahony opened the proceedings at a Fenian Hall located on the corner of Rush and Randolph Streets with a rosy welcoming address. The soon-to-be-called "Men of Action," however, carried motions that would dramatically alter executive control of the global movement. By unilateral declaration, the IRB was redesignated as a Fenian Brotherhood subsidiary instead of as its parent organization. A president and five-member board, more importantly, would henceforth be annually elected to lead the organization. O'Mahony dutifully resigned his position of head centre when these administrative changes were adopted and openly pledged to assist the organization in whatever capacity seemed fitting. Because he tactfully endorsed the creation of a new American-style power structure within the Brotherhood, O'Mahony was unanimously chosen to lead his reconstituted organization on condition that he subjected his work to administrative review.

Although the Chicago convention was a political embarrassment for O'Mahony, its most lasting significance was the reintroduction of a two-decade old proposal to organize an Irish American invasion of Ontario and Quebec. As nationalists believing that they were the principal leaders of the transatlantic Irish republican movement, the Men of Action argued that an effort to seize Canadian territory by force would be more effectual than previous Brotherhood intentions to support a republican rebellion in Ireland.[67] In his capacity as chairman of the new Fenian executive committee, Brotherhood newcomer William Randall Roberts began to extol the merits of a cross-border foray, which had originally been suggested in 1843 by the members of the defunct Philadelphia Repeal Association.[68] Whether O'Mahony's intra-Brotherhood opponents were aware that their predecessors had also offered to deploy shiploads of armed soldiers to Ireland is unknown, but global Irish militant strategy had been modified in a Midwest meeting hall. Young men not yet born when antecedent expatriates had first suggested that the fight for Irish freedom could be waged on Canadian soil would soon march into Ontario and Quebec under arms.

Fenian convention delegates emulated O'Mahony's dualistic nationalist views by openly expressing patriotic loyalty to Ireland and the to United States when they met in downtown Chicago. Memorial toasts to comrades who had died while fighting in the Civil War and to Polish revolutionaries then in the midst of an ultimately unsuccessful rebellion against Russia were the highlight of a closing night banquet. The twenty thousand published copies of the Chicago convention minutes, likewise, emphasize the duality of American Fenianism. In pledging their commitment to emancipating Ireland, the formulators of the reconstituted Brotherhood saluted their patriotic predecessors by declaring their "entire allegiance to the Constitution and laws of the United States of America."[69] No American law would be violated, according to the declaration, in the struggle for Irish independence.[70] As the editors of the pro-Irish *Chicago Tribune* accurately claimed, "The Fenian Brotherhood are the only class of Irish Catholics who heartily support the Government in its struggle with the rebels; the only class of Irish Catholics who volunteer to fight for the Union; the only class of Catholic Irish who are unconditionally loyal and true to the American flag."[71] Conversely, John Mitchel complained that Irish Southerners were victimized by such expatriate devotion to the Union. Ever the Confederate apologist, Mitchel wrote on the same day that the declaration was published that "green flags lie torn on many a battlefield, and the bones of those who were to liberate Ireland whiten the plains of the continent from Galveston to the Potomac."[72] Coincidentally, some nativists inaccurately accused the Brotherhood of abetting the Draft Riots and the proliferation of antiwar sentiment among the Irish community in the North.[73]

Nationalist activity among female expatriates became increasingly noticeable after the Chicago Convention. Irish American women had previously expressed their patriotic sentiments by establishing female auxiliaries of the Worcester Emmet Guards, the 69th New York militia, and other predominately Irish regiments in the Union army. But a nationwide organization ideologically comparable to the defunct ICMRU Ladies Committee did not surface until an intriguing convention resolution appeared as an *Irish People* editorial on December 5, 1863. While thanking the Irish women of Chicago for presenting delegates with a flag, a Lafayette, Indiana native called for greater female participation in the Fenian movement by somewhat condescendingly saying, "We know the Irish woman is peerless in all charms save one—she loves her country, but she is not national."[74] Whether this snide remark was viewed as a gentlemanly provocation is uncertain, but the nascent Fenian Sisterhood became increasingly popular in the months that followed. Most middle-class females did little outside the home during the mid-nineteenth century besides occasional philanthropic activity, but Sisterhood members raised money for Fenian militants by hosting several picnics as well as balls. Although a Chicago Sisterhood assignment to prepare meals before the 1864 Saint Patrick's Day parade typifies many of the menial tasks female Irish nationalists were asked to perform, other women organized medical dispensaries in emulation of Irish Brigade Nurses Association members.[75] Another early project included collecting funds to purchase a monument for the tomb of a popular Crawfordsville, Indiana parish priest who had escorted MacManus's remains to Ireland and who had organized many circles in his home state before dying in the summer of 1863 at the age of forty-five.[76] Sisterhood fundraising, however, remained much more important than posthumously honoring Father Edward O'Flaherty. By one estimate, between 1858 and 1863 the Fenian Brotherhood forwarded only $7,500 to its colleagues in Ireland.[77]

The peaceful conclusion of the Chicago Fenian convention and the establishment of Sisterhood auxiliaries were counterbalanced by preexisting and emerging problems within the transatlantic Irish nationalist movement. Disparate members of the Fenian Brotherhood were now espousing two different military strategies. IRB organizational preparedness also remained clouded in fabrications offered up by Stephens and others. O'Mahony was warmly received at a December meeting of Polish nationalist sympathizers in New York as a firm opponent of global imperialism, but loud applause at the beginning of his remarks did little to advance the Fenian cause.[78] Evidence of increasing grassroots manipulation of the Irish republican cause was concurrently revealed when a Nashville circle raised funds to build an orphanage in its community rather than forward additional money to the IRB war chest.[79] Of more immediate concern, the Union army had seized the Mississippi River Valley as well as vast portions of Tennessee and the Atlantic seacoast, but expatriate enthusiasm for the Union war effort continued to decline. The December 22 death of Michael Corcoran was particularly upsetting to both ardent Fenians and tepid Irish nationalists. The talented thirty-six-year-old might have one day led a republican army into battle on Irish soil. Instead, he died near Fairfax, Virginia in a riding accident with Meagher that may have involved alcohol. With New York City flags at half-mast two days after Christmas, thousands of Irish men and women gazed silently as O'Mahony and seventeen other pallbearers escorted Corcoran's body to and from his December 27 funeral at the original Saint Patrick's Cathedral.[80] A former Crown revenue officer, Corcoran had renounced his native government and become both an Irish and an American hero.[81]

The Catholic Church–sanctioned Michael Corcoran memorial service masked increasingly significant ecclesiastical efforts to stymie lay and clerical support for the Fenian Brotherhood. On January 17, Philadelphia bishop James Frederick Wood issued the first of several anti-Fenian pastorals that compared the Brotherhood to Vatican-proscribed organizations such as the Masons.[82] The bishops of Hamilton, Toronto, and Montreal similarly denounced the Fenians over the following months, while ultramontanist curates reiterated conservative anti-Brotherhood criticism that the editors of the New York City Catholic establishment journal, *The Tablet*, had published a year earlier.[83]

Only a handful of priests emerged as pronationalists in the wake of these censures. South Side Chicago Pastor John Waldron antagonized his Irish-born anti-Fenian superior, Bishop James Duggan, by permitting local members of the Brotherhood and other nationalist organizations to conduct meetings in his rectory.[84] In the spring of 1864, Bishop Wood demanded that Father Patrick Moriarty renounce his pro-Fenian views, but the former Augustinian President of fledgling Villanova College continued to endorse the Brotherhood and, the following December, insisted that Ireland become an American state. He refused to admit that he had abetted the Fenian movement, however, when he apologized for his disobedience in an open letter.[85] The presence of less vocal pro-Fenian clerics in various locations around the country was evident when Cleveland Bishop Amadeus Rappe later wrote to Cincinnati archbishop John Baptist Purcell that many of his clergy had secretly encouraged Ohio Fenians.[86]

Several clergymen pragmatically refused to ferret out IRB members in the confessional or to deny the sacraments to suspected Fenians out of fear of losing the respect of their parishioners.[87] Dominican brothers residing in a Louisville friary openly expressed their Irish nationalist sympathies because they belonged to an autonomous religious congregation. The bishop of their diocese, Martin John Spalding, was slightly more reserved. Although he would ask the Vatican to condemn the movement within a year, he initially allowed priests under his supervision to administer sacraments to local Fenians.[88] Alton, Illinois bishop Henry Damian Juncker similarly informed Purcell in an April 3, 1864, letter that Fenians would remain in the good grace of his diocese "until he [learned] how the other prelates are treating the matter."[89] More cautious clerics attempted to balance the wishes of their superiors with those of their Irish nationalist congregants.[90] Private correspondence revealed that many pastors tailored political statements to the collective views of their parishioners.

Increasing Catholic Church efforts to suppress the Fenian movement compounded the impact of Irishmen, who continued to immigrate rather than remain in Ireland and potentially join the IRB. False rumors of "puritanical, Cromwellian" abolitionists forcing the Irish to fight for the Union were common throughout Ireland, and the *Irish People* editorial staff tried to stem the exodus of prospective Fenian recruits by suggesting that emigration was "a very good thing in the eyes of our Irish masters."[91] While writing of his March 1864 arrival in Portland, Maine, Thomas McManus informed his parents that "there were hundreds of civilians there to meet us: and they gave us brandy, whisky, pies, puddings, cigars or any other thing we wished for to enlist."[92] McManus himself resisted all the strings-attached offers initially presented to him and joined the army after he traveled to Massachusetts. One hundred and two of his fellow passengers were neither as resolute nor as fortunate. After a scheming recruiter conned them into joining the Irish Brigade, almost all the men who had traveled to America with McManus were arrested and transported back to Ireland when British officials protested that they had been illegally mustered into military service.[93] As such instances were rare, most wartime emigrants fulfilled their desire to become American citizens. In the contemporary words of County Monaghan–born Toronto Bishop John Joseph Lynch:

> When the Irish come to America and see the freedom the people enjoy, and the laws protecting the poor tenants as well as the rich landlord, and no compulsory support of [a] state church which they detest, their feelings of exasperation against their former ruler know no bounds; they take the oath of allegiance to the United States almost immediately upon their arrival and renounce their former allegiance "with a vengeance."[94]

Although the majority of wartime Irish immigrants had no desire to be British subjects, they also expressed no discernable desire to be Fenians. By immigrating, in Lynch's opinion, they demonstrated the desire to become Americans.

Undeterred by lackluster recruiting initiatives and ecclesiastical opposition, the Chicago-based Men of Action dramatically enhanced the political stature of the Fenian Brotherhood in the spring of 1864 by staging a hugely successful "Great National Irish Fair" without O'Mahony's approval. Although Fenian leaders had had little rapport with American political leaders to date, several public officeholders accepted invitations to attend the festival's opening day ceremonies. Illinois Lieutenant Governor Francis Hoffman joined a municipal delegation that included Mayor Francis Sherman and several city aldermen when the fair officially began at two downtown locations on Easter Monday, March 28. Rather than attend the celebration themselves, House Speaker Schulyer Colfax, Postmaster General Montgomery Blair, Republican Minnesota governor Steven Miller, and three high-ranking Union army generals were among the many people who sent cash contributions and letters of encouragement to the event's organizers.[95] Such political patronage boosted Fenian morale, but such support was to be expected; 1864 was an election year, and control of the federal government would determine the future prosecution of the Union war effort.

The highlight of the fair was a massive auction featuring thirty cases of imported items that had been donated by Irish men and women, as well as a wide selection of American-made products.[96] In addition to Irish-made clothes, "fancy articles," and jars of moonshine, fair-goers could bid on curios reputedly from the 1798 United Irish uprising, a toothpick that had supposedly belonged to the Great Emancipator, Daniel O'Connell, and three autographed pictures of Irish archbishop John MacHale. High bidders could also claim a McCormack Reaper, a marble bust of the recently deceased General Michael Corcoran, and several pairs of footwear that had been individually handcrafted by each member of the local boot and shoemakers guild.[97] Entertainment activities included a circus performance, a night when the Brotherhood collected all Chicago theatre box office revenue, and a boastful public address by Stephens. Although well received, Stephens strained his already uneasy relationship with the Men of Action by insisting in his remarks that Irish militants were ready to mobilize for battle if Great Britain defended Danish claims to the then-disputed North European provinces of Schleswig and Holstein. By one modern-day calculation, about 40 percent of the fifty-five thousand dollars raised during the fair was eventually transferred to the *Irish People* newspaper office in Dublin, despite increasing calls for Fenian military action in North America rather than Ireland. If true, money that was not spent on event preparation costs—or dishonestly diverted—should have provided Stephens with more than enough funds to purchase a sizable number of firearms. Yet it was more likely that whatever the total amount, most of this revenue was squandered. As an indication that graft and mistrust were present within the Fenian movement, the Men of Action prohibited O'Mahony from shepherding any of this money through his New York headquarters.[98]

Needing to reestablish his personal credibility as a nationalist leader in the months that followed the Chicago Fenian Fair, O'Mahony fulfilled his earlier desire to serve in the Union army when the all-Fenian Phoenix Zouaves were mobilized for one hundred days of active duty service at the beginning of August. Renamed the 99th New York National Guard, O'Mahony's unit received some basic training on Governor's Island and was then dispatched upstate to a notoriously disease-ridden prisoner of war camp in Elmira. As an indication that they were not blindly obsessed with defeating the South, the men of the 99th gained the respect of the inmates through frequent demonstrations of compassion.[99] By delegating day-to-day supervision of the regiment to his second-in-command (Patrick J. Dowling, a former Irish subversive recently released from a British prison), O'Mahony continued to supervise Fenian activities occurring throughout the United States. In addition to appointing talented recruiters who were dispatched throughout the Northeast and the greater Ohio Valley, he sent an early September telegraph to delegates attending a two-day Pacific Coast Fenian convention in San Francisco.[100] He never acquired the military experience needed, however, to boost his credibility as a revolutionary leader; nevertheless, he was often addressed as "colonel" in deference to his Civil War service and past experience as the leader of an Emmet Monument Association militia unit.

Rising expatriate nationalist expression at the time O'Mahony was ostensibly on active duty obscured harbingers of the Fenian movement's ultimate demise.

Stephens raised significant amounts of cash and established several new circles on a five-month tour through the Midwest and federally occupied sections of the South. Armed with passes from Union and Confederate officers, he was also allowed to cross enemy lines and meet with Rebel soldiers.[101] Such success was compromised, however, by the battlefield deaths of many fervent Irish American nationalists. In a testament to his dual patriotism, the eldest son of John Mitchel was quoted before dying during a July 20, 1864, Union navy bombardment of Fort Sumter, "I die willingly for the South, but oh, that it had been for Ireland."[102] Thirty-seven-year-old Fenian sympathizer Patrick Cleburne was killed in Franklin two months after Stephens visited nearby Nashville. A devoted defender of individual liberty, Cleburne had remained in Rebel uniform despite longing for his fiancée, his profound dislike of his commanding officer, and the fact that two horses had been shot underneath him just before he died.[103] Having acquired the epitaph "Stonewall Jackson of the West," Cleburne would have boosted Fenian support if he had had the opportunity to lead Irish nationalists into battle. The dwindling presence of other Irish nationalists in the Union and Confederate army commands was equally devastating to the Fenian movement. Twenty-four officers of the New York Irish Legion were killed during the penultimate year of the war.

The number of ideal Fenian recruits in the Union army continued to decline around the time of Cleburne's death. Fifty percent of all 1861 three-year enlistees rejoined the army in 1864, but only three probable Milford Fenians remained in the service for the duration of the war, even though Ninth Massachusetts casualty rates had been relatively low.[104] Atypical émigré disrespect for American government officials also suggested that politically empowered expatriates would increasingly question Stephens and O'Mahony's authority. Thomas Francis Meagher crossed political party lines to endorse Abraham Lincoln's re-election bid, even though the commander in chief had become widely unpopular among Irish soldiers in the Union army after the formal introduction of the Emancipation Proclamation. One Irish Brigade recruiting officer predicted a month before the 1864 Federal elections that "If [the Democratic Party nominee George] McClellan is defeated, and he can only be defeated by Foul means, a Revolution in the North will be inevitable."[105] Such prognostication proved false when Lincoln secured a second term in office, but expatriate antigovernment angst continued to be evident. Charles G. Halpine delighted men and women in attendance at an 1864 Irish Brigade ball when he recited his two-year-old racist poem, "Sambo's Right to be Kilt." Initially hinting of interethnic respect, the poem closes by indirectly censuring the Lincoln administration for extending greater civil rights to African Americans. Because Stephens and O'Mahony had never exploited racial prejudice to win support, the possibility that thousands of disaffected expatriate soldiers would immediately mobilize into Fenian paramilitary units once the war was over became remote. Thousands of Irish American women had been similarly disgruntled with Union officials ever since one Irish Brigade wife had complained in December 1861, "You have got me man into the soldiers, and now you have to kape us from starving."[106] Yet the Fenian leadership had also opted not to actively recruit women who expressed such sentiments.

In late 1864, members of traditionally Irish regiments continued to be the best prospective Fenian filibusterers, as Stephens was more successfully recruiting civilians than enlisted personnel. Even though most of their comrades had not re-enlisted, only three of the seventy-eight suspected Milford Fenians were ever identified as deserters.[107] Despite expatriate resentment that the depleted Irish Brigade had been dissolved in June 1864, hundreds of New York expatriates joined the army late in the war. By November, Robert Nugent had enticed enough new volunteers to warrant the re-establishment of the famous military unit, even though he had helped suppress the New York City Draft Riots a year earlier. Veteran Brigaders who remained or returned to service were permitted to join their reconstituted unit, and Nugent ultimately had the personal honor of presenting the first Union armistice offer to Robert E. Lee.[108]

Stephens might have continued to successfully recruit new supporters once he returned to Dublin in late 1864 if he and his IRB colleagues had not been so averse to the ongoing socioeconomic modernization of Ireland. *Irish People* editors ignored that industrial expansion and political activism became interrelated in the nineteenth century. The creation of new transportation networks expedited the dissemination of Fenian propaganda, but IRB leaders did not develop a reform platform that was consistent with the growing power and influence of Irish towns. Many ideal Fenians were peasants who, upon reaching working age, had relocated to small market centers in search of employment. Although these men would have preferred to farm, they were also concerned about greater labor equity. *Irish People* staff members, nevertheless, published several editorials that pertained to rural issues. Foreshadowing his widely acclaimed romantic 1879 novel, *Knocknagow, or the home of Tipperary,* Charles Kickham particularly loathed how an emerging market economy and technological innovations had irreparably influenced Irish society. Like his Fenian colleagues, Kickham demonstrated that his politics were geared toward the future, while his economic outlook was oriented toward the past. Few nineteenth-century revolutionary movements, however, received constructive support from rural sustenance communities.[109]

Demographic data demonstrates that Kickham's interest in agrarian issues primarily appealed to urban and municipal residents who aspired to own a small farm. During the mid-1860s, the largest concentrations of Fenian supporters were in cities. Fenian expression was insignificant in predominately rural Connaught except in Ballina. Over one thousand men, or 39.2 percent of the town's entire male population, were reported members of the organization in the mid-1860s.[110] A high per capita number of Fenians resided in Leinster and Munster municipalities, where employment was available to young men who were unable to purchase arable land because their personal aspirations were often frustrated by cyclical recessions. Tipperary, Cork, and Dublin were the birthplaces of many Fenian leaders, whose parents had migrated to larger cities during the Famine. Kickham's bucolic sentimentality did not resonate in densely populated Ulster, however, because of long-standing religious tensions. Presbyterian tenant farmers who resided in the province were largely content with the sociopolitical status quo, moreover, because they had long benefited from exclusive economic and civil protections. A thirty-four-year-old son of a well-to-do farmer named Charles Rice led a somewhat sizable Fenian organization in County Monaghan, and a Londonderry circle was established in early 1863.[111] Additional manifestations of Irish nationalist activity in the north, however, were uncommon and largely limited to rural and urban areas, which were predominately Catholic.

Irish nationalist sentiment within cities throughout the British Isles was most prevalent among young lower-middle-class workers. Dry goods clerks, commonly known as drapers' assistants, were omnipresent in Dublin and Cork circles. The proprietors of McSwiney's and its two primary competitors in Dublin were known for hiring young men who had been raised in peasant families; thus they unknowingly employed dozens of militant nationalists. The IRB front organization, the Brotherhood of Saint Patrick, likewise, was actually more popular in England than in Ireland because variously trained expatriate tradesmen primarily resided in urban émigré enclaves.[112] Separated from their relatives and childhood friends, these men tended to join Irish nationalist organizations because they felt socially disoriented in their adopted urban homes. The IRB also attracted recruits by providing a social outlet to alienated city dwellers. Although the possibility of being allotted a smallholding in a postrevolution independent Ireland remained distant and uncertain, IRB membership offered instant camaraderie to men who shared Kickham's pastoral sentimentality. The organization might have been even more popular if its leaders had circulated a prolabor agenda in addition to advocating peasant interests.

Several economic factors dissuaded more prosperous Irish men and women from supporting the Fenian movement. John O'Leary argued that the Irish middle class was too obsessed with its own self-preservation to be truly nationalistic.[113] Bourgeois conservatism was understandable among a segment of the Irish population that had increasingly relied on inter-island trade. Comparatively inexpensive English, Scottish, and Welsh goods had been consistently available for purchase in Irish towns ever since an Act of Union provision to abolish inter-island tariffs had decimated the Irish manufacturing sector. Hibernian consumers also increasingly shopped in foreign-owned "monster stores" that underpriced Irish family-owned businesses with cheaper mass-produced products.[114] British investors, moreover, financed almost all the major industrial projects in Ireland during the nineteenth century. Irish subcontractors and suppliers recognized that they would likely lose revenue and have to furlough employees if political unrest disrupted cross-channel commerce and the flow of venture capital. John O'Mahony and William Roberts were two of only a few Fenian leaders from wealthy backgrounds, because Anglican and Catholic aristocrats would most likely have lost more than they would have gained in a mid-nineteenth century Irish republic led by people who might have supported massive land reform schemes after achieving independence. Although an expanded consumer economy inspired some materialistically driven members of the Irish lower classes to fight for a better life by rebelling against the government, it primarily fostered political contentment among the bourgeoisie and the aristocracy.

Already fearing that lower class leisure activities encouraged unwarranted self-confidence among commoners, reactionary Irish aristocrats correctly assumed that IRB leaders recruited and trained aspiring nationalist soldiers at sporting matches and other traditionally masculine diversions. Fenian meetings were often disguised as Sunday strolls, hurling matches, public debates, and afternoon hunting excursions. Playing English games would be considered unpatriotic once the Gaelic Athletic Association was established two decades later, but a group of Dunnamaggin Fenians enjoyed a friendly round of cricket and a postmatch picnic during one of their 1864 meetings. IRB operatives in Leinster, likewise, often conducted clandestine activities at thoroughbred racetracks, because large crowds offered good cover from the police, and the lure of recreational gambling attracted the type of adventuresome young men the IRB hierarchy wanted in its organization. Yet unlike legendary Fianna warriors, who were supposedly recruited at market fairs, most Irishmen became members of the IRB in pubs. Constables were easy to identify in taverns frequented by a loyal clientele. Alcohol also encouraged congeniality between IRB recruiters and prospective Fenians who were relaxing after a strenuous day or week of work.[115]

The need for more vigorous IRB recruiting throughout Ireland became more important at the end of the American Civil War. Thousands of Irish American men and women would participate in innocuous Fenian activities during the two years that followed the restoration of peace between the North and South. A much smaller percentage of expatriates, however, were actually willing or available to fight for Irish freedom. In addition to the deaths of Michael Corcoran and of several other Irish Brigade officers who were Irish nationalists, the highest-ranking Fenian in the Union army, General Thomas A. Smyth, died from a bullet wound on the same day that Lee surrendered at Appomattox. The County Cork native and former coach-maker would have likely been a highly competent Fenian general.[116] Smyth's death, however, highlighted that the IRB could not over depend on American supporters for military assistance. Irishmen would have to compose the bulk of any revolutionary army that had a chance of securing their independence from Great Britain.

The dearth of Fenians who actually volunteered for paramilitary service after the Civil War was over, once again, suggests that O'Mahony might have had more recruiting success if he had compromised his principles and reminded prospective Fenians that they were marginalized American citizens. Nativist sentiments were declining, but many Protestants still despised Irish Catholics. Hibernian ethnic pride was assaulted, for example, in an October 1864 *Atlantic Monthly* editorial comment that read, "the emancipated Negro is at least as industrious and thrifty as the Celt, takes more pride in self-support, is far more eager for education, and has fewer vices."[117] Potentially exploitable, low Irish American morale was also evident in a blackface minstrel song entitled "The Bonny Green Flag." In reference to Antietam, Fredericksburg, and a myriad of other battles, one line read, "They say the Irish need not apply, but when soldiers they want, in the front Pat is seen."[118] The Fenians could have made further political capital from the fact that Irishmen who had served in Minnesotan and, presumably, in other state volunteer regiments had received fewer promotions than native-born Americans during the war.[119] O'Mahony and his comrades, nevertheless, had remained loyal to the Union not only in the hope that they would be better able to recruit grizzled expatriate veterans with ample combat experience, but also so that the IRB would receive diplomatic recognition from State Department officials in the event of an Anglo-American War. A proclamation issued during a January 1865 Fenian convention in Cincinnati read, "We deem the preservation and success of the American republic of supreme importance not alone for ourselves and our fellow citizens, but to the extension of democratic institutions, and to the well-being and social elevation of the whole human race."[120] Noble as these goals may have been, they would not provide the Fenian Brotherhood with enough manpower and matériel when they engaged the British on Canadian and Irish battlefields in 1866 and 1867.

4

Fenian Renaissance

Although impaired by limited manpower and internal conflict, the transatlantic Fenian movement briefly challenged British suzerainty over Ireland after the culmination of the American Civil War. Contrary to widespread expectations, Fenianism became popular within the global Irish community, because it psychologically transitioned expatriates from a violent to a peaceful social environment. Few IRB and Brotherhood supporters were truly devoted militants during this brief interlude, even though they belonged to an organization that endorsed a violent struggle for Irish independence. Expatriates in the United States continued to assimilate, while Irish families residing throughout the British Isles pragmatically limited their contact with the IRB at a time when Stephens was purchasing footman's pikes because he could not afford to buy rifles. Yet members of the Fenian Sisterhood and a Dublin-based Ladies Committee demonstrated that committed male and female republicans would willingly donate time and money to the nationalist cause if a credible revolution appeared imminent. Delaying an IRB-orchestrated insurrection exacerbated Irish political apathy and expedited ongoing expatriate assimilation into an American society that was becoming increasingly receptive to Catholic immigrants and their descendents.

In mid-1865, a steep decline in public drunkenness reportedly encouraged British bureaucrats to expand an official investigation of the IRB that had begun the previous August.[1] In the common parlance of the era, undercover Dublin Metropolitan Police detectives "decked" Fenian leaders and recruited spies from the handful of people who were employed as part-time *Irish People* printers. Obtaining compromising information was easy; little effort was made to keep conversations

confidential inside the Parliament Street IRB headquarters. Nationalist operatives from all parts of Dublin would often banter with *Irish People* editors and
writers for hours without knowing that one or more informants were in their
midst.[2] With suspicions of a seditious transatlantic movement mounting, Irish
customs inspectors—who had typically spent their workdays arresting tobacco
smugglers—started detaining Americans who had revolvers and military drill
books in their possession.

Extant British government documents suggest that many Fenians inadvertently disclosed their subversive activities at the same time that IRB leaders were
under investigation for committing treason. In filed reports, suspicious foreigners
with distinctive "Yankee swaggers" were noted for their ample supply of money
and their propensity to buy drinks for potential recruits. Over the next three years,
expatriate visitors from the United States often drew attention to themselves, in
fact, because of their preference for double-breasted coats, broad-brimmed felt
hats, and square-toed boots.[3] American citizens with no discernable employment
piqued the interest of vigilant British detectives when they booked accommodations in luxury hotels.[4] The most personal indication of the influence of expatriate
Fenians in Ireland, however, was the increasing tendency of pronationalist Irish
men to grow mustaches in the same New World style as Civil War veterans who
were recruiting new IRB members in their respective communities.[5]

British authorities were well prepared for a potential revolt in Ireland, having
planted several resourceful informants throughout the United States while monitoring IRB activity in major Irish cities. Expatriates who valued money more than
patriotism easily compromised the Fenian movement from 1865 onward. Some
security was assured by printing the names and descriptions of Irishmen who had
betrayed the IRB in *The Phoenix*. O'Mahony refused, however, to heed the advice
of colleagues who insisted that he dismiss a deceitful assistant named Red Jim
McDermott.[6] Other spies variously provided accurate information and fantastic
rumors. Satisfied in knowing almost every significant decision and action rendered
by the Fenian leadership in New York City, British diplomatic officials routinely
declined solicitations from disloyal Fenians who offered to become turncoats.

Heightened British interest in the IRB coincided with the emergence of a
licit Irish nationalist movement that initially threatened to draw supporters away
from James Stephens. Several influential Irishmen, including Cardinal Cullen,
endorsed the so-called National Association because they had long insisted that
all Irish constitutional reforms be secured through nonviolent means. As always,
Stephens believed that reform petitions and legislative initiatives were doomed
to failure, so he strived to maintain IRB preeminence within the Irish republican
community. Stephens started disrupting National Association meetings shortly

before John Blake Dillon was elected as one of three MPs who represented the organization in the British Parliament. Stephens's activities were particularly directed at John Martin. In public meetings, whenever Martin and other Association leaders predicted that the "Fenian delusion" would not last longer than another six months, IRB men occasionally outfitted in Union army uniforms would heckle them.[7] The IRB leader also drew would-be National Association members into the IRB by dissimulating their objectives through the superficially benevolent Brotherhood of Saint Patrick. Initiates in Ireland and England (who variously did, or did not, know that they had joined a front organization) were gradually introduced to militant republicanism by the popular vice-president of the fraternal association and MacManus funeral homilist, Patrick Lavelle.

Rising Fenian influence in the transatlantic world was further evident when another series of ecclesiastical censures of Irish militant republicanism began in March 1865. Encapsulating the sentiments of colleagues who aggressively censured bellicose Irish nationalist activity, Newark, New Jersey bishop James Roosevelt Bayley declared that Fenianism was "a cancer that needs to be cut-out."[8] Such diatribes were largely counterproductive. The minority of Irish men and women who supported the Fenian movement were not dangerous militants. An agnostic IRB military recruiter named Patrick "Pagan" O'Leary, moreover, was the only member of the Fenian hierarchy who could arguably have been called a heretic. The Mexican War veteran despised Saint Patrick for Christianizing Ireland and long espoused the reintroduction of premodern mysticism into Irish spiritual life. In addition to developing a druidic equivalent to the Holy Trinity, he often regaled his associates with a personal belief that the Celtic concept of heaven, a paradise called Tír na nÓg, was far superior to the Garden of Eden. Yet, O'Leary was well versed in scripture and was employed by a Dublin parish church in the 1860s. More significantly, he returned to Catholicism in his waning days at an Old Soldiers' Home in Georgia.[9]

Several other Fenian leaders openly displayed their spiritual beliefs throughout the Fenian era, while they criticized ecclesiastical intervention in temporal political affairs. John O'Mahony would conclude an important August 1865 fundraising letter with the peroration, "The rest we leave to you and to heaven."[10] Such sentiment echoed that of an Ohio Fenian who had closed an open letter three years earlier with the petition, "May the great ruler of the Universe hasten this glorious consummation."[11] James Stephens displayed even greater respect for the church by marrying a publican's daughter named Jane Hopper in a small Catholic ceremony in November 1863—even though one of his parents was Protestant, and Stephens himself had not been known to practice his faith, despite being baptized in the church.

Ecclesiastical attempts to suppress the Fenian movement elicited several spates of negative reaction in Ireland and America. IRB operatives in Skibbereen burned a conservative local priest in effigy. Cullen himself was once challenged when a group of Fenians drowned out one of his cathedral sermons with loud coughing.[12] Fenians residing in the northwest corner of Ireland, meanwhile, inserted a false report into an early 1865 edition of the *Connaught Patriot,* declaring that the papacy had instructed Irish and American bishops to refrain from censuring all IRB members.[13] Philadelphia Fenians, similarly, circulated a forged papal letter in January 1865 instructing Bishop James Frederic Wood to stop condemning Irish militants in his diocese.[14] Belfast native Frank Roney adamantly defended his nationalist ideals after the Bishop of Down and Connor, Cornelius Denvir, requested that he disassociate himself from the budding insurrectionist movement in 1865:

> I felt that it was a God-given privilege and a sacred duty to work and suffer and die that others might be blessed and happy, and no Church censures could change or convert, stultify or deny what God had so firmly planted in my mind and soul. I told the bishop that he could, if he chose, publicly excommunicate me, but that if he did he was doing the work of England by singling me out for arrest.[15]

Because ultramontanist Irish Church leaders were given great respect and authority by the vast majority of their parishoners, millions of Irish Catholics abided by the wishes of anti-Fenian clerics. Irish republican leaders were becoming increasingly vocal, but they remained a minority segment of the transatlantic Irish population.

The New York headquarters of the Fenian Brotherhood was inundated with donations from around the United States, at the same time that IRB members were involved in their tit-for-tat struggle with the Catholic Church. One hundred ninety-eight circles and sixteen Sisterhood chapters forwarded membership dues and other funds to O'Mahony's office during a one-month reporting period that began on May 10. With the exception of donations from Alexandria, Virginia and Nashville, Tennessee, all the $8,850.02 raised that month came from Northern states. The Union army occupied both of these southern commercial centers from early in the war until the end of Reconstruction, so it is quite likely that the members of these two circles were at least partly comprised of Yankee servicemen. Antebellum Fenian circles in the Deep South, primarily located in coastal towns such as Charleston and Savannah, had either disbanded or been reestablished, as former members were killed while in uniform or had migrated elsewhere in search of employment.[16] The list of contributors reveals a distinct correlation between Fenianism and mill-town America. The vast majority of the eighty-seven New England circles were located in small and midsize manufacturing communities, such as Lewiston, Maine and New London, Connecticut. Fifty-two Mid-Atlantic and thirty Ohio Valley circles generally represented regional commercial centers.[17]

In terms of total Fenian membership in mid-1865, it is likely that a contemporarily published newspaper report of 379 active circles was only a slight exaggeration.[18] Many cities with large Irish American communities did not submit any contributions to Fenian headquarters during the May 10 to June 10 reporting period. In particular, not one Upstate New York community was identified on the list, even though Fenianism was very popular in Troy, Buffalo and other cities located in relative proximity to the Erie Canal. This discrepancy may be because of the rising influence of William Roberts and his fellow "Men of Action." In the midst of the May–June collection period, nineteen-year-old Galway native and former 99th New York Regiment volunteer, John F. Finerty, wrote to O'Mahony, "Indiana not now as ardent in the cause of the FB as she once was."[19] Fort Wayne Bishop John Luers had written two years earlier that his diocese was replete with Fenian supporters, thus such apathy likely surfaced because many staunch nationalists had become frustrated by continued inaction in Ireland.[20] The members of the Constitutional Brotherhood, as Roberts's organization was called on rare occasion, accordingly, had recruited many expatriates in Indianapolis and other communities in the Great Lakes region. Finerty himself defected to the emerging militant wing of the organization and soon thereafter was censured by O'Mahony for joining a group of dissident Fenians who wanted John Mitchel or Meagher to assume control of the Brotherhood.[21]

Improper allocation of Fenian financial resources may have also dampened expatriate support for the Irish nationalist movement, but a proposed Fenian salary structure reveals that O'Mahony did not provide lavish compensation to his subordinates. Under a sliding pay scale devised the previous June, O'Mahony minimized anticipated payroll expenditures by offering deferred compensation to Fenian officers. All men below the rank of captain would have 50 percent of their income automatically invested in yet to be distributed Fenian bonds that had been approved for public sale after a favorable report about IRB military preparations had been presented during the Cincinnati convention. Fenian field commanders, moreover, would be given a bond payment in addition to receiving the same monthly stipend as captains. A colonel would thus be slated to earn two hundred and fifty dollars a month but only seventy-five dollars would actually be offered in cash.[22] Because none of these bonds was issued until late 1865, Brotherhood volunteers were more motivated to fight for ideological than remunerative reasons.

Brotherhood provisions also prohibited the redemption of any Fenian bonds until six months after the establishment of an Irish republic, so militant members of the Brotherhood were not mercenaries. Accusations of financial impropriety would nevertheless haunt the Brotherhood for many years. In early 1870, the editors of *The Nation* would write that a gang of "impudent and impecunious persons" had long raised money "for their personal use."[23]

A sense of urgency was critical if the Fenians hoped to launch a successful rebellion in the months after the Confederate surrender at Appomattox. Discharged Civil War veterans had already started to readapt to a peacetime economy by returning home or relocating. Postwar employment on the incomplete Union Pacific railroad was one of several opportunities attractive to mobile adults. Former County Monaghan IRB leader Charles Rice went to work alongside expatriate Billy Yank and Johnny Reb navies in Nebraska, for example, after he was released from Mountjoy Prison in September 1866.[24] Other would-be recruits started homesteading in sparsely populated sections of the Great Plains. Once given the opportunity to secure a good job, expatriates became less inclined to join an Irish paramilitary organization of questionable credibility. By mid-1865, therefore, the Fenian Brotherhood was already in danger of becoming little more than a social forum through which a few thousand battle-scarred veterans slowly restored frayed or severed psychological and social ties to their communities.[25] Only a minority of the expatriate community in the United States and Canada concurred with an August 1865 editorial in the Toronto-based *Irish Canadian* that read, "[Fenianism] is the germ, the hope, the means of a *future* harvest that shall give us life, strength and health."[26]

Zealous men, such as young Patrick Hasson of Philadelphia, epitomized Fenian recruits who offered their skills to the organization solely out of a personal commitment to Irish independence. In a July 22, 1865 letter addressed to O'Mahony, Hasson noted his past service as a Union quartermaster and stated his hope that "sooner or later a day would come when I could use such knowledge for the benefit of that country which I have never forgotten nor never disowned."[27] Although his views were not widely shared in the expatriate community, men like Hasson heightened public fears in Ireland that a revolution was imminent. Several resident magistrates and private subjects emphatically appealed for British troops to be stationed in their communities.[28] Equally frightened upper-class Irish Protestants in Counties Limerick and Clare reportedly locked their valuables in bank vaults, and others later armed loyal tenants.[29] By February, particularly nervous landowners would request that the government dispense grenades to reputable subjects who were worried about their own safety. Seeking more professional protection, descendents of Daniel O'Connell who resided on a County Kerry family estate demanded police and military protection.[30]

All these requests were an overreaction to the actual threat the IRB presented to Irish loyalists and British government stability. As reported to O'Mahony in a letter that summer, a dozen or so republicans in Glanmire drilled every other night, but were often forced to disperse after only five minutes to avoid arrest.[31] Elsewhere, many IRB circles were still without weapons. Several operatives also made careless mistakes. In late July 1865, a young boy found a cache of confidential Fenian correspondence and cashiers' checks in a rail station just south of Dublin. Although the misplaced papers betrayed no information that was not already available to Irish constabularies and Dublin Metropolitan Police officers, the loss of the bank drafts became a serious problem. O'Mahony was not immediately informed that one of his envoys, P. J. Meehan, had failed to notice when the documents had fallen out of his underwear, so he continued to forward expatriate donations to the same recipient listed on the seized materials. British officials thus intercepted multiple money transfers destined for IRB coffers toward the end of the year. The incident also exacerbated distrust within the republican movement. Meehan was allowed to remain in the Fenian Brotherhood, even though he had lost the incriminating documents, but an attempt was made on his life several years later, because many colleagues believed he blundered deliberately to disguise his activities as a British spy. Despite rising reports of militant activity, the Fenian movement, in sum, was of modest consequence to the British government in late 1865, because the militant organization lacked guns and properly trained men.

Irish aristocratic fears of a looming insurrection proved additionally unfounded, as American Fenian leaders did little more than organize large-scale social events and raise money during the summer of 1865. Washington, D.C. members of the Brotherhood sponsored a mid-July picnic on what today is known as Roosevelt Island, but was then remembered as the boyhood residence of former *HMS Trent* emissary James Murray Mason.[32] The fourth annual Manhattan Fenian picnic held at Jones's Wood a week later, on July 25, was a massive affair, possibly as a reflection of O'Mahony's young adult admiration for the political mobilization efforts of Daniel O'Connell. Dancing throughout the day coincided with a host of lectures and Gaelic-oriented contests, such as a rock-heaving competition.[33] In the midst of such festivities, the only incident of Fenian provocation occurred when an O'Mahony emissary returned to New York City to report Stephens's insistence that with proper stateside support, a credible rebellion could be launched in two weeks' time. Pursuant to a strategic agenda previously endorsed by the IRB leader and ratified by Fenian delegates in Cincinnati the previous January, O'Mahony subsequently announced a "Final Call" for volunteers and donations on August 10. Expatriates responded with remarkable enthusiasm as the fund drive over the next fourteen days raised thirty thousand dollars; ultimately, between February 25 and September 23, over $122,000 was sent to Fenian headquarters.[34] A handful of American ship owners concurrently offered to ferry Irish filibusterers to Ireland.[35] Yet, recreation and Irish nationalism continued to be intertwined. A reported 1,405 Fenians, representing ten of thirteen Rhode Island Brotherhood circles, marched in a parade that preceded a downtown Providence celebration on August 11.[36]

College of the Holy Cross archival records show that the Worcester Irish community was highly receptive to O'Mahony's funding request. A "Last Call" meeting at the local Mechanics Hall was filled "to overflowing" with generous donors. Altogether, 1,020 people and two businesses raised $2,207.14. Additional statistical analysis of an extant list of contributors who attended the rally reveals significant demographic information about the Fenian movement a few months after the Civil War. If it is assumed that the twenty-two contributors identified as a "friend" or simply as "cash" were men, about 88.1 percent of all donors were male. Such a presumption is probably accurate, as one anonymous person is specifically referred to as "a lady friend." On the other hand, if all unidentified donors were female, roughly 86 percent of the contributors were men and 14 percent were women. The total number of female contributors may also be higher, but the full names of the people included on the roll are unknown. Many people are identified only by their surname and first initial. Notably, of the women on the list, fifteen are denoted as married (8.1 percent of the total number of women in the sample). Single Irish women, who composed the largest single group within the American expatriate community, were more sympathetic to the Irish nationalist cause than wives and widows. This approval is presumably because their residence in America had been of shorter duration at the time of the fundraiser. The high proportion of modest contributions also suggests that poorer Irish residents of Worcester were more supportive of Fenianism than their more established expatriate kinsmen. Seventy-six percent of all donors offered two dollars or less to the "Last Call" fund. A private business, conversely, was one of only three benefactors that matched the highest single contribution of $25. On average, men donated $2.22, whereas the $178 dollars raised by women equates to $1.47 per female.[37]

How much of this eleventh-hour money reached the IRB is uncertain. Stephens continued to lambaste his American counterparts for failing to provide him with more money. Printing expenses were a significant financial burden. Little profit was made from the two-year-old *Irish People,* despite a respectable peak circulation of 8,000 copies. Because money was also needed to print pamphlets and handbills, many of the paper's freelance contributors were never paid for their submissions.[38] Yet, the *Irish People* was the leading Irish nationalist newspaper in England by the spring of 1864, thus demonstrating that publication of the paper facilitated wide dissemination of IRB ideology. In each weekly edition, land reform issues were only overshadowed by constant editorial censure of ecclesiastical interference in temporal affairs.[39] As a devoted Catholic, Charles Kickham contradicted his otherwise conservative social sentiments by writing essays that highlighted Fenian antipathy toward the church hierarchy's influence on secular issues.[40] Other writers occasionally made caustic remarks about bishops and priests who were opposed to republican initiatives. Church leaders countered these attacks by publicly denouncing the political bent of *Irish People* poets, such as the sixteen-year-old sister of future Irish parliamentarian Charles Stewart Parnell.[41] Circulation suffered as a result, and an IRB-coined mantra, "The Land for the People," did not become widely used until the Land League was organized in the early 1880s.[42] Stephens had once said he believed that "every child born in a free state should have a place on his native soil whereas to gain an independent livelihood."[43] Kickham, likewise, postulated that an independent Irish republic would have to be established so that patriarchal British laws could be replaced by equitable social and commercial customs that were rooted in Brehon traditions.[44] Cooperative property ownership, in his estimation, would produce lower and more equitable rents by undermining well-endowed landholders, who often maintained near oligarchic control of rural economies. Contrary to claims by the noted labor historian David Montgomery, the Fenians were not "totally oblivious" to the agrarian question in Ireland.[45] They failed, however, to arouse nationalist expression in rural areas because most peasants were either politically apathetic or skeptical of IRB leaders, who had yet to demonstrate their capability to challenge British suzerainty over Ireland even though they were receiving expatriate financial support.

A Dublin Metropolitan Police raid in mid-September 1865 irreparably impaired the IRB at a time that the cash-strapped *Irish People* was becoming increasingly popular. Having been tipped by an informant that a drunken Fenian had warned fellow nationalists in Clonmel to prepare for rebellion, a detachment of constables obtained a search warrant and raided Stephens's headquarters shortly after midnight on September 15. Securing the building proved effortless, but Twentieth Massachusetts veteran James Murphy insisted that he could not be arrested for seditious activity because he was an American citizen. The concomitant pretrial detention of many republican operatives in Munster also embarrassed the British government when it was publicly revealed that Brian Dillon and John Lynch of Cork were among many lower-middle-class Fenian prisoners who were brutally mistreated while in prison.[46] Yet these problems were overshadowed by key pieces of admissible evidence that incriminated several IRB conspirators. In addition to thirty-eight thousand dollars worth of bank notes payable to Fenian financial agents, police officials obtained a letter that designated Luby, Kickham, and O'Donovan Rossa acting heads of the IRB when Stephens was out of the country.[47] Having already been typeset, the September 16 edition of the *Irish People* made no reference to the previous night's raid.

The proscription of the *Irish People* and the arrests of forty-one IRB suspects could have been an opportunity rather than a setback for the Irish republican movement. Fenian activities to date had not been definitely treasonous. Leading nationalist defendants could argue in court that they had been denied civil protection from unsubstantiated arrest. In addition, with the European press having condemned the raid as an unjustified suppression of free speech, losing the capacity to print a newspaper was trivial, if the leaders of the organization had the courage to retaliate. Few rank-and-file members of the IRB, or Irish American soldiers who had returned to Ireland to participate in a widely anticipated rebellion, were detained. Republican men around the country waited for the call to mobilize even though most of them had no weapons. Fenian support within the greater expatriate community remained meager in per capita terms, but seven thousand energetic New Englanders did attend a September 19 Fenian picnic in Framingham, Massachusetts.[48] Several Irish American priests, including the Dublin-born, Cleveland cleric, Thomas Thorpe, openly supported the Brotherhood.[49] Even John Martin anticipated a Fenian revolt. As he wrote in a letter to a colleague at the time, "I would be relieved from heavy anxiety if I felt confident that the arrests will prevent any attempt at a rising."[50] If Stephens had been aggressive, a series of small strikes against government outposts, whether successful or not, might have precipitated a groundswell of grassroots military activity similar to the United Irish Rebellion a half-century earlier. Stephens, however, remained largely silent while he hid on the southeastern outskirts of Dublin in a rented Sandymount country house.

With Stephens and Kickham sequestered and the rest of the *Irish People* editorial staff awaiting trial, a twenty-three-year-old emerging nationalist hero named John Devoy temporarily became the most active Fenian operative who remained at large. Devoy possessed impeccable republican credentials. Of primary importance, he was the son of a nationalist farmer who had later become a brewer. He had also allegedly been expelled from the Marlborough Street National School when he was ten for refusing to sing "God Save the Queen." As a teenager, he had affirmed the Fenian oath before serving as a French Legionnaire in North Africa for a year to obtain military experience.[51] Upon his return to Ireland, Stephens, who had long been concerned that IRB members in uniform would resist following orders from civilians, placed the former infantryman in charge of co-opting members of the British military. Devoy's natural charm, strong personal convictions, and daring courage served him well in this capacity. Recruiting

members of the only volunteer army in mid-nineteenth century Europe was unquestionably difficult. Despite low pay and arduous work, rank-and-file morale, in
the absence of war, was rarely so low that disgruntled enlisted men would risk being sentenced to death for defecting.[52] Nevertheless, Devoy, who sneaked onto a
British army base at night on at least one occasion to recruit enlisted men of Irish
descent, provided what is most likely an inflated estimate in his memoirs that he
swore eight thousand servicemen into the IRB.[53] There is no doubt, however, that
he and other nationalist operatives secured the support of a few hundred, if not a
few thousand, of the seventeen to twenty-six thousand troops variously stationed
on the island between 1864 and 1867.

IRB inability to truly infiltrate British military and Irish law enforcement
entities compounded the simultaneous negative impact of heightened opposition
from Archbishop Cullen and other leaders of the Irish Catholic Church. Most
Irish bishops and priests, like their American counterparts, continued to condemn
the IRB for violating canonical prohibitions against individual participation in secret societies and the temporal administration of oaths. Initially a nuisance, the
growing Fenian movement now modestly compromised the extraconstitutional
authority of the Church by offering the laity an alternative conduit to vent its
economic and civic grievances. It was plausible that diocesan leaders would be politically emasculated if the IRB were eventually able to fulfill Irish Catholic social
aspirations. Reminiscent of when the Jacobins controlled French government in
the 1790s, conservative Irish Catholic clerics feared that the highly secular IRB
would curtail an ongoing post-Famine devotional revolution that had been largely
orchestrated by Cullen. Countless nonpracticing Catholics re-embraced their
faith during the mid-nineteenth century, and this seeming devotional revolution
brought the building of new churches and parochial schools. The clergy feared,
however, that a revolution in Ireland might cause havoc in the Irish social system
and lead to the secularization of the nation.[54] If such secularization of Irish society
were to occur, the Irish Church might suffer financially. By writing a pastoral condemnation of the organization in October, Cullen thus acted contrary to his South
Leinster ancestors, who had defied British rule since the seventeenth century.

Nationalist operatives waited in vain for instructions from Stephens, as
Cullen's censure of the IRB occurred at the same time that detained republican
suspects were pressured to accept prosecutorial immunity in exchange for becoming state witnesses. It can be argued, of course, that Stephens and his cohorts were
caught off guard. Before the seizure of IRB headquarters, proactive nationalists
had been accustomed only to mild government harassment. Some state-employed
schoolteachers had been dismissed for reading the *Irish People* before the previous
September, but there was little indication that the Dublin Metropolitan Police

would launch a major strike against the organization.[55] In addition, the Fenians received information from spies planted within the British bureaucracy; whether these people were unaware of pending arrests or were unable to warn IRB leaders is uncertain. Stephens's true dereliction as a nationalist leader was thus his unwillingness to retaliate. Throughout the fall, he tended to his seaside hideout garden and constantly demanded briefings from operatives who risked arrest each time they fulfilled his often-unnecessary orders to obtain information. Yet, as the IRB leadership had always maintained a certain veil of secrecy, Stephens's continued inaction did not initially affect Fenian Brotherhood bond sales. Between mid-September and the end of October, $130,905 was received from entities, such as the sixty-member Fenian circle in Toronto and the New York Longshoreman's Protective Association.[56]

Stephens's lack of resilience further compromised O'Mahony's stature within the transatlantic republican movement when a third Fenian Brotherhood convention was held in Philadelphia during mid-October. Perturbed that the IRB leader had absconded rather than rebel after the *Irish People* offices were raided, Men of Action supporters among the six hundred assembled delegates insisted on the short-term implementation of a military operation and internal organizational reforms. In an effort to ascertain how the federal government would respond if the Fenians launched an invasion north across the American border, William Roberts dispatched three envoys to Washington during the convention to confer with President Andrew Johnson and Secretary of State William Seward. A former Missouri state senator named Bernard Doran Killian and the other members of the Fenian delegation later reported that successful Irish infiltration of Canada would be officially recognized as a *fait accompli*. Such federal posturing was intentionally ambiguous. Whether the Fenians would be freely allowed to violate American neutrality laws was uncertain. Anglo-American relations had improved since the recently concluded Civil War but bellwether state elections were looming in New York. Politicians and appointed leaders in state capitals and city halls around the country shared a desire with the dignitaries who had attended the Chicago Fenian Fair to placate Irish American constituents without entangling the United States in a bloody transatlantic war.

Harbingers of a mercurial relationship between the Fenians and United States government officials also surfaced when Seward further attempted to appease the Irish nationalist community at the time of the Philadelphia convention. As a secretary of state who strongly supported American territorial expansion, Seward was particularly mindful of the need to accommodate the British government and the Fenians alike. While previously serving as a United States senator from New York, he had acquired the appellation "friend of the Irish" in part for donating one hundred dollars to William Smith O'Brien in 1848. The Whig/ Republican Seward had also garnered popularity in the expatriate community by publicly endorsing Repeal during an 1853 visit to the old Irish Parliament in Dublin.[57] An inaugural member of the Lincoln administration, he had mused in the early 1860s that an Anglo-American war might allay domestic political tensions between the North and the South. When the Confederacy surrendered, he made the same proposal under the presumption that a war with Great Britain could heal a fractured nation. Seward soon recognized, however, that most Americans wanted peace after four arduous years of internecine warfare. Reluctant to allow any Fenian violation of Canadian territory to metastasize into a full-scale transatlantic military conflict, the secretary of state attempted to retain Irish voter support by furloughing John Mitchel from federal custody. Brotherhood members appreciated that Mitchel was released after spending four-and-a-half months in a Tidewater Virginia military prison for publishing incendiary antigovernment remarks in a New York newspaper shortly after the war. Mitchel himself wanted to sue the United States government for false imprisonment after his release. He instead settled in Paris two weeks after he parted company with fellow Fortress Monroe convict Jefferson Davis so that he could serve as a Fenian financial agent.[58] Contrary to his long-held belief that Irish militant activity was futile at a time when Great Britain was not at war with another world power, Mitchel expressed new confidence in the Brotherhood's potential and became actively involved in the Fenian movement for the first time.[59]

The Men of Action proceeded to undermine John O'Mahony's organizational authority, once they assumed that they had received a blanket endorsement from the Johnson administration. Dressed at the convention in his Civil War uniform, O'Mahony had to accept a new constitution that provided the Fenian President with a two thousand dollar salary but almost no autonomous powers. All executive appointees, henceforward, also had to be approved by an annually elected, fifteen-member senate that would be comprised of people who had been nominated by a larger Fenian House of Delegates. The aura of Independence Hall (which was only a few yards away from the building in which the Fenians deliberated) may have influenced members of the convention to further approve a system of checks and balances that allowed the two houses of the newly created Fenian legislative branch to override executive appropriations and strategic decisions.[60] Grassroots initiatives were to be channeled through House of Delegates members, who would represent each United States congressional district. In a struggle for control of the Fenian movement, O'Mahony's opponents demonstrated that, even though they were committed to Irish independence, they too admired American constitutional democracy. British law was rebuked, moreover, with an additional provision that prohibited the passage of any *ex post facto* laws. Cognizant of the legal chicanery that had led to the transportation of John Mitchel to Australia in 1848, the Fenians remained wary of arbitrary bureaucratic power.[61]

William Roberts quickly emerged as an attractive alternative Irish nationalist leader to O'Mahony after he was elected the first president of the Fenian Senate. Born in 1830, Roberts was a Protestant from Mitchelstown, County Cork who had emigrated to the United States at the age of nineteen and become a merchant employee of the extremely wealthy commercial magnate A. T. Stewart. Working in the Ulster native's famous and elaborately decorated Marble Palace department store was a tremendous stepping-stone for the undereducated Roberts. During the Panic of 1857, he had opened a rival establishment in Lower Manhattan at 252 Bowery, calling it the Crystal Palace. As he had joined the Fenian Brotherhood only two years earlier, Roberts's recently obtained wealth and influence (rather than his previous experience as the president of the fraternal New York Knights of Saint Patrick and as a former militia lieutenant colonel) boosted his credibility within the nationalist community. His outstanding oratory skills contrasted starkly with O'Mahony's dour public persona. Unlike Roberts, O'Mahony had become progressively poorer rather than richer after he had deeded his Munster property to a brother-in-law and escaped to France in 1848. Because he had never been compensated for translating *Foras Feasa ar Éirinn*, a public subscription had been raised for him in June 1863.[62] Described in the 1850s as "one of the finest looking of men in New York City," O'Mahony's once brawny physical appearance had declined over a decade to a threadbare resemblance of an "overworked assistant book-keeper in some second or third rate . . . jobbing house."[63] Thus, even though O'Mahony was better qualified, a large faction within the Fenian rank-and-file supported Roberts because he was breaking organizational precedent in both strategy and style.

The appointment of a new chief military commander and the relocation of Brotherhood headquarters best demonstrate that a new era in the history of the Fenian movement began after the Philadelphia convention. Nominated by O'Mahony, Thomas William Sweeny was widely welcomed into the Brotherhood as the revamped organization's secretary of war. The expatriate Union army general had ample combat experience and tremendous confidence that an army of Irish American filibusterers could capture populated sections of Ontario and Quebec. It was fitting that, as a man of change, Sweeny helped Roberts and Killian select the large, four-story townhouse of pharmaceutical magnate William Moffat as the Brotherhood's new primary office. O'Mahony had based his operations in a nondescript building located in the tawdry Lower East Side. Deferring to Roberts's luxurious tastes, however, Fenian supporters would now subsidize a one thousand dollar a month lease and a twelve thousand dollar security deposit, so that their leaders could conduct their affairs in lavish green-and-gold upholstered offices in upscale Union Square. By also purchasing new mahogany furniture, the Brotherhood presented a stately aura of power and authority to impressionable outsiders.[64]

Anecdotal evidence suggests that the Irish American community was either unaware of or unopposed to such ostentatious spending. No mention of Fenian activity in Manhattan appeared in the New Orleans press while Louisiana Brotherhood leaders were receiving favorable coverage for holding meetings throughout the Crescent City.[65] At the same time, Chicago-area expatriates routinely sang verses of the pro-Fenian anthem, "The Green Above the Red," when they attended Irish theatrical performances in late 1865.[66] The widespread postwar popularity of Dion Boucicault's nationalist-tinged play, *Arrah-na-Pogue*, additionally suggested that many expatriates were, at the very least, casual Fenian supporters. Loosely translated as "Exchanging Kisses," the romantic comedy set during the 1798 rebellion included a popular new rendition of "The Wearing of the Green," a nationalist tune that had actually originated in mid-eighteenth century Scotland.

The arrest of Stephens, Kickham, and two other nationalists on the same day that New Orleans Fenians held a sizable rally at the Saint Charles Street Opera House temporarily overshadowed the many changes that were occurring inside the American-based Brotherhood. Frequent constabulary spotting of Stephens's wife, Jane, persuaded British law enforcement officials to obtain an arrest warrant and execute an early-morning raid by politely knocking on the front door of the IRB leader's presumed Sandymount hideout. Stephens's ensuing attempt to deceive the authorities failed miserably. Identifying himself as Mister Herbert and initially refusing to open the door, he did not admit his true identity until several minutes after he reluctantly opened the lock wearing only a nightshirt, and then repaired to his bedroom.[67] Remanded into custody after insisting that he would have resisted arrest if he had been better prepared, Stephens refused his right to defense counsel in a calculated effort to appear a martyr of British justice. Retaining a lawyer—as he told the court—might be construed as personal acknowledgment of British jurisdiction over Ireland.[68] With the Fenian leader detained, there was little possibility of a revolt. Most likely hyperbolized newspaper reports, moreover, damaged IRB morale by indicating that the private residence where Stephens had been hiding was well maintained, received frequent deliveries of foodstuffs, and was graced by a wine cellar that "no gentleman might feel ashamed of displaying to his friends."[69] Once incarcerated in Richmond Bridewell, Stephens further disappointed zealous Irish nationalists by again ordering his men to stand-down and by fostering internal dissension among militant republicans. With the assistance of a sister-in-law who repeatedly smuggled his orders out of prison, Stephens prevented one of his critics within the organization from assuming control of the Fenian movement by dispatching him to New York. Although County Tyrone native Francis Frederick Millen obeyed Stephens's order, he offered his services as a spy to the British consul soon after he arrived in Manhattan. The IRB was again deprived of a volunteer who had been a high-ranking officer in the Union army.[70]

John Devoy's resourcefulness was further evidenced when he and a Galway-born Tenth Ohio Infantry veteran named Thomas Kelly led a team of prison employees and other reliable IRB members to help Stephens escape from his Dublin prison cell two weeks after he had been captured. Just after 1:00 a.m. on the rain-drenched morning of November 24, a prison medical orderly and a night watch-man released Stephens from his third-floor hospital ward cell and ushered the Fenian leader to an inner courtyard partition that was only surmountable after a hidden ladder was hastily placed on top of two tables. With the aid of a rope that was thrown over the outer prison wall and held by a pair of accomplices, Stephens scaled the final barrier to freedom and fled the complex in the company of a small entourage. Overall, the execution of the entire operation was nearly flawless. Co-workers never discovered the identities of the two prison employees who had used a beeswax impression to copy the key to Stephens's cell. A young pretrial prisoner in an adjacent cell, moreover, had disobeyed a warden's order to ring a gong if he heard suspicious noises, because he feared that any prison infiltrators might slit his throat if he sounded an alarm. By the time the accomplice night watchman had informed his superiors of an escape at 5:00 a.m., the Fenian chief and his liberators were already celebrating their tremendous coup in a Dublin safe house within view of the prison. Five other locations also remained available if Stephens needed to be moved on short notice.[71]

Stephens's escape produced widespread speculation that a revolution in Ireland would finally occur. As people on the street spread rumors of anticipated Fenian activities, Stephens squelched near-unanimous support for an insurrection among the IRB hierarchy during a seminal meeting that was held two days after he was rescued from Richmond Bridewell. All but one of the assembled expatriate military advisors and leading Irish circle heads insisted that now was as good a time as ever to revolt. Devoy, in particular, called for immediate action by arguing that IRB stockpiles of pikes could be easily augmented by stealing firearms from inadequately defended British military installations.[72] Stephens reversed his previous boastful predictions of "insurrection or dissolution in 1865," however, because he believed his men were still unprepared for battle.[73] Inadequate training, in his estimation, had undermined the Young Ireland movement in 1848. Perhaps with weakened resolve after his brief incarceration, Stephens ironically expressed concern for the safety of the Irish people. Writing to Cincinnati Archbishop John Purcell on December 2, the Irish prelate compared an Ireland potentially in political turmoil to an uprising that had occurred in Jamaica two months earlier: "Our orangemen [in the event of a rebellion] would treat our poor people, as the blacks were lately dealt with [during the Morant Bay uprising]."[74] Despite the irreversible damage to the IRB leader's reputation, Vincent Comerford argues that Stephens can be credited for not fulfilling his pledge to revolt. Insistence on delay was in the best interest of greenhorn insurgents who might have been killed.[75] Unaware that IRB forces would not be mobilized soon, British officials continued to compromise the nationalist movement by arresting militant suspects and by deploying two additional infantry regiments to Ireland.

Dissension between Stephens and his advisors was relatively insignificant compared to an irreparable conflict that erupted within the American Fenian movement toward the end of 1865. Searching for a pretext to obtain total executive control of the Brotherhood, Roberts initiated impeachment proceedings against O'Mahony on December 2 by accusing his adversary of illegally authorizing the sale of Fenian bonds, providing William Sweeny with only 20 percent of the funds that he had committed to Fenian defense funds, and refusing to submit his records for an independent audit.[76] Originally offered in five to five hundred dollar denominations, a preprinting public sale of the bonds at a prevailing market rate return of 6 percent had stalled when Roberts's operatives had coerced Fenian treasury secretary Patrick Keenan into resigning before he could endorse sixty-eight thousand dollars worth of certificates.[77] O'Mahony's subsequent decision to unilaterally transpose his signature on an engraving plate so that the promissory notes would be available for delivery, sale, and compensation as planned was technically illegal under the provisions of the recently adopted Fenian constitution. With only a few supporters among the fifteen senators, the Brotherhood founder and his colleague, Doran Killian, were impeached on December 7, even though O'Mahony's only moral error of judgment had been arbitrarily granting himself a twelve hundred dollar pay raise as compensation for assuming Keenan's former responsibilities.[78]

Besides refusing to formally answer the charges brought against him, O'Mahony publicly announced that he was still legally at the head of the expatriate nationalist movement. Roberts's machinations, in O'Mahony's estimation, violated the Brotherhood's regulations.[79] In retaliation, O'Mahony barred any senators from entering his headquarters and unsuccessfully ordered Sweeny to acknowledge his authority. Scathingly, he also publicly accused his detractors of "perfidy, treason, disobedience of orders, and conveyance of information to the enemy."[80] Members of circles that did not immediately fall into disarray were left to decide whether to support one of the two splinter groups that emerged after the Philadelphia convention or become independent organizations like the Irish National Fund Association of Corry, Pennsylvania.[81] Although his rivals had outmaneuvered him, O'Mahony may have expedited the Fenian Brotherhood schism in a letter he had penned six months earlier. Writing in confidence to a Cleveland Fenian who had joined the Roberts faction during the bond crisis, the former Young Irelander candidly admitted, "I am not a bookkeeper and I know nothing of buying and selling goods. I would be a fool in an auction room."[82]

The debilitating organizational struggle between O'Mahony and Roberts continued to unfold as thousands of expatriates displayed solid nationalist loyalties in late 1865. Collateral evidence suggests that a traveling theatre company successfully presented a revue entitled the *Hurley Tour of Ireland* to raise money and propagate Fenian ideals during the Christmas season.[83] In a January 1866 report to the royal governor of New Brunswick, a Canadian militia commander noted that he had witnessed ardent demonstrations of Irish patriotism when he attended two Fenian productions at the Harvard Theatre during a recent visit to Boston. Besides describing the audience as a crowd of "rowdies and roughs," he noted that actors were rousingly applauded each time they made a favorable reference to Fenianism. Cheers and a standing ovation ensued when the star actor proclaimed, "Hurrah for Stephens and ould Ireland."[84] A Chicago-based reporter for the *La Crosse Daily Democrat*, likewise, noted that a pro-Irish independence lecture by the psychologically unstable millionaire orator George Francis Train had been sold out.[85] The bulk of the $228,000 that O'Mahony raised in 1865 had been received in the latter portion of the year, because the expatriate community was no longer distracted by the Civil War and had yet to fully readjust to a peacetime economy.[86] Many Irish Union army veterans who would have preferred to remain in uniform gravitated toward the Fenian movement as the postwar United States military was downsized.[87]

William Roberts also received increased expatriate support after internal dissension roiled inside the Brotherhood. The *New York Times* reported on December 13 that members of a Manhattan circle who had defected to Roberts en masse diplomatically lauded O'Mahony as "a ship deeply anchored in Irish hearts" and "a shining star in the heavens, receiving new luster from the clouds."[88] Saint Louis Fenians most likely aligned with Roberts also sponsored a successful banquet featuring an inebriated General Frank Blair shortly before New Year's 1866. Slurring his words, the former Union officer repeatedly addressed dinner party attendees as "Finnegans" and unwittingly predicted how O'Mahony's allies would launch a transatlantic filibuster from Manhattan to Ireland two years later.[89] Saint

Louis Fenians who had organized the Blair dinner were also among the thousands of expatriate Irish nationalists who increasingly defied their spiritual leaders. At the end of the previous August, Archbishop Peter Kenrick had announced, "Members of the Fenian Brotherhood, men and women, are not admissible to the sacraments of the church as long as they are united with that association."[90] A month later, moreover, he prohibited community expatriates from displaying any Fenian insignias when former Brotherhood national secretary Henry O'Clarence McCarthy was buried in the local Calvary Cemetery.[91] Similar Fenian defiance surfaced in Buffalo. Unfazed by the possibility of ecclesiastical retaliation, local members of the Brotherhood issued a November 24 public letter that censured their Gaelic-speaking bishop, John Timon, for having openly criticized area members of the Fenian Sisterhood.[92] Calling the auxiliary a "plague" in private correspondence to another bishop, Timon had apparently been additionally upset that the female organization met at night.[93] Such disobedient behavior was fostered by a variety of factors, including fleeting nativist sentiments. The former president of the Union army–affiliated United States Sanitary Commission Henry W. Bellows stated in December 1865, for example, "We owed little to Irish regiments and [their] commanders."[94]

In late 1865 and early 1866, nationalist activity in Ireland revolved around the occasionally contentious trials of several Fenian suspects. Conflict-of-interest issues notwithstanding, Independent Irish Party defector John Keogh was appointed to serve on a two-man Court of Common Pleas tribunal because few members of an elderly Irish judicial bench had the knowledge or physical stamina to preside over what many court spectators believed would be a protracted courtroom affair. A Catholic, Keogh proved to be largely impartial, but some of his pretrial rulings reflected his newfound loyalist sentiments. A court order prohibited the popular nationalist newspaper publisher and barrister P. J. Smyth from serving as defense counsel for Luby, O'Leary, and O'Donovan Rossa, because he himself was under investigation for engaging in seditious activities. Former Young Ireland counselor Isaac Butt, likewise, had difficulty getting defense motions approved after he agreed to represent Stephens's closest colleagues pro bono. Butt's strategy to have Luby countersue the Dublin Constabulary for illegal search and seizure before his trial began, for example, was summarily rejected by Keogh—as was his request for a change of venue, even though Keogh recognized that certain biased press reports might prevent Fenian defendants from receiving a fair trial. Yet Butt—whose cyclical popularity had recently increased when he secured an acquittal for an expatriate O'Mahony emissary named John McCafferty—deftly used his preemptory challenges to dismiss potential jurors with possible loyalist sympathies. As a County Donegal Protestant who had defended Young Ireland suspects before becoming a member of parliament, Butt recognized that representing IRB operatives overshadowed his current reputation for squandering money on gambling and women. More importantly, his public re-emergence reinforced simultaneous IRB efforts to foster an ecumenical Irish nationalist coalition. In December, a republican sympathizer wrote in an open letter, "We embrace Protestants, Catholics, Dissenters, and all who love Ireland."[95] Outside of a few leaders and a handful of circles comprised mainly of Presbyterians and Anglicans, however, the IRB was always predominately comprised of Irish Catholics.

Butt's skill at deposing jurors failed to insure that he would win acquittals for his clients. By utilizing flimsy evidence, such as a nationalist-tinged poem that was written by Fanny Parnell and published in the *Irish People*, crown lawyers secured guilty verdicts against most of the defendants; only five suspects were acquitted. Although unschooled as a barrister, the irascible O'Donovan Rossa defended himself in an effort to provide Kickham with more time to prepare for trial and to save Butt and his able assistant from the embarrassment of defending a client who would undoubtedly be found guilty. With occasional impromptu advice from another lawyer named John Lawless, the Phoenix Society founder repeatedly mocked the British judicial system by exercising his right to read submitted evidence verbatim. Such insouciance—and the young Miss Parnell's attempt to throw flowers to him—tested the patience of Keogh and his judicial colleague. O'Donovan Rossa was promptly sentenced to penal servitude for life after he completed an eight-hour-long closing argument.[96]

Several female Irish nationalists filled a leadership vacuum within the IRB after the first Fenian suspects were tried and sentenced to prison. The wives of Luby, O'Leary, and O'Donovan Rossa occasionally smuggled Brotherhood documents to John Mitchel in France. With the help of another woman, who assisted a Fenian operative until he was arrested shortly after the *Irish People* press offices were seized, they also established a female-led Fenian prisoner's defense fund. By defying the so-called Victorian "cult of domesticity," these four women and other female Irish republicans raised money to offset Fenian legal fees and ultimately provided financial support to 110 families of convicted nationalist conspirators.[97] On her own initiative, Delia Parnell, the mother of Charles Stewart Parnell, aroused the attention of Irish police inspectors by donating money to fellow Americans who had been detained on suspicion that they were Fenians. Like their male counterparts, female nationalists had to be wary of other women. A spy only identified as Mrs. Johnstone provided British officials with information that led to the detention of several IRB members.[98]

Rightfully skeptical that the Fenian movement had been contained once the *Irish People* editorial staff was in prison, British officials continued to retaliate against the IRB by conducting additional constabulary investigations, sending more nationalist suspects to prison, and reassigning two more army regiments to Ireland.[99] With rumor of an impending Irish American naval invasion circulating throughout the North Atlantic world, Royal Navy gunboats remained off the west coast of Ireland throughout the winter, despite relentless rough weather.[100] One hundred and fifty soldiers were ultimately court-martialed for seditious behavior. Many people found guilty of yelling "Hurrah for the Irish Republic" were flogged in front of their regiments.[101] Prosperous Philadelphia wheelwright John Fleming informed his nephew in late January 1866 that he would not be returning to Ireland for a visit, because he had heard that British authorities had been mistreating Irish American travelers suspected of Fenianism. Fearing that he might be mistaken as an Irish American military officer, he wrote, "I did intend to go on to See ye but in concequince of how Setezens ar trated there I made my mind up not to go for sum time untill I see sum better chance."[102] Fenians who belonged to British regiments stationed in Canada and Ireland also risked severe punishment if they expressed militant political views.

By rallying his supporters at a New York convention three weeks before Fleming wrote to his nephew, O'Mahony partly stemmed rising expatriate interest in Thomas Sweeny's plan to lead a Fenian army into Canada. In conjunction with his personal efforts to regain influence with the expatriate nationalist community, O'Mahony repealed the Fenian constitution that had been approved in Philadelphia; remaining members of the original Brotherhood would respect bylaws adopted in Chicago two years earlier. Recognizing that a severe conflict had erupted within the Brotherhood, the veteran of the contentious 1855 EMA split also ordered fellow members of the predominately Fenian 99th New York Militia regiment to prevent pro-Roberts rabble-rousers from demonstrating on the convention floor. William Sweeny was invited to the well-attended proceedings, however, as O'Mahony hoped to publicly disgrace one of his most prominent rivals. Suspecting a trap, Sweeney initially demurred from attending the convention. He changed his mind, however, when he decided that his appearance might facilitate the reunification of the Brotherhood. Confirming his earlier suspicions, Sweeny was denounced for having never taken the Fenian oath after he asked the delegates who had cheered him upon his arrival to seek accommodation with the Men of Action. Sweeny left the speaker's platform before sergeants-at-arms were called to remove him, but personal attacks against his character persisted for several weeks. The former newspaper publisher and underexperienced Union infantry officer B. Doran Killian was particularly virulent, repeatedly ridiculing Sweeny in public. The Roberts faction, however, continued to gain greater expatriate support.

Undiscouraged by his experiences at O'Mahony's convention, Sweeny finalized an elaborate plan that would deploy thousands of Roberts-faction Fenians across the Canadian border. After mustering in various locations throughout the United States, Hibernian filibusterers would fight to establish an expatriate republic in southern Quebec, which potentially could be ransomed for Irish independence. After revealing snippets of his plan to nationalist sympathizers throughout the Upper Ohio River Valley in late January, Sweeny avoided arrest as he traveled with Roberts through Hamilton, Ontario, and later submitted a full invasion proposal to forty-eight people who attended a breakaway Fenian gathering that began in Pittsburgh on February 19.[103] Even though Killian had arrived in the city to organize a public demonstration against the Men of Action, the assembled delegates approved Sweeny's wintertime operation plan by a landslide vote of forty-four to four. If executed as planned, ten thousand expatriate infantrymen and three artillery batteries would seize a vast section of Canadian territory stretching from Lake Huron to the Saint Lawrence River Valley. By waiting eight to twelve months, Sweeny would have time to equip and train an army that would utilize otherwise impassable rivers as frozen conduits into British-controlled territory.[104]

Fenians who had endorsed William Roberts siphoned additional money and media attention away from O'Mahony and other Fenians by increasingly disseminating their intention to organize an invasion of Canada. The Men of Action, or senate wing as they were also called, drew its greatest support in the Midwest. John Looby reported to O'Mahony from Newburgh, Ohio in January 1866 that dissension within the Fenian leadership had fostered apathy within his community, "The indifference that exists among the members at the present on account of our late troubles is obvious, our Circle is shattered at the present time a good deal, but we live in hope."[105] Continuing negative financial implications of the schism were evident a month later in a letter from Thomas Siske of Abington, Massachusetts to the former Missouri State Senator turned O'Mahony confidante, B. Doran Killian. In reference to a fifteen dollar loan, Siske apologized for not repaying the money sooner: "I have not been able to collect it before this, in consideration of the great many of our members seceding . . . we are not fairly organized, the Secretary, Treasurer, and the Chairman of the Committee of Safety having left the organization."[106] As Roberts's popularity rose, O'Mahony supporters became primarily concentrated in New England and the Eastern Seaboard of the Mid-Atlantic States.

Such conflict within the Brotherhood greatly compromised IRB efforts to obtain more weapons. Stephens had instructed a resourceful Union army veteran named Richard O'Sullivan Burke to begin conveying a small stash of IRB firearms in England to Ireland the previous November. However, once many Fenians started supporting Roberts, even less money was available to sustain this operation. In the midst of such ideological and financial disarray, the Fenian movement was desperate for a leader who could reunite the two factions and reestablish funding for illegal firearms purchases; yet the most eligible people were unavailable or unwilling to serve the Brotherhood. Meagher had left New York to become the Acting Territorial Governor of Montana. Mitchel, meanwhile, was content to remain in Paris, where he received a substantial quarterly stipend of $625.00 in gold for serving as a financial intermediary between the Brotherhood and the IRB.[107] The only other possibility of an intra-Brotherhood reconciliation was a significant strategic crisis in Ireland.

Such an event occurred when the British Parliament suspended *habeas corpus* protections in Ireland on February 17, 1866. Two hundred eighteen people, including John Devoy, were arrested within a week after a newly elected Tory government almost unanimously authorized Irish constables and detectives to arrest nationalist suspects without probable cause for six months.[108] The Dublin Temple Street home of Delia Parnell was searched even before the legislation officially became law. A Cambridge University student at the time, Charles Stewart Parnell was acutely incensed that his mother and sisters had been harassed. Years later, he would say his decision to become politically active like his poetess sisters was rooted in his anger that law enforcement authorities had had the audacity to enter his mother's bedroom when she was indisposed.[109] The slightest hint of suspicion also landed many Irishmen in jail for prolonged periods. One man was arrested in Cavan merely for shouting, "Here's health to the Fenians all around."[110] Additional arrests were secured by pressuring incarcerated suspects to reveal the names of other nationalist sympathizers. Even the most resolute nationalist detainees often agreed to compromise the militant republican movement in exchange for their release from prison.[111] Such strong-armed tactics were repeatedly used over the following years, as the Suspension Act was renewed on multiple occasions.

Recognizing that the imprisonment of untried Fenian suspects angered even nominal Irish nationalists, O'Mahony issued a well-received plea for additional financial assistance when word of the *habeas corpus* suspension first reached the United States on March 2. Reprinted with various minor vocabulary differences in newspapers throughout the country, his urgent request in the Lowell *Daily Courier* read:

> *Brothers:* The hour for action has arrived. The *habeas corpus* is suspended in Ireland. Our brothers are being arrested by hundreds and thrown into prison. Call circles together immediately. Send us all

the aid in your power at once, and in God's name let us start for our destination. Aid! Brothers, help for God and Ireland. God save the Green.[112]

Nationalist exuberance remained relatively high in the United States despite disunited and inadequate leadership. Both factions of the Brotherhood continued to raise money, even though counterfeiters had begun to circulate bogus copies of Fenian bond certificates that depicted an expatriate soldier grasping a sword off American soil while the female allegorical form *Hibernia* beckoned him east across the Atlantic to an Irish battlefield.[113] Press reports that some vendors coerced expatriates into purchasing Fenian bonds also failed to dissuade many expatriates from supporting the Brotherhood.[114] New recruits joined the organization every day. At least twenty Fenian circles were active throughout sparsely populated Wisconsin by February 1866.[115]

The organization of Fenian demonstrations in other American cities elicited a variety of public responses. Temporarily ignoring their differences, New York members of the O'Mahony and Roberts factions both attended a February 12 Cooper Union rally that featured the influential former Copperhead New York City mayor and Manhattan congressman, Fernando Wood, as well as George Francis Train.[116] Hundreds of latecomers were turned away from the Lawrence City Hall a few weeks later after an estimated crowd of two thousand expatriates filled the building "to suffocation." Considering that the Irish population in the northeast Massachusetts mill town was 8,200 in 1875, it is reasonable to estimate that perhaps 20 percent of the entire local expatriate community listened to a 105-minute keynote address, brief remarks from other speakers, and the North Andover Brass Band's rendition of the increasingly popular anthem "The Green above the Red."[117] Yet such enthusiasm was openly mocked by several establishment newspaper editors and by the widely admired humorist Artemus Ward. In a witty short story that was written shortly before he traveled to England and became the editor of the popular London magazine *Punch*, Ward accurately depicted the folly and falsity of many Fenian rallies. One character in the vignette is a Union veteran who vocally supports Irish independence because he wants to be elected county clerk. Other attendees speak heavily accented dialogue as they debate whether they will support "O'McMahony" or equally corrupt members of the "McO'Roberts" faction.[118]

Fenian recruiting in the South remained more modest at the time *habeas corpus* rights were suspended in Ireland. Other than an occasional public lecture, Irish nationalist activity in the defeated Confederacy was still primarily limited to expatriate population centers, such as New Orleans and other cities that had been occupied by Union troops early in the war. A widely traveled organizer known interchangeably as Godfrey Massey and Phillip Condon reported from the Crescent City that it was "Not easy to organize an Irish element here; there is much bitterness against the Irish of the North on account of their being regarded by the southern people, Irish included, as the chief cause of the destruction of the Confederacy."[119] Of course, Massey may have attempted to disguise his lackluster talents as a recruiter and bond agent by scripting a report that boosted Irish American pride at Fenian headquarters. Southerners were undoubtedly leery of purchasing promissory notes from itinerants after Confederate treasury certificates had recently been rendered worthless. The Irish working class in Dixie was also hard-pressed for income after the war was over. Former rebel Joseph Witherow informed his cousin in Ireland, "I was left without anything but the suit of clothes and it half worn that was on my back I had plenty of Confederate money but as soone as we surrendered it was no acct one hundred thousand Dollars of it would not buy one meal vituals."[120] In a devastated economy, securing a reliable source of income was more important than political activism.

Massey mentioned in his letter to O'Mahony that naming circles after Irish Confederate heroes had rekindled some nationalist fervor along the Gulf Coast. One of the five New Orleans circles in existence in early 1866 was named in honor of John Mitchel, while circles in Algiers and Mobile were christened in commemoration of the recently deceased Patrick Cleburne.[121] A Fenian ball held six days before the Louisiana state Fenian convention in early March was also widely attended. Governor J. Madison Wells was among the many well-dressed attendees who mingled with friends in the midst of a lavishly decorated meeting hall.[122] By late spring, moreover, a circle dedicated to John O'Leary had been established in Brownsville, Texas, and an estimated one hundred Irish Americans belonged to a group of nationalists in Galveston that may have later become aligned with the Roberts faction.[123] Some noted former rebels would soon become influential Fenian military leaders in England and Ireland, but Southern defeat and general wartime Confederate affinity for the British government continued to restrain greater Fenian support in the South.

Public demonstration of Irish nationalist sentiment continued to increase in the North over the following months. A massive Fenian picnic at Jones's Wood attracted an estimated one hundred thousand attendees despite the open opposition of Catholic Church leaders. John Hughes's successor, Archbishop John McCloskey, had instructed diocesan priests to inform their parishioners that attending a nationalist-oriented rally during Lent would be a "profanation of the Lord's Day" and "an outrage to the feelings of all good Catholics."[124] Nevertheless, four hours before the picnic's main program was scheduled to begin, roads leading to the Upper East Side recreation area were clogged with pedestrians and overcrowded streetcars.[125] A journalist reported that Saint Patrick's Cathedral was full during mass, but that the congregants in the pews were primarily elderly.[126] To what extent O'Mahony was able to propagate his agenda "to put munitions of war in the hands of the Irish army ... [and] to put Irish ships upon the sea" is a matter of conjecture, because alcohol was available for purchase. *New York Times* correspondents also reported that few people standing at the back of the crowd could hear orators speaking from the main platform.[127] However, in light of recent tensions within the movement, any display of Irish patriotism was reassuring to the militant nationalist leader. In November 1864, the head centre had received a complaint that Fenian meetings in Indianapolis were "monotonous."[128] Sympathetic journalists throughout the North wrote of boisterous, overcrowded nationalist gatherings. Among a handful of peripatetic Fenian speakers who toured New England, the twenty-two-year-old future Irish Catholic mayor of Boston, Patrick Collins, addressed several crowds and organized many circles throughout the spring.[129] An O'Mahony representative was also well received at a late March public meeting in Saint Paul. His recruiting efforts were stymied, however, when future archbishop John Ireland responded to a nomination to serve as secretary of a new local circle by informing the three to four hundred people in attendance that it was foolish of them to support an organization that was marred by factionalism.[130]

Expatriate interest in the Fenian movement encouraged hundreds of newspaper publishers to comment and report on the myriad of Irish nationalist activities occurring in their respective communities during the spring of 1866. The editors of the anti-Irish *Peoria Daily Transcript* implied that Fenianism was popular in central Illinois when they sarcastically encouraged former "draft-dodging" expatriates to participate in a Fenian invasion of Canada. Presuming that any protracted military engagement would lead to a decreased number of expatriate voters in the First, Fourth, and Sixth wards, the essayists predicted that rents would drop and "This city will go Republican *sure.*"[131] Unfazed by such derision, a Fenian sympathizer wrote a week later in the *Peoria National Democrat,* "Let no Irishman or woman think that they can escape [*sic*] the disgrace [if the Brotherhood fails]."[132] Evidence that female expatriates were answering similar calls around the country is corroborated by various community newspaper articles indicating that special seating was being set aside for Sisterhood members during crowded Fenian meetings.[133] Thousands of Irish Americans, in other words, did not care that a large anti-Fenian demonstration had been held in Manhattan on Saint Patrick's Day or that anti-Fenian jokes were circulating in American newspapers. They had also ignored Saint Paul bishop Thomas Langdon Grace's comment that Fenianism was "the laughing stock of the whole world."[134] On March 17, Winona

Fenians, particularly, had marched with "the banners of the Union and of Ireland flying gaily" to a local Catholic Church, where they attended mass and then resumed their procession.[135]

Close examination of other contemporaneous Fenian initiatives reveals that thousands of Irish Americans were willing to at least offer token gestures of sympathy to their more zealous nationalist comrades. Expatriates meeting in Lowell, Massachusetts on the same day as the Jones's Wood rally reaffirmed their support for the IRB by voting not to celebrate Saint Patrick's Day that year because, they said, "so many of our brothers are suffering in English dungeons for the cause of their country."[136] In a more festive mood five weeks later, however, the local circle and its Sisterhood affiliate raised somewhere between three and four thousand dollars by sponsoring an Easter week fair that included an opening procession and a market.[137] Having already invited the Irish nationalist owner/editor of the influential *Freeman's Journal,* James Alphonsus McMaster, to address their predominately Democratic Party circle, Rochester, New York Fenians agreed to boycott Canadian and English goods. Manhattan Fenians unanimously resolved only to patronize tradesmen who bought Fenian bonds.[138] Not to be outdone, Men of Action supporters continued to prepare for an invasion of Canada. The British consul in New York reported on March 9 that the governor of New York had authorized Roberts to recruit an all-Fenian state militia regiment.[139] A *New York Herald* reporter wrote a few days later, furthermore, that Sweeny staffers had received three thousand dollars in contributions during the first twenty minutes of his visit to their office.[140]

Much of this enthusiasm was based on the propagation of misleading information regarding the whereabouts of James Stephens. Philadelphia Fenians who gathered to hear O'Mahony speak in front of Independence Hall on April 6 were inaccurately informed that Stephens was at the head of an IRB army anxiously waiting to rebel.[141] In truth, the IRB leader had effectively emulated the 1607 Flight of the Earls by inexcusably leaving Ireland three weeks earlier. At a time when charismatic leadership had already been desperately lacking, Stephens had convinced himself that he could best serve the Irish nationalist movement by traveling to the United States and attempting to reunify the divided factions of the Fenian Brotherhood. He began his transatlantic journey by secretly traveling to France on March 14, even though wanted signs with his name had been posted throughout Dublin, and the presence of a British revenue cutter had prevented him from starting his cross-channel voyage a day earlier.[142] In the company of Thomas Kelly, IRB operative John Flood, and a sea captain whose grandfather had piloted the United Irishman Archibald Hamilton Rowan to France in 1794, the IRB leader boarded a collier and departed from a River Liffey wharf unnoticed.

A brutal storm in the Irish Sea subsequently blew their vessel north to Ulster. Stephens and his companions thus arrived in Paris by taking a ferry to Scotland and a train to England, and spending a portion of Saint Patrick's Day in a hotel located next to Buckingham Palace.[143] Four months earlier, a fellow nationalist had asked Devoy whether the potential benefits of rescuing Stephens from Richmond Bridewell justified the considerable risk his liberators would have to take to succeed. Initially, the young Fenian protégé had correctly predicted that Stephens would arouse nationalist sentiment as a fugitive. His mentor's decision to flee Ireland irreparably damaged the republican movement, however, and left republican collaborators with little possibility of redeeming their reputations in an envisioned Irish republic. A Dublin dressmaker who is remembered today only by the name "Mrs. Butler" lost the patronage of her affluent Protestant clientele, for example, when the public discovered that she had harbored Stephens and some of his associates in the spring of 1866. She subsequently died in poverty.[144]

The Fenian Sisterhood continued to expand in early 1866 despite Stephens's flight from Ireland and the leadership dissension within the expatriate nationalist community. Several thousand women utilized their socially suppressed professional talents after they pledged that they would respect the constitution and bylaws of their organization.[145] In addition to the establishment of other chapters throughout the country, new auxiliaries were chartered in New York City at the beginning of February and in Boston and Lowell two months later.[146] An early achievement of the Philadelphia chapter was the 1866 Saint Patrick's Day presentation of green silk flags to the leaders of eastern Pennsylvania circles.[147] The national "Directoress" of the organization, Ellen A. Mahoney, received a fifteen hundred dollar annual salary. As an added bonus, she was assisted by a clerk who earned about fifteen dollars a week.[148] Because she only endorsed militant action in Ireland, the Quincy, Illinois native and former principal of the Chicago Normal School encouraged fellow expatriate women to side with the O'Mahony wing. In editorials published in New York newspapers, she called for expatriate women to purchase Fenians bonds to help support rebellion in Ireland. In one letter, she argued that expatriate remittances to family members in the homeland destabilized the nationalist movement because most of the money was used to pay rent to landlords who supported the British government.[149] Her polemics appear to have had some influence. The June 1865 list of Fenian contributors shows that female Irish American nationalists had raised more money than their male counterparts during the four-week reporting period. Two Illinois Sisterhood chapters, in particular, forwarded the second ($698.00) and third ($600.00) largest single contributions to O'Mahony at this time. Interestingly, few letters of receipt to Sisterhood chapters survive to this day.

The peripheral role that these and other women played in the transatlantic Fenian movement reflected the limited extent of female empowerment in mid-nineteenth century Ireland and Irish America alike. The Irish Women's Suffrage and Local Government Association was not established until 1876, and the 1848 Seneca Falls convention had been dominated by middle-class Protestants who supported abolition. With the exception of post-Risorgimento Italy, moreover, feminism and patriotism were almost mutually exclusive during the Victorian period.[150] Hypothetically, some of this sexism may have been linked to O'Mahony and Stephens's experiences in France. Reform-minded French women were often welcome to attend the meetings of radical clubs and underground societies during the mid-nineteenth century. Yet, with few exceptions, they were not allowed to speak. A handful of Parisian women participated in nationalist demonstrations, but most played ancillary roles like Mahoney. Similar to countless other women who had spurred European men to rebel through either positive or negative psychological reinforcement, the Directoress once wrote, "We have nerved our men, if possible, to fierce energy."[151] The patriarchal structure of the Fenian movement on both continents was thus a reflection of male perceptions that women were nurturers rather than provocateurs. Contemporary Irish illustrators often depicted the feminized embodiment of the Irish nation *Erin* as a strong resourceful woman. Many Fenians, however, perceived Irish women in the same manner as contemporary British artists who allegorically depicted Ireland as a somewhat docile female.

Although one influential Fenian leader later complained that Stephens's wife, Jane, had been an unbearable presence during a secret late 1865 meeting in Dublin, female participation in Irish nationalist activities may have augmented male membership in the Fenian Brotherhood and, to a lesser extent, in the IRB. Social contact between single Irish males and females was limited in the post-Famine era. Courtship declined as Hibernian women throughout the North Atlantic world forsook or delayed wedlock, because they believed that the domestic prevalence of alcoholism, poverty, and spousal abuse demeaned the sanctity of marriage. Convents on both sides of the Atlantic attracted thousands of novices, as institutional life provided young women with a host of benefits otherwise unavailable to the unmarried during the mid-nineteenth century. Women averse to structured vocational life tended to remain at their childhood homes and delay marriage into their mid-twenties. When spare time was available, young males would have had little choice but to fraternize in masculine settings, such as taverns, religious fraternities, and fire brigades. Gender-specific participation in the Fenian movement might thus have been enhanced by a young adult desire to flirt at picnics and parades.

Increased Fenian activity throughout the transatlantic world in early 1866 encouraged British cartoonists and journalists to portray all Irish Catholic males as disreputable thugs rather than as honorable suitors of Irish females. Although court records show that the per capita number of murders and assaults was higher in England, the British public generally associated violent crime with the Irish during the mid-Victorian period because incendiary editorial cartoons typically depicted Hibernian males as wild, whiskey-swilling subhumans with simian physical features. A March 3 illustration by the famed editorial cartoonist Sir John Tenniel depicts Irish nationalists as comically foolish ape-men who threatened the chastity of *Hibernia*, a feminine personification of Ireland similar to *Erin*. In an accompanying caption written below "The Fenian Pest" when it appeared in *Punch*, a brief dialogue between the innocent Irish maiden and the matronly *Britannia* further demeans the Irish by suggesting that the best recourse against the Fenians is to do nothing. Then, if the brutes remain a nuisance, the reader may assume that the mighty British army will insure that the IRB is destroyed. Yet such propaganda did not foster overconfidence within the British government; police and military officials continued to monitor Fenian activities closely. A prevailing assumption was that domestic disturbances were very possible.

Continued internal squabbling within the Fenian Brotherhood during the first half of 1866 fortified Tenniel's cartoon messages. Besides dispatching the roguish Red Jim McDermott to heckle Sweeny when he presented his proposed invasion of Canada at a Newark Fenian assembly in late January, it was rumored that O'Mahony had been paying "roughs" to disrupt the springtime activities of other circles that were aligned with Roberts.[152] McDermott, ironically, was simultaneously encouraging dissension amongst O'Mahony and Roberts's respective supporters by spreading exaggerated reports of bad-mouthing and deceit between the two leaders.[153] In what may actually have been further demonstration of Roberts's skillful ability to manipulate the press, a story was circulated that an independent group of Fenians had been rebuffed by O'Mahony but warmly received by his adversary when they respectively asked both men to review the financial records of their organizations. Roberts-produced misinformation further compromised the overall integrity of the Fenian Brotherhood by insinuating that the founders of the movement were duplicitous. One pamphlet author accused O'Mahony cohorts of constantly opening and packaging their modest supply of weapons in the front office of their headquarters so that visitors in the building would presume that matériel was constantly flowing into the Fenian arsenal.[154] At an early meeting of a small Roberts circle, which was established by a few dozen Lawrence, Massachusetts Fenians in April, one speaker received enthusiastic applause when he suggested that both Roberts and O'Mahony should step down if a better leader could be found.[155] In hindsight, this proposal was sound, because both parties wasted resources in an attempt to disgrace one another.

Once expatriate outrage over the suspension of *habeas corpus* in Ireland subsided, an Irish American invasion of Canada increasingly seemed a more logical utilization of Fenian resources than abetting a decimated republican movement in Ireland. The organizers of the Chicago Fenian Fair had demonstrated that they could raise money and enthusiasm for Irish militant endeavors. Fenianism, more significantly, actually rose in relative popularity after the Civil War despite bitter infighting within the Brotherhood. Ignoring continued Catholic Church censure of militant political activism, a small faction of men and women within the expatriate community increasingly endorsed Thomas Sweeny's elaborate strategy to secure Irish independence by capturing southern portions of Ontario and Quebec. With Roberts warmly received in Peoria and other cities where he spoke in early 1866, even John O'Mahony would become convinced that a Fenian military incursion into Canada was a prerequisite for the onset of a republican rebellion in Ireland.[156] The mid-nineteenth-century struggle for Irish freedom would thus be fought in North America as well as in the British Isles.

5
FENIAN FIZZLE

John O'Mahony and William Roberts authorized their supporters to launch separate invasions of Canada during the spring of 1866—both of which ultimately failed and irreparably tarnished the global Fenian movement. Recognizing the near-term infeasibility of an IRB-led rebellion so soon after *habeas corpus* rights had been suspended in Ireland, O'Mahony reluctantly amended his long-standing organizational strategy. During a Saint Patrick's Day meeting in Manhattan, the beleaguered Fenian leader approved B. Doran Killian's several months–old plan to organize a brigade of expatriate soldiers that would cross two miles into New Brunswick territorial waters from Eastport, Maine and capture rustic Campobello Island. While O'Mahony tried to regain lost expatriate support and precipitate an Anglo-American war through this venture, the Men of Action finalized their preparations to orchestrate a more elaborate multipronged invasion of Ontario and Quebec. Yet this foray was easily contained shortly after it began six weeks later, despite an initial flurry of modest Fenian military victories. Lacking United States government support, in addition to other organizational shortcomings, the two attacks expedited the unification of a traditionally divided Canadian population under a single confederated government. About ten thousand Irish expatriate zealots willingly risked their lives under the largely false assumption that they were assisting the Irish republican movement in their homeland, while Canadians throughout the provinces rallied to defend their property and a collection of colonies that would soon become one of the primary dependencies in the British Empire.

From December 1865 until the following spring, Canadian public reaction to incessant rumors of a Fenian invasion varied. A short-lived bank run that occurred in Saint John, New Brunswick in 1866 foreshadowed several instances of collective panic throughout British North America. More widespread fear of a Fenian attack did not arise, however, because O'Mahony and his supporters had openly declared that a sortie across the American border would be a worthless endeavor.[1] While Roberts and Sweeny spent the latter half of the same month trying to secure stateside support for their invasion plans, Nathaniel Carrothers, an Irish Protestant residing in Westminster, Ontario, wrote to his brother:

> Ther has been some feer that the[y] woud cros the lines this winter
> and rob and plunder and carry what the[y] could a way with them,
> but I think the poor devils is putting their time and money to a bad
> use as the[y] never will be able to do either; the thing that is causing
> the greates excitement in this part of the country is the discovery
> of oil which is under the earth in large quantiteys in this part of
> Canada which is going to become a sourse of welth as great as the
> gold miens in California and Austrila.[2]

Carrother's prediction that material pursuits would continue to be of greater Canadian public interest than national security issues proved false when a spell of new invasion rumors circulated in February 1866. Initial predictions of a March 17 raid were supplemented with outlandish reports that Fenian marauders would poison Montreal reservoirs and distribute disease-laced clothing. A widespread trichinosis outbreak in New York City apparently incited speculation that Fenian operatives would infect Canadian hogs with the potentially deadly parasite.[3] False sightings of Fenian ships on the Great Lakes were also common.[4] In response, community leaders throughout Canada reconstituted or bolstered local defenses. Men residing in the small town of Saint Catherines placed cannons on the roads leading to their Lake Erie harbor town.[5] Militias were mustered throughout distant Nova Scotia.[6] Upper-class patronage was evident in the St. Lawrence River port of Brockville. Affluent members of the community donated their spare time to lead working-class enlistees, who were modestly paid for serving in the town rifle company.[7] Many recruits received small bounties or a thirty-five cent stipend for each day in uniform. Pay was sporadic, however, so most of the estimated ten to fourteen thousand men who reported for service became de facto volunteers. If invasion rumors proved true, the people of Canada were determined to defend themselves, even if they were not compensated for their efforts.

Anti-invasion precautions appeared to have been unnecessary when no Fenian disturbances occurred in Canada on Saint Patrick's Day.[8] As sentries posted at Toronto banks and on bridges leading to Montreal became less vigilant, some militias had to draft men to conduct border patrols away from their homes before all Canadian units were ordered to stand-down at the end of the month. By early April, several newspaper editors (who were now able to obtain information from a second telegraph line that had been specifically constructed between Kingston to Montreal in the event of a Fenian invasion) declared that the Brotherhood was all but dead. As William O'Brien noted in an April 6 letter to his cousin, "Since the excitement has passed away several of the companies have been dismissed. The news says it is the conviction of sane Americans that the Fenian leaders do not intend to fight but will content themselves with the money they can wring out of their dupes."[9] Somewhat more cautious Canadians surmised that national defense could be adequately maintained by the British Army. Many of the soldiers who had been dispatched to North America in the early stages of the American Civil War remained in Canada.[10] Yet mild Fenian hysteria in early 1866 heightened provincial security by galvanizing Canadian nationalist sentiment. Local militia forces remained undersupplied and poorly trained, but the March scare had inspired citizens throughout Ontario, Quebec, and the Maritime provinces to defend their communities if they were threatened by O'Mahony or Roberts supporters. As H. D. McKenzie wrote in a private letter on April 15, "I guess you fellows will have to shoulder the musket i hope the provinces will give them a devilish good licking."[11]

O'Mahony sanctioned Killian's proposal to seize Campobello Island at the height of Canadian militia mobilization on March 17, because, like Roberts and Sweeny, he presumed that ostensibly Anglophobic United States government officials would welcome a cross-border attack. Many congressmen had recently demanded that the United Kingdom cede Canada to the United States in reparation for British support for the former Confederacy; this appeal gave American Fenians hope that they would receive the support of elected officials. Resolution of the *Trent* crisis notwithstanding, Palmerston had allowed Liverpool-based shipbuilders to skirt British neutrality laws by building a dozen Rebel warships that were outfitted with everything needed for naval warfare, except artillery. Once provided with cannons, the predominately British crew of the then record-fast *Alabama* and the men onboard its sister ships ultimately sank just over half the Union-registered merchant fleet. In addition, London- and Midlands-based insurance agencies had indemnified rebel blockade-runners. The Laird Shipbuilding Company, furthermore, was only belatedly prohibited from selling two 230-foot, battering ram–equipped ironclads to Confederate purchasing agents.[12] Countless Americans were outraged that parliamentary officials permitted such practices at the same time they professed diplomatic impartiality. Maurice Woulfe had written to his uncle in September 1863: "If the English were to make war against the Country I am sure that there would a Million of men be enrolled before a week"[13]

Many Americans in the North were also still bitter that Canadian citizens had repeatedly rendered indirect assistance to the Confederacy during the Civil War. Rebel navy ships had frequently been allowed to dock in Canadian ports, and Southern guerrillas had successfully commandeered an American steamer called the *Philo Parsons* after boarding the vessel in Malden, Ontario. Southern POWs were granted unofficial asylum, moreover, if they were able to escape across the border. The Canadian government's refusal to extradite twenty-two Rebel guerillas who had killed a man and stolen two hundred thousand dollars from three Saint Albans, Vermont banks on October 19, 1864, caused tremendous friction. Besides sheltering the alleged culprits, Quebec officials incensed Americans by only offering an $88,000 reparation payment and the establishment of a frontier patrol to prevent similar attacks in the future.[14] With additional grievances, radical republicans such as Chicago Fenian Fair attendee Schuyler Colfax and senate president Henry Wilson (who once said that, he too, was a Fenian because the Brotherhood supported the cause of liberty everywhere) were already pressing for a settlement of what became known as the *Alabama* claims. Even though the Canadian public had responded to the assassination of Abraham Lincoln the previous April by expressing sincere condolences to the American public, several politicians in Washington recognized that a northward-oriented sense of Manifest Destiny was popular among many constituents.[15] Although they bantered about imperialistically annexing Canadian territory in restitution for Civil War grievances, their actual attitudes toward the British government were not truly bellicose.

In addition to the premise that executive and legislative branch officials would welcome any filibuster across the Canadian border, O'Mahony and his colleagues made questionable geopolitical assumptions when they authorized Killian to seize Campobello Island. Imaginative Fenians envisioned a captured Campobello as a staging area for an expatriate invasion of Ireland and a safe haven for Fenian sea captains who would menace Royal Navy and British merchant marine vessels in emulation of legendary Irish privateers. Somewhat more pragmatic nationalists hypothesized that the IRB would benefit whether or not Killian captured the sparsely populated, twenty-nine-square-mile island. Parliamentary leaders, in Fenian estimations, would declare war on the United States once a part of its sovereign territory had been violated. In the midst of a military conflict between the two world powers, an IRB recently paralyzed by the suspension of *habeas corpus* and the timorous flight of James Stephens would be able to attack a compromised foe. Yet, because more contentious events, such as the outfitting of the *Alabama*, had not resulted in war, it was unlikely that a Fenian foray into Canada would immediately precipitate an international conflict.

The potential strategic advantages of seizing Campobello were counterbalanced by several factors. Of foremost significance, the Fenian marauders would not be able to surprise the one company of American solders stationed on the southern edge of the Maine/New Brunswick border.[16] Besides recent reports of a pending attack, Canadians had been cognizant of expatriate aspirations to capture provincial territory ever since the emerging Men of Action started espousing the establishment of a New World Irish republic in 1863. Rumor of a specific advance into New Brunswick, moreover, originally surfaced in December 1864 and then reappeared the next November, when O'Mahony had written to Mitchel that Brotherhood-led military engagements in North America would be "a mere diversion . . . Unless it drag the U.S. into war with England it can only end in defeat for those who engage in it. But it is worth trying in the hope that it may lead to such a war."[17] After the end of the Civil War, the *New Orleans Daily Crescent* reported that imprisoned Confederate president Jefferson Davis and one of his Irish American guards had reportedly discussed whether the Fenians were capable of seizing Canadian territory.[18] Boston Fenian leaders had also brazenly announced during rallies that they intended to participate in an invasion across the eastern Maine frontier.[19] Pre-invasion media attention included *New York Herald* reports that seventy Fenians left New York City on April 4 and arrived in Portland, Maine four days later. Although Killian had announced that he and his cohorts were off to invade Bermuda, informed readers knew otherwise.[20]

The County Down–born Killian may have been nonchalant about such publicity because he expected to receive assistance from many New Brunswick residents after he mobilized his forces. Unwilling to relinquish autonomous political powers, many inhabitants of the Maritime Provinces ardently opposed a pending proposition to establish a federalized Canadian government. Many of these anticonfederationists, however, had already demonstrated their determination to thwart the Fenians by joining local militias and home guards earlier in the year.[21] The descendents of 14,000 Tories who had been banished from the newly formed United States and subsequently victimized by Continental privateers during the late 1770s, as well as during the War of 1812, were more than willing to assist British marines stationed in nearby Halifax if any attack occurred. Killian also incorrectly assumed that Irish Catholic Canadians would support a Fenian invasion, even though they paid low taxes in a social environment where nativist violence was less common than in the United States.[22] Despite recruiting efforts that included an initiative to co-opt established immigrant fraternal organizations, such as the Society of Saint Patrick, only a handful of Fenian circles had even been established in Canada.[23] Most Irish Catholic Canadians, like the former Young Irelander Thomas D'Arcy McGee, refused to betray an adopted homeland that had guaranteed Catholic voting rights since the adoption of the 1774 Quebec Act.[24] Killian was destined to confront people who had as much motivation to maintain their vested interests under the British crown as his charges had to terminate centuries of monarchical rule in Ireland. As a lawyer and former publisher of a Saint Louis newspaper called *The Western Banner*, Killian presumably recognized that his plan would provoke legal tensions and generate significant press attention. As a man who had also briefly served as a Union army officer in hotly contested Missouri, he had apparently forgotten that local civilians do not usually welcome invading armies.

Either ignoring or oblivious to the logical reasons why his intention to seize Campobello would likely fail, Killian hurriedly prepared to lead Fenians into battle before members of the Roberts faction could initiate their more substantial invasion plan. Acquiring weapons proved relatively effortless. Dues and donations in record amounts had been channeled to O'Mahony's headquarters over the past year and were used to purchase rifles from the army and to acquire a former Confederate blockade runner called the *Ocean Spray* from the United States Customs Service. As the vessel proved to be too small and not entirely seaworthy—it had recently been painted black for scheduled artillery practice—Killian divided his newly acquired weapons into several shipments and instructed the majority of his men to proceed to southeastern Maine in small groups at their own expense.[25] These measures attracted additional attention to an operation that had never been a well-kept secret. A spy had been present when O'Mahony authorized the invasion, and the mainstream press later issued several reports that hundreds of filibusterers were destined for Campobello. Killian and other expatriates of equal significance unwisely arrived in northern New England two weeks before the captain of the *Ocean Spray* delivered a sizable consignment of Fenian weapons.

Provided all these warnings, Canadian authorities promptly reactivated several militia units and detained Irish nationalist suspects in early April. Ontario Fenian leader Michael Murphy (who had demonstrated his misgivings about an expatriate invasion across the American border by professing his loyalty to Canada at the Toronto Saint Patrick's Day celebration and by billeting militiamen in his boarding house during the mid-March Fenian scare) was peremptorily arrested, along with a former Confederate army officer and five other revolver-toting companions who were also en route to Eastport on April 10.[26] Placed in jail, Murphy escaped five months later by digging a tunnel; he fled to Buffalo, where he opened a tavern that was shunned by Fenians who believed he had participated in a staged escape after agreeing to become a spy.[27] Displaying greater tolerance for anti-British sympathies, Halifax militia leaders allowed two Irishmen in their ranks to pledge an oath to defend Nova Scotia rather than to profess their loyalty to Queen Victoria as a prerequisite for mustering into service.[28]

Fighting boredom rather than British and Canadian soldiers, most of the Fenians who had quit their jobs and left home to join Killian in Maine spent much of their time dawdling in boardinghouses where vigilant British agents and United States marshals had also rented rooms. Expatriates drilled on a beach and paraded through the streets of Eastport, while the portly Killian held meetings in rented town halls to sustain morale.[29] Fenian mischief subsequently became increasingly common. *Philadelphia Inquirer* and *New York Herald* reporters predicted a momentous military operation, but a local Canadian reporter described the interlopers in mid-April as "villainous cut throat[s] . . . who would be in their native element in the midst of rapine and murder."[30] In one of the more noteworthy instances of the filibusters' impatience, two boatloads of Irishmen rowed across the Saint Croix River on the night of April 13, but abandoned an attempt to land in the Canadian community of Saint Stephen when they were detected by a group of women. Two days later, a group of nine men ventured to unguarded Indian Island at about 2:00 a.m. and stole a British Revenue Service flag from the home of a Canadian Customs official.[31] Falsely trumpeted by pro-Irish nationalist journalists as a significant victory, the incursion onto "enemy" soil—and all the precursor incidents—actually insured that Killian and his supporters would be swiftly contained.

Canadian, British, and American entities intensified their efforts to suppress Fenian activity on the Maine/New Brunswick border after Killian's men "attacked" Indian Island. Local militias were swamped with additional recruits, while the Royal Navy enhanced its presence in the Bay of Fundy. At this time, the former Union commander at Gettysburg, General George Meade, assumed control of a combined army-navy detachment that was ordered to prevent any further violations of Canadian territory. Killian subsequently recognized that additional Fenian forays might lead to the arrest of expatriate filibusters on the frontier. On the evening of April 16, O'Mahony's deputy told a curious crowd of one thousand men and women who had gathered in the town of Calais that his men had assembled in eastern Maine because several Canadians who opposed provincial confederation had requested their protection. Killian, moreover, pledged to respect all American laws.

Federal government officials were equally determined to prevent the Fenians from precipitating an international conflict. Although a midterm election looming in the fall made them reluctant to offend their Irish constituents, Johnson administration officials upheld the seizure of the *Ocean Spray* and its cargo when the vessel arrived in Eastport on April 17. Despite ensuing protests from the pro-Fenian United States district attorney in Portland, the naval captain of the *USS Winooski* unilaterally transferred 129 cases of Fenian matériel to a nearby American military installation. In an unsuccessful attempt to regain control of the confiscated firearms and ammunition, Killian assured General Meade that the weapons were intended to be used in self-defense when the Fenians embarked on a planned fishing expedition to offshore shoals that had been hotly contested ever since the recent abrogation of a bilateral tariff agreement. Conventional lobbying for the return of the equipment proved equally unproductive. Killian deputy and former United States congressman James Kerrigan rushed to Washington from northern New England but received little sympathy when he met with former Capitol Hill colleagues and other politicians.

O'Mahony attempted to portray himself as a peacemaker once it became apparent that Killian and his fellow filibusterers would not succeed in their effort to overshadow the Roberts faction and instigate a transatlantic war. Having already recalled an ironclad containing additional weapons before the arrival of the *Ocean Spray*, O'Mahony had also prohibited several hundred Boston Fenians from proceeding to eastern Maine.[32] More importantly, O'Mahony instructed an emissary to deliver a request for a rapprochement to Roberts. The millionaire merchant never considered the offer, however, because he was not identified in any part of the letter as "President of the Fenian Brotherhood."[33] Ignoring some fellow Men of Action who believed that all personal differences between the two leaders should be overlooked at a time when Fenian volunteers were attempting to attack the British Empire, Roberts allowed his own vanity to compromise an opportunity to unify and strengthen a damaged, but still potentially powerful, expatriate nationalist movement.

Another series of unlawful Fenian antics highlighted the closing moments of the Campobello escapade. On April 21, a band of men violated Killian's pledge to respect all American laws by setting fire to a bonded Indian Island warehouse owned by a local liquor exporter who had publicly demanded that United States military personnel seize all Fenian arms in the area.[34] Another sortie to the unfortified island was later deterred when the *HMS Niger* arrived in Passamaquoddy Bay. With the delayed transfer of news information to Manhattan, the editors of the once pro-Fenian *New York Citizen* later wrote that Killian and his Indian Island interlopers "might just as well have 'captured' a British hen roost or two red flannel shirts and a pair of drawers which some British fish wife had hung out to dry for her husband's use the next morning."[35] A final Fenian initiative was equally ineffective. In early May, about fifty Fenians commandeered a chartered schooner called the *Two Friends* shortly after the captain of the vessel set sail. Steering the ship into Canadian waters, the Fenian buccaneers evaded pursuit from a Royal Navy vessel and two American Revenue cutters before returning to port without having landed on foreign soil. Because the incident was locally regarded as an act of piracy rather than a display of Irish patriotism, one of the Fenian participants was later tried as a brigand and sentenced to three years' hard labor.[36]

The Fenians never attempted a full-scale invasion of Campobello Island because they were always outnumbered. When seven hundred Royal Marines disembarked from an eighty-one gun British warship on the same day that the *Ocean Spray* and the *Winooski* docked in Eastport, there were only six British soldiers stationed along the Maine/New Brunswick frontier for every Irish American scheming to precipitate a global conflict. American newspapers, moreover, printed false reports in early May that the *USS Shamrock* and four additional United States Navy vessels were headed to Eastport.[37] To the relief of most locals, virtually all the Fenians dispersed by mid-May. A handful of boardinghouse owners and other merchants had profited from the influx of strangers into their communities, but most Canadians and Americans residing in the border region were elated that the threat of violence had passed. Commended by both United States and Canadian citizens, George Meade returned to his Philadelphia home after convalescing from a protracted illness in Eastport.[38] The departure of the *Winooski* was more dramatic, as three sailors, including an Irish-born seaman named Thomas Burke, received the Medal of Honor for rescuing two of their crewmates from drowning off the coast of Maine on May 10.

In a marginally successful attempt to protect his reputation from an onslaught of criticism after the Campobello fiasco came to an end, O'Mahony accused Killian of being a British spy by circulating a public letter throughout the country in late April. It is uncertain how many people believed the Fenian leader's dubious allegation that Thomas D'Arcy McGee had helped coax Killian into organizing an invasion that would supposedly persuade a frightened populace to support provincial confederation. Killian was court-martialed by a panel of Fenian leaders, however, and banished from the Brotherhood shortly after he publicly denounced O'Mahony and endorsed his erstwhile rival, Thomas Sweeny.[39] O'Mahony realistically deserved the same punishment for having lied to his supporters throughout the spring of 1866. At a one-day conference in New York City on March 3, he and 117 other Fenians had publicly reiterated their commitment to aid a rebellion in Ireland. While addressing one of the largest gatherings ever assembled in Lowell a week later, he told three thousand people "the men who propose to invade Canada have no right to call themselves Fenians."[40] Speaking before a standing-room-only audience in the Lawrence City Hall the next day, he had warned about "bringing woe upon a people innocent of the wrongs which have been heaped upon Ireland . . . we owe them no enmity and [I] trust that the banner of Ireland would never be used as that of her oppressor, as an emblem of robbery, piracy, and subjugation."[41] Like Killian, who had informed a crowd assembled at the early March Fenian picnic in Jones's Wood that the original wing of the Brotherhood would "not take [Canada] if they could," O'Mahony had either ignored his better judgment or had been intentionally lying in an attempt to deceive Canadian military and civilian leaders.[42] In either case, the initiative failed, and Campobello Island is better remembered today as the site where a vacationing Franklin Roosevelt contracted polio in 1921 than as the location of a futile 1866 attempt to secure Irish independence from Great Britain.

The motive behind O'Mahony's actions mattered little to the many Fenians who believed that they had been betrayed by the expatriate nationalist leader. The *Cincinnati Enquirer* reported that two Campobello veterans had entered the Moffat Mansion in late April, put a gun to O'Mahony's head, and vowed to kill him unless he agreed to reimburse filibusterers for lost wages and travel expenses.[43] The same investigative committee that dismissed Killian impeached O'Mahony upon the conclusion of a two-hour closed inquiry at Fenian headquarters on April 30, 1866.[44] O'Mahony, who was bombarded with insults during the deliberations, eventually regained some of his lost stature, but for the next two years he only served as a member of a Manhattan circle named in honor of Michael Corcoran. By coincidence, the second edition of his *History of Ireland* was published not long after Campobello. What should have provided an eloquent author with additional recognition aroused sarcasm among an Irish American community that believed it had been cheated and betrayed. A May 1866 snippet in the *Lowell Daily Courier* read, "Col. John O'Mahony, the Head Centre is claiming notoriety as an author."[45] Because Fenian supporters desired a charismatic statesman more than a literary talent, expatriates who continued to espouse exclusive Fenian support for a revolution in Ireland decided to vest Stephens with control of the organization upon his anticipated mid-May arrival from France.

Roberts and his supporters had initially reacted to the Campobello debacle with some anxiety. Meeting on April 16, the members of the breakaway Fenian senate persuaded Thomas Sweeny that their credibility as leaders of a militant nationalist organization would be lost if they did not expeditiously surpass what had been dubbed in the press as the "Eastport Fizzle."[46] Over the following week, this concern was increasingly overshadowed by collective smugness, as wire reports revealed that none of the Fenians assembled in Maine would ever launch a legitimate attack. Killian's embarrassing failure, however, tarnished the reputation of all Fenians, because the futility of invading Canada had been clearly demonstrated to the public. Even if government officials had not enforced American neutrality laws, the Fenians who ventured to northern New England would still have confronted a formidable army of British regulars and Canadian militia. Consequently, Roberts had to boost the confidence of his supporters before mounting skepticism evolved into widespread indifference among members of the expatriate community.

Forced to abandon his plan to invade Canada during the following winter, Sweeny quickly adapted his existing battle plans for a summer campaign. In an effort to divert enemy forces away from where his main army would infiltrate southern Quebec, Midwest Fenian regiments would gather in Milwaukee, Chicago, and Detroit, and then initiate the multipronged attack by proceeding to western Ontario via the Great Lakes. Fenian contingents from Ohio and Buffalo would likewise cross into Canada by boat shortly thereafter and attempt to envelop British and Canadian forces in the vicinity of Toronto, while guerrilla units destroyed segments of the strategically important Grand Trunk Railroad. Even if stymied in their attempt to disable the primary east-west transportation conduit between the provinces, the middle column of the Fenian army would still attempt to lure Canadian troops away from the principal front by securing a large swath of land between Lake Erie and Lake Ontario. Sheltered by two bodies of water and a twenty-six-mile-long canal that bisected the Niagara peninsula, a Fenian army could entrench and withstand a protracted siege if supply lines to Buffalo were properly maintained. Farther east, the Saint Francis and Richelieu Rivers would serve as de facto moats around a provisional Irish republican capital in the market town of Sherbrooke.[47]

Sweeny had never devised or led a large campaign during his extensive military career, but he wisely presumed that early skirmish victories would draw expatriate fence-sitters into Fenian regiments. With many Irish American Union and Confederate veterans still resettling into civilian employment and peacetime family life, Sweeny anticipated that an initial force of 10,000 men would eventually expand 150 percent. Having witnessed greenhorn recruits become competent soldiers after receiving rudimentary training in Saint Louis at the beginning of the Civil War, he also believed that dedicated Fenian drill sergeants could expeditiously mold expatriate civilians into competent infantrymen.[48] Sweeny's willingness to divide his men into small mobile groups that could effectively orchestrate random military strikes—at the risk of being easily outnumbered by Canadian forces—was perhaps more a reflection of his own courage than of widespread beliefs about an innate Irish fighting prowess. Having lost an arm to a bullet wound during the Mexican War, Sweeny had been nearly killed on several occasions

while fighting Native Americans in Southern California. Ulysses S. Grant reportedly once quipped during a Civil War engagement to the "man with the armless
sleeve," "How is it Sweeny, that you have not been hit? There must be some mistake. This fight will hardly count unless you can show another wound."[49] Whether
other expatriates would be as daring as their leader would partly determine the
outcome of the forthcoming Fenian incursion into Ontario and Quebec.

Paltry contributions to Roberts's Irish National War Fund throughout the
spring of 1866 compromised Sweeny's amended battle plan. Even though Roberts-
issued bonds offered an attractive 8 percent return, prospective donors did not respond to the Men of Action's "Special Call" with any enthusiasm. Campobello had
raised doubts about the practicality of another Canadian invasion. Many expatriates also resented Roberts for refusing to assist Killian when he needed assistance
on the frontier. The bonds—which in symbolic reference to the divided patriotic
loyalties of many expatriates included silhouettes of Robert Emmet and Abraham
Lincoln—accordingly sold poorly.[50] Ultimately receiving only 22 percent of his
requested four hundred and fifty thousand dollar budget, Sweeny would never
have been able to outfit a large army. The ten thousand Enfield rifles, 2.5 million
ball cartridges, and miscellaneous supplies from the United States Army would
not be enough to sustain a contingent of filibusterers for very long.[51] Sweeny additionally had to presume that sympathetic Irish boardinghouse owners and private
citizens would graciously accommodate unpaid Fenian volunteers en route to the
frontier. Irish American businessmen residing in urban centers along the international border, furthermore, would presumably provide transportation and sundries
at attractive prices. Sweeny, in short, had to hope that supplemental money, like
additional recruits, would become available once his men actually started fighting.

Despite recent United States military enforcement of American neutrality
laws in eastern Maine, Roberts and Sweeny erroneously assumed that their acquisition of surplus Union army equipment tacitly confirmed Johnson administration
and Congressional Radical Republican approval of a more credible engagement
of Canadian forces.[52] Yet, unbeknownst to the two Fenian leaders at the time,
it was the brinksmanship threat of an invasion, rather than an attack itself, that
most American statesmen believed would coerce their British counterparts into
a favorable settlement of the *Alabama* claims. Usually confrontational, Seward
had moreover already informed his British counterparts that the United States
government would limit support for the Fenians. Other than insisting that detained expatriates receive due process in British courts, State Department officials
would honor the 1819 American Neutrality Act.[53] Many otherwise Anglophobic
newspaper editors similarly refused to endorse any Fenian military operation on

Canadian soil.[54] American soldiers and police officers would therefore likely stifle another Fenian attempt to establish an Irish republic in the same way they had contained Killian and his men earlier in the spring.

Historical precedent demonstrated that the Sweeny invasion plan would fail regardless of federal government assent or whether the Fenians mobilized a formidable army with limited funds. Resolute volunteers, including the thousands of Canadians who had just mustered to defend Campobello, had repeatedly thwarted military incursions into British North American territory since the beginning of the Anglo-French colonial wars in the mid-seventeenth century. The last major foreign victory on Canadian soil had occurred when General James Wolfe led a triumphant English army into combat against French adversaries on the famed Plains of Abraham outside Quebec City in 1760. Early in the American Revolution, Continental Army forces led by County Dublin native Richard Montgomery captured a British Army garrison at Montreal, but his forces were expelled from the Saint Lawrence River Valley the following summer because Benedict Arnold failed to capture Quebec City. Ominously, a large monument that commemorated a British War of 1812 victory over New York State Militia forces stood near the site where Sweeny intended to advance several Fenian regiments from Buffalo into eastern Ontario. British capability to resecure modern-day Toronto and the surrounding countryside after losing two substantial battles in 1813 was equally foreboding to the Fenians. If they succeeded initially, Sweeny's men would eventually be counterattacked by regiments stationed throughout the British Empire.

In more contemporary decades, British subjects residing throughout Canada had continued to defend their country by containing New York- and New England-based rebels who often received aid from American citizens. Members of the Orange Order and other Canadian loyalists had largely blamed Irish Catholic fellow countrymen for instigating a brief rebellion against increasingly domineering government officials in 1837. In truth, people on both sides of the border acknowledged that the insurgents had received stateside assistance from people who opposed the expansion of bureaucratic power within Ontario and Quebec. Most notably, a group of Buffalo residents ferried supplies to the so-called patriots, until their vessel was captured and destroyed on United States soil by a combined force of fifty British and Canadian soldiers. Other Americans in Vermont abetted a Patriot affiliate organization called Les Frères-chasseurs. Organizationally similar to the Freemasons, the Frères attempted to precipitate an Anglo-American war by staging a cross-border raid into Quebec, but their effort was thwarted by a United States Army detachment. In appreciation, Canadian officials refrained from attacking Patriot outposts in northern New England.[55]

Foreshadowing the Johnson administration's reaction to the Fenian invasions two decades later, Canadian leaders exercised restraint when the possibility of a bloody bilateral altercation arose.

A distinct, unassimilated minority of Irish American men and women supported Roberts's invasion plans despite Killian's failed Campobello expedition, Sweeny's lack of resources, and ominous historical precedent. Patrick Foley reported in an April 1866 letter to a friend in Newfoundland that the number of members in a Waterford, New York circle had doubled over the past year and that forty to fifty men from nearby Troy were ready to fight. Foley himself noted that he had "said nothing about my name yet but I suppose if required I will jump in the Ring."[56] Hundreds of junior and middle grade officers who had served in the Civil War expressed interest in joining the Fenian army. Once prescreened by a state military inspector, all people requesting a commission were vetted by a three-man review panel in Manhattan.[57] With the pledged financial support of local Irishwomen, thirty men from Milford extemporaneously organized a Fenian company immediately after a state representative and former Ninth Massachusetts infantry officer named John W. Mahan delivered a pro-invasion address during a town hall meeting.[58]

Increasing expatriate talk of a massive Fenian invasion across the Canadian border coincided with the dramatic arrival of James Stephens from France. On May 10, the IRB founder was warmly welcomed to Manhattan; crowds of admirers thronged Pier Fifty when he descended along the gangplank of a transatlantic steamer. A simultaneous artillery salute from the New Jersey shore preceded a flurry of activity that occurred at Stephens's Metropolitan Hotel over the following days.[59] A military band serenaded Fenian supporters with renditions of "Hail Columbia" and "The Wearing of the Green" after the Irish leader briefly addressed well-wishers who remained outside his lodgings until midnight. An Irish standard was hoisted atop the hotel flagpole on the following day to suggest that the president of a future independent Ireland was in residence. The showman and politician P. T. Barnum was one of several dignitaries who called on the IRB chief, while telegrams of welcome arrived from around the country.[60] In the aftermath of O'Mahony and Killian's deceitful blunder, Stephens's continued insistence on military revolution in Ireland temporarily relieved Irish nationalists. Stephens, moreover, could demonstrate that his intentions were sincere. His strategic plans had never wavered, and he had recently secured the professional services of Gustave Cluseret, a French officer who had been promoted from colonel to general while serving in the Union army from January 1862 until March 1863. Yet many expatriate Fenians rejected Stephens's overtures to reunite the fractured Brotherhood. Roberts supporters completed their final preparations for an invasion of

Canada. Other émigrés continued to co-opt Fenianism as a leisure activity. A multiday Fenian festival in New Orleans featured foot races and orations instead of recruiting and martial training. Some of the most popular attractions at the celebration, moreover, were temporary beer and whiskey tents with names including "Stephens' Rendezvous," "Irish Republican Headquarters," and "Erin go Bragh."[61]

In a dramatic reversal of expatriate sentiment, Stephens's popularity declined as he commenced a speaking tour at the same time that the New Orleans fair closed and Sweeny girded for war. In sharp contrast to the Fenian gathering at Jones's Wood two months earlier, a small partly drunken crowd of somewhere between two and six thousand people paid fifty cents to hear the Irish nationalist leader deliver a seventy-five minute address on Tuesday, May 15. In the midst of his remarks, Stephens exonerated O'Mahony and Killian, extended a truce offer to Roberts, and chastised Irish Americans for failing to support an IRB army that he said would be in the throes of battle before the end of the year.[62] Follow-up public appearances featured a question-and-answer session that highlighted Stephens's strengths and weaknesses. During a New York meeting, Stephens smoothly answered a question about the nationalist sentiments of Irish women as a self-declared "lover of the ladies" by stating, "The girls at home are not only trumps in the cause, but are the ace of hearts itself."[63] His public address in Philadelphia a few days later, however, became "a scandalous scene of confusion" when one person in the crowd reiterated accusations made by Roberts, as well as by the popular expatriate writer Charles Halpine, that Stephens was a British operative.[64] Sweeny's related allegation that prison officials had staged Stephens's escape from Richmond Bridewell diminished the credibility of the IRB leader as he continued to travel up and down the East Coast.[65] A *Waterbury Daily American* reporter wrote that the number of people who came to hear Stephens speak at the New Haven Music Hall was "not large probably on account of the high price of admission."[66]

Rising public skepticism of Stephens encouraged many people to question the integrity and organizational structure of the Brotherhood itself. By late spring, word had reached northern California that a New York Protestant preacher had publicly denounced Fenianism as an elaborate scam that Southern Democrats and Catholic Church prelates had organized to gain control of the United States government. After forwarding one-half of the recently acquired proceeds to both Fenian factions, the state head centre of California telegrammed the recently deposed O'Mahony, "If you unite with Roberts we can do much; without union little."[68] A less optimistic Bay Area newspaper publisher suggested that the fifteen thousand expatriates who attended a Fenian picnic in San Mateo on May 21 form their own independent organization because neither of the two wings was prudent, realistic, or deferential to one another.[69] This proposal proved prophetic; a new Irish American nationalist organization would be formed in just over a year.

Female expatriate support for an invasion of Canada rather than rebellion in Ireland became more apparent as Stephens failed to reunite Irish American nationalists under his leadership. Sisterhood chapters in Cleveland, Waterbury, Connecticut, and booming northern California continued to establish nursing units, wrap bandages, and collect medical supplies in preparation for combat. In the spirit of Betsy Ross and other American women who had sewn battle flags in the past, the Buffalo Sisterhood presented an enormous fifty-four square foot green silk standard to the large local contingent of Roberts Fenians at the same time that Sweeny dispatched a deployment order to Fenians throughout the country who had pledged to lead Irish American volunteers into Canada.[70] On the eve of the mobilization, his colleague Patrick Meehan issued a public letter that included the passage, "Let our women go to work for the soldier in the field; the necessities of the late war will teach them what will be required now. The sick and the wounded will need delicacies; the ladies can supply all."[71] Now serving as the archbishop of Baltimore, Martin John Spalding informed Cullen at the time that it was unwise to censure the Fenian movement, because the expatriate community and the United States government enthusiastically endorsed current Brotherhood activities.[72]

Lingering tensions within the American Fenian movement impeded the mobilization of Sweeny's forces in mid-May. John O'Neill of Nashville had been one of the first Brotherhood commanders to receive the coded message, "You may commence working," but he had to delay his departure so that he could raise enough money to pay travel expenses for himself and several men. Fenian units from the south and north central United States had similar problems. By the end of the month, volunteers who arrived at their designated muster points in Wisconsin, Illinois, and Ohio discovered that some ranking officers had either failed to report for duty or that transport across the Great Lakes was unavailable.[73] Of equal concern, government entities had begun seizing Fenian weapons and equipment. United States Army detachments confiscated several railcars full of equipment at the De Kalb Junction and Richville stations in Upstate New York. Artillery was also impounded in Pittsburgh, and government agents in Erie, Pennsylvania took possession of a steam-powered vessel that the Fenians apparently intended to use as a transport ship.[74] United States marshals and customs officials, meanwhile, reportedly prevented a Manhattan-bound freighter from leaving Galveston with 1,280 weapons and crates of ammunition that Fenian agents had originally stolen from a federal garrison in Texas.[75]

Hastily, Sweeny decided to move all the men who had mustered for duty in the Midwest to Buffalo, where local Fenian leaders had successfully secured tugs and canal boats to ferry men across the Niagara River. Although sensible, these orders compromised morale. About one-seventh of the Fenian contingent that had reached Cleveland returned home when they were informed that their initial battle plan had been changed. Other Fenians scattered throughout the Great Lakes region were indecisive about proceeding farther north to fight for Ireland and possibly obtaining a one hundred pound bounty and a two hundred acre Canadian farm in exchange for their efforts.[76] Some members of the Brotherhood, alternatively, never received new orders. Chicago merchants complained that many Fenians had made a nuisance of themselves by squatting in vacant buildings and at the largely abandoned Fort Douglas Union army training camp. Other expatriate strangers were reported in various communities throughout the next week.[77]

With marginal success, Fenian volunteers attempted to draw public attention away from their activities in the days immediately before their advance into Canada. Assuming that principal western New York railroad stations were replete with spies and newspaper reporters, O'Neill instructed the 342 men who had remained with him to disembark from their Buffalo-bound train a few miles south of their destination on May 30 and walk to the city in small groups. These filibusters, like all their other comrades from around the United States, had been ordered to tell any inquisitive strangers that they were either laborers hoping to secure Canadian railroad construction jobs or soldiers en route to California.[78] Such precautions were largely unnecessary, because border towns throughout the northeast were already inundated with hundreds, if not thousands, of filibusterers ranging, like O'Neill's men, between fifteen and fifty years of age.[79] The distribution of weapons to volunteers under the semblance of an army surplus auction fooled no one, because the well-known local nationalist leader who owned the Pearl Street warehouse, Patrick O'Day, unwittingly employed a Canadian spy.[80] A Fenian sympathizer posing as the owner of a foundry two miles north of the city had greater success disguising his efforts to procure transportation across the Niagara River when he told a leasing agent that he needed two tugs and four canal boats to convey his employees to a company picnic.[81] Wherever possible, Fenian soldiers were billeted in the homes of sympathetic expatriates, but with finite bed space, about five hundred men slept in two rented town halls near the waterfront.[82]

With a smaller number of subordinates than expected, William Sweeny authorized the Tennessee Fenian John O'Neill to lead a sizable vanguard across the

Niagara River on the night of May 31. O'Neill had the requisite experience for the mission, although it had initially been assigned to a higher-ranking officer who fell ill with fever a day earlier. Quickly promoted within the Union army ranks, despite having temporarily deserted his cavalry regiment during the 1857 Mormon War, O'Neill had been publicly praised by Archbishop Purcell in 1863 for leading attacks against Morgan's Raiders. O'Neill later served under William Tecumseh Sherman in Georgia and eventually led a Negro regiment before being wounded near Nashville in 1864. Assisted by an equally competent staff, O'Neill organized a staggered dispatch of his men just past midnight. Groups comprised of roughly fifty people intermittingly arrived at the Pratt Iron Works and preceded one thousand yards across the Niagara River in tug-pulled scows that were laden with equipment. The first Fenian contingent arrived at a wharf located roughly a mile north of the small Canadian village of Fort Erie around 3:30 in the morning. Not worried that their boisterous cheers could be heard as far away as the Buffalo side of the river, several Fenian officers bedecked in old, somewhat tattered Union army uniforms assembled ragtag enlisted filibusterers around green battle flags embroidered with the insignia of the Irish republic.[83] By safely landing on foreign soil, O'Neill had done more to expedite Irish independence over the course of a few hours than Killian had accomplished after a month in Maine.

Initial Fenian actions on the Niagara Peninsula proved that the filibusterers were more committed to the ideological and strategic objectives of the raid than to simple plunder. Shortly after arriving in Fort Erie, Lieutenant Colonel Owen Starr placed sentries outside all the taverns to discourage his advance troops from pilfering alcohol and distributed a Sweeny-authored declaration of friendship to the Canadian people. In accordance with the text of the document, Fenians described as religiously reverent and morally upright cut telegraph lines, burned a railroad bridge, and dismantled fence lines to build breastworks around a make-shift campsite in the interest of security rather than malice.[84] O'Neill also offered to compensate the inhabitants of Fort Erie in Fenian bonds after he demanded that members of the town municipal council provide breakfast for his estimated seven hundred men. Considering that 47,000 Canadians had fought in the Union army, it is understandable (beyond the unnecessary risk of further antagonizing the civilian population of eastern Ontario) why O'Neill only wanted to provoke government and military officials. Yet raising a Fenian flag over the Fort Erie courthouse did little to foster congeniality with Niagara Peninsula residents.

Canadian militia volunteers had received little more than basic infantry drill instruction at the height of the March invasion scare, but they were determined to safeguard their homeland. In all, twenty-five hundred novice soldiers mustered to guard the Welland Canal when word of a pending attack was delivered to British officials shortly before O'Neill landed north of Fort Erie. Most of these men were inappropriately and inadequately equipped. Some members of the Queen's Own regiment who departed Toronto with much public fanfare on the morning of June 1 were provided with Spencer repeating rifles, even though they were generally more proficient with older muzzle-loading Enfields. Provided with a meager twenty-eight rounds of ammunition, they would at best impede, but not repel, any substantial attack. Only the British enlisted regulars in the Canadian vanguard were as battle-hardened as the many grizzled Irish American veterans in the Fenian ranks. Many of the first Ontario volunteers to report for duty were teenage university students. Neither leader of the expedition, moreover, had ever been in combat. British Regular Army colonel George Peacocke had mostly served in administrative positions during his extensive military career. His subordinate civilian commander, a wealthy Hamilton, Ontario merchant named Alfred Booker, had only led his men in drills. To their advantage, however, Canadian morale was exceptionally high. Sixteen-year-old private Fred McCallum was so afraid that his parents would not let him fulfill his strong desire to serve during the invasion that he ran away from home a few hours before he was supposed to report for duty.[85] Canadian troops were also supported by thousands of devoted civilians. Community leaders residing in Welland Township empanelled a committee of safety that remained in session for seventeen hours beginning on the afternoon of June 1, while farmers and merchants donated food to many of the undersupplied volunteer regiments.[86]

John O'Neill was concerned about obtaining more manpower at the same time that Canadian and American government officials were preparing to encircle his primitive advance camp in a farm orchard near Fort Erie. After three weeks of monitoring Fenian activities along the border, as ordered by the United States secretary of the navy, the commander of the paddle frigate USS Michigan unilaterally decided to obstruct maritime traffic originating from the Pratt Iron Works shortly after O'Neill and his men had successfully crossed into Canada.[87] Public transportation also became unavailable to Fenian reinforcements in Buffalo when the anti-Irish mayor of the city, Chandler T. Wells, simultaneously halted all commercial ferry service to Canada. As further precaution, the local United States district attorney, William Dart, mandated that all ships docked in Buffalo had to be inspected during business hours before being allowed to leave the city. Accordingly, only a small number of resourceful Fenians, some American journalists, and a few adventurous curiosity-seekers crossed onto the Niagara Peninsula after sunrise on June 1.

On the basis of reports he had received from mounted scouts, O'Neill recognized that he would have to attack one of the two approaching Canadian armies with the men he had available in order to initiate a credible feint before the main Fenian army invaded Quebec as planned. At 9:00 p.m., he roused his men and prepared for a quick departure by destroying nearly one thousand firearms that had been earmarked for reinforcements from New York and for Irish Canadians who, as previously mentioned, had been expected to support the Fenians.[88] Although his repair to the northwest from his secure position near the confluence of Frenchman's Creek and the Niagara River was tactically pragmatic, the Fenian leader had arguably squandered an opportunity to seize the Welland Canal by not moving inland when he had been completely unopposed earlier in the day.[89] Twelve hours of inactivity had also provided several of his subordinates an opportunity to desert.

As O'Neill anticipated, Peacocke wanted nearly all the British and Canadian soldiers on the Niagara Peninsula to engage the Fenian filibusterers in unison. Booker thus received an order on the night of June 1 to have his deputy commander, Colonel J. S. Denis, muster a small group of men that would patrol the nearby Niagara River from the deck of a tugboat called the *W.T. Robb*. The remainder of Booker's army was to rendezvous with Peacocke's men a dozen miles to the north, in Stevensville, before 11:00 a.m. the next day. Booker preferred to attack the Fenian camp near Fort Erie because repairs had already been made to a railroad bridge that the Fenians had damaged earlier that day. A messenger reported that some of the marauders had been drinking in the town all afternoon. Peacocke, however, rejected this counterproposal via telegram at 2:00 a.m. Although a larger section of the Welland Canal was temporarily more vulnerable to seizure, Peacocke may have been concerned that Booker's inexperienced force would be overwhelmed if it were forced to fight the Fenians single-handedly.[90] With limited and conflicting information, Peacocke had devised a sound strategy to confront an invading army that would remain a formidable opponent until large numbers of additional Canadian volunteers arrived on the Niagara Peninsula. In addition to his mounted scouts, O'Neill had superior geographical knowledge of southeast Ontario, because at least one Fenian spy had earlier established residence in Fort Erie and surveyed the Niagara Peninsula throughout the spring.[91] Peacocke and Booker, conversely, had to rely on less detailed postal route maps.[92]

Having rested for a few hours beside another creek, O'Neill and his men briefly consumed a predawn breakfast and resumed their march inland. Turning south, they covered just over four miles as the sun rose over the horizon. Upon proceeding along the spine of a thirty- to forty-foot hill, expatriate reconnoiterers returned to the Fenian column to report that Booker's troops had just arrived by rail in the nearby village of Ridgeway. Subsequent locomotive engine whistles echoing from roughly two miles away prompted Fenian officers to dispatch a forward guard one hundred and fifty yards ahead of a hastily constructed defensive perimeter that stretched from an open field to a copse of trees on the opposite side of the Lime Ridge Road. Area farmers and a reputed smuggler from Fort Erie, in the interim, rushed into Ridgeway to inform Booker that a Fenian contingent had situated itself on high ground just east of the town. Skeptical that such reports were true, Booker inadvertently started moving his forces straight toward the Fenians an hour before Peacocke had ordered him to depart for Stevensville. Just fed, but with only a few water bottles, the Toronto volunteers were about to become the first Canadians to fight a conventional battle on native soil in over fifty years.

The best-trained members of the Queen's Own regiment were the first Canadian volunteers to engage O'Neill and his fellow filibusterers. Once guns started firing at about 8:00 a.m., Booker advanced his front lines and deployed flankers, who flushed out Fenian ambuscades in the nearby woods. A methodical ninety-minute assault weakened Fenian resolve. Despite being informed by telegram that Peacocke had yet to vacate his temporary camp in the town of Chippawa, Booker skillfully pressed forward. Many Fenians had deserted, even before the sustained militia attack had begun. Others fled to safety when Buffalo native Peter Lanagen and a handful of other Fenians were critically wounded. As a twenty-three-year-old Canadian Fenian named Thomas Ryall later testified while on trial in Toronto for treason, "While we were marching a man, who was addressed as captain, came running back saying we were going into action, I then thought it was about time to leave."[93] Portents of Canadian victory proved false, however, shortly after Booker's reserves were ordered to relieve their comrades on the front lines. At a moment when O'Neill was contemplating retreat, several inexperienced Canadian soldiers spotted a group of Fenian officers rounding a bend in the Ridge Road on horseback and mistakenly yelled "watch out for cavalry." Following standard drill book procedure, Booker lined most of his men up in square formations to minimize their exposure to mounted attack. The complicated maneuver led to mass confusion. Many of the Canadians were unfamiliar with the orders they received or were uncertain where they were supposed to position themselves.[94]

Soon realizing that no cavalry charge was forthcoming, Booker countermanded his previous order, but his bugler initially resisted sounding new commands because he was tired. The militia infantrymen then had difficulty reassembling in a straight line under fire.[95] Panic ensued in the center of the Canadian defenses, while many members of a Highlanders regiment stopped engaging the Fenians in the nearby woods under the incorrect assumption that they had been ordered to retire. O'Neill capitalized on his adversary's blunder by instructing a company of Fenians from Indianapolis to charge. Within minutes, almost every Canadian along the ridge had been frightened away by an aggressive attack that included a cacophony of Union and Rebel yells.[96] Nearly three-dozen casualties and several dead comrades were abandoned, as Booker's men and several onlooking civilians began a ten-mile retreat to a town called Port Colburne.[97]

Recognizing his failure, Booker later arranged for a relief party to aid wounded men remaining on the battlefield and then requested to be immediately relieved of command. As the relative immobility of Peacocke's troops had greatly abetted the Fenian advance, Booker was later cleared of any wrongdoing during a military inquest, but he eventually moved to Montreal to avoid continued public criticism of his poor tactical decisions during the engagement.[98] With better maps, Booker would have averted a Fenian altercation by proceeding along a more direct road to Stevensville. Instead, paramilitaries that lacked substantial support from the expatriate population they purportedly represented had killed nine Canadians. The Fenian ability to reload and fire faster than their adversaries had resulted in a dozen Canadian casualties. One percent of Booker's men had been killed in action, while two other people died from injuries within the following month. Despite the then-common preventive practice of amputation, only three wounded men had to have limbs removed.[99]

The victorious Fenians did not pursue Booker and his men for both practical and shameful reasons. Advancing fatigued soldiers any closer to the Welland Canal was now dangerous without additional manpower and secure supply lines. Time was thus allotted for the Fenian army to relish its victory for a few hours at the expense of the local civilian population. After posting a picket line on a hill just west of Ridgeway, Fenians stole food and drink from the twenty-odd homes and two taverns in the community. Several meals, including freshly slaughtered pigs and chickens, were prepared in the same kitchens that had been used to make breakfast for Booker's soldiers three hours earlier. The concurrent looting of small objects, such as handkerchiefs and stockings, suggests that the Fenians were more interested in collecting mementos in the same manner as Civil War soldiers than in ransacking Canadian homes out of nationalistic spite. The presence of questionable men in O'Neill's army was confirmed over the following years when one Connecticut filibusterer raped a woman and was imprisoned, while another murdered his mistress and was executed—but few people purloined anything of substantial value or senselessly vandalized private property at the time.[100] Moreover, one Fenian intervened when a fellow filibusterer tried to steal a sword from a town doctor who had served as a Union army surgeon. O'Neill himself threatened to bayonet any Fenian he caught attempting to steal a black woolen shawl.[101]

The Fenian invaders started marching to the relative safety of Fort Erie after O'Neill received no word by the early afternoon that he would obtain reinforcements from Buffalo. Dividing into two groups so that they could destroy all the bridges to their rear, O'Neill and his men returned to their embarkation point by way of a farm road and the Buffalo & Lake Huron railroad tracks. The retreat was uneventful until the first Fenians to reach Fort Erie encountered the one hundred–man detachment that Booker had ordered to patrol the Niagara River. Already having disobeyed orders to remain onboard his vessel, Colonel Denis further endangered the members of the Welland County Militia when he ordered his men to attack after a mounted Fenian emissary carrying a white truce flag was shot by a Canadian soldier.[102] An afternoon-long skirmish ensued. Because he had incorrectly presumed that the Fenians in his midst had been defeated earlier in the day, Denis was quickly overwhelmed as more of O'Neill's men reached Fort Erie. By 5:00 p.m., most of the Canadians had evacuated to the *Robb,* but the vessel remained in rifle range because it was burdened by the weight of fifty-seven Fenian prisoners, in addition to Denis's men.[103] Spectators crowded along the Buffalo shoreline strained their eyes to watch a shoot-out near the Fort Erie post office and the desperate actions of a wounded Canadian officer, who unsuccessfully attempted to avoid capture by dragging himself into the fast-moving Niagara River.[104] With a bullet in his ankle, Richard King would have been swept out from under a pier if he had not been rescued by a group of Fenians, who later had him transported to a Buffalo hospital where his leg was amputated at the knee. Denis was slightly more fortunate; court-martialed for fleeing into the woods as O'Neill gained control of the town, he was later acquitted of cowardice on a split vote.[105]

O'Neill established a camp within the crumbling stone walls of an old War of 1812–era stronghold south of Fort Erie after he defeated Denis's men. He abandoned this position hours later, however, in recognition that he and his men would soon be surrounded by a vastly superior number of adversaries. An estimated nine fatalities during the day had not significantly weakened Fenian military strength, but the sluggish General Peacocke was due to arrive with a large force of men who had remained in remarkably good spirits despite facing tremendous adversity. Bridges unable to sustain the weight of Peacocke's field artillery had collapsed throughout the day, and many of his men were suffering from dehydration.[106] With no other recourse, many of the soldiers under his command had consumed stagnant mud puddle water. The fatigue-related death of one soldier, moreover, might have been the first of several ancillary fatalities if Afro-Canadian families living in a tiny village of New Germany had not provided buckets of cold water as the militia passed through their community at midday.[107] Yet, despite suffering from heat exhaustion, the volunteers approaching Fort Erie had sung anti-Fenian lyrics set to the tune of "Tramp, Tramp, Tramp" and other compositions throughout the day. Peacocke also had his six artillery pieces. Fenian retreat would be nearly impossible in the probable event that these well-armed men and hundreds of additional volunteers from greater Ontario and western Quebec attacked. Contrary to what a Saint Louis Fenian had been told when he agreed to participate in the invasion, the majority of the Canadian population had not supported the Irish republican agenda.[108]

Diminishing supplies and limited manpower also convinced O'Neill to retreat. Fenian ability to withstand a siege would be impossible unless a significant number of reinforcements confined to Buffalo were able to cross the Niagara River without interference from the crew of the *USS Michigan*. The few Fenians who had reached Canada, either by swimming or by navigating tippy boats across the swift-moving river without drowning, barely augmented O'Neill's forces.[109] In contrast to an editorial that appeared three days later in the *Philadelphia North American and United States Gazette*, Sweeny had not "greatly mistaken the capacity of the man to whom he entrusted the command of the Fenians."[110] O'Neill had executed his orders effectively and had secured two military victories to his credit. Logic now dictated that he return to American soil lest Fort Erie become, as he feared, "a slaughter pen."[111]

A Fenian retreat was also honorable because O'Neill had accomplished several components of his original mission. A superfluous number of Canadian soldiers were now en route to the Niagara peninsula, and the intended main Fenian attack had yet to begin near Lake Champlain. As Sweeny had correctly predicted, thousands of expatriates from around the country had volunteered for Fenian military service the moment they heard that O'Neill had defeated Canadian forces at Ridgeway. Recently returned from Campobello, James Kerrigan had established a "labor" recruiting office at Tammany Hall, which buzzed with activity for the next several days while a green Fenian flag flew from an outside balcony.[112] In the Midwest, sixty-four Irishmen from Fond du Lac, Wisconsin marched to Chicago, while Irishwomen in Milwaukee sold some of their jewelry so that 150 expatriates from their community could purchase equipment and proceed to Canada.[113] Willing to do more than sell some of her possessions, sixteen-year-old Molly Mahan volunteered to become the departing company's field nurse.[114] Davenport, Iowa Fenians (who had recently invited local couples of all nationalities to attend an April 18 fundraising ball for the Brotherhood) mustered two separate detachments of several dozen armed and provisioned men, who embarked for Chicago by evening trains on June 4 and 5.[115] The departure of 140 Fenians from the roughly two thousand–member Peoria Irish community on June 5 forced the leaders of a local Baptist church to postpone an excursion to nearby Eureka because members of the Brotherhood had rented all the passenger railcars that were usually available for private use.[116] Expatriates in Lawrence, Massachusetts volunteered at a City Hall rally that had been preceded by a procession led by a town resident who was an O'Mahony circle color guard.[117] With such nationwide expressions of Irish patriotism, O'Neill could reasonably presuppose that he would lead a new Fenian army into Canada within a few days of his return to Buffalo.

Fenian treatment of Canadian prisoners in the hours before O'Neill's retreat from Fort Erie further suggests that Irish nationalist filibusterers were more idealistic than brutish. Queen's Own lance corporal William Ellis noted in a retrospective article that "the Fenians treatment of myself and the other prisoners was kind and considerate in the extreme."[118] Captured soldiers were the first men to receive water each time the invaders rested during their retreat to the Niagara River. O'Neill also purchased a glass of beer for each Canadian POW at a Fort Erie tavern on the evening of June 2. Although ominous, his subsequent threat to summarily shoot ten Canadian prisoners for every one Fenian executed by provincial authorities was reactive. His preretreat vow to lead another foray into Ontario or Quebec, furthermore, occurred at the same time he shook hands and released all the Canadian soldiers from his custody.[119]

O'Neill's decorum may have been inspired by the knowledge that several Canadian soldiers had served under his command when he was a Union army officer, but such chivalry had also been common during the Civil War.[120] The Fenians, however, were long remembered throughout the provinces as immature, lower-class freebooters rather than as freedom fighters. Fenian prisoners captured in Quebec were described in the Montreal press as "little scamps as one sees about the streets of all great cities."[121] Biographical information printed in the *Toronto Leader* on June 5, 1866, shows that the average age of nineteen Fenians captured at Ridgeway was 26.15 years old. Discounting forty-eight-year-old painter James Spalding of Cincinnati and forty-two-year-old Buffalo native Henry Mourin, the average age would be 23.9. The majority of the men in the sample were semi-skilled laborers.[122]

Fenian mobilization back to American territory during the predawn hours of June 3 led to increased federal government efforts to contain Irish militarism. Unlike the series of minor disturbances that had occurred along the Maine/New Brunswick border six weeks earlier, Fenians affiliated with Roberts had demonstrated over the previous two days that their organization could compromise American security. Politicians affiliated with both of the major parties recognized that unbridled Irish republicanism might lead to a war that even many Anglophobic citizens of the reconstituted United States did not want. O'Neill and his men, accordingly, were detained in the middle of the Niagara River after the crew of the Revenue cutter *Harrison* fired a warning shot across the bow of the Fenian-leased tug that was towing filibusterer-filled scows back to Buffalo. Whereas expatriate officers were later sequestered in cabins onboard the *USS Michigan*, all the enlisted men who did not escape by swimming ashore were detained in their open-air vessels until Canadian officials announced late the following day that they would not submit extradition requests for any Fenians in American custody.[123] As future President Grover Cleveland and other influential local lawyers prevented William Dart from bringing any Fenian to trial in Buffalo, one of the few punishments for the Battle of Ridgeway victors was knowing that 150 Fenian pickets and several wounded comrades had been left behind in Canada.[124] When released from custody, O'Neill announced that he was returning to Tennessee immediately, even though hundreds of other Fenians remained in western New York. Sweeny, nevertheless, promoted him to the rank of brigadier general in recognition that the former Union army deserter had led the largest independent Irish army into combat since 1798.[125]

Fenian incursion onto the Niagara Peninsula affected several different expressions of Canadian nationalism. Thousands of people were reverently silent along the streets of Toronto one moment and jeering the next, as the coffins of several Canadians who had been killed at Ridgeway were paraded through city streets in front of several well-guarded Fenian prisoners.[126] Mourners were also in abundance at a joint funeral for the fallen members of the Queen's Own regiment. Inspired by the bravery of the deceased and of battlefield survivors alike, an additional eighteen thousand Canadians volunteered for militia service.[127] Communities all along the route from Windsor to Toronto warmly welcomed about sixty-five members of the Chicago Canadian Protection Society, who were fulfilling a pledge they had each made during the first Fenian convention to return home and defend their native land if it was attacked. Farther east, soldiers affiliated with militia units in predominately Catholic Quebec were generally eager to engage the Fenians, even though some of their coreligionists in Ontario were arrested and charged with treason and others were summarily dismissed from their jobs.[128] Combined, these manifestations of anger and respect buoyed Canadians to unite under a single confederated government.

Expatriate nationalist resolve remained strong throughout the United States despite heightened Canadian opposition and aggressive federal government efforts to restore peace along the border. Several hundred militant Irish Americans remained in Buffalo, Chicago and other cities that had earlier been designated as Fenian mobilization points. On the same day that Ohio Republican congressman Reader Clarke submitted a House bill that would have granted the Fenians belligerent status, 100 of 160 total volunteers from Lawrence assembled at the local train station before proceeding to Saint Albans, Vermont by way of Manchester, New Hampshire.[129] The press likened the scene on the railroad platform to a moment in 1861 when wives and sweethearts bade fond farewell to loved ones destined for Union army training camps. Many cried as a rousing three cheers were raised for the young men who were "predominately under twenty years of age."[130] Many of these men were presumably naturalized Americans, because four of five documented members of the Fenian Brotherhood who served in the predominately Irish Ninth Connecticut Infantry during the Civil War had been born in Ireland.[131] A few Fenians who mustered in New England were older and more prosperous. Albert E. Matthews, for example, had been an antebellum cobbler, but he had become the head of the Milford circle upon the January 1862 death of Robert Peard and had entered the middle class when he became a private grocer in 1865. In deference to his social stature, he was commissioned as a Fenian major, whereas most of the retinue from Lawrence was comprised of volunteer enlistees.[132]

Similar instances of Irish nationalist expression occurred throughout the rest of the country. The day after an energetic meeting produced $1,300 in donations and forty new recruits, somewhere between 1,000 and 1,500 men and women gathered at the Lowell city rail depot to part company with roughly 110 mostly teenaged Fenians destined for the frontier.[133] As in Worcester a year earlier, subscriptions to a Waterbury, Connecticut special fund ranged from spare change to twenty-five dollars.[134] Celebrations slightly delayed by the intracontinental transmission of information to California included the festive uncorking of several champagne bottles in a San Francisco saloon on June 7.[135] Among the many instances of volunteerism in the South, 20 women joined the Nashville chapter of the Fenian Sisterhood and about 150 New Orleans expatriates followed 200 Memphis expatriates, who had departed for New York several days earlier.[136] Similar to fellow Irishmen who headed east from Leavenworth, Kansas and several other Midwest cities, these men were members of a distinct minority within the expatriate community in that they were willing to leave their jobs and families for an indefinite period on behalf of the Irish nationalist cause.

The intervention of United States government officials prevented a large number of these last-minute volunteers from crossing the Canadian frontier. On June 6, President Johnson authorized his attorney general, James Speed, to enforce American neutrality laws so that "public peace as well as the national honor" would be maintained.[137] General George Meade was once again called on to quell Fenian disturbances. Whereas *USS Michigan* commander Andrew Bryson had heretofore detained Fenians and seized weapons largely at his own discretion in western New York, members of the Brotherhood henceforward were arrested anywhere, under the pretext that the United States government was bound by the Monroe Doctrine not to interfere in what Johnson administration officials referred to as a "European" political matter. By midnight, Sweeny and some of his staff members had been apprehended in a Saint Albans hotel room, while seven prominent Irish nationalist leaders from Missouri were being arraigned in a Saint Louis Federal District Court.[138] Roberts (who refused a courtesy offer to surrender himself at the Manhattan offices of the United States marshals service) was taken into custody the following day and held in the renowned Astor House until insurers informed the hotel management that any damages caused in the event of a Fenian rescue attempt would not be reimbursed. After refusing bail and insisting that he would continue to assist his comrades in battle, Roberts succeeded in his efforts to appear a political martyr when he was subsequently incarcerated with common criminals in the Ludlow Street Jail for a few hours.[139]

The June 6 arrest of Sweeny and his principal advisors in Vermont left West Point graduate Samuel Patterson Spears in charge of leading two separate expatriate detachments into Quebec from both sides of Lake Champlain. At 10:00 a.m. on June 7, the former Union army cavalry officer, and perhaps as many as one thousand men, marched one mile across the Canadian border and started building a hilltop camp. Similar to events that had transpired in Fort Erie six days earlier, Spears and his men were initially unimpeded by adversaries. Most civilians who resided in the area had hidden their valuables in buried mason jars and evacuated their homes days earlier. In addition, two local militia companies had refused to report for duty, and a Canadian border patrol had retreated fifteen miles inland on June 4, fearing that it would soon be attacked.[140] Besides brief, inconsequential encounters between Fenian scouts and small homeguard units, the frontier remained quiet. At the end of his first day on foreign soil, Spears boastfully reported that his well-fed men had secured control of four hamlets. Such modest success later came as some surprise to San Francisco residents who initially received exaggerated telegraph reports that green flags had been raised all over Montreal after the Fenians had used one thousand ironclads to capture all of Canada.[141] Spears's command over a sliver of the British Empire was temporary, moreover. Canadian and American officials were already organizing countermeasures that would force the expatriate marauders back into Vermont within hours.

An uneasy calm prevailed over Spears's camp on Friday June 8. Throughout the day, Fenian foraging parties scoured the area for food. On at least one occasion, they offered Fenian bonds as payment for the supplies they confiscated, but they also looted some small items. Although proud that they had stolen a British flag, the marauders reportedly resisted the temptation to tap several kegs of liquor that had been intentionally left in the open by Canadian militia forces in an attempt to intoxicate and weaken their enemy.[142] Contrary to Fenian expectations, Yankee farmers did not openly abet the insurgents, even though memories of the "Vairmont Scare Party" that had raided Saint Albans during the Civil War were still vivid. Local Irish Canadians who respected their neighbors, moreover, said that they would join the Fenians only if they marched well inland. Insightfully, Spears noted by nightfall that his filibusterers were "in excellent spirits, but the fact of the Canadian militia being ordered out makes some uneasy."[143] It would have been equally appropriate if he had also mentioned that his men were discomforted by the presence of a United States Army detachment that was waiting on the border to arrest anyone who was suspected of violating the 1819 Neutrality Act.

By the evening of June 8, it was obvious that the Fenians would not be able to occupy Canadian territory indefinitely. Inexplicably, Spears, who had been an army officer for thirty years, had not attempted to impede approaching Canadian infantry, cavalry, and artillery units by ordering the destruction of unprotected rail lines in the vicinity of his camp. Well aware that they were in danger of death or imprisonment, all but two hundred filibusterers deserted when a large number of adversaries appeared the next morning. Despite disarming themselves in the hope that they would be mistaken for civilians, nearly all the retreating Fenians were detained as they returned to the United States, because they had significant amounts of clothing and other pilfered goods in their possession.[144] A more determined group of expatriates, who primarily hailed from Norwich, Connecticut, held their position until they were about to be shelled by cannons.[145] With only a few random shots fired and a volunteer Canadian cavalry observing an order to strike adversaries with the flat ends of their swords, no one was killed or wounded during the brief encounter.

The 1866 Fenian invasions ended later the same day when General Meade authorized the dispersal of a few hundred Fenians who had gathered fifty miles almost directly to the west of Saint Albans at an abandoned army barracks in Malone, New York.[146] Expecting strong American government support, Brotherhood military leaders were unable or unwilling to offer resistance once the 1819 Neutrality Act was enforced. The only Fenian provocation on United States soil occurred when a group of militants boldly attempted to commandeer a commercial locomotive and steal two boxcars of Brotherhood weapons that had been confiscated in Watertown, New York. The initiative was abandoned when the culprits learned that a contingent of soldiers was in pursuit of their small train.[147] With peace restored on the south side of the border, Quebec residents vented their anger toward the Fenians, reprising what had occurred in Toronto a few days earlier by yelling "hang them, hang them" as a captured group of Spears's men were escorted into Montreal.[148]

The evacuation of Fenians from the northern frontier was replete with silent homecomings, inappropriate behavior, outright lies, and Canadian celebrations.

Even though most Fenians had been lauded by friends and loved ones before they ventured north, many defeated filibusterers returned to their hometowns unnoticed and unappreciated.[149] Other men who had no money could apply for transport subsidized by the United States Army and Boss Tweed if they signed an affirmation to "desist from any further attempt to invade Canada and to return quietly to their homes."[150] Recalcitrant Fenians accused cohorts who complied with these stipulations of being cowards. Passenger cars full of dejected Brotherhood members were rolled out of Buffalo and other cities to the sounds of catcalls and obscenity-laced tirades. Determined to disperse the last of Sweeny's supporters, General Meade announced on June 12 that any member of the Brotherhood could receive free passage home without pledging good conduct. Yet, several disenchanted Fenians (among the approximately five thousand who were disbanded at government expense) fired at cattle as the trains that were transporting them back to their communities passed by farms and stock pens.[151] Issuing a circular in Buffalo on June 14, Fenian General M. W. Burns deviated from usual Irish republican declarations of American patriotism by arguing "it was the United States and not England, that impeded our onward march to freedom."[152] False rumors also circulated that Canadian soldiers, "who were worthy of the brutal Saxons," had scalped Edward Lanergan's head after the twenty-one-year-old Fenian lieutenant died at Ridgeway on his birthday.[153]

Compared with activity in other sections of the country, expatriate support for the Fenian movement was remarkably strong along the Gulf Coast during the weeks that followed the failed Canadian invasion. Perhaps not yet aware that Spears had retreated from Quebec, pronationalist Irishwomen in New Orleans emulated fellow female expatriates in other American cities by presenting a green silk battle flag to the members of a local circle.[154] Godfrey Massey, moreover, successfully recruited men and raised money in Houston and other southeast Texas locales throughout early June. Combined with propaganda being circulated by Fenian leaders in New York, such activity in the former Confederacy provided Canadian officials with ample reason to remain cautious. Many militias units were not disbanded until mid-June. Two warships and two gunboats were deployed, moreover, to Victoria Harbor in case West Coast Fenians attacked British Columbia, as was rumored.[155] Nonetheless, many communities organized postinvasion celebrations around the official beginning of summer, and one man apparently of Gaelic ancestry became the first Canadian recipient of the Victoria Cross, in recognition of his role in extinguishing a fire that had ignited onboard a boxcar loaded with ammunition.[156]

Pervasive Anglophobic and anti-Canadian sentiment notwithstanding, many Americans were equally pleased that the 1866 Fenian invasion had been repulsed. A *New York Times* editorial published shortly after the Buffalo raid reveals noticeable empathy between Americans and Canadians of the upper classes:

> If there is one thing that we Americans have prayed earnestly for since these bandit gangs were first formed, it was that every ruffian that crossed the frontier might be straightway caught and hung. The prospect of this was a sort of compensation for the intolerable nuisance of being obliged to listen to their blather day after day.[157]

The editors of the *Atlantic Monthly* similarly dismissed Fenian arguments that their invasion had been conducted in the spirit of the American Revolution: "All the qualities which go to make a republican, in the true sense of the term, are wanting in the Irish nature."[158] Mention of O'Neill's actions also precipitated barroom brawls in a Baltimore Turnpike tavern and in the mining community of Grass Valley.[159]

With federal elections now only five months away, many politicians ignored anti-Irish sentiments and resumed espousing Fenian objectives during the summer of 1866. On the same day that many discouraged Fenians returned home to Lawrence, Reading, Pennsylvania Democrat Sydenham E. Ancona submitted a bill that would have required his House of Representatives colleagues to review the 1819 Neutrality Act. Although complemented by corollary legislation that was sponsored by a Republican who had served as a Union army general, the proposal died in committee. In the ensuing week, Schuyler Colfax once again courted pro-Fenian voters by escorting Roberts on a tour of Washington. The Fenian leader had been released from jail three days earlier and was still under indictment, but Colfax, nevertheless, introduced him to several Capitol Hill powerbrokers. Stephens declined a similar Colfax invitation a few days later, because he believed it was demeaning for him to accept an honor that had already been extended to Roberts. The most provocative gesture, however, was undertaken by the former Know-Nothing and Union general turned Fenian advocate, Nathaniel Banks. As the sponsor of an annexation bill that would have delighted Fenians and Manifest Destiny supporters alike, the Massachusetts congressman introduced legislation on July 2, 1866 to annex eastern Canada to the United States.[160] An Anglo-American war could have been provoked if the House Foreign Affairs Committee had not promptly rejected the proposal. British diplomatic sensitivities were re-aroused shortly thereafter by an ensuing resolution favoring the release of Fenian prisoners in Canada and a provision that allowed the Brotherhood to use a federally owned building in Washington for organizational activities.[161] Because Irish voter support was crucial, political leaders pretended that militant Fenian objectives were admirable in theory, if not in practice.

Relatively few Irish Americans were willing to endorse revolution in Ireland after the two Fenian invasions of Canada were over. Park officials denied Stephens access to Jones's Wood in late June, but he was allowed to address a relatively small gathering outside the gates of the private Upper Eastside recreation area.[162] Boos and hisses often drowned out Stephens's haughty and bombastic public addresses. To his personal embarrassment, Stephens was arrested in Massachusetts, on July 11, for disregarding a civil charge that he owed an influential New England Fenian five thousand dollars worth of lecture honoraria incurred in Maine during the Campobello escapade. Stephens posted bail a few hours later and, apparently, the charges were later dropped.[163] When compared with Sisterhood contributions to O'Mahony fourteen months earlier, an August 1866 donation of $108.15 to Stephens from female Irish residents of Tarrytown, New York Irish appears somewhat paltry.[164] William Barry of White Plains, New York indirectly demonstrated that he was among the few expatriates who still had faith in the increasingly unpopular IRB founder, when he wrote to his parents in County Cork three months later that he was hoping to "go home before Christmas . . . to do some good for Old Ireland."[165] Although both factions of the Brotherhood had suffered irreparably debilitating defeats, the Men of Action would command greater expatriate support in subsequent years.

Roberts and his allies sustained limited expatriate interest in their endeavors through the fall of 1866 by aggressively censuring United States government officials for obstructing their paramilitary operations in Canada. O'Neill openly complained for several months that he and his fellow officers had been contained by "fire in the rear, not fire in the front."[166] Cincinnati Fenian leader James Fitzgerald echoed these sentiments in a private letter by arguing that Seward and Johnson "had broad enough shoulders" to "father the entire failure."[167] Expatriates who attended a July 4 Fenian demonstration in Dubuque similarly loathed a president who had labeled the Fenians "evil disposed persons," guilty of committing "high misdemeanor[s]," in his June 6 neutrality proclamation.[168] Johnson's efforts to commission several Irish officers after the United States Army underwent a dramatic peacetime expansion in mid-1866 also failed to appease Fenian supporters, who refused to accept collective responsibility for Sweeny's inability to capture any Canadian territory earlier in the year.[169]

Partisan politics continued to elicit Fenian angst in the later half of 1866. Two years away from being elected Ulysses S. Grant's vice president, Schuylur Colfax announced at an August Brotherhood gathering in Chicago, "Johnson is now the friend of the English government."[170] Milwaukee newspapers reported that three thousand Irishmen attended a local Radical Republican rally a month before hundreds of their fellow countrymen heckled the president in Indianapolis so fiercely that he was unable to speak more than a few words. Somewhat ironically, Irishmen in the crowds called on General Grant to speak at the Indiana gathering, even though the Union war hero had earlier stated that the United States would not invade Canada unless the British government supported efforts to refortify diminishing French control over Mexico.[171] Other Lincoln administration holdovers who accompanied the president on his "Swing around the Circle" were similarly entreated to present addresses, despite their previous unwillingness to sanction the recent Fenian incursion into Canada.[172] The accidental commander in chief was simultaneously lambasted at Fenian picnics, which often featured public speakers and a skewed Battle of Ridgeway re-enactment. To the delight of expatriate crowds, a dashing actor—or John O'Neill himself—would lead Fenian troops against fellow expatriates, who portrayed Canadian soldiers and a bumbling Alfred Booker.[173] Considerably less entertaining was an October pro-Roberts rally on Staten Island, which featured a Spanish-language address by the aging Santa Ana.

Protracted Fenian opposition to Andrew Johnson ultimately impaired rather than abetted the Roberts faction. Thomas Sweeny was forced to resign from the Brotherhood during a September gathering of Roberts supporters in Troy, New York, because the Fenian general was unwilling to abandon a Democratic ticket that had granted his release from prison and dropped indictments against him in mid-August.[174] Out of a collective need to find a scapegoat, most Irish American nationalists, unlike Sweeny, forgot that their newfound Radical Republican friends had done nothing for either faction of the Fenian Brotherhood until the April and June invasions were contained. As a result, John O'Neill succeeded Sweeny when the Union army hero Phil Sheridan reportedly declined an offer to become the newest Fenian secretary of war.[175] Reelected by the assembled delegates to another term as president of his organization, Roberts, henceforward, had to manage with less qualified leadership and decreasing grassroots support. Accordingly, Roberts initiated a lobbying campaign on behalf of the Brotherhood in Washington and later entertained the possibility of forming an alliance between his supporters and the IRB.[176] Sweeny, in the interim, traveled to Nashville and reassumed his former position in the United States Army's Sixteenth Infantry Regiment.

Andrew Johnson reversed several of his anti-Fenian executive orders after his disastrous fall 1866 whistle-stop campaign. All Brotherhood members still under indictment for violating American neutrality laws were pardoned in an attempt to counter anticipated strong expatriate voter support for Radical Republican candidates during forthcoming federal elections. In addition to the captain of the tug that had fired at O'Neill's retreating Fenians, Buffalo-based United States district attorney William Dart was forced out of office for having attempted to prosecute expatriate filibusterers the previous June.[177] A separate executive order irked Canadian and British officials by instructing army quartermasters to return all Fenian-owned weapons seized at the time of the raid in exchange for a bond that would be forfeited if the arms were reused contrary to federal law.[178] The president additionally dismissed a Canadian request to pay for damages incurred at Ridgeway and endorsed continued State Department legal assistance to Irish American citizens who had been detained in Ontario, Quebec, and Ireland on suspicion of treason.[179] Although Irish American nationalists appreciated these gestures—a Fenian who had been wounded at Ridgeway led a jovial parade of Buffalo expatriates who retrieved their firearms from a nearby United States military installation on December 4—they did not signify the establishment of a full-fledged alliance that Irish militants had long desired to forge with American government officials. Johnson's initiatives also failed to insure favorable election results for the president and his congressional allies. Johnson's restitution programs were largely ineffectual. Many Republican-leaning Irishmen and women abstained from voting in the 1866 federal election rather than betray their longstanding political affiliation with the Democratic Party.[180] The merits of defending Fenian actions also proved of questionable value, in hindsight, as Sydenham Ancona, a Democratic congressman from Pennsylvania, lost his seat in the House of Representatives in the fall, despite having supported revision of the 1819 Neutrality Act. The policy change also emboldened B. Doran Killian to solicit a government job. Writing to the president on September 19, the disgraced Fenian noted that he was qualified for federal employment because he had once been nominated to run for Congress. More interestingly, he masked his recent involvement in the Campobello foray by alleging once again that he had ventured to eastern Maine the previous April as an advocate of American fishing interests near the Bay of Fundy.[181]

Johnson administration concessions to the Fenians were unnecessary, in retrospect, as the fractured Brotherhood became a fringe group within the greater expatriate community. Readmitted to Jones's Wood after a visit to Saint Louis in the fall, Stephens assured women in attendance at an outdoor Fenian Sisterhood gathering that he would be leading an insurrection on his native soil by the beginning of the new year. During his last public appearance on October 28, moreover, he reemphasized his commitment to Ireland by noting that he had risen "from his bed of fever" to inform supporters that he would be fighting in the midst of two hundred thousand IRB soldiers before the beginning of the new year.[182] Even though he was described a month later in the *Missouri Democrat* as a future Garibaldi or Bismarck, Stephens had already become another failed Irish revolutionary who commanded dwindling public respect.[183] Maurice Woulfe later boasted in a May 1867 letter to his uncle that he had once thrown a rotten apple at the balding five-foot-three Stephens when the Fenian leader addressed a crowd at an outdoor Washington, D.C. rally.[184]

Such lackluster support for a nationalist leader who had been widely adulated six months earlier was due as much to Stephens's personal ineptitude as to the increasing Americanization of the Brotherhood and its members. During a territorial convention in September 1866, Colorado Fenians had adopted a constitution that began with wording which nearly replicated the first sentence of the preamble of its American counterpart. Additional provisions mandated that each Colorado circle conduct meetings using a democratic parliamentary procedure. A Jacobinesque-sounding Committee of Safety was charged with vetting prospective members of the organization. An accompanying set of bylaws revealed how the Brotherhood was intended to serve both as a benevolent society and as an Irish nationalist advocacy group. Article IX mandated that people who neglected to share responsibility for keeping vigil over sick members would be assessed a five dollar fine. Attendance at the funerals of deceased compatriots was defined in Section 16 of Article V as "an imperative duty," but transgressors, interestingly, were not subject to any defined penalty.[185] The professional success of many Fenians further suggested why Irish nationalist expression declined precipitously during the closing months of 1866. Men with increasing vested interests in their local communities had little incentive to remain involved in the Brotherhood. Rather than from working-class Irishmen and expatriates, some of the strongest support for Fenian activities was offered by the myriad of local, state, and federal politicians who were trying to woo Irish constituents in the weeks leading up to the 1866 midterm elections.

Canadian judicial officials had to gauge the integrity of American politicians who made pro-Irish republican statements in public when the first Fenians were tried in Toronto and Sweetsburg during the fall of 1866. In the interest of fairness and impartiality, Canadian judges had delayed the formal adjudication of all the accused suspects so that public antipathy toward the "youthful, hard-looking" Fenians, as they were described in the Canadian press, could subside over the summer. Twenty-two expatriate suspects were also discharged during preliminary hearings owing to insufficient evidence or to witness inability to identify defendants whose once bearded and bronzed skin was now clean-shaven and pale.[186] Such probity largely vanished when an all-Protestant jury was empanelled for the trial of the first Fenian defendant, and one of the attorneys selected as a member of the Ontario provincial prosecution team was the grand master of a local Orange Lodge.[187] Aided by Canadian and American lawyers, eighty-five

Fenian defendants constructed elaborate and sometimes far-fetched alibis out of fear that they might be executed for committing treason or found guilty of violating an obscure capital charge originally authorized as a means to curtail United States involvement in the 1837 rebellion.[188] As two-thirds of the defendants were Catholics being tried before Anglophiles, any of the accused who paraphrased United Irish hero Robert Emmet's courtroom recitation was likely to receive a death sentence.[189]

County Galway native Robert Blosse Lynch and an Irish-born priest from Indiana named John MacMahon were among the first defendants who attempted to distance themselves from the Fenian Brotherhood. Lynch, who was an affluent Union army veteran and a former Milwaukee city clerk, unsuccessfully contended that he had been a reporter under the employ of the *Louisville Courier* at the time of the attack. While an actual *New York Tribune* correspondent had been mistakenly arrested and released earlier through American diplomatic intervention, one witness testified that he had seen the approximately forty-five-year-old Lynch on Canadian soil with a sword strapped to his waist. Transcripts from the Lynch trial also show that the accused had answered to the title "colonel" when he first met a witness on the Niagara Peninsula. MacMahon presented a similarly tenuous alibi when he claimed that he was present at Ridgeway largely by coincidence. In court, the forty-eight-year-old cleric testified that he had coincidentally encountered a group of Fenians while crossing the Niagara River into Canada on a commercial ferry and had offered to serve as a chaplain before proceeding to Montreal on a personal matter. In truth, he had been in the company of a Fenian contingent at Brotherhood expense from the moment he left his parish. In addition, Buffalo mayor Chandler Wells, as noted, had suspended all public transport across the Niagara River when the threat of an invasion appeared imminent. MacMahon could not possibly have encountered Fenians by chance, as he testified. To his credit, MacMahon had remained on the battlefield and assisted in the burial of dead expatriate filibusterers after a Canadian officer offered him the opportunity to escape back to the United States. The jury, however, concluded that such magnanimous concern for the spiritual welfare of others did not exonerate anyone from having abetted Fenian marauders.[190] MacMahon was sentenced to be hanged, while the Fenians' Protestant field chaplain—a reputed drunk from Syracuse—was acquitted because he had inexplicably attempted to rally the residents of Fort Erie against the Fenians after O'Neill and his men retreated from Ridgeway.[191]

Irish nationalists throughout the United States were outraged as Canadian magistrates sentenced five more Fenian prisoners to death during the fall of 1866. In addition to carrying out public demonstrations beginning earlier in the fall, the expatriate community demanded that politicians fulfill campaign promises to secure the release of republican militants who had been condemned to the gallows. As a goodwill gesture to the Johnson administration and to Catholics residing in Quebec who were particularly opposed to the execution of a priest, MacMahon and all the other Fenians convicted of treason during the fall assizes were granted a three-month stay of execution shortly before a Christmas court recess began on December 13. In an apparent interim attempt to embarrass Roberts, an incendiary letter supposedly written to Lynch by the department store magnate was printed in the December 17 edition of the *Toronto Globe*. Scripted to incite anti-Fenian sentiment among all Canadians, the most noteworthy sentence in the missive read, "I regret to tell you that you are not going to be hanged. So great a crime upon a non-combatant like yourself would make every Irishman in America a Fenian, and furnish our exchequer with the necessary means to clear Canada of English authority in short order."[192] Most likely, however, Roberts was not disappointed that Lynch and his incarcerated comrades received some clemency. In a letter that was printed in a Buffalo Fenian newspaper at the time of the trials, the millionaire nationalist wrote, "I am satisfied they will never hang one of them."[193] The fate of colleagues yet to be tried remained uncertain, however, because Canadian patriotic resolve was fortified by Fenian threats to retaliate if one of their comrades were to be executed.[194]

Whether O'Neill was of the same opinion as Roberts is difficult to assess. The *Cincinnati Enquirer* reported that the "Hero of Ridgeway" accused Lynch of cowardice during a mid-December speech in Nashville for not wanting to die for Ireland. Yet, in a demonstration of his own pusillanimity, O'Neill, like General Spears, refused to travel to Canada under the threat of arrest to testify on behalf of men who had served under his command.[195] Eighteen additional death warrants were signed, as more Fenians were sequentially placed on trial in Toronto and Sweetsburg.[196] As the editors of the *New York Herald* predicted, British government officials who administered the Canadian court system were not "so foolish as to execute the condemned Fenians."[197] The hanging of any Irish nationalist prisoner might invite another expatriate invasion of Canada. In a foreshadowing of treatment of republican prisoners in the United Kingdom, the death sentences of all Fenians convicted before the new year were eventually commuted to twenty years' hard labor.[198] Several other colleagues had yet to be tried, however, and some desperate Fenians, unlike Roberts, sincerely hoped that some of their comrades would be executed. In reference to MacMahon and Lynch, James Fitzgerald had privately written in mid-November, "Prompt the Canadian government to hang those two men [sic] then there is some hopes of the future but if they are smart enough to pardon them as I fear they will then indeed I tremble at the fate of the organization."[199]

Stephens's role within the transatlantic Fenian movement, in the interim, was irreparably altered. The IRB leader's popularity had been somewhat resilient in Ireland and England, as several IRB circles had been able to raise money in late 1866 by claiming to collect funds for "distressed families."[200] The former Young Irelander became a political liability when he proved unable or unwilling to instigate an Irish rebellion at the end of 1866. Francis Millen publicly accused Stephens of cowardice in a lengthy letter to the *New York Times* in early December.[201] Disillusioned Fenians based in England voiced their desire for new, aggressive leadership in private forums by insisting that an armed insurrection begin immediately. Because many American and Irish militant republicans concurred with these sentiments, the rise of a new Fenian hierarchy was imminent.

The downfall of James Stephens was, appropriately, triggered by a lie. Instead of immediately departing for Ireland as promised, the IRB leader remained hidden in a West Eleventh Street apartment in Manhattan as the adjudication of Fenian prisoners in Canada continued throughout the fall.[202] Unsatisfied with the excuses Stephens offered for remaining in the United States when he was summoned to a private meeting on December 29, the former Isaac Butt client John McCafferty placed a revolver next to the erstwhile provisional dictator's temple and demanded his resignation. Stephens, by his own account, offered to surrender himself to the British as proof of his patriotic fervor before he acquiesced to his frustrated subordinates' demands. He instead was relegated to the powerless post of civilian organizer. In disgrace, he subsequently returned to Paris after he apparently missed the early January departure of a ship carrying the new Fenian leadership to Europe by two hours. As a political exile, he would play no part in the forthcoming Irish insurrection, even though he wrote in a private letter at the time that he would "return to Ireland and face certain death" on a moment's notice if it would expedite Irish independence.[203] The longtime conspirator would make many unsuccessful attempts to regain control of the IRB, but his days as an influential republican leader were over.

Unaware that a coup had occurred within the Fenian movement, most Irish nationalists and British government officials still believed that Stephens was the leader of the IRB and of the O'Mahony faction of the stateside Brotherhood at the beginning of 1867. Devoted Irish men and women who presumed that the Fenian chief would fulfill promises he had made at Jones's Wood continued to await the resurfacing of their leader through the following spring. Such optimism, however, was counterbalanced by disgruntled nationalists, who spread idle threats and outlandish gossip. A group of Manchester Fenians threatened to kill Stephens in December if a revolution was not immediately forthcoming.[204] According to one rumor that surfaced not long after Canadian judges spared the lives of another group of convicted Fenians, the ousted IRB founder was traveling around Ireland in French clothes with a fourteen-year-old boy.[205] British authorities were some of the few people who still worried that Stephens was a credible force within the Irish republican movement. At the end of 1866, the British government Home Office had hired detectives to investigate a rumor that the IRB chief had disguised himself as a sailor working aboard one of the three yachts that had been entered in the first transatlantic regatta.[206] Still convinced that Stephens was a leading member of the Fenian movement when he was sighted in France at the end of January, British officials assigned several people to monitor his public and private activities over the following year.[207]

The legacy of the 1866 Fenian invasions and qualified American government endorsement of Irish nationalist initiatives led to the creation of the Canadian Dominion on July 1, 1867. Negotiations with Foreign Office representatives in London coincided with weaning the Canadian military from imperial dependence. Several vessels that had been utilized when O'Neill and Spears led expatriate filibusterers across the Fenian border were commissioned into a newly formed Canadian navy, and thousands of aging single-shot muzzleloaders were replaced with modern repeating rifles.[208] Upon receiving final legislative approval from the British Parliament, the peoples of already-unified Ontario and Quebec became the fellow countrymen of New Brunswick and Nova Scotia residents a month before Fenian nemesis George Meade was warmly received during a brief tour of the new nation.[209] Although it received substantial support because it promoted internal economic growth at a time when recently reestablished American tariff laws had stifled bilateral trade, Confederation was mainly endorsed because it better protected the newly aligned provinces from the possibility of another foreign invasion or a paramilitary attack. The Fenians had thus expedited the formation of a sovereign state other than their own. They would also facilitate the geographic expansion of the new Canadian nation three years later, when John O'Neill led an expatriate foray into Manitoba shortly after the frontier territory officially became a Dominion possession.

Despite limited expatriate support and the unforeseen crystallization of Canadian nationalism, Irish American patriotic expression had flourished in the months immediately following the February 1866 suspension of *habeas corpus* provisions in Ireland. Notwithstanding the improbable chance of establishing a "New Ireland" on foreign soil, as many as eleven thousand Fenian militants had volunteered to fight the British army and provincial militia forces between April and June. On the home front, a roughly equal number of expatriate women had demonstrated their nationalist sentiments by preparing bandages and raising money for the Brotherhood. Like Irish nationalist males, members of the Sisterhood hoped that the establishment of an independent Ireland would psychologically compensate for years of arduous living in unpleasant émigré enclaves. Even some normally tepid nationalists had endorsed the Fenians during the invasions. Many expatriate men and women later honored O'Neill and his men, moreover, by touring the Ridgeway battlefield. Although the establishment of the many taverns near the battlefield site suggest that a visit to Ridgeway was also an expatriate leisure activity, these trips were primarily undertaken to see the location where Irishmen had won their first victory over the British in sixty-eight years.[210]

John O'Mahony. From *The Felon's Track: History of the Attempted Outbreak in Ireland, Embracing the Leading Events in the Irish Struggle from the Year 1843 to the Close of 1848*, 1914.

James Stephens. From *The Felon's Track: History of the Attempted Outbreak in Ireland, Embracing the Leading Events in the Irish Struggle from the Year 1843 to the Close of 1848*, 1914.

William Roberts, president of the Fenian Brotherhood, ca. 1866. Library of Congress.

Michael Doheny. From *The Felon's Track: History of the Attempted Outbreak in Ireland, Embracing the Leading Events in the Irish Struggle from the Year 1843 to the Close of 1848*, 1914.

William Smith O'Brien. From *The Felon's Track: History of the Attempted Outbreak in Ireland, Embracing the Leading Events in the Irish Struggle from the Year 1843 to the Close of 1848*, 1914.

The Battle of Ridgeway, June 2, 1866. The Fenian Brotherhood under the command of Colonel John O'Neill charged the retreating Queen's Own Rifles of Canada commanded by Colonel A. Booker at Ridgeway, Ontario, during the Fenian invasion of Canada. Library of Congress.

The "Cuba" Five. *From left to right:* John Devoy, Charles Underwood O'Connell, Harry Mulleda, Jeremiah O'Donovan Rossa, and John McClure. These five Irish Fenian prisoners, who under general amnesty were released by the British to America on January 5, 1871, were shipped together aboard the *Cuba*. Printed below the image are signatures of each of the men along with two stanzas of a poem which begins: "They hither came with confidence / They hither came in banishment." Library of Congress.

The Fenian Banner. Library of Congress.

6

"No Event of Any Importance"

The cadre of expatriates who deposed Fenian leader James Stephens in December 1866 attempted to bolster the Irish nationalist movement over the course of the following year by organizing three ultimately unsuccessful military initiatives. A mid-February attempt to steal firearms from a Lancashire arsenal preceded an ineffectual March revolt in Ireland and a transatlantic filibustering operation launched from New York City in early April. Expeditious British suppression of these and some smaller scale militant activities further suppressed Irish militant expression throughout the North Atlantic world. Thousands of male and female Fenian supporters of similar socioeconomic standing were subsequently drawn into more licit nationalist movements. By the latter half of 1867, would-be Fenian soldiers and Sisterhood auxiliaries were likely to be demonstrating for the acquittal of comrades who had been indicted for treason or for the release of convicted nationalists who had been incarcerated.

The newest leaders of the militant Irish nationalist movement lacked the resources to mobilize thousands of poorly prepared IRB activists for battle before the spring of 1867. The sale of Killian's Campobello supply ship, *Ocean Spray,* provided Kelly, Cluseret, and other members of a newly formed IRB provisional government with fourteen thousand dollars to travel to London and begin activating Fenian units. Stephens, however, had only stockpiled an estimated four thousand firearms over the previous two years and several salaried Fenian officers had been consistently underpaid.[1] Although O'Mahony and others had enjoyed the amenities of the Moffat Mansion, Kelly and his colleagues were forced to live in a modest Bedford Square boarding house. The headquarters of the self-declared Irish republic thus doubled as a residence for everyday Englishmen.

Kelly's coterie was unable to sustain IRB manpower as desertions mounted and public criticism of the organization increased. Many Irish American officers had gradually returned to the United States after Stephens refused to initiate a rebellion upon his escape from prison two years earlier.[2] An equally skeptical John Mitchel had similarly refused an offer to become president of a reunified Brotherhood at roughly the same time that a scathing anti-Irish nationalist letter appeared in the Philadelphia *Catholic Herald*. In addition to arguing that the Fenian agenda was futile, the author of the missive rhetorically suggested that benevolent domestic community service had become more important than underwriting the IRB: "When you cannot effectively assist those in Ireland, why not extend the hand and lift up from misery, degradation, and ruin those in America?"[3] As in the past, members of reputable Roman Catholic Church–affiliated, expatriate benevolent organizations were some of the strongest critics of Fenian enterprises.

IRB efforts to reverse declining support for the Irish republican movement were also stymied by British radicals. Several former leaders of the protoprogressive Chartist movement curtly rebuffed a Gustave Cluseret–led delegation during a meeting in London at the beginning of February, even though the French mercenary had presented a letter of introduction from Mazzini.[4] Charles Bradlaugh, the London-born founder of the National Secular Society, hindered, rather than assisted, the IRB shortly thereafter when he revised a proclamation that the Fenian hierarchy intended to distribute as it mobilized its forces at the beginning of March. Although Fenian political objectives remained rather nebulous, IRB militants were falsely presented to the public in the *Proclamation of the Irish Republic* as nondenominational nationalist champions of a disenfranchised working class. In addition to excluding any reference to past instances of state-sponsored anti-Catholic oppression, the final version of the document demanded universal suffrage from "the aristocratic locusts whether English or Irish who eat the verdure of our fields."[5] As Stephens had learned when he courted Chartist veterans in 1865, Poles, Italians, and other people opposed to the imperial rivals of the British Empire were the only nationalist insurgents who received sympathy from the English general public. At a time when radical leaders did not want to jeopardize passage of the pending Second Reform Bill, which would enfranchise the male working class in England and Wales, Fenian operatives were denied external support.

Provisional government inability to quickly rectify IRB shortcomings fostered dissension and confusion within the global Fenian movement. Denied formal endorsement from Mazzini, Garibaldi, and aforementioned British radicals, the once-impatient Kelly recognized that his underprepared men were not ready to rebel on Monday, February 11, as he had originally planned. In an apparent effort to not appear as dilatory as James Stephens, he delayed the mobilization of his forces only until the scheduled March 5 execution of several Fenians in Toronto. For reasons that remain unclear, John McCafferty ignored this order by leading a large band of Fenians, who attempted to steal several hundred rifles from a British government–controlled arsenal in the Midlands city of Chester on the same day that the nationwide insurrection was originally supposed to have begun. Having affiliated himself with a splinter nationalist group called the IRB Directory, McCafferty apparently planned to infiltrate the eight-hundred-year-old armory, commandeer a train to Holyhead, and then ferry several prepackaged crates of expropriated weapons across the Irish Sea to County Wicklow on a stolen steamship.[6] Because the proposed night-time operation was logistically outlandish, the former Confederate guerilla may have had the ulterior motive of leading a mission--almost certainly doomed to failure--that would nonetheless rally more of the Irish community to the Fenian cause. As had happened during the Roberts wing invasion of Canada almost a year earlier, morale was likely to rise both within the IRB and among nationalists throughout the North Atlantic world if a large group of republican militants openly attempted to challenge British authorities. The acquisition of even a limited number of stolen rifles with the help of coconspiring sentinels alone would be considered a success.

A relatively large number of Fenian volunteers ventured to Chester on February 11. About thirteen hundred of the estimated twenty thousand expatriate nationalist sympathizers in Lancashire joined McCafferty for many of the same reasons that Irish American militants had willingly invaded Canada eight months earlier. Noted heretofore, English nativists despised first- and second-generation members of the Irish community in Great Britain for their willingness to work for low wages, their cultural mannerisms, and their demographically disproportionate propensity to commit crime. Irish men, moreover, were often stereotyped as verbose effeminates and uncouth drunkards who spoke the "foul" Gaelic language.[7] As one English aristocrat once lamented, "I am more like a woman than a man, but that's Irish."[8] By participating in the attack, marginalized Irishmen, primarily in their late teens and early twenties, demonstrated their masculinity and vented their frustration with social discrimination.[9] In addition, *habeas corpus* protections were still guaranteed in England. The one-armed future leader of the Irish Land League, Michael Davitt, and other Fenians who otherwise might have been reluctant to fight for fear of arbitrary imprisonment were therefore willing to participate in a massive weapons theft.

Forewarned British officials prevented McCafferty from leading an attack by assembling an array of constables and soldiers throughout Chester several hours before the raid was supposed to occur. On the basis of information received the previous day from John Joseph Coridon, a well-placed informant inside the IRB, hundreds of civilian volunteers were temporarily deputized. Infantry regiments from as far away as London were simultaneously rushed to the North Midlands. As key locations in the city were secured, young adults with Irish brogues were summarily detained. McCafferty himself never reached the arsenal, because the passenger train on which he was traveling was delayed so that British army officials could maintain right-of-way on all railways leading to Chester. Once they realized that their commanding officer had failed to appear, most of the men wisely evaded arrest by throwing their revolvers into canals and ponds. A handful of people were incarcerated for a few days. One suspect was remanded for an extended period. McCafferty himself was apprehended twelve days later in Dublin harbor, after he was spotted onboard a collier inbound from Whitehaven.[10] Cash-strapped militants, who had anticipated proceeding directly to Ireland with the weapons they intended to steal, pawned some of their clothes so they could purchase train tickets to return home and avoid suspicion.

Lack of coordination within the IRB was additionally evident in County Kerry two days after the aborted Chester raid. Unaware that Kelly had postponed the start of the uprising, Irish-born Union army veteran John J. O'Connor led a group of several dozen insurgents who stole a cache of arms and ammunition from a Kells Coast Guard station on the morning of February 13. After subduing a lone constable shortly thereafter, O'Connor ascertained from reading police dispatches that the provisional Fenian government in London had actually delayed the start of the insurrection until early March. When another communiqué revealed that government officials had already identified many of his men as subversives, O'Connor decided to lead the Americans and Irishmen under his command into hiding. Engaging government entities without external support and anonymity unnecessarily risked arrest and loss of life.

In another demonstration of Fenian magnanimity, O'Connor attended to his prisoner before he and his men fled into the nearby hills. Although conscious, the detained constable was clearly suffering from a Fenian bullet wound, which had prevented his brave attempt to avoid capture. O'Connor provided the constable with brandy from his own flask. A messenger was then dispatched to fetch both a priest and a doctor, while a couple of men carried the wounded policeman to a nearby cottage. Aided by widows and other civilians who provided food and shelter, most of the Kerry Fenians remained on the run for the ensuing week.[11] Several people were arrested, but most of the insurgents returned to their homes with partial assistance from prorepublican enlisted members of the 73rd Scottish Highland regiment.[12] O'Connor himself eventually fled to America disguised as a cleric. Later venturing to Louisiana, he became a sheriff and the son-in-law of a wealthy ex-Confederate general. As in Chester, committed republicans had been willing but unable to fight for political agency and economic opportunity because IRB leaders failed to coordinate the deployment of their supporters.

The Chester and Kerry disturbances further impaired Fenian Brotherhood efforts to secure United States government support for the Irish republican movement. With only spotty and often censored telegrams arriving via the recently completed transatlantic cable, émigrés were uncertain whether McCafferty and O'Connor were the vanguards of a full-scale revolution. As a gesture of solidarity, a new Fenian leader, who had assumed control of the O'Mahony faction after Stephens's deposition, sold some rifles to raise money for the provisional Fenian government and publicly attempted to recruit one thousand men who could defray the first one hundred dollars of their own filibustering expenses.[13] James Gleeson's initiative did not significantly bolster Fenian military rosters, however, because most Irish Americans had rarely donated more than a dollar or two to the Brotherhood at any given time. Moreover, by soliciting their long-term benefactors for even more assistance, Gleeson appeared to be just as ineffectual and corrupt as his predecessors. Maurice Woulfe would note, in another letter to his uncle in County Limerick three months later, that he was offended by prominent Fenians acting like a "Pack of Scoundrels going around picking the pockets of their foolish countrymen."[14] As during the Campobello escapade, the Roberts faction refused to aid fellow nationalists at a time of pressing need. O'Neill, in fact, assembled his supporters in Utica on February 27 to determine the feasibility of reinfiltrating Canada without once again provoking American military intervention.[15] Unswayed by earnest expatriate demonstrations in New York and Philadelphia, ostensibly pro-Irish politicians in Washington, D.C. ignored the IRB by offering little more to the Fenians besides the submission of bills and resolutions that had little chance of approval in the House of Representatives and the Senate. Instead of securing military assistance from private and public sources in America, insurgents belonging to the Directory and the IRB received tepid expressions of appreciation for their efforts.

Fenian provisional government leaders continued to prepare for a rebellion, even though McCafferty and O'Connor were forced to disperse their men. While former Fenian Brotherhood recruiter Godfrey Massey quickly conducted an inspection tour in Ireland, the forty-four-year-old Gustave Cluseret modified his original battle plans and agreed to assume overall command of IRB forces when half of the ten thousand Irish Fenians he originally requested were ready to fight. By stationing guerilla units in the principal Irish mountain ranges, rather than trying to fight a conventional campaign against the British, the former French general anticipated dividing his troops into ten- to fifteen-man units that would pester their enemy by cutting telegraph lines and raiding government outposts. Assuming that a series of small-scale victories would attract new recruits and instill greater confidence among skeptical IRB members, Cluseret would progressively engage more substantial targets until his army received diplomatic recognition from the United States. Massey, however, concluded that thirty-three thousand armed Irishmen were ready to mobilize, so he returned to London and persuaded his colleagues that implementing Cluseret's amended strategy was unnecessary.[16] Infuriated that Civil War veterans within the IRB hierarchy believed a full-fledged republican army had suddenly and inexplicably materialized, an exasperated Cluseret permanently severed his ties with the Fenian movement, returned to France, and became actively involved in French politics. His two aides-de-camp, however, remained willing to follow Massey into battle. Former Union army colored regiment colonel Octave Fariola and Victor Vifquain, a Belgian-born Nebraska resident who had won the Medal of Honor and had attempted to kidnap Jefferson Davis in 1862, were two of the IRB's most experienced military leaders on the eve of the revolt. Ironically, neither man was of Irish descent, but unlike Massey, they were not former blackmailers nor had they greatly exaggerated their credentials.

The loss of Cluseret was devastating. A *Légion d'honneur* recipient who had held field commands on three continents, the Paris native was also a republican idealist who had fought in the Crimea, Algeria, and France before he received his Union army commission.[17] Massey, at best, was an underexperienced cavalry officer ethically blemished by a past attempt to reap financial reward by threatening to reveal that he was the bastard son of an Irish aristocrat and a peasant girl. On the basis of his general demeanor, Massey had probably fought for the British in the Crimea and for the Confederacy during the Civil War, but in what capacity and for how long was clouded in mystery. Throughout the mid-1860s, he variously claimed that he had served in Texas and Virginia cavalry regiments, but a New Orleans police chief (who doubled as a local Fenian Brotherhood leader) reported in an October 1866 letter to O'Mahony that Massey had no proof of military service and, by his behavior, "most certainly was an English detective."[18] The possibility that he was an informant may have also been reflected in his illogical insistence that he use IRB forces to conventionally engage vastly superior British adversaries. Cluseret wrote in a magazine article five years after his resignation from the IRB that he had encountered a drunken Massey smoking expensive cigars and flaunting money on the night before he was to depart London to assume command of nationalist forces in Ireland.[19]

The greater wisdom of the rejected Cluseret guerrilla strategy was evident even before the IRB rebellion began on the night of March 5. Correctly forewarned by Coridon and other informants of imminent disturbances, British authorities preemptively arrested Massey inside the same Limerick Junction rail station through which the body of Terence MacManus had passed without incident five-and-a-half years earlier. Transferred to Kilmainham Gaol after a supposedly anti-Fenian draft newspaper article had been found in his possession, he soon abandoned an alibi that he was a *New York Herald* reporter, and agreed to become a prosecutorial witness because he feared prolonged separation from his wife. No other arrests occurred for several hours, however, because British authorities believed it would be easier to contain Fenian units in the open countryside. Romantic nationalists had erected imposing barricades across narrow thoroughfares in Paris and other European centers of revolutionary activity throughout 1848. Sunken roads and stone fences, conversely, would, at best, offer modest defensive cover to undertrained Fenians.[20]

Fenian and British expectations of an imminent military engagement proved unfounded when full IRB mobilization was impaired by a series of strategically insignificant shootouts. Inadequately trained and poorly equipped IRB men lacked the discipline to muster at predesignated locations without incident. Volunteers assigned to gather near the site of a brief 1798 skirmish had been instructed to avoid the Tallaght village police barracks. However, a contingent of about 150 Fenians approached the garrison from Roundtown at about 1:00 a.m. and ordered the fifteen occupants of the building to surrender.[21] When none of the constables complied, the twenty men within the group who had rifles instigated a brief gun battle, which resulted in the death of two nationalists and the seizure of a Fenian standard that was loosely modeled after the American Stars and Stripes.[22] Several weapons and at least six wagonloads of ammunition were also lost as the assailants fled. Besides weakening morale, the altercation fostered confusion in two other large bands of Fenians that had followed flares to gathering points in the Wicklow Mountains. Many rebel volunteers who had mustered in mild expectation of being led into battle by Stephens were flustered when they heard disturbances in the distance.[23]

Other Fenian initiatives on the outskirts of the Irish capital were equally inconsequential. One large contingent of men did nothing more than congregate on a private estate in Killakee. After a bullet struck him during an inconclusive skirmish in Dundrum village, former Union army colonel Michael Kerwin delegated command to a fellow Irish American named Patrick Lennon. Lennon, thereafter, started to set a community police barracks in Stepaside on fire so that the five occupants would be forced to surrender. These prisoners were later used as human shields in a firefight that began when the Fenians reached nearby Glencullen at 7:00 a.m. and engaged rifle-wielding officers who were defending the local police station. The safety of the detained constables was ultimately guaranteed, in exchange for the few weapons kept inside the facility. Having lost two more men to nonfatal bullet wounds and with no indication that the insurrection could be sustained through the morning, Lennon assigned a handful of men to guard the several constables he had captured, while the remainder of his troops dispersed.[24] Many of these rebels, like their colleagues who had deserted earlier in the night, safely returned to their homes, however, 207 predominately lower-middle-class Catholic Fenians were arrested within a day of the uprising.[25] Despite isolated reports that some circle leaders had vowed to shoot anyone who failed to report for duty, most of the estimated one thousand volunteers who mustered in greater Dublin had demonstrated an unequivocal commitment to the nationalist cause.[26] Yet only those people who were later indicted for treason would suffer for their nationalist beliefs.

A replication of the County Dublin Fenian strategy produced equally lackluster results throughout southern Ireland. Despite having no long-range plans and few weapons, Union army veteran William Mackey Lomasney led a reported one thousand men from Prayer Hill outside Cork on a long nighttime march through wind and heavy snow to a private residence. In search of firearms, the Cincinnati native and his men requisitioned a damaged pistol, a double-barreled bird gun, and five pitchforks. Recognizing later that their efforts to disable local rail and telegraphic lines were just as inconsequential as their capture of the Ballyknockan police barracks, Lomasney decided to disband his forces. Tipperary Fenians under the leadership of a locally born man who had served as a private in the Confederate army established a makeshift camp inside the earthen walls of the ancient Ballyhurst ring fort. Handicapped by an insufficient number of rifles and by conflict among his men, however, Thomas Francis Bourke, like Lomasney, could do little except attempt to forestall deteriorating morale. Irishmen unaccustomed to military discipline had become unnerved the day before, when an expatriate officer shot an IRB man as he tried to desert. Although many men escaped arrest when British forces overran his defenses the following morning, Bourke was captured and indicted for treason.[27] A fellow Irish American known only by the last name Dunne was more fortunate, as he and several of his men avoided arrest after shooting two civilians and unsuccessfully assaulting the Kilmallock police barracks.[28]

The eleven other Fenian disturbances that occurred throughout Ireland on March 5 were fairly insignificant. Assaults on two County Clare Coast Guard stations, a brief heated skirmish in Drogheda, and other random incidents all failed to sustain the rebellion any longer than O'Neill's foray onto the Niagara Peninsula a year earlier.[29] No activity whatsoever occurred in Connaught. Fenians in the predominately rural province had been promised that the former Cluseret aide-de-camp, Victor Vifquain, would lead them into battle. The thirty-year-old Belgian American had failed, however, to arrive in the province before the uprising began. Left to his own devices for the remainder of the summer, he eventually escaped to his native Belgium and was temporarily sheltered by a sister in Brussels.[30] Dublin government officials accordingly informed their London counterparts by telegraph on March 6 that "no event of any importance took place last night." The Home Secretary thus discounted rumors circulating in Parliament that martial law would need to be imposed in the four Irish provinces. *Hansard's* transcripts show that at the time British MPs were more concerned about an ongoing revolution in Crete than about an apparently fleeting domestic uprising.[31] Whereas politicians in England had dismissed the Fenian rebellion, the wives and daughters of several Anglo-Irish aristocrats residing near Mallow crowded into a local hotel for several days for their own safety.[32] If the Fenians had been better trained and equipped, affluent families throughout the rest of Munster might have been just as timid. One undercover Irish constable noted immediately before the uprising that even though he had not witnessed any outright instances of treasonous activity, a "frightful feeling of disloyalty" had been rampant among peasants and small-farm owners in the Iveragh Mountains.[33] A Tuam Fenian named William Faulkner had also betrayed the members of his circle before March 5, because some of his compatriots threatened to pike all defiantly loyalist members of the local gentry once the rebellion began.[34]

The rapid collapse of the IRB rebellion permanently eliminated any possibility that Irish nationalists would be able to establish a strategic alliance with the United States government. About ten thousand New Yorkers gathered outside Fenian Brotherhood headquarters on a rainy night, and an assembly of Bridgeport, Connecticut expatriates waited at the town train station to receive telegraph reports of the insurrection. These demonstrations probably swayed some congressional leaders to sign a joint resolution on March 11, calling on the Canadian government to release John MacMahon.[35] President Johnson rejected a request to recognize IRB insurgents as belligerents in mid-March, however, because he believed the Fenian provisional government in London lacked political legitimacy. Capitol Hill politicians, similarly, offered the rebels little more than a few Saint Patrick's Day sympathy resolutions. Hoping for immediate émigré financial assistance, thirty-four-year-old Thomas Kelly had written to the O'Mahony wing at the time of the rebellion that Irish independence would be a "fixed fact," if the expatriate community did not wait until "the last man [was] slaughtered before sending aid."[36] By the time such support became available, however, hundreds of Fenian expatriates had been arrested. One exception was William Barry. As he had promised, the relatively affluent Irish American had booked passage to Queenstown with arms for the IRB, but the rebellion was already over by the time he arrived. Left with little to do for the nationalist cause, Barry eventually fulfilled the dream of many Irish immigrants by returning home permanently. Over the following years, he found a bride and raised five children in County Cork.[37]

Aggressive British government efforts to capture Fenian suspects prevented determined Irish nationalists from sustaining the IRB revolt until assistance arrived from North America. The 10th Hussars (which Devoy had claimed was replete with republican partisans) and other army regiments formed "flying columns" that captured several Fenian fugitives in the countryside while detectives patrolled the cities.[38] Thefts attributed to Fenians continued for almost a year, but the last violent incident linked to the rebellion occurred at the end of March. Caught in a mountainside shoot-out near Kilclooney, twenty-one-year-old Civil War veteran John McClure surrendered to British authorities after his thirty-four-year-old compatriot, Peter O'Neill Crowley, was shot in the back and killed as he attempted to ford a stream. With the exception of the Scottish Highlands infantrymen who had helped John J. O'Connor and other Fenians flee into the West Kerry hills six weeks earlier, almost all government employees had remained loyal throughout the disturbances. In recognition of their dutiful service, Queen Victoria later conferred individual awards on several civil servants and exercised her monarchial right to acknowledge collective meritorious service to the United Kingdom by renaming Ireland's national police force the Royal Irish Constabulary.[39] British public opposition to the IRB was further evident in early May when John Bright and other Radical members of Parliament had no success passing a bill that would have provided for the lenient treatment of Fenian prisoners.[40]

Arrest records and press reports show that British authorities arraigned demographically similar nationalist suspects at the time of the March rebellion. Several IRB provincial operatives were identified in the *Cork Examiner* as laborers and carpenters. One butcher and one baker were also detained.[41] All but two of the overwhelmingly literate prisoners sent to Fremantle onboard the last convict ship to Australia in October 1867 were Catholics in their twenties. Predominately transporting former soldiers, such as future Boston-based journalist John Boyle O'Reilly, the *HMS Hougoumont* also conveyed several clerks from Munster. Only ten of the sixty-two Fenians on board were married.[42] This high percentage of educated felons was a reflection of the technological modernization that had occurred throughout Ireland since the 1830s. Improved commercial networks had greatly expedited the dissemination of newspapers and other sources of information to every province except Connaught. Exposure to the *Irish People* and other nationalist-oriented journals, in particular, had inspired Irishmen throughout the British Isles to express their political sentiments by joining the IRB.[43]

The limits of a general Irish civilian willingness to participate in nationalist activities, however, was also evident after the rebellion. In contrast to the relatively few Irishmen who had mustered for battle on the night of March 5, large crowds appeared along a County Cork roadside, as the body of the wealthy farmer Peter Crowley was transported from Mitchelstown to Ballymacoda for interment. Teams of pallbearers and a large cortege of cottier families also accompanied the deceased Fenian grandson of a United Irishman on an overland funeral procession that ultimately traveled over forty miles.[44] Although the interment of Terence MacManus demonstrates that such collective mourning was not unprecedented, it was becoming increasingly common. Irishmen perceived as nationalist martyrs would be similarly celebrated in death in the coming decades, as well as at the time of the Easter Rebellion and the Troubles in Northern Ireland.

The ensuing adjudication of 169 Fenians suspected of participating in the March 5 revolt crippled the IRB. Overall, seven Irish nationalists were acquitted, whereas 110 pled no contest and 52 others were sentenced upon the conclusion of their largely uncontroversial trials in Dublin and Cork.[45] Besides a bench decision by Justice John Keogh that denied courtroom translation assistance to two defendants who only spoke Gaelic, Fenian defense lawyers had difficulty arguing that judicial officials had mistreated their clients. Incriminating testimony provided by Coridon (whose name was commonly misspelled at the time with a "y") and his fellow informant, Massey, swayed many juries to convict several prominent Fenian defendants.[46] Altogether, eight men, including McCafferty, Bourke, and McClure, were sentenced to be hanged, drawn and quartered for committing high treason.[47] Many others were imprisoned for a blanket noncapital offense of attempting to overthrow the English monarchy.[48] Irate that one of their leaders had abetted the conviction of several IRB members, many Fenians coined the slang word "Masseyism" as a synonym for betrayal.

British subjects responded to the adjudication of Fenian suspects with a new, more permissive attitude toward the use of informants in criminal investigations. Detectives traditionally had been expected to obtain evidence in a spirit of "fair play" rather than through bribing greedy turncoats. Victorians were typically disgusted by men who valued their own self-interests more than the sanctity of mutual trust.[49] Whereas the twenty-six-year-old Coridon unsuccessfully demanded one half the value of all seized IRB weapons in exchange for his cooperation, an aristocrat briefly taken prisoner by a group of Tipperary Fenians refused to assist local constables after he was released by Bourke, because he did not want to "debase [himself] to the level of a common informer."[50] Henceforward, however, British subjects who had become acutely concerned about public safety did not object when law enforcement officials offered financial incentives to double agents in exchange for insider information that compromised the Irish republican movement.

Undeterred by the rapid collapse of the IRB rebellion and the prosecution of many Fenians suspects, O'Mahony faction leaders in New York organized a transatlantic military expedition in April 1867. Former Union army officer James Kelly purchased an impounded 138-ton hermaphrodite brigantine called the *Jacmel Packet,* as well as an accompanying cargo of rifles and ammunition at the same time that he recruited a large contingent of filibusterers. Christened in honor of its original owner, the Nassau-registered *Jacmel* and its contents had been confiscated by the United States Customs Service the previous December in Panama on suspicion that the ship had been used for smuggling arms to insurgents then at war against the Mexican emperor, Maximilian I. Several devoted volunteers still shared the same desire Patrick O'Brien had expressed a year earlier. In a March 12, 1866, letter to one of his local Fenian superiors, the Clinton, Iowa native had written, "I do not ask any favor from you all that I ask is to be sent on board a vessel of war and have the pleasure of saying i served my country in the capacity i was brought up."[51] Kelly recruited professional sailors or lower-middle-class Civil War veterans who were highly active members of New York and New England Fenian circles. Only three preselected volunteers failed to report for duty when the *Jacmel* was ready to sail. Yet these men were true die-hard members of a declining organization. One of the only other significant Brotherhood activities that occurred in North America in the weeks following the March revolt was an organized attempt to heckle Thomas D'Arcy McGee at a Montreal campaign rally.

Conveying valuable freight and several men to Ireland was well within the capability of the *Jacmel Packet*'s newly appointed captain, John Francis Kavanagh. A former member of the United States Navy who had served under the legendary David Farragut and other decorated captains, the Fenian mariner had begun his career as a seaman onboard the 234-foot *U.S.S San Jacinto* in 1859. Among the highlights of his first tour of duty was the liberation of 616 African slaves, who were rescued from a vessel near the mouth of the Congo River, and the early Civil War interception of a Confederate ship captained by future *C.S.S. Alabama* commander, Raphael Semmes. After indirectly participating in the controversial November 1861 high seas abduction of Mason and Slidell, Kavanagh returned to civilian life for two months and then reenlisted as an ensign. Detailed to the *U.S.S. Racer,* he participated in the capture of New Orleans, the shelling of Vicksburg, and the blockade of Charleston before receiving an honorable discharge in December 1865. Unlike the majority of the men under his command, who were single, Kavanagh had been married for one year when he was assigned to ferry the first of several anticipated Fenian contingents to Ireland on a small ship with a twenty-foot beam.[52]

Just as Kavanagh had enough maritime experience to transport Irish insurgents and weapons across the Atlantic, the field commander of the expedition, James E. Kerrigan, was qualified to lead the filibusterers once they landed in County Sligo, as initially planned. A lifelong New Yorker who had participated in a gang fight with the Dead Rabbits a decade earlier, the thirty-nine-year-old had twice parlayed his adventurous personal experiences to secure political office.[53] Having defied unpopular United States neutrality laws by escorting twenty-eight Irish American "vagabond" supporters of William Walker to Nicaragua in early 1856, the then-pro-Southern and proslavery Kerrigan temporarily became the mayor of Managua and later secured a seat on the New York City Council.[54] A subsequent one-year stint as a Union army colonel preceded election to Congress, where Kerrigan represented a predominately Irish section of Manhattan. On the basis of charisma alone, the one-term Independent Democrat was an asset to the *Jacmel* expedition.[55] His martial acumen, however, was somewhat lacking compared with that of his colleagues, as his only other military service had occurred during the Mexican-American War.[56]

Kerrigan's subordinate officers were equally devoted Irish nationalists who, with one exception, had considerable combat experience. William J. Nagle had fought in several harrowing altercations against Confederate forces during the Civil War. The Lewiston, New York-born Fenian had survived the bloody Battle of Antietam and been thrown to the ground three months later when a shell fragment ripped a haversack off his back during the reckless Union assault up Marye's Heights.[57] Present thereafter at Chancellorsville and other less significant skirmishes, Nagle had risen from the enlisted ranks to regimental colonel and had been mentioned as President Johnson's choice to serve as the United States Consul in Waterford before he became the military Inspector General of the O'Mahony wing.[58] The third officer assigned to the expedition was more of a Fenian intellectual than a soldier. John Warren had joined the Irish Brigade in August 1861, but had been dishonorably discharged as a captain after only six months in uniform. Eventually cleared of any misconduct by an Act of Congress, the thirty-one-year-old County Cork native had then edited a short-lived militant newspaper in Boston called *The Fenian Spirit*. He subsequently represented Massachusetts as a state head centre at the 1863 Chicago convention before venturing to Campobello with Kerrigan and serving as an O'Neill deputy during the Roberts faction's invasion of Canada.[59] Fenian appointments were not solely based on merit. George Richard Phelan, a former ranking officer in the Fifth United States army cavalry, and S.R. Tresilian, a thirty-eight-year-old County Cork Protestant who had been an Army Corps of Engineers veteran and prominent Sweeny deputy during the May 1866 Canadian invasion, were both subordinate to Warren and Kerrigan.[60]

Kelly instructed his five ranking officers and their underlings to prepare for their mission in secret. Members of the Roberts faction, whose headquarters were also located on the Lower East Side, had every incentive to sabotage rival initiatives that compromised their efforts to reinvade Canada. Federal law enforcement officials and British spies, moreover, continued to monitor Fenian activities. All the filibusterers were sequestered in a safe house for several days before their departure. They also boarded two separate vessels in several small groups when they embarked for Ireland on April 12. Men dispatched to the *Jacmel* were instructed to sail their ship no farther than the outskirts of New York harbor. Kavanagh was well enough known within the expatriate community to have aroused suspicion if he was spotted near any ocean-going ship, so he was among the many men who intermittently boarded a tugboat at a Canal Street wharf. By not carrying luggage, Brooklyn circle head John F. Fitzsimmons and journeyman shoemaker Daniel Lee appeared to be among similarly disposed friends who were preparing to enjoy a brief pleasure cruise.[61] Yet, instead of venturing to a nearby island for an afternoon picnic, the Fenian contingent traveled eighteen miles south to a preselected rendezvous point off Sandy Hook, New Jersey. However, Kavanagh did not see his vessel for the first time until the next day. The departure of the *Jacmel* may have been delayed by outfitting projects, because carpenters were still onboard the *Jacmel* as it passed the western edge of Long Island. The skeleton crew onboard the *Jacmel*, alternatively, may have postponed setting sail in the interest of stealth. In an attempt to avoid bureaucratic scrutiny, clearance papers had not been filed for the *Jacmel*, and such chicanery may have required an unusual departure time.[62] While the filibusterers were still in sight of land, the British diplomatic consul in Manhattan forwarded information to a fellow government official in Dublin that a weapons-laden Fenian ship was prepared to set sail.[63] The Roberts faction compromised the expedition by bribing a courier whom James Kelly had dispatched to Thomas Kelly. Instead of traveling across the Atlantic to promptly notify the provisional government that the *Jacmel* was en route to Connaught, the insubordinate messenger idled in England for two weeks per Roberts's instructions before he delivered a barely decipherable missive that announced Kavanagh's forthcoming arrival.

Kavanagh took additional security precautions as he cleared the Eastern Seaboard. With such a large cargo, the former United States Navy ensign would have no means of concealing his weapons stores in the event of a high seas inspection. By initially plotting a course for Bermuda, he thus hoped to avoid American and British ships that might be dispatched to the primary transatlantic shipping lanes as word of the Fenian expedition inevitably reached government officials. Although Kavanagh did not know that spies were already aware of his plans, he did wonder if observant Manhattan dockworkers might become suspicious when the steamer that had carried most of the filibusterers to Sandy Hook returned to port without passengers. Presumably, he also worried about the trustworthiness of the several carpenters who were transferred to a Boston-bound vessel after they finished building berths in the compact holds below deck on the first day of the expedition. These erstwhile passengers would presumably have known all about the vast number of weapons onboard the *Jacmel*. Besides three pieces of three-pound artillery, five thousand rifles of various manufacture and quality had been stowed on board the brigantine. Supplemented with crates full of revolvers, sabers, and 1.5 million rounds of ammunition, the *Jacmel* was a true arsenal. From afar, however, the ship appeared to be a nondescript merchant craft. Conforming to standard practice, the professional sailors onboard the poorly rigged *Jacmel* continued to communicate with the crews of other vessels they encountered to exchange information and confirm their nautical position.[64]

The highlight of the *Jacmel* voyage occurred during a noontime ceremony on Easter Sunday. After assembling all of the ship's hands on the quarterdeck, Kavanagh unsealed written orders he had received from James Kelly and the Fenian navy secretary John Powell before departing New York nine days earlier. Barring any unforeseen circumstances, the filibusterers were to unload their multi-item cargo near the northwest port city of Sligo, and then join their Irish comrades in battle while the *Jacmel* sailed back to the United States. Before their arrival, Kavanagh was at liberty to attack small British vessels and to scuttle his ship in the event of imminent capture.[65] Kavanagh was also instructed to confer promotions to each one of the filibusterers. Two recipients of midgrade Fenian commissions, thirty-three-year-old County Fermanagh–native Andrew Leonard and Boston painter Michael J. Green, were both brevetted to captain from their Union army rank of infantry lieutenant. William C. Nugent also deserved the lieutenant's commission that he received. Having lied that he was eighteen so he could enlist in the Seventy-Fourth New York Volunteers at the beginning of the Civil War, Nugent later reenlisted in the Second Massachusetts Artillery regiment at the height of the New York City Draft Riots and spent considerable time on guard duty at a Union fort in North Carolina before he had turned twenty.[66] Like their comrades, all three of these men cheered with fervor when Kavanagh concluded the ceremony by rechristening his vessel *Erin's Hope* and subsequently instructing some of his crewmen to replace the Union Jack that had been flying on the *Jacmel* mainmast to avoid unwanted attention with a green Irish standard. Once the Fenian sunburst emblem that had similarly adorned many Irish regimental flags during the Civil War was visible on the new ensign flying overhead, one bullet was fired in honor of each Irish county. Formality, as one eyewitness later testified in an Irish courtroom, was then followed by a morale-boosting afternoon of "amusement, fun, and frolic."[67] As a short story about a northern California Fenian was simultaneously being published in Mark Twain's first book, *The*

Celebrated Jumping Frog of Calaveras County and Other Sketches, a small ardent group of Irish militants was attempting to fulfill the original mission of the stateside Brotherhood.

Having covered twelve hundred miles before Easter Sunday, Kavanagh estimated at the time of the promotion and rechristening ceremony that he would reach the Irish coast by early May. Instead, an unsettling week-and-a-half of inclement weather slowed his progress, as the *Jacmel* passed roughly 350 miles south of Newfoundland on April 21. Sturdy enough to reach Australia a year earlier, the six-year-old brigantine had deteriorated after it was used primarily as a short-range Boston-New York transport ship. With poor sails and a heavy cargo, it rode low in the water as it crossed the Atlantic. Because of the ship's relative lack of mobility, Kavanagh barely avoided colliding with another vessel, as he spent prolonged periods sailing through thick fog.[68] When fair skies returned and their vessel was intact, the *Erin's Hope* crew resumed its preparations for arriving in Ireland. Weapons were transferred from crates and barrels into small, easy-to-unload boxes with bills of lading falsely marked for Cuba. Although the extended time at sea had diminished food stores to the point that everyone on board was occasionally allowed to consume only one meal a day, the sole report of conflict during the entire voyage had occurred at the beginning rather than at the end of the transatlantic crossing. Voicing his displeasure when he discovered that clearance papers had not been filed before the *Jacmel* was towed out of port, former infantry officer James Prendergast had demanded that the filibusterers return to shore so that they would not risk the ignominy of being arrested for piracy and, potentially, hanged. Incensed by such insubordinate behavior, Kerrigan had stripped Pendergrast of his Fenian commission, but Kavanagh later restored it as a conciliatory gesture.

Misinformed British authorities and Irish peasants vigilantly awaited the arrival of a Fenian flotilla while the *Erin's Hope* crew continued to sail across the Atlantic. As in 1865, Royal Navy ships patrolled the west Irish coast, while many Connemara and Munster peasants worried that they would be victimized in the event of an expatriate invasion. Rural laborers knew through oral tradition that foreign marauders had burned crops and slaughtered livestock; other Irish men and women welcomed a Fenian invasion. French victory at Castlebar in 1798 had demonstrated that even an undersupplied army had the capability to challenge superior British forces on Hibernian soil. Either by coincidence, or as an indication that hypervigilant Irish detectives assumed that the Fenian Brotherhood was smuggling firearms across the Atlantic, one British informant called attention to a national school pupil who had drawn a picture of a fictitious vessel with the christened name "Yankee Clipper" inscribed across its bow.[69] In truth, British officials and Irish peasants had nothing to fear. The crew of the *Erin's Hope* was plagued with problems over the ensuing three weeks. Assuming that he was near the mouth of the River Shannon when a crewman first spotted land just after dawn on May 10, Kavanagh turned his vessel north but overshot Sligo Bay a few days later. Reversing direction upon reaching the coast of County Donegal, Kavangah sailed southward for almost a week. Anxious to establish contact with Fenians on shore, he continuously transmitted coded signals by lantern, in the hope that IRB men were waiting to receive hundreds of Enfield and Spencer rifles in addition to Burnsides and Sharps breechloaders. Frustrated because the only attention they drew was from Coast Guard station hands requesting general information, the leaders of the expedition ultimately decided to send scouts onto the mainland.

Conveying filibusterers to the Irish coast proved as difficult as crossing the Atlantic and locating IRB operatives. Phillip Dougherty and Jeremiah O'Shea were rowed ashore on May 23, but failed to return the next day.[70] Kavanagh and Kerrigan then decided that their declining food supplies obligated them to land a raiding party in Sligo. A crewman accordingly hailed a local pilot at noon. Welcomed aboard, Michael Gallagher was immediately escorted to a cabin, where Warren and Nagle assessed the trustworthiness of their new acquaintance. Gallagher readily revealed that he was genuinely apolitical and knew nothing of nationalist activity in the area. The two filibusterers subsequently asked him to recite the Fenian oath as a security precaution. Initially refusing because he was a married man with children, Gallagher relented when Warren pointed a gun at his head and demanded that he formally join the Brotherhood before he manned the helm of the *Erin's Hope*.[71]

Kavanagh's plan to supervise an amphibious landing was thwarted by two incidents that occurred shortly after Gallagher was forced to join the IRB. Free of injury or accident throughout the entire transatlantic voyage, two crewmen were wounded when four-year Union army veteran Daniel Buckley unintentionally discharged a firearm that he was cleaning in preparation for their scheduled assault. James Connor was struck in his thigh and a ship's cook from New York named James J. Nolan was wounded in one of his ankles by the same bullet from Buckley's weapon. The appearance of IRB messenger Richard O'Sullivan Burke that evening occurred at the same time that many *Erin's Hope* filibusterers were worried that the accidental shooting was an ominous harbinger. They were correct. The twenty-seven-year-old Burke had only bad news to deliver when he hailed his fellow expatriates in code from the deck of a chartered fishing boat. In addition to reporting that no new rebel activity had occurred since the *Jacmel* had departed New York City, Burke informed his fellow expatriates during a one-hour briefing that the messenger who had been dispatched to the provisional government in April had dawdled in London for twelve days before delivering tampered messages to the IRB leadership.[72] The *Erin's Hope* mission had been made in vain. Now, at best, Kavanagh and his men could provide the IRB with some assistance and hope that Irish Fenians would rally again shortly.

The men of the *Erin's Hope* hastily prepared their return to sea after Burke departed for Sligo with three ranking filibusterers in his company. Both Connor and Nolan required prompt medical attention, so Kavanagh instructed Gallagher and two escorts to ferry them to a safe house that Burke had identified. Time permitting, they were to search for Dougherty and O'Shea, but without fail return to the ship before sunrise.[73] Kavanagh's efforts were compromised when Gallagher abandoned the wounded Fenians as soon as their other escorts departed. The filibusterers later requested assistance from a seaweed farmer, but a Coast Guard officer arrested them before he could return with a cart. Under subsequent interrogation, the twenty-five-year-old Nolan said that he and Connor had been transported ashore after being shot during a fight onboard a Spanish ship that was conveying fruit from Malaga to Glasgow.[74] Such a dubious alibi aroused much suspicion. Kavanagh, however, had avoided an altercation with a Royal Navy warship by two hours and reached open waters without Dougherty and O'Shea before the detainees were linked to the Fenian movement. Burke himself was equally fortunate as he fled Connaught without formally vacating the Sligo Imperial Hotel lodgings he had rented in the company of a hired valet. Many local aristocrats had invited the apparently wealthy vacationer into their homes for dinner and billiards; not until the end of the year did they learn that their guest was an IRB operative.[75]

Disappointment and danger continued to plague the remaining members of the *Erin's Hope* crew over the next few days. Kavanagh followed Burke's earlier instructions to signal County Kerry IRB scouts by lowering his jib-sail once he reached Toe Head, but no contacts were ever established. With food and water rations continuing to diminish, thirty-two of the lower-ranking filibusterers unilaterally voted in favor of returning home by slightly more than a two-to-one margin. When informed of this quasi-mutinous decision, Kavanagh retorted that the remaining supplies onboard could, at best, sustain a small crew back across the Atlantic. Other than depositing several men onshore immediately, the only possible way of keeping everyone together, he argued, would be to seek shelter among the Gaelic-speaking population of the distant Scottish Herbides.[76] The latter option was risky because the daily ration had been reduced to little more than one biscuit and a pint of rainwater. The filibusterers accordingly agreed to escort their cargo ashore. The urgency of this initiative was evident almost immediately. Outrunning a Coast Guard rowboat near a beach between Glandore and Gally Head was a mere nuisance compared with a more threatening early evening encounter with an ironclad frigate called the *HMS Black Prince*. The former Young Irelander and Freemason S. R. Tresilian moved the three field cannons from the cargo bay to the top deck. With enveloping darkness, however, none of the weapons needed to be fired, and the Fenians slipped away from a naval engagement they likely would have lost.[77]

While the men onboard the *Erin's Hope* were sailing farther eastward, Thomas Bourke almost became the first Fenian political martyr. Even though he had been sentenced to death for his role in leading Tipperary Fenians during the March 5 rebellion, Bourke had believed that British radicals would fight to have his sentence commuted to penal servitude. Bradlaugh and his colleagues had done little to abet IRB forces the previous spring, but they had later interceded to prevent seven republicans from being hanged because they did not want Fenian prisoners to be treated in the same brutal manner that captured Jamaican rebels had been a year earlier. Bourke, moreover, was not guilty of a heinous crime.[78] He and his men had only dismantled some telegraph poles and fired one return volley at approaching British soldiers before they were captured at Ballyhurst. In addition, he had promptly released the local aristocrat whom some of his men had taken prisoner.[79] Nevertheless, he came within one day of execution, in part, because he had refused a conditional pardon from the British government after being convicted of seditious activity and deported in 1865. Through the efforts of Secretary of State Seward, Mazzini, and Cardinal Cullen (who usually declined to meet with British officials unless the occasion was of utmost importance), Bourke was saved from being hanged, drawn, and beheaded a day before his scheduled execution on May 29.[80] With a transatlantic diplomatic crisis averted, a gallows was dismantled and Bourke prepared to spend the rest of his life behind bars. The Bourke case, however, foreshadowed extensive State Department assistance to both the *Erin's Hope* filibusterers, who were then off the Munster coast, and other Fenians who were already incarcerated.

Continued misfortune and bad judgment led to the arrest of several additional *Erin's Hope* filibusterers when they attempted to land in Dungarvan Bay on June 1. As initially planned, Nagle and Warren were to establish contact with local IRB representatives in County Waterford, while most of the other men encamped on nearby Ballycotton Island to await further instructions.[81] Tresilian would remain onboard the *Erin's Hope* with a sick Kerrigan and a few crewmen in expectation of overseeing the off-loading of their arms and ammunition stows or of supervising the sinking of their ship if they were attacked by a superior vessel. Kavanagh decided to send his entire landing party directly to the Irish mainland, however, when the onset of heavy morning fog provided good cover. Accordingly, the crew of a small fishing boat was hailed and an agreement was reached whereby two men were to be ferried to a nearby beach in exchange for two pounds sterling. To the surprise of Patrick Whelan and his two sons, however, twenty-four men scurried onto the two-ton launch moments after both vessels pulled alongside one another. Instead of proceeding directly ashore, moreover, the Fenian passengers informed the fishermen that they would remain at sea until they could land that evening under cover of darkness.

Such duplicity expedited the final collapse of the *Erin's Hope* expedition. Angered that he had been swindled, Whelan retaliated by steering his craft directly toward a Coast Guard station after his passengers decided that continued poor visibility permitted them to disregard their orders to remain in the bay until nightfall. When the sky abruptly cleared not long thereafter, however, the Fenians realized that they could easily be spotted. Crouching beneath the gunwales, they demanded to be deposited elsewhere. After another two-mile leg across the harbor, the overcrowded vessel ran aground on a sand bar called the Ring Strand. Impatiently, the Fenians tossed some coins to their escorts and waded to the beach in waist-deep water that occasionally swelled to their armpits.[82] Although reaching land was somewhat reassuring, the arrival of the filibusterers had been witnessed by a British official who thought it was unusual to see so many men abruptly disembark from such a small craft.

Irish constables apprehended almost all the remarkably conspicuous Fenian filibusterers within a day of their arrival onshore. The filibusters had divided into small groups by the time they passed through a fishing village called Ballinagoul, yet they remained easy to identify. Many of the expatriates were distinguished by their abundant facial hair, personal possessions, and soaked American-style apparel. With a "luxuriant" mustache, John Warren drew attention to himself and William Nagle even before they were arrested in Ringville.[83] Having spent the last two months at sea, other filibusterers with distinctive beards and thick whiskers awkwardly walked westward through the Drumlin Hills toward Kiely's Cross and Youghal. Former Manhattan circle head and 99th regiment veteran Augustine E. Costello had only been ashore for two hours when he was detained. New York City natives John Cade and John F. Fitzsimmons eluded capture until they drew undue attention by taking refuge in a local tavern. Patrick J. Kain unwittingly betrayed himself and another fellow 99th New York veteran named Frederick Fitzgibbon, meanwhile, by retaining an opal-inlaid gold ring, as well as an ornate watch guard, after he and his cohort exchanged their damp clothes for some threadbare shirts and trousers.[84] Traveling twelve miles before they were apprehended, Munster native Daniel Buckley and James Lawless were arrested by a subconstable on a bridge spanning the Blackwater River. In all, twenty men who came ashore inadvertently traded cramped berths and scant nourishment for jail cells fouled by drunks and petty felons.[85] Four other men avoided capture, with one man returning to the United States by traveling under an assumed name.[86]

Local reaction to the landing of the expatriates varied along class lines. Aristocratic magistrates presiding over the Petty Sessions trials of a sheep stealer and an army deserter in Dungarvan summarily adjourned after a flustered constable rushed before the bench to announce that sixty-four Fenians had just landed. The soldier in the dock promptly escaped.[87] Less affluent ladies residing in the town, on the other hand, provided home-cooked meals with ham, mutton, and beef to the "well-dressed . . . fine, able, intelligent [and] young" filibusters before they were identified in court by the ubiquitous John Coridon.[88] It is possible that this aid was inspired by a degree of amorous attraction, as the prisoners were predominately single and, according to press reports, ranged in age from eighteen to twenty-eight.[89] Dungarvan protesters who rioted in support of the filibusters counterbalanced previous reports that Irish peasants feared an expatriate invasion. A bacon salter died and thirty-eight others were injured when an estimated mob of eight thousand threw rocks and shoes at the forty-two policemen assigned to escort the prisoners and Coridon to Dublin on June 14.[90] Warren, who had claimed that he was a nonpartisan journalist, later wrote that an occasional old woman also appeared either to say prayers for the prisoners or to utter "maledictions" at their guards as they were marched through the Leinster countryside. In essence, the detained *Erin's Hope* filibusters became nationalist heroes, because they had been remanded without clearly committing any crime on British soil.

The men who stayed onboard the *Erin's Hope* initially suffered just as much as their imprisoned former shipmates. Despite limited supplies, Kavanagh hovered south of Dungarvan Bay for two days, hoping that the weapons and ammunition stored in his ship's hold could still be transferred ashore. When no word came from any of the filibusters on land, Kavanagh sailed past his native County Waterford to the English Channel, where he remained in sight of the Cornish coast for four days. As during the previous week, Royal Navy frigates were a constant nuisance to the former United States Navy ensign, in part because one of the captured filibusters, William F. Million, had immediately offered information about the *Erin's Hope* that was forwarded to Admiralty officials.[91] Kavanagh also had to fend off commission-seeking harbor pilots by saying that he was a merchant sea captain who was waiting for a strong breeze to propel his vessel out to open water.[92] As prearranged with Nagle, Kavanagh returned to the southeast Irish coast and waited near Mine Head in hope that a signal would be sent from shore. When none came after another four days of anxious waiting, Kavanagh decided that he could no longer delay his return to the United States without obtaining additional supplies. With little left in their original stores, besides six barrels of various foods, a box of fish, and one-third standard water rations, the remaining men onboard the *Erin's Hope* headed home with their mission unfulfilled.[93]

Alone for several weeks in the open Atlantic, Kavanagh and his crew were finally relieved from their hunger and thirst when they received desperately needed foodstuffs from a fishing vessel off the coast of Newfoundland. With additional provisions from another ship just east of Boston, they were able to return to New York on August 1. At sea altogether for 103 days, the returning filibusterers had traveled 9,265 miles and suffered no casualties, besides having to put a deathly ill pilot named William Sweetman ashore in Connecticut.[94] Although a failure, the mission was long portrayed as a success. Kavanagh later falsely claimed in the New York edition of the *Irish People* that he and his men could be credited for the sinking of three British gunboats. The Irish American public, however, had no reason to believe otherwise at a time when newspaper reporting was often inconsistent.[95] Public lectures offered by Kerrigan and Tresilian, moreover, neglected to reveal that the only significant outcome of the *Erin's Hope* expedition had been British government allocation of additional state funds to the military and the royal court system.

The crew of the *Erin's Hope* returned to an expatriate nationalist community that continued to be divided by the remnants of the two Fenian Brotherhood factions. William Roberts had dispatched a series of Paris-bound deputies, while the *Erin's Hope* was en route to Sligo to negotiate an agreement with the remaining members of the British-based IRB. Roberts himself sailed for France on June 1 to finalize an accord between the two parties in Paris on July 4 and to visit the fairgrounds of the acclaimed 1867 Exposition Universelle.[96] Under the terms of the accord, Roberts agreed that any future American-based invasion of Canada would coincide with a rebellion in Ireland.[97] Yet the conclusion of this pact did little to revive an organization that had lost so much political clout over the previous year. Irish public confidence in the movement had diminished so significantly that Fenian bonds sold for twenty cents on the dollar.[98] Worse yet, Thomas Francis Meagher mysteriously drowned in the Upper Missouri River on July 1, 1867. A Men of Action convention in Cleveland the following September is remembered today for little more than O'Neill's election as a Fenian senator and a rejected floor motion to admit women as full members into the organization. Despite the vigorous efforts of their female colleagues, a majority of the members determined that the "fairer sex" could not keep secrets.[99]

Such dissension facilitated the establishment of a new rival Irish nationalist organization called the Clan na Gael. Founded by a Cork native who was later killed during a widely publicized Arctic expedition, the Clan (which was also known as the United Brotherhood) was committed to fulfilling the original objectives of the IRB. In emulation of the Freemasons, each Clan member voted in favor or against the admission of new members. Approved recruits placed their left hand on a pocket-sized prayer book and recited a loyalty vow that was intended to be less offensive to Catholic Church leaders than the oath of the Fenian Brotherhood. Initiates were taught how to communicate covertly. Although some of these measures were laughable (the Clan used a pedantic written code, in which all messages were encrypted by substituting each character with the next highest number or the letter that followed it in the alphabet), they were positive steps away from bad Fenian precedents.

Die-hard O'Mahony wing supporters attempted to aid the detained *Erin's Hope* filibusterers and other Fenians in British penitentiaries throughout the remainder of 1867. Only United States diplomatic officials, however, had the political muscle to call for the humane treatment and expedited release of Irish nationalist prisoners. The Dublin-based United States counsul to Ireland, William West, questioned the continued incarceration of many expatriate Fenians by writing several hundred letters to high-ranking British officials. In addition to providing many reasons why the expatriates should be furloughed, West requested that all Fenian suspects be transferred from Kilmainham Gaol to the somewhat more salubrious Mountjoy Prison. Such an initiative was of utmost importance to the physical and mental health of several *Erin's Hope* filibusterers. British prison regulations distinguished little between remanded suspects and convicted felons, so Fenians awaiting adjudication were provided with meager rations and little time to exercise. Nagle reported in a letter to West, written while he was in pretrial detention, that he suffered from intermittent fever and was kept in solitary confinement at all times of the day except during his two-hour recreation period. In isolation, he said, "his own words had become strange to him."[100] Warren suffered from diminishing eyesight, as he was subjected to a similar daily schedule in an inadequately lit eight-by-ten-foot cell.[101]

Irish nationalist leaders had ample opportunity to use alleged British government maltreatment of Fenian prisoners for propaganda purposes. Prison guards threatened to corporally punish several *Erin's Hope* filibusterers in early December, after they twice disobeyed a rule that prohibited inmates from placing their hands in their trouser pockets when they were outdoors.[102] William C. Nugent was beaten with a lead rod and then placed in solitary confinement for seventy-two hours after he provokingly raised a stool during a verbal altercation with a deputy warden. The Irish-born, Dennis O'Connor, a former plumber, compromised his normally strong physical appearance, moreover, when he received nine weeks bread and water rations for disobeying an order to remove his hat.[103]

Serving as an intermediary between the American Fenian community and politicians in Washington who still wanted to curry Irish votes, West thus eventually became the recipient of several hundred letters from expatriate families and diplomatic officials in the United States. One such missive addressed to him on August 27, 1867, read, "You would grant a favor to the mother of Daniel J. Buckley by pleading on his behalf, as he was great help to support a widowed mother and family."[104] As subsequent events would prove, West would have aided the Fenians and eased his official diplomatic workload if he had promptly attended to Mrs. Buckley's appeal.

Prolonged deprivation and psychological baiting weakened the patriotic resolve of many incarcerated *Erin's Hope* filibusterers. Upon their eventual return to their native New York, John P. Murray and former cabinet-maker Patrick Coogan submitted affidavits, later published in the Irish American press, that they and another detainee named John Cade had been offered £100 and government employment upon their release if they incriminated their fellow prisoners.[105] Some of their comrades, however, were less resilient. To the dismay of more stalwart filibusterers, Daniel Buckley became the second member of the *Erin's Hope* expedition to betray his peers when he agreed, in September, to become a crown witness in exchange for unspecified future compensation. Having been a devoted Fenian in his twenties with no dependents, Buckley was an unlikely turncoat. Yet having witnessed the Campobello fiasco firsthand before participating in the failed *Erin's Hope* expedition, he may have decided that further privation was pointless because the Fenians had no chance of securing Irish independence. He may have also been a truculent individualist. During the Civil War, he had resigned a cavalry commission and reenlisted as an infantry private after he began to suspect a promotion board had intentionally underscored one of his exams.[106] Somewhat more resolute prisoners refused to betray their comrades but eventually agreed to sign confessions in exchange for their release. The wounded Nolan admitted that he had participated in a subversive military expedition so that he could be deported and returned to his wife and only child.[107] No different from past experiences, Irish nationalist initiatives had been thwarted by insiders who lacked the resolve to protect their comrades from arrest and from British strong-arming.

Traitors, such as Buckley, Coridon, and Massey, were exceptionally self-interested people among steadfast militants who attempted to establish an Irish republic. Despite the embarrassing failure of two Fenian incursions into Canadian territory and the lackluster March rebellion in Ireland, the global Irish community increasingly lauded nationalists who had distinguished themselves from dishonorable informants and sunshine patriots. William Mackey Lomasney gained favorable notice for robbing gun shops. Released prisoners, including

Patrick Hasson, were regarded as innocent victims of tyranny.[108] Arrested in Ireland before he could fulfill his dream of assisting the IRB, the former quartermaster had been routinely harassed while incarcerated for six months in a Belfast prison. Before reenlisting in the United States Army as a lieutenant upon his return to America in September 1866, he wrote to Secretary of State Seward that he had been threatened with punishment merely for writing a letter that encouraged a female friend to toast the United States on the Fourth of July. He also noted "visitors . . . were constantly admitted to gratify their curiosity in having a look at the Fenian prisoners."[109] Fenian critics, of course, still abounded. Whereas British journalists portrayed the IRB as a collection of people inferior to civilized Anglo-Saxons, Cardinal Cullen wrote just after the insurrection that the rebels had acted like "foolish children, prattling about everything.[110] Yet even some longstanding IRB opponents acknowledged the patriotism of the March 5 rebels. In private correspondence, the Fenian critic John Martin wrote nine days after the uprising:

> I regard [the rebellion] as an insane attempt of patriotic and virtuous men. Their leaders I suppose to have tempted them by misrepresentations and exaggerations of the provision in arms, etc., and of the numbers pledged to obey Mr. Stephens. . . . Surely never were more innocent and generous rebels than these; not a single act of pillage, of cruelty, or injury to person or property, have they committed since they have been up as outlaws.[111]

Retrospective admiration and accolades for the IRB masked that the Fenian movement became a defensive rather than an offense-oriented organization after mid-1867. Instead of launching rebellions, Irish republican leaders would henceforward devote most of their time to rescuing colleagues from prison and entreating longstanding donors to underwrite increasingly foolhardy initiatives. Occasional successes during a period of slow decline energized Irishmen and expatriates who remained unswervingly committed to the establishment of an independent Ireland.

7

FENIANISM ON THE DEFENSIVE

The most significant Fenian activity occurred in England and Canada after the failed *Erin's Hope* expedition. Increasingly operating on the defensive, IRB members primarily devoted their collective energy to liberating comrades from prison, while other militants enunciated their republican sentiments as defendants in British courtrooms. The open-air rescue of Thomas Kelly and an associate from custody in September 1867 was a tremendous nationalist victory that was overshadowed two months later when three questionably guilty perpetrators of the crime were hanged in Manchester. An attempt to liberate Richard O'Sullivan Burke from a London prison at the end of the year was an outright disaster that led to the death of a dozen civilians and the execution of another Fenian. Despite widespread English revulsion toward the Irish after these two events occurred, British prime minister William Gladstone emerged as a sincere advocate of Irish reform in the late 1860s. As part of a longstanding desire to rectify past injustices against the Irish people, the powerful Liberal party leader furloughed several republican prisoners who had been arrested in accordance with the *Habeas Corpus* Suspension Act and abolished state subsidies to the Church of Ireland. After a decade of Fenian efforts to lead Ireland into a new era, a British statesman—ironically—became a principal instigator of the slow process that eventually led to the creation of the Irish Free State in 1922. John O'Neill, conversely, embarrassed Fenians throughout the world when he once again attempted to invade Canada in May 1870.

A new era in the history of the Fenian movement began after a routine arrest in the fall of 1867. Having been reconfirmed as IRB leader at a clandestine convention in Manchester the previous summer, Thomas Kelly had conducted underground activities in England throughout the early fall. On the night of September 11, Kelly and expatriate assistant Timothy Deasy had just departed an intra-Brotherhood court-martial when they were arrested for loitering in a city park. Presumed to be vagrants, the two Fenians would have been booked under the aliases they had provided and released if a constable had not discovered a keepsake inscribed with the name "Kelly" in the possession of the Tenth Ohio Infantry veteran. When Coridon was summoned from London thereafter to identify the two mystery prisoners, British authorities confirmed that they had captured the most powerful Irish republican in the United Kingdom as well as a resourceful Fenian who had served in the Ninth Massachusetts Infantry. Irish nationalist republicans still at large recognized that the already tenuous future of the Fenian movement was in jeopardy if their two colleagues were not promptly extricated from custody. The number of IRB circles in Manchester had already dropped from nine to three since the previous March.[1] Without a morale-boosting rescue, the organization might disintegrate not only in the Midlands, but also throughout the British Isles.

The rescue of Kelly and Deasy was simple, quick, and inadvertently tragic. On the night of September 17, Edward O'Meagher Condon, Toronto Fenian circle founder and Irish Brigade veteran, devised a plan to rescue his two compatriots the following afternoon. After their arraignment in the Manchester Municipal Court, Kelly, Deasy, and a few petty criminals would be transferred to the nearby Bellevue Gaol in a horse-drawn carriage by way of Hyde Road. While waiting for a messenger to signal that the two expatriate IRB leaders were in transit, preselected Fenian volunteers would loiter in one of several saloons located near a railway arch between the two facilities. At the time of the briefing, all the designated assailants were instructed to avoid bloodshed and use their revolvers sparingly. The dozen constables assigned to escort the detainees, conversely, had taken limited precautions to protect themselves before the prisoner transfer began at about 3:00 p.m. Sergeant Charles Brett, the lone officer armed with a cutlass, rode inside the coach with the prisoners while his eleven associates carried truncheons. Why all the officers were not better armed is puzzling given that a knife-wielding Irishman unaffiliated with Condon had caused a brief disturbance as Kelly and Deasy were led down the front steps of the courthouse.[2] Accordingly, many members of the guard detail fled when two Fenians darted out into the road and shot over the reinsmen and at one of their horses. While dodging rocks thrown by civilian onlookers, several assailants were able to wedge open a portal on the roof of the vehicle before they demanded that Brett surrender his keys. A Fenian fired at the trapdoor padlock when he refused to comply with the order. The door to the coach held, but a bullet fragment fatally ricocheted into Brett's head. In fear for her own life, one of the female detainees hurriedly stripped the keys from Brett's body and passed them through the window to the attackers. Gates to individual compartments respectively holding the two IRB prisoners were opened, and the two Fenians fled to a safe house. Kelly and Deasy were free men once bricks were used to break manacles from their wrists. A prolonged period of organizational torpor ended, as the IRB achieved its greatest success since the rescue of Stephens two years earlier.

British authorities mobilized a massive manhunt for Kelly and Deasy in conjunction with an aggressive attempt to ferret the murderers of Charles Brett out of the Midlands Irish immigrant community. Security details patrolled ports and railway stations. Constables, in the meantime, were ordered to inspect coffins, because government-paid informants had reported that IRB operatives were using funeral corteges to secretly convey fugitives to safety.[3] Peripheral rescue team members (such as a Fenian who escorted two would-be female accomplices away from the scene of the crime before the carriage approached) were promptly arrested. Kelly and Deasy, nevertheless, both escaped to the United States. Journalists later reported that Kelly lived lavishly as the husband of a rich Italian heiress; in reality, the Galway native worked for several years with other former Fenians as a federal customs official in New York.[4] Deasy parlayed his military experience as a Battle of Cold Harbor veteran and leader of the IRB uprising in Cork into a successful political career. In addition to becoming a city councilman in his hometown of Lawrence, the former IRB operative and Sweeny invasion filibusterer was elected to the Massachusetts state legislature in 1876.[5] Many Fenians who had risked their lives so that these two men would not wallow in a British prison for years were considerably less fortunate. An English public that had generally feared the outbreak of an insurrection since the height of the Chartist movement readily assisted British government efforts to apprehend the people responsible for Charles Brett's death.[6]

Practically every man in Lancashire who spoke with a brogue was suspected of treason in the fall of 1867, in large part because the English press published a barrage of anti-Irish rhetoric. On October 1, the editors of the *London Times* promulgated a Darwinian argument that the Irish republican movement had to be contained because "The Fenian conspiracies [were] carrying [an otherwise advancing society] back a whole century."[7] By linking militant Irish nationalists to mischievous labor radicals and a giant ethereal goddess of death in an incendiary October 12th illustration called "The Order of the Day; or Unions and Fenians,"[8] John Tenniel concurrently suggested that IRB operatives were a threat to English society. In the *Punch* editorial cartoon, beastly looking Irishmen obey a phantom behemoth who stomped on a scale of justice that lay in front of a fallen constable. Yet despite a prejudiced media, only five of twenty-eight indicted Irishmen were actually found guilty of murdering Sergeant Brett. The conviction of these suspects, moreover, was questionable. Thomas Maguire protested to a presiding judge that he had been falsely incriminated by inconsistent and illegally obtained evidence. Edward Condon, William Allen, Michael Larkin, and Michael O'Brien, likewise, insisted that they were innocent, but were sentenced to death.

The contentious trial of three *Erin's Hope* filibusterers in Dublin at the same time as the Charles Brett murder trial strongly suggested that British government leaders were unlikely to commute the capital convictions of Kelly and Deasy's rescuers. Because he was an American citizen, William Nagle initially attempted to win a procedural acquittal in emulation of his Fenian compatriot John McCafferty. The mastermind of the aborted Chester Arsenal raid, McCafferty had been released from British custody in 1865, when court officials could not accommodate his right to be tried for sedition by a jury equally comprised of foreigners and British subjects. Nagle, however, was bound over to a later date when bailiffs failed to empanel a so-called jury *de mediatate lingue*. John Warren's similar petition to have a group of multinationals determine his guilt or innocence proved as ineffectual as when Thomas Francis Bourke had unsuccessfully submitted the same request during his trial five months earlier. By the provisions of an extant English feudal law that unequivocally prohibited anyone born in the United Kingdom from ever renouncing fealty to the British sovereign, the naturalized American was officially recognized as a native Irishman shortly before crown prosecutors started to present their case against him.

Warren was unable to secure an acquittal once his trial began because he unwisely dismissed an attorney that American consular officials had retained for him at the behest of William Seward.[9] Over the course of several hours, Coridon, Massey, and the Irish harbor pilot Michael Gallagher supplemented the signed confessions of other *Erin's Hope* filibusterers by testifying that the defendant had committed treason in the United States and while crossing the Atlantic Ocean the previous spring. Convicted and sentenced to fifteen years of hard labor after he strained to read an inflammatory anti-English personal statement, Warren was assigned to Millbank Prison.[10] Augustine Costello was similarly unable to avoid incarceration. A mixed Catholic and Protestant jury failed to return a verdict against him at the end of a daylong trial, but he was retried the following morning and sentenced to twelve years of hard labor. The County Galway native was eventually transferred across the Irish Sea under tight security to prevent another Manchester rescue attempt. After serving a standard six-month period of solitary confinement, Costello was assigned to a full-time work detail, like Warren and other Fenian convicts.

The plight of Warren, Costello, and dozens of other Fenian prisoners was overshadowed in the closing weeks of 1867 by the looming execution of the men who had been convicted of murdering Charles Brett. Eight people were treated for head wounds at the Birmingham City Hospital after they participated in a brawl between local expatriates and Tory fanatics who demanded that Kelly and Deasy's rescuers be hanged.[11] English constables arrested Richard O'Sullivan Burke and a cousin of James Stephens without a warrant five days later, while the two IRB men were attending a Charles Bradlaugh–led clemency demonstration in the Clerkenwell section of London. Members of the English working class were noticeably present at these and other pro-Fenian public meetings. Friedrich Engels (who decorated his Manchester home at the time with the mid-nineteenth-century Irish republican colors of green and black) wrote to a colleague on November 8, "The London proletarians declare every day more openly for the Fenians."[12] Many of these urban laborers had just obtained suffrage with the passage of the 1867 Reform Bill. Educated middle- and upper-class Englishmen ultimately determined the fate of the Manchester convicts, however. The Royal Marine Thomas Maguire received an unconditional pardon on November 21, for instance, when several English journalists and politicians openly criticized the highly suspect conviction of an active-duty soldier who had spent much of the previous decade either at sea or at British military outposts in Asia. Although the same evidence had been used to incriminate all five defendants, Condon, Larkin, Allen, and O'Brien were not automatically granted any mercy. This judicial inconsistency was primarily the product of incendiary press reports and a reactionary British bureaucracy. Rumors of a planned Fenian strike in Holyhead and a tall tale from Paris that IRB operatives were preparing to attack British naval vessels helped sustain anti-Irish feelings in Great Britain.[13] English authorities concluded, moreover, that harsher punishment of Fenian criminals was in order, because militant activities had continued to occur despite the lenient sentencing of other IRB members earlier in the year.[14]

The exoneration of Maguire ultimately facilitated last-minute American diplomatic efforts to save Condon from the gallows. As part of his ongoing commitment to aid detained Fenians who had loyally served in the Union army, William Seward instructed the United States ambassador to Great Britain, Charles Francis Adams, to request that Condon and O'Brien be resentenced to hard labor. Adams had considerably more sympathy for the English than the Irish, but he did secure a commutation for Condon because he was a first-time offender. Adams ignored additional instructions to intercede on behalf of O'Brien, however, because American legation officials had helped ensure that the Civil War veteran would not be imprisoned after he had been convicted of illegal weapons possession during the previous Winter Assizes in Liverpool.[15] Irish republican militants, in Adams's estimation, did not deserve second chances. As a result, O'Brien and his two alleged accomplices resigned themselves to prepare for death at Salford Prison. Anticipating large crowds and a possible Fenian disturbance during the November 25 execution, the official British hangman, William Calcraft, supervised the construction of a fenced, thirty-foot-high scaffold that rested on an exterior prison wall. Manchester police officials used a detailed city map to determine where they would deploy about 2,500 security officers and where they would erect several four-foot barriers.[16]

The patriotic resolve of the three Fenians awaiting execution was highly evident during their final hours of life. Several relatives and a trio of Catholic priests consoled Allen, Larkin, and O'Brien when they were not writing defiant professions of innocence. Although Allen was not allowed to visit with his fiancée one last time, O'Brien was permitted to speak with some relatives, and Larkin was able to bid his immediate family farewell. Arising well before dawn, the men attended Mass and ate a few slices of toast before they were marched to the gallows at 8:00 a.m. with a clergyman at each of their sides.[17] Newspaper reports issued the next day noted that Kelly and Deasy's rescuers confidently confronted their fate through prayer. Allen repeatedly uttered, "Lord have mercy on us," as he appeared before a crowd enveloped in a thick fog. O'Brien, meanwhile, gazed at a crucifix and said, "Christ hear us, Christ graciously hear us." Spiritual supplications continued to be heard over a din of jeers and feminine lamentations as Calcraft and his assistant covered the Fenians' faces and bound their ankles. Sharing a few last words of fraternity among themselves, the men were then hanged for rescuing two Irish Americans who shared their transnational dream of an independent Ireland. Allen died instantly, but Larkin and O'Brien continued to gasp for air as their bodies convulsed just off the ground. Remorselessly, Calcraft climbed down inside the enclosed base of the gibbet and strangled Larkin by jumping on his back. One of the priests prevented the hangman from killing O'Brien in the same coarse manner. The devoted Fenian, who had helped organize MacManus commemorations in Cork and had once told Kelly that he was willing to die for him, thus slowly suffocated as he swayed in the air for the next forty-five minutes. The three bodies were then removed and immediately buried under quicklime in the unconsecrated Salford Prison graveyard.[18]

An outpouring of sympathy and protest arose as word of the Manchester executions spread around the world. Working-class men and women donned shamrocks and green ribbons before they marched through rain-soaked streets to Salford Gaol and to the home of Larkin's widow a week after the hangings.[19] A crowd of four to five thousand people followed delegates carrying trade association and school banners during a procession through Allen's hometown of Cork on the same day.[20] Commemorations in Dublin were delayed until the second week of December so that Stephens's longtime antagonist John Martin could take precautions to prevent the violation of any laws during the scheduled march and public address. Several off-duty British soldiers seditiously tipped their hats when they passed the spot where Robert Emmet had spoken his last words before he was hanged at the beginning of the century, but the rest of the sixty thousand sash-bearing mourners were not overtly political.[21] Martin, nevertheless, was arrested and later acquitted for violating the 1850 Party Processions Act. While the Anglican archbishop of Dublin joined his fellow members of the Irish Privy Council in banning any additional demonstrations, Cardinal Cullen permitted priests and parishioners under his purview to pray for the souls of the three men, who quickly became known as the "Manchester Martyrs."[22] An estimated eighteen Dublin parish churches ultimately honored the three executed Fenians. Archbishop MacHale of Tuam similarly demonstrated his sympathy for the condemned by helping establish a relief fund for the Martyrs' surviving family members.[23] As an enduring tribute, T. D. Sullivan adapted Larkin's courtroom plea, "God Save Ireland," into a song that immortalized the deceased as unblemished heroes of Irish freedom. Set to the ubiquitously popular melody of "Tramp, Tramp, Tramp," the score served as the unofficial Irish national anthem until 1926.[24]

Veneration of the Manchester Martyrs was equally spirited in British colonies and in the United States. One thousand expatriate miners staged a mock funeral procession through a large goldfield on the south island of New Zealand. Other Irish émigrés organized marches in Australia, Canada, and the Cape Colony.[25] Fenian-sponsored protests in America were laced with symbolism and theatrics. New York City mayor John T. Hoffman accompanied several city council members who officially reviewed a large parade of mourners the day after the execution. A previously postponed January 8, 1868, commemoration in Philadelphia featured an enormous cortege and fiery anti-British eulogies. In the midst of a winter afternoon, an estimated seven thousand Irish Pennsylvanians defied Bishop Wood by walking behind three coffin-laden hearses for five hours before congregating around courthouse steps at the corner of Chestnut and Broad streets to hear speakers, including the Fenian general Samuel Spears, address the assembled crowd.[26] Less than a week later, the same Maurice Woulfe who had once thrown an apple at James Stephens acknowledged a renewed sense of Irish American patriotism in the United States. In a letter sent to his uncle from a military fort in the Dakota Territory, Woulfe wrote, "The news of the Murder of them three Irishmen was [reported] by the 'Press' & people of this Country with indignation, This reduction of the Army will help to Swell the Fenian ranks to a large extent and all fighting men. I am no Fenian yet and don't intend to be one, But if a blow is Struck for Irish independence. . . . I will bear a part."[27] To the detriment of the IRB and the stateside Brotherhood, however, the belated nationalist sympathies of Woulfe and thousands of others were of little benefit to their cause in the aftermath of repeated military failure.

Any chance of galvanizing the outpouring of sympathy for the Manchester Martyrs into grassroots militant nationalist activity was also negated by a deadly, unsuccessful attempt to rescue the recently arrested Richard O'Sullivan Burke from the Clerkenwell Detention House. Ever resourceful, the Fenian operative had spent the better part of his three weeks in custody devising a primitive escape plan. In accordance with instructions that had been written in invisible ink and smuggled out of the prison by Burke's lawyers and some female operatives, Twentieth Massachusetts Infantry veteran James Murphy and a few associates attached a fuse mechanism to a thirty-six-gallon, gunpowder-filled beer barrel on the night of December 11. The bomb was rolled in front of a thirty-foot exterior prison wall at 1:00 p.m. the next day and lighted at the same time a white ball was thrown into the detention house bull-ring to warn Burke of the pending explosion. As the Fenian prisoner pretended to remove a pebble from his shoe so that he could crouch down for protection, his aspiring rescuers took cover in the midst of several unsuspecting pedestrians. Expecting a thunderous blast, the would-be rescuers instead became frustrated when the fuse to the bomb twice failed to fully combust. Nonchalantly, the two men ultimately had to remove their deadly contraption when Burke's daily exercise period ended. Nationalist operative Ann Justice visited Burke early the next morning to inform him that she and her fellow accomplices would once again attempt to rescue the resourceful IRB weapons smuggler in the same manner later that day.

The dramatic precedent in the history of the Irish republican movement occurred when Murphy and Sullivan were finally able to detonate their homemade bomb on the afternoon of December 13, 1867. An eighteen-hundred-square-foot section of the detention house wall was instantly reduced to rubble and almost every structure in the surrounding area was damaged. Two adults and a seven-year-old girl were killed within seconds of the explosion. Another nine fatalities and countless injuries followed. Journalists later reported that over three dozen expectant mothers went into premature labor and that the blast was heard forty miles away.[28] Burke, however, never reached the rubble-strewn street. Forewarned by an informant of a second possible rescue attempt, the Clerkenwell warden had reassigned his already notorious Fenian prisoner to a midmorning recreation period. When the explosion occurred, the man who had effectively posed as an affluent gentleman while awaiting the arrival of the *Erin's Hope* in County Sligo was soundly confined in his cell. In the ensuing mayhem, Justice and three male accomplices helped distract the police as the two principal bombers began their protracted flight to the United States.[29]

The Clerkenwell explosion unleashed scathing criticism from pro-working-class intellectuals and from dogmatic English Hibernophobes. Charles Bradlaugh wrote a categorical public condemnation of the bombing less than two weeks after espousing lenient sentencing for the Manchester rescuers. Karl Marx, meanwhile, wrote to Friedrich Engels as a platform schism between pro- and anti-IRB supporters was continuing to develop within the Reform League and the International Working Men's Association: "This last episode of the Fenians is very stupid. . . . It is not to be expected that the mass of the Londoners who had shown much sympathy with Ireland . . . will allow themselves to be blown up for the greater honour and glory of the emissaries of the Fenians."[30] John Tenniel censured the Clerkenwell attack from the conservative side of the political spectrum by sketching a new illustration for *Punch* called "The Fenian Guy Fawkes." The December 28, 1867, cartoon linked a simian-looking IRB operative to the foiled English Catholic perpetrators who had attempted to blow up the House of Lords during the 1605 opening of Parliament. Yet more importantly, the image conveyed powerful messages through the placement of allegorical figures. One of the six well-groomed youngsters in the scene plays with a toy that resembles a Trojan horse. To reinforce this warning, Tenniel situated a nursing infant and her young mother to the left of a torch-bearing Fenian and a large barrel.

In recognition of these and several other contextual analogies that were published after the botched Clerkenwell rescue, the British public temporarily became even more jingoistically suspicious of Irish men and women. Although republican operatives did not plant another bomb in England until 1871, the sound of fireworks was often mistaken in the late 1860s for a Fenian attack. Containers of dirt were placed in government office buildings in case a detonated IRB bomb started a fire that needed to be extinguished. Sand was spread on the floor of the London Board of Trade for the same preventive reasons.[31] "Terror took possession of society," as one House of Lords member later recalled.[32] Clerkenwell, unlike any previous Fenian operation, left a lasting imprint on the collective English psyche and dissuaded many Irish men and women from ever supporting militant nationalist activities again.[33] The legacy of Fenian terror in England may have also encouraged an American expatriate residing in London to murder an innocent passerby. Having reluctantly carried out an order to brand a "D" on the face of an Irish American soldier who had deserted during the 1864 Battle of the Wilderness, discharged Union army physician Doctor William Minor had increasingly suffered from delusion. Convinced that the Fenians intended to kill him in retaliation for permanently blemishing the face of a comrade, Minor shot and killed a man named George Merrett with his service pistol on the night of February 17, 1872. Thereafter committed to the newly built Broadmoor Asylum for Criminal Lunatics, Minor ultimately became known as the "madman" who passed his time under medical observation by writing thousands of definitions that were accepted for publication in the first edition of the *Oxford English Dictionary*.[34]

At the end of the year, the British government took many additional precautions to protect subjects from potential Fenian violence. All military and police personnel vacations were prohibited at the same time that one hundred and sixty-six thousand civilians were registered to serve as special deputy constables. Detectives assigned to scrutinize rumored Irish terrorist activity were particularly busy processing a myriad of false information reports, which were forwarded to several government entities.[35] Confidential Canadian reports that a Fenian assassination team was traveling to London onboard a Danish ship to murder Queen Victoria also generated attention throughout the British bureaucracy.[36] The editors of the *London Times* stressed the need for heightened domestic security when they speculated that the Clerkenwell bombing would precipitate copycat crimes. An opinion piece from January 8, 1868 also indirectly dehumanized the Irish race, as the editors wrote, "There are not only wild and savage spirits among the Fenians, but a time of commotion like the present is sure to excite the brains of a great number of half crazy people."[37] Several Irishmen and English radicals were summarily detained for questioning owing to heightened public anxiety, but well-placed spies had little knowledge of the Clerkenwell perpetrators. Lack of progress in the investigation was evident when a police detachment mistakenly assaulted a paid informant during an interrogation.

Condemnations of the Clerkenwell attack from within the transatlantic Irish community prevented the already problem-plagued Fenian Brotherhood and the equally disorganized IRB from further traumatizing the English people or capitalizing on potential propaganda opportunities. In mid-December 1867, Roberts and the newly elected head of the O'Mahony wing, John Savage, provisionally resigned their executive positions on condition that John Mitchel would change his mind and become the president of a reunified Fenian Brotherhood. The former Confederate apologist, in his own words, once again "respectfully declined" "to knit up the two ragged fag ends of an organization originally rotten, and now all tattered and torn."[38] Disinclined to resume his leadership responsibilities, Roberts delegated control of his organization to John O'Neill at the end of the year and temporarily returned to private life. The death of an *Erin's Hope* filibusterer was thus hardly noticed as the Fenian Brotherhood remained in disarray. Unable to recover from the gunshot wound he received the previous May, Halifax native James Connor had declined a pardon because he could not afford private medical care. He succumbed to internal hemorrhaging on December 29, despite physician supervision, and was buried in Richmond cemetery with only a Catholic clergyman and a few prison employees at his graveside.[39]

The dire state of the global Fenian movement was also evident in the chance British government arrest of an alleged Clerkenwell bomber. The deposition of a suspect, who was threatened with a death sentence unless he implicated accomplices, led investigators to Scotland, where Michael Barrett and another man had been recently detained and released for inexplicably firing pistols on Glasgow Green. Although James O'Neill was eventually released, Special Branch (which had been specifically established to counter Fenian activities after the Burke escape attempt) secured formal indictments against Barrett and five other people shortly after *London Times* editors had forecast that the Clerkenwell explosion would incite emotionally unstable people to commit terrorist attacks throughout England.

Neither the belated trial of William Nagle nor the acquittal of five other *Erin's Hope* filibusterers during the Sligo Spring Assizes aroused any significant displays of Irish nationalist sentiment. Upon being found guilty by a *de mediatate lingue* jury, Nagle was sentenced to fifteen years of hard labor, but British prosecutors were largely unable to convict other Fenians who had participated in the *Erin's Hope* expedition. The adjudication of William Nugent for treason felony and for an additional charge of assaulting a warden with a stool was stymied, in fact, not because the defendant had become an American citizen in 1864, but because a Fenian-sympathizing subsheriff persuaded an empanelled juror to excuse himself from court by feigning illness.[40] At a time when the Fenian movement was in clear decline, any form of public protest or celebration would have at least temporarily precluded the republican cause from further disappearing into de facto obscurity. Yet such activity did not occur, in large part, because of general apathy and because remaining members of the IRB concurrently abrogated the so-called Treaty of Paris that had temporarily united the Roberts's wing of the Fenian Brotherhood with their Irish counterparts.[41]

By early 1868, Irish nationalist agitators were concentrated within isolated communities throughout the transatlantic world. Evidence abounded that both Brotherhood factions lacked the resources and resolve to reestablish popular support for the Fenian movement. The French-born bishop of the Colorado and Utah territories, Joseph Machebeuf, wrote to Archbishop Purcell two years after removing a pro-Fenian pastor from a Center City parish, "My Irish Catholics have frequently manifested a strong dislike to my administration, caused first by my quick and passionate temper . . . by a scandalous Irish priest who I had to dismiss [and] my opposition to the Fenian Brotherhood." Such a statement, however, was hardly evidence of widespread militant nationalist activity. Rocky Mountain–based expatriates may have resented Bishop Machebeuf's political views, but Irish nationalist expression had abated in conjunction with increasing expatriate assimilation into American society.[42] Expatriate Fenians, accordingly, failed to exploit the release of the professional sailor Thomas Fruen. Other than some press notices, the *Erin's Hope* expedition member and Limerick native had become a virtual nobody.[43] John O'Neill similarly failed to attract more than cursory attention in the national press as he offered lectures around the country in the spring of 1868. One of the only noticeable Irish nationalist initiatives at the time was the introduction of pure Virginia dark leaf "Fenian Comfort Smoking Tobacco." Whether this product sold well is uncertain.[44] Yet Canadian government officials remained vigilant. In June, the Irish-born governor general, Viscount Charles Stanley Monck, petitioned the State Department to allow Canadian vessels to patrol Lake Champlain. Seward later denied the request at roughly the same time that he submitted a letter to Congress calling for Warren and Costello's release. A large number of United States soldiers were transferred to military installations near the border that summer, however, so they could train in relatively cool weather and serve as Fenian deterrents.[45]

Sentencing several additional IRB convicts to prolonged periods of hard labor was perhaps justified by isolated violent incidents that occurred in Australia and Canada during the spring of 1868. Mentally deranged Irish nationalist sympathizer Henry O'Farrell shot Queen Victoria's third eldest son in the back during a March 12 charity picnic being held just north of Sydney in Clontarf Park. Prince Alfred recovered quickly, and magnanimously favored lenient treatment of his assailant, but attempted murder was a capital offense in New South Wales during the mid-nineteenth century. O'Farrell, consequently, was hanged six weeks after he committed his premeditated crime.[46] Irish Catholic Canadian Patrick J. Whelan additionally foreshadowed instances of Fenian terrorism when he fatally shot forty-three-year-old Thomas D'Arcy McGee in the neck on April 6, 1868. The same Grand Master Orangeman who had prosecuted Fenian suspects in Toronto skillfully defended Whelan by challenging specious witness testimony. John Hillyard Cameron failed, however, to provide mitigating reasons why his client had stalked McGee, was outside the Ottawa boardinghouse where McGee was murdered during the early morning of April 7, and had hidden a gun of the same caliber as the murder weapon in his residence.[47] Sharing the consensus opinion of her subjects, Queen Victoria informed Home Office bureaucrats shortly before O'Farrell and Whelan were sentenced to death that "we begin to wish that these Fenians should be lynched-lawed and on the spot."[48]

The criminal actions of O'Farrell and Whelan increased the possibility that at least one person would be convicted for participating in the bungled Clerkenwell rescue attempt. With a modest defense fund raised by Irish newspapers, the suspected bombers retained several promising junior councilors. Although inexperienced, these lawyers accepted reduced fees for the opportunity to challenge top-notch crown barristers in a high publicity trial that began on April 20. Plausible alibis were constructed for four of six suspects who, unlike Ann Justice, were not freed by the presiding magistrate when the prosecution rested. Michael Barrett, however, was found guilty. Pending the outcome of an official review of his conviction, the twenty-six-year-old Catholic native of County Fermanagh was to be hanged because he had attempted to liberate an incarcerated American who shared his patriotic ideals. Like the Manchester Martyrs, Barrett pronounced his innocence and his undying devotion to the Irish nation before his sentencing. Through the intercession of liberal reporters and influential politicians who questioned Barrett's guilt, Burke's alleged rescuer received two temporary execution stays over the course of the next four weeks. While Barrett's ultimate fate remained unknown, John Mitchel incidentally wrote that Fenianism was "an enormous sack of gas."[49] At roughly the same time that one little-known nationalist had pronounced his undying devotion to Irish independence, the more famous Mitchel had indirectly censured thousands of like-minded countrymen for supporting an organization that had helped secure his release from United States custody three years earlier.

In what was foremost the result of United States government intervention rather than of Fenian agitation, many *Erin's Hope* prisoners were furloughed before they were adjudicated while investigators reviewed Barrett's conviction. Reluctant to have another questionably guilty filibusterer die behind bars, British officials released and expelled Patrick J. Kain shortly after the twenty-one-year-old County Westmeath native became deathly ill. A married boilermaker and Civil War veteran who had collected several bullet wounds and saber scars as he was gradually promoted from Irish Brigade drummer boy to artillery captain, Kain had been familiar with incommodious living conditions in Union army camps. Incarceration had plagued his body, however, with a festering skin infection and other ailments.[50] Only a toddler when he immigrated to New York during the Famine, he was deported with few adult memories of his beloved homeland besides imprisonment in a dingy jail cell. Most of the other filibusterers were thereafter paroled on condition of signing the same confession that Nolan and several others had already affirmed. The wife of William Nagle was thus rewarded for her extensive efforts to aid Fenian prisoners when her devout Catholic husband was furloughed in early May.[51] Known for his intelligence as well as for his muscular stature, the twenty-five-year-old Eleventh Massachusetts infantry veteran Dennis O'Connor departed Queenstown shortly thereafter with the memory of a dockside rally that George Francis Train had organized on his behalf. In the midst of a European tour and always hungry for attention, Train presented O'Connor to the crowd, spoke highly of the Irish nationalist movement, and then provided the released Fenian with a one-way ticket home.[52]

The release of O'Connor and other Fenians was offset by the upholding of Michael Barrett's death sentence. Home Office officials announced on May 25, 1868, that the Ulster Fenian would be publicly hanged at 7:00 a.m. the following morning. Despite the short notice, a lively crowd started gathering outside London's Newgate Prison throughout the night. Affluent curiosity seekers paid up to £10 to rent expensive hotel rooms in clear view of a scaffold that had already been erected. Regardless of their sentiments about Irish independence, thousands of English men and women watched as Barrett was executed shortly after dawn.[53] As had happened upon the death of Allen, Larkin, and O'Brien, Barrett's execution temporarily sparked expatriate interest in the Fenian movement. The hosts of a July Fenian picnic in northern California failed to reserve enough passenger space on a train for all the Brotherhood supporters from Sacramento who wanted to attend an afternoon of festivities in a Folsum-area park.[54] Such enthusiasm, however, was once again fleeting.

The continued detention of many Fenians did little to expedite John O'Neill's efforts to recruit rich and poor people who were willing to participate in another invasion of Canada. While IRB insurrection veteran Michael Kerwin contemplated potential incursion strategies in conjunction with his other Fenian secretary of war responsibilities, O'Neill unsuccessfully petitioned recently impeached President Johnson for diplomatic and military support during a meeting at the White House. Continued insistence by the so-called Hero of Ridgeway that he would return to Canada did little to bolster expatriate financial backing of another foray across the border. Internal treasury reports suggest that the remnants of the Roberts faction only raised five thousand dollars more than the ninety-six thousand they spent throughout 1868. Delinquent contributors were a particular problem. Two-thirds of the $167,450 that had been pledged the previous year was never received.[55] Such declining support was because of American Fenian social mobility as well as of public distrust. Of the twenty-two suspected Milford members of the Brotherhood who appear in an 1869 city directory, fifteen had become residential property holders instead of prewar renters. All these men were still bootmakers, but they generally specified a subspecialty such as bottoming.[56] Canadian citizens, nevertheless, remained keenly prepared for a potential outbreak of more hostilities. As an Irish Protestant resident of Sherbrooke wrote to an Irish acquaintance in July, "We are prepared here—almost every one has his rifle and no quarter will be given any more than to wolves or rats. If they come here they will find no soft Southern people to deal with—but stern hardy sons of the forest and they will feel the hug of the northern bear."[57] O'Neill, in other words, would likely find himself once again surrounded by unsupportive American soldiers and provoked Canadian citizens if he led another series of forays into Ontario and Quebec. Events surrounding ongoing Fenian fundraising activities also suggested that his men would be of questionable integrity. A Fourth of July Fenian picnic in New York City's Bellevue Gardens was marred when a fight between large groups of expatriates expanded into a riot against policemen who had been called out to restore order.[58]

The declining influence of the Fenian movement became increasingly evident during the latter half of the year. Rather than addressing recruiting and strategic matters, Buffalo resident John O'Brien continued his antebellum practice of asking for job placement assistance each time he wrote to fellow Irish nationalist leader Frank Gallagher.[59] The United States Senate refused to confirm John Savage as United States consul in Leeds.[60] Contrary to the actual state of the Fenian movement, the O'Mahony wing war department concurrently issued a circular to delinquent members, which included a statement in the body of the text that their organization "was never, during any period of its existence, so strong in numbers and resources." In actuality, the first sentence of this letter provides a more accurate reflection of diminished Fenian influence: "Among the records of this office, your name appears as that of one who has taken an active interest in promoting the cause of Ireland; but having not heard from you lately; it is natural to conclude that you do so no longer."[61]

Irish nationalist activities became increasingly linked to leisure pursuits as interest in the Fenian Brotherhood continued to decline. Some of the former supporters referred to in the O'Mahony wing missive may have limited their patriotic expression to social events. Several hundred Manhattan residents attended a fundraising concert at the end of the year that featured a celebrity vocalist named Mina Geary, who was married to an expatriate who had fought at Ridgeway. A continued feminine presence within the Fenian movement was also apparent when a young girl was designated to portray an "Irish Goddess of Liberty" during a parade that O'Neill supporters organized in Philadelphia at the end of November. With bands also assigned to play the still-popular tune "The Green above the Red," the procession was a boisterous contrast to the efforts of a popular scholar who concurrently raised money for New York Fenians by twice presenting the ambiguously titled lecture, "Panoramic Tour of Ireland."[62] Fenian publication of a romantic adventure novel in December 1868 further demonstrates that O'Neill's supporters were employing several different methods to raise money and public awareness for their cause. However, relatively few people purchased the over sentimental and virulently Anglophobic story of a young Fenian male who fights at Ridgeway moments before he is reunited, at long last, with the Irish love of his life.

Statistical data compiled by British authorities up until the time of Tresilian's death confirms that most of the 1,005 IRB operatives who had been apprehended between 1866 and 1868 were demographically similar. Like the Milford, Massachusetts, and Tenth Ohio Infantry Fenians, 60 percent of Irish nationalists arrested under the provisions of the *Habeas Corpus* Suspension Act were young lower-middle-class males.[63] Many journeymen tailors who had been participating in a nationwide strike against garment industry owners had also mustered on the night of the March 5 rebellion. These men had been joined by at least 105 Dublin dry-goods clerks who were absent from work the morning after the rebellion.[64] A draper's assistant had also served as the IRB head in Connaught, and another with ties to the organization had alerted British officials after John J. O'Connor, as mentioned heretofore, had mistakenly raised a Fenian army in County Kerry a month before the actual rebellion began.[65] Yet many Fenian supporters were unique; in addition to being a Protestant and a reputed former Orangeman, *Erin's Hope* expedition veteran S. R. Tresilian had earned enough education and professional experience to secure employment as a Hudson Railroad civil engineer before he died of tuberculosis at his Hoboken, New Jersey home on January 5, 1869.

While men with a limited degree of money and free time for leisure activities had been ubiquitous within the IRB, farmers (who usually did not venture far from home when their crops were in the ground) and poor laborers had largely disregarded the Fenian movement.[66] Substantial numbers of urban militant republicans had been raised in modest farm families that had suffered through a prolonged boom-bust agricultural economy, but only 10.8 percent of the men in a government index of IRB criminal records were definitely rural laborers.[67] A mere 6.4 percent of the arrested Fenians, moreover, were unskilled workers. Corresponding to reports in the Dublin press that the majority of the rebels were between eighteen and twenty years of age, 87 percent of the men in the government index had not reached their thirty-sixth birthday. Many detainees were artisans who fell significantly below the average age of twenty-seven.[68] Teens from the lower classes, in sum, were most likely drawn to Fenianism when they left home and became economically independent workers in metropolitan environments.[69]

First-term prime minister William Gladstone attracted almost as much criticism as approval when he furloughed forty-nine of the eighty-one Fenians who remained in prison in early 1869. Even though anti-Irish sentiment in England was still pervasive fourteen months after the Clerkenwell explosion, die-hard Irish militants were disappointed that Charles Kickham, John Warren, and Augustine Costello were the only prominent Fenians among the initial group of nationalist parolees who were released in February. Among the many Fenian notables who remained incarcerated were Jeremiah O'Donovan Rossa and Thomas Francis Bourke. Additional pardons were possible. Isaac Butt and the other leaders of the one-year-old Amnesty Association had already exerted some influence in Parliament through grassroots agitation, while American politicians continued to serve as advocates for Fenian convicts who were United States citizens.[70] Just under 50 percent of the three thousand Catholic priests in Ireland, moreover, had eschewed their earlier aversion to the IRB by signing a petition that called for the release of all Fenian prisoners.[71] In the interim, however, most of the republican prisoners broke rocks in prison quarries or separated old rope into threads that would later be used to make a naval caulk called oakum.

Gladstone continued his campaign to "kill Irish nationalism with kindness," despite mildly subversive reactions to the early release of several Fenian prisoners. Cheers erupted in the gallery of a Dublin courtroom after a bench furlough was issued to Costello.[72] Gladstone, nevertheless, appointed the first Catholic lord chancellor of Ireland since the seventeenth-century reign of James II. The Liberal Party leader's spirit of reform was further evident eighteen days after Patrick J. Whelan became the last man to be publicly executed in Canada. In an effort to wean Irish churches from state subsidies, Gladstone submitted an April 1869 parliamentary bill that would render all Irish religious institutions financially independent. Popularly referred to as disestablishment, the Irish Church Act would officially become law the following July despite the opposition of Queen Victoria and the Conservative Party Parliamentary caucus. Having quipped the previous summer that Gladstone would be a more effective head centre than James Stephens was, John Mitchel had, ironically, foreseen a British prime minister unilaterally offering political concessions to the Irish that the former IRB leader had been unable to secure through idle threats of revolution.[73]

Fenian celebrations continued to surface in Ireland and America as Gladstone contemplated his next effort to "pacify Ireland." Costello was feted in his native Galway before he and Warren were the guests of honor at a Cork banquet that was held the night before the two men started their early May voyage home to America.[74] Both of the *Erin's Hope* filibusterers were similarly honored upon their arrival in the United States. Warren, who had recently been introduced to Susan B. Anthony and Elizabeth Cady Stanton at a Manhattan reception, was presented to President Grant and almost every cabinet secretary during a visit to Washington. Republican officials provided Costello with an overnight postal clerk position in New York, but he was fired after only a few days on the job because his supervisors discovered that he had attended a Fenian prisoners' relief meeting at Tammany Hall.[75] Even though he had only resided in the United States for two years before the *Jacmel* expedition, Costello presumably received Democratic Party machine support thereafter because the one-time professional entertainer was soon hired by the New York City Police Department.[76] Continued political machine patronage of Fenian leaders proved to be a wise move, as the Brotherhood briefly regained public attention when Canadian penitentiary officials furloughed several Ridgeway filibusterers in a goodwill gesture to the Grant administration. Canadian conciliation toward the Fenians at the time the Irish Anglican Church was officially disestablished, however, would ultimately assist Gladstone in his effort to pacify Ireland with kindness.

Warren and Costello remained in the spotlight when one of their former associates died before he could fully capitalize on his recent notoriety as an Irish nationalist leader. Accompanied by Boss Tweed and nine other men, the two former prisoners served as pallbearers at William Nagle's funeral in August. Suffering from mental derangement, Nagle had been working as a tax clerk when he committed suicide at his Madison Avenue residence by jumping through his bedroom window. Although he had once organized a Father Mathew Temperance Society chapter, Nagle may have been inebriated at the time of his death.[77] He died instantly and was buried at a Brooklyn cemetery.[78] Unlike Warren and Costello, Nagle was soon forgotten, despite the hazards he had risked for the Union and the IRB. More memorable was the thoroughbred that won the third running of the Belmont Stakes. In recognition of his long-time financial relationship with the Brotherhood, German-born banker August Belmont owned a mount called *Fenian,* with whom he won the New York track race that still bears his name. A solid mount, *Fenian's* record of success was more akin to those of the legendary Fionn MacCumheill than those of most mid-nineteenth century nationalist leaders.

Nagle's death occurred when a new series of ideological differences arose within what remained of the Fenian movement. Hints of a more complacent Brotherhood surfaced when an O'Neill deputy wrote to Archbishop Spalding, "if there is anything in our organization which is in conflict with the doctrines of the church it shall be so changed to be in harmony with such doctrines."[79] Father John MacMahon appeared ungrateful, however, shortly after several hundred clemency supporters, including William Seward and the Irish-born, anti-Fenian Archbishop of Halifax, Thomas Louis Connolly, successfully petitioned for his release from a Canadian prison in August 1869.[80] Commencing a lecture tour at Cooper Union by addressing a five thousand–member audience that included Horace Greeley, MacMahon falsely claimed that he had been mistreated while in custody. In truth, Canadian records show that all the Fenian prisoners detained in Ontario and Quebec received utmost consideration. The September 24,

1869, death of one republican prisoner named Thomas Maxwell was due to natural causes. Two furloughed Irish Americans, more significantly, later thanked the warden for his professionalism.[81]

Actual incidents of Fenian prisoner abuse in England precipitated a series of Amnesty Association–led protests, the appointment of an independent prison review committee, and some additional furloughs. An embellished rumor that O'Donovan Rossa had been forced to consume meals with his hands shackled behind his back for disciplinary reasons inspired nationalist sympathizers in Tipperary to nominate the incarcerated former *Irish People* editor as a parliamentary candidate in a November 1869 by-election. Although the cantankerous Rossa could not serve as an MP while in prison, he outpolled all the other candidates. Irish defiance also surfaced two months later when Denis Cashman and a handful of other Fenian prisoners who had been released from Australia were welcomed to San Francisco with a parade.[82] Karl Marx argued at the time, moreover, that the Fenians who were furloughed under Gladstone's pacification scheme had served the same proportion of their sentences as common criminals who were routinely paroled for good behavior.[83]

Gladstone's unparalleled concessions and divided sentiments within the Brotherhood were two of several reasons why John O'Neill was unable to mount a credible invasion of Canada in late May 1870. Most Fenian leaders had been ardent supporters of the separation of church and state. The possibility of reviving nationalist expression within the expatriate community was inhibited, however, by a papal condemnation of the Irish republican movement on January 12, 1870. Many North American ecclesiastical leaders had feared that a Vatican edict would provoke otherwise quiescent militants.[84] Instead, Paul Cullen's decision to allow his colleagues to excommunicate Irish militants within their respective dioceses at their discretion was accepted by the laity.[85] As a further indication that the Fenians were no longer a threat, it is not known if any bishops ever invoked this authority.

O'Neill's efforts were further impeded by the ever-rising social influence of the Irish American community. In a January circular, Roberts wrote that he believed many Fenian senators were affiliated with the Irish nationalist movement only because they wanted to "profit politically" from their, albeit declining, position of influence within the expatriate community.[86] P. J. Meehan received a letter that contained similar sentiments a few days before a fellow Fenian senator shot him during a heated mid-February Brotherhood meeting in Manhattan. Among other matters, the author of the missive wrote to the infamous former Fenian courier, "I beg to state that some of the Senators are too much engaged in American politics to have the cause of Ireland at heart."[87] It is thus assumed that few people abided by O'Neill's February 17 request to forward weapons to James O'Hara's Boston property on 79 Blackstone Street or to other designated intermediaries residing in other locales.[88]

Ongoing tensions among die-hard expatriate nationalists additionally impeded O'Neill's efforts. In reference to the Clan na Gael, Boston expatriate nationalist leader George Cahill reported to one of his colleagues on February 19, 1870 that disgruntled former Fenian supporters were forming societies that claimed to represent the true spirit of the original IRB.[89] Philadelphia nationalist leader James Gibbons subsequently complained when the vestiges of the old Roberts faction split into pro and anti-O'Neill camps in April 1870. In a private letter to a colleague, he wrote, "I am now an old man. My business ruined. I must go at once and sell all to pay my debts. Too old to work and ashamed to beg. My hopes for Ireland blasted."[90] O'Neill's best source of volunteers during this continuing period of Fenian decline was among middle- and lower-class people residing in northern industrial centers. Sixteen members of a forty-nine-member strong circle that was active the previous March were variously identified as shoemakers, saloon-keepers, laborers, painters, and sailors. One person was a police officer; the professions of their compatriots are unknown.[91]

The signing of a May 1870 Anglo-American naturalization accord was yet another blow to the Fenians. By exempting British-born American citizens from perpetual fealty to the United Kingdom, Foreign Office and State Department negotiators prevented the ninety-year-old *de mediatate lingue* jury issue from precipitating a transatlantic war. Fenian membership was in such a state of decline that former nationalist hotbeds became progressively assimilated expatriate communities. A four-hundred-man-strong organization at the time of the 1866 invasion of Ontario and Quebec, the Lowell Fenian Brotherhood circle had declined 90 percent by May 1870. Few men and women in a town of fifteen thousand expatriates were willing to support an organization that had been marred by controversy for several years.[92]

Undeterred by such setbacks, O'Neill informed his relatively small retinue of die-hard followers in mid-May that they would invade Canada through the same corridors Sweeny had exploited four years earlier. Recognizing that he would need an early victory like Ridgeway to generate wider support, O'Neill deviated from his predecessor's goal of establishing an Irish republic in the town of Sherbrooke by selecting two small Quebec villages as his initial targets. Fenians embarking from Saint Albans would drive across the border to the French-speaking village of Saint Jean. Their counterparts in northeast New York would attempt to capture a Grand Trunk railroad junction near Richmond. A preliminary feint across the Niagara River would also be used again to draw Canadian troops into Ontario. Inadequate preparation and poor timing rendered even this scaled-down plan unlikely to succeed. Few circles had regularly drilled of late, and surreptitiously distributing the Brotherhood's remarkably large amount of military supplies would once again be a logistical challenge.[93] Because the invasion was originally scheduled to begin on Queen Victoria's May 24 birthday in an affront to Anglophiles throughout the world, O'Neill's men would most likely be contained within a matter of days, if not hours, by militia forces that would already be assembled to parade in honor of their sovereign.

O'Neill would also have to contend with thousands of Canadians who remained committed and well prepared to defend their native land. Reports of a looming Fenian invasion led the Canadian government to suspend *habeas corpus* protections and unleashed a flurry of military mobilizations throughout Quebec and Ontario.[94] Niagara Peninsula home guards and French Canadian militias were dispatched towards Fort Erie, while civilians residing along the frontier girded for battle by burying their valuables and driving their cattle inland.[95] Provincial scouts hindered the possibility of a surprise attack by repeatedly visiting a growing Fenian camp in Malone and by patrolling strategic locales. Among the many Canadians who returned home to protect their nation and property, three men en route to Ontario traveled by rail in the company of several inebriated Fenians bound for Buffalo.[96] As before, the services of Canadians residing in the United States would not be needed because precaution prevailed north of the border. A female Canadian Protestant taught several children how to make the sign of the cross, under the assumption that invading Fenians would not harm youngsters who knew how to bless themselves like Catholics.[97]

The impracticality of O'Neill's strategy failed to deter an estimated six thousand Fenians from appearing in various locations in Upstate New York and northern Vermont in late May. Irishmen described as young, well behaved, and only distinguished by their urban mannerisms initially slept in makeshift accommodations at the Malone fairgrounds because no rooms were available in the town hotel. The subsequent establishment of a military camp on a private farm offered volunteers more amenities. Bland provisions were complemented by homemade pies and breads that were donated by local families who sympathized with the Irish republican agenda.[98] The Fenian capability to cut Canadian telegraph lines and reconnoiter territory across the border from Malone were additional morale boosters at a time when bands of volunteers ventured northward with minimal equipment and ammunition. As the Fenians aroused press attention throughout the country, newspaper reports were replete with both accurate and erroneous information. Many journalists and editors detailed the appearance of Fenian contingents at railroad stations. Other newsmen circulated a false story that famed Confederate guerrilla John Singleton Mosby was among the hundreds of New England Fenians who had embarked for Saint Albans.[99] Fenian critic Bartholomew Wolfe also ventured to the Canadian border. Offended that IRB operatives had wounded a former acquaintance who had become an Irish constable, Wolfe had written to his cousin that the "Fenians [were] doing a great deal of injury to Ireland instead of a great deal of good."[100] Nevertheless, he promptly traveled 150 miles north from his Brattleboro, Vermont home to serve under Fenian general J. J. Donnelly when circles around the country were instructed to dispatch volunteers to Upstate New York and northern Vermont. John H. Gleeson also participated in the Fenian invasion, despite rumors that he had been arrested for stealing five hundred dollars while impersonating a federal revenue collector in West Virginia two months earlier. While possibly free on bail, the Fenian leader temporarily commanded Fenians who mustered in Malone before O'Neill deputy Owen Starr arrived.[101]

O'Neill remained confident that he would be able to capture Saint Jean and Richmond, even though his invasion plans were undermined long before he ordered men across the Canadian border. Anticipating that he would assume command of over one thousand volunteers when he arrived in Saint Albans on May 24, he instead was welcomed into the northern New England hamlet by roughly one hundred poorly equipped supporters.[102] President Grant concurrently redeployed military service personnel all along the frontier and issued a neutrality proclamation that authorized federal prosecution of any American citizen who unlawfully threatened Canadian domestic security. As O'Neill marched his small contingent roughly fifteen miles north to establish an advance camp near a small village called Franklin a day later, battalions of Canadian soldiers proceeded directly from Queen Victoria birthday celebrations to the border. O'Neill would soon be outnumbered by adversaries stationed in key defensive positions. Several hundred eleventh-hour recruits were en route to northern Vermont, but O'Neill did not have the financial resources to properly equip a large army. Aware of speculation that famed Civil War general William Tecumseh Sherman had ordered his arrest, the Hero of Ridgeway decided to attack immediately rather than wait for reinforcements.[103]

The May 25 beginning of the 1870 Fenian invasion was more of a multi-act spectacle than a genuine military engagement. Early in the day, United States marshal George P. Foster infuriated the forty-six Canadian volunteers and active-duty British soldiers who were protecting Eccles Hill by delivering a handwritten letter from O'Neill that included a personal guarantee to respect the standard codes of warfare. O'Neill and his men arrived on the border shortly thereafter. Sparing little hyperbole, the Hero of Ridgeway began a pep talk in which he identified his charges as the "advance guard of the Irish American army for the liberation of Ireland." However, the expatriates assembled on the border in green and yellow braided blue uniforms that morning were perhaps not irreproachable nationalists. One Canadian journalist reported that the filibusterers on the scene were "approximately twenty-five years-old and the scum of American cities."[104] Unscrupulous local teamsters had transported Fenian equipment to the border and remained in the vicinity in hope of eventually hauling pilfered Canadian goods to Franklin and Saint Albans.

The first Fenian approach toward Eccles Hill began when forty expatriates from Burlington, Vermont marched across the border in rows of four while their comrades moved into reserve positions. With their adversaries in clear view, Canadians hiding in the nearby woods fired in unison moments after the last Fenian crossed a little over one hundred feet inside Canadian territory. A twenty-five-year-old mechanic named John Rowe was shot through the head and died instantly. Intermittent gunfire ensued until a ranking expatriate officer, who may have been a Montreal military academy graduate, fell wounded within fifteen minutes of Rowe's death. O'Neill emerged from the second story of a nearby farmhouse to berate his soldiers, who had fired errant shots as they retreated in panic to the American side of the border. "Men of Ireland," O'Neill yelled, "I am ashamed of you. You have acted disgracefully, but you will have another chance of showing whether you are cravens or not." O'Neill, however, did not have any opportunity to demonstrate his own valor, as he was arrested moments later by Foster for violating Section Six of the American Neutrality Act.[105] While being led past farmers and local townspeople who had ventured to the frontier in hope of witnessing a rare spectacle, the quixotic Fenian general delegated command to John Boyle O'Reilly, a former Devoy aide who had escaped imprisonment in Australia.[106] Employed as a *Boston Pilot* correspondent at the time, the Drogheda native was long believed to have declined to become a combatant. Because he was briefly detained later the same day, however, it is more likely that he actually assumed command of the Fenians under the alias General G. Dwyer.[107]

Fenian soldiers assembled on the Quebec/Vermont border were mostly immobile in the hours after a United States marshal took O'Neill into custody. Random firing persisted throughout the afternoon, as members of both forces stationed themselves in secure positions. Even under a flag of truce, O'Neill's men were unable to recross the border for the rest of the day because a veteran British officer of the 1866 Fenian invasion rejected a Brotherhood proposal to remove the dead and wounded under a temporary cease-fire. Such an agreement, in his estimation, might signify de facto recognition of the Fenians as a foreign army. The 4:30 p.m. arrival of one hundred men from New York did not lead to another

Brotherhood foray across the border. Missisquoi Volunteers instead ventured onto American soil shortly before suppertime and captured a rifled field gun that was the lone piece of Fenian artillery. Every filibusterer in the vicinity thereafter retreated to his base camp in Franklin. Estimates of total Fenian deaths vary between two and five people. Up to twenty expatriates may have been wounded. No Canadians sustained injury.[108] Additional casualties did not occur on either side of the battlefield in large part because a well-planted British spy named Thomas Billis Beech had surreptitiously disobeyed an O'Neill order to lead four hundred New York expatriates to the frontier on the day of the attack.

As eyewitnesses later wrote in local historical journals, a day of repeated Fenian blunders might have been avoided if O'Neill had entered Canada at a flatter, less defensible crossing point that was only a mile away from Eccles Hill. Yet initial Fenian success also might have landed O'Neill in a Canadian prison for several years instead of a Windsor, Vermont, penitentiary for four months. After being indicted for committing high misdemeanors, O'Neill smiled contently when he pled guilty and declared that he would discourage any other Fenians from organizing another invasion of Canadian soil.[109] Imprisoned with seven co-defendants, O'Neill remained behind bars until President Grant suspended his sentence in a political gesture to the Irish community in the midst of the 1870 midterm election campaign.[110] No different from their Johnson administration predecessors, White House Republicans were willing to give the Fenians some latitude in exchange for expatriate voter support. In the coming years, moreover, Seward's successor, Hamilton Fish, would routinely announce that English maltreatment of the Irish was the root cause of lingering Fenian mischief.[111]

O'Neill deputy Owen Starr was similarly defeated when he led a foray into Huntingdon County, Quebec a day after fifty "soldier boys" from Providence had departed for northern Vermont by rail in the company of several Boston Fenians.[112] In need of a morale-booster more than a strategic victory, Starr had advanced about 220 men eight hundred meters into Canada around 7:00 a.m. on May 26 and supervised the construction of a 125-yard-long, three-foot-high breastwork that snaked from a wood thicket to a nearby river.[113] Holding the position under attack, Starr reasoned, would reinstill confidence among hundreds of dispirited Fenians. Provoking prepared Canadian forces proved unwise, however; a combined force of Home Guard volunteers and British regulars (who were much better trained and confident than their 1866 counterparts) attacked the Fenian breastwork within minutes of its completion at 8:30 a.m.[114] Ordered to lead a charge under the premise that they would be highly motivated to defend their property, local farmers and merchants advanced with such determination from a field of hop vines that the undertrained Fenian contingent fired three rounds before their adversaries were even in gunfire range. The Fenians subsequently retreated, and the skirmish was completely over within thirty minutes. Casualties, as at Eccles Hill, were minimal; one Fenian was killed, another was wounded, and one was taken prisoner. The only Canadian to leave the battlefield wounded was a soldier whose forehead was scarred by a bullet fragment.[115]

Rallies rather than combat marked the end of the 1870 Fenian campaign. Continuing to defy Catholic Church leaders, Father John MacMahon traveled from his new, predominately German American parish in Indiana to address a large crowd of filibusterers on Saturday, May 28.[116] His many prevarications failed, however, to precipitate another attack. Fenians to the west in Buffalo never entered Canadian territory because no ferry operator was willing to risk being arrested or fined for violating United States neutrality laws. In addition to the return presence of the USS Michigan, United States Army companies patrolled the eastern shore of the Niagara River. Preemptively detained Fenian rabble-rousers once again hired Grover Cleveland as legal counsel. The rising Democratic Party star's insistence on working pro bono for Fenian defendants arrested in western New York (as he had done four years earlier) was little consolation for expatriates in Malone and Ogdensburg, who started returning home after purchasing reduced rail fares with money from Tammany Hall coffers.[117] Before being presented with the Fenian uniform of Eccles Hill casualty John Rowe, IRB assassination attempt survivor Prince Alfred inspected Starr's overrun defensive positions near Huntingdon while several expatriate filibusterers were still encamped ten miles to the south, in Malone.[118] The last Fenians to depart the two border communities on June 9 subsequently abandoned a substantial military arsenal that Canadian journalists estimated was worth two hundred and fifty thousand dollars[119] Devoid of funds, personnel at O'Neill's Manhattan headquarters reportedly had been unable to pay for a telegram that was sent from the Canadian border on May 31.[120] In celebration, Quebec and Ontario residents began joking that the still-uncommon acronym IRA was an abbreviation for "I Ran Away."[121] Adding further insult to Fenian injury, sectarian violence erupted in New York City the following July when Orange Order members taunted working-class Catholics near the southeastern end of Central Park by yelling and singing "To Hell with the Pope" during a Battle of the Boyne commemoration parade.[122] Eight people were killed during the demonstration and other sporadic instances of nativist violence continued to occur in the United States, but the Fenian Brotherhood had still failed to recruit a sufficient retinue of expatriates.

Notwithstanding defense appropriations costs, one of the only inconveniences the Canadian people experienced during the May 1870 Fenian invasion was a lagging stock market and a five-day bank run.[123] The recently established

Canadian nation had weathered a significant early challenge to its political legitimacy. Canadians of all ethnicities had remained just as loyal to their homeland as they had been to their native provinces during the first two Fenian forays. The popular upstart Montreal newspaper, *The Evening Star*, reported that several Irish nationalist sympathizers did not report for work when they received word that O'Neill had led another attack across the border, but no outright instances of collaboration were widely reported.[124] Of equal importance, the conclusion of another Anglo-American rapprochement treaty the following August further negated the possibility that the Fenians would ever be able to mount another comparably sized foray into Canada.

Rather than retaliate for Fenian activities that had occurred across the Atlantic, or for rumors that James Stephens was still attempting to conclude a Franco-Fenian alliance with Napoleon III, William Gladstone continued to offer concessions to the Irish people in the aftermath of the 1870 attack. A land reform bill was undermined shortly after it was passed on August 1. Reactionary Irish landlords had little desire to honor expanded peasant protection from arbitrary eviction.[125] The start of the serialized publication of Benjamin Disraeli's anti-American novel *Lothair* in November also discouraged English men and women from relinquishing their prejudices against Irish Catholics, as two characters in the satire distinctly resembled James Stephens and Gustave Cluseret.

Current and former members of the increasingly marginalized Fenian Brotherhood were involved in a variety of activities during the year that followed the 1870 Canadian invasion. Several filibusterers further demonstrated that they were romantic nationalists with a penchant for danger and adventure by enlisting in the French Army upon the outbreak of the Franco-Prussian War. James J. O'Kelly organized an Irish Brigade that was led in Flanders by Wexford native Michael Kerwin.[126] Other former Fenian leaders also began to command respect at the ballot box. Even though he had endorsed several Radical Republican candidates two years earlier, William Roberts became the Tammany Hall nominee to replace retiring fellow Fenian and former heavyweight boxing champion, John Morrissey, in Congress. After winning 14,566 of 16,930 total votes cast in a predominately expatriate Manhattan congressional district, Roberts, like most greenhorn politicians in a minority party, served on the marginally influential coinage and postal service expenditure committees.[127] He did secure, however, a West Point appointment for the only son of the deceased Thomas Francis Meagher.[128] San Francisco Fenian leader Thomas Mooney secured the Democratic nomination for governor despite having once been accused of embezzling approximately two hundred thousand dollars from patrons of a bank he owned.[129] Another California Fenian became a state Supreme Court justice. Irish Canadian politician

John O'Connor, conversely, condemned the Fenians in a series of public letters in order to secure constituent support and the good favor of provincial government leaders.[130] John O'Mahony's public life was more subdued; the former expatriate powerbroker served as a floor delegate for two circles at an 1870 Fenian convention and worked as a writer for a publication called *The Sunburst* a year later. He started a two-year stint as the editor of a new nationalist newspaper called the *American Gael* in May 1873, and recruited members of a military-oriented affiliate of the Brotherhood called the Legion of Saint Patrick.[131]

Battlefield failure and rising Fenian participation in American election campaigns necessitated Brotherhood media exploitation of relatively unimportant events. In early January 1871, veteran Irish republican leaders affiliated with both major political parties competed for the right to formally welcome the first group of furloughed prisoners who were transported to New York onboard the *SS Cuba* at British expense.[132] Not wanting to offend any of their expatriate supporters, Rossa, Devoy, and three colleagues politely declined to be ferried ashore on either William Roberts's Tammany Hall tender or a launch John Warren and the British spy Francis Millen had chartered on behalf of the Republican Party. The released convicts likewise refused complimentary lodging and meals in luxury hotels, but they did agree to meet with President Grant on the steps of the White House a month later. Thomas Francis Bourke also became a temporary celebrity in the United States after he was freed from British custody on January 3, 1871.[133] Joined by nationalist orator Lizzie O'Brien, the man who had escaped execution by one day became a popular fixture on the Fenian lecture circuit. Bourke promoted the commercial benefits of supporting the Irish republican movement when he concluded a Cooper Union address by reminding members of the audience to buy their pianos from a local storeowner who had provided one of his instruments for the ceremony. Whether he endorsed local merchants when he addressed a Lawrence, Massachusetts crowd on March 25, 1871 is uncertain.[134] Ironically, the release of Fenian prisoners from British penitentiaries may have decreased already-minimal expatriate support for another invasion of Canada.[135] With their comrades free, many Fenians felt less obligated to support a lost cause.

Final Anglo-American resolution of outstanding Civil War grievances overshadowed the pittance of Irish nationalist activities that occurred throughout the United States in mid-1871. Despite having once argued that British authorities could solve their "Fenian problem" if they ceded Canada to the United States, Hamilton Fish signed an agreement with Foreign Office representatives in May that designated a Geneva-based panel of international arbiters to resolve all outstanding Union reparations claims.[136] British officials also agreed to apologize for supplying war matériel to the former Confederacy, in accordance with a pact that became known as the Treaty of Washington. These concessions proved financially worthwhile to the British and Canadian governments. Radical Republican Charles Sumner had once demanded a minimum restitution payment of two billion dollars. Other members of the United States Senate had also previously joined Sumner in denying a Canadian reimbursement request for expenses incurred during the 1866 Fenian invasion. The 15.5 million dollars that was ultimately awarded to the United States in compensatory damages was thus a token amount, and British government officials eventually quieted Canadian restitution claims by subsidizing the construction of a transcontinental rail link to Vancouver.[137]

An outbreak of sectarian violence in New York City at the time the Treaty of Washington further suggested that other matters besides Fenianism had always had a more pressing influence on the mid-nineteenth century expatriate community. By once again commemorating the 1690 Battle of the Boyne with a parade, Manhattan Orangemen provoked a bloody altercation with an unruly mob of Catholic Irish Americans who had gathered along Eighth Avenue. Then serving as a police captain, the former *Erin's Hope* filibusterer Augustine Costello had shared the sentiments of local Church leaders by issuing a pre–July 12 plea for peace and order. Local Ancient Order of Hibernians (AOH) leaders, however, had vowed to stop any Orange Order demonstrations in Lower Manhattan.[138] Many deaths thus occurred when city law enforcement officers fired on Catholic protestors. During a period of significant Anglo-American diplomacy and senseless street violence, Fenian Brotherhood leaders once again appeared as charlatans who routinely lied about their capability to liberate Ireland. Occasional Fenian boasts that militant expatriate activity would elevate the social status of the Irish American community were also unfounded. Expatriate service in the Union army had negated nativist sentiment in the United States. Fenian invasions of Canada, on the other hand, had been widely mocked as the machinations of men and women who belonged to an inferior race.

Continued tensions between Canadian government officials and mixed-race inhabitants of modern-day Manitoba unexpectedly precipitated a third Fenian foray across the northern United States border shortly after the mid-July Orange riots. Two years of intermittent hostilities in what was then known as Rupert's Land had provided John O'Neill with a remote opportunity to secure an alliance with intermarriage descendents of French trappers and Native Americans. The large local population of so-called Métis had resisted annexation and colonization of their lands by seizing a Hudson's Bay Company trading post near the soon-to-be incorporated city of Winnipeg in 1869. To demonstrate his resolve, Métis leader Louis Riel had also court-martialed and summarily executed a Scots-Irish hostage. Yet few Irish militants besides O'Neill actually believed that the creation of a Fenian-Métis alliance would be worthwhile. Riel had already demonstrated a willingness to negotiate with Canadian officials. A former priest and college professor named William O'Donoghue, moreover, had failed to secure an American government guarantee to aid Riel, even though many United States senators and a handful of upper Midwest railroad magnates hoped to annex unsettled lands north of the Dakota Territory.[139]

John O'Neill was the only East Coast Fenian leader who was intrigued when O'Donoghue traveled to New York and Washington, D.C. to propose a collaborative agreement between the former Roberts wing and the Métis. The Hero of Ridgeway resigned from the Brotherhood in September so that he could raise an army that would travel halfway across the United States and invade the northern end of the Red River Valley. As O'Neill headed west at the beginning of the fall, he distanced himself physically and intellectually from the contrite nationalist efforts of the Amnesty Association. In contrast to O'Neill's objectives, P. J. Smyth signed an ornate, oversized clemency petition, which depicted a crestfallen Hibernia and a docile wolfhound, on behalf of all demonstrators who assembled in Phoenix Park on September 3, 1871.[140] O'Neill also parted with a New York expatriate community that would soon be revisited by the disgraced James Stephens. While working as a sales agent for a Le Havre–based wine merchant, Stephens would be accused of being a British spy. Within a year he would be unemployed and on his way back to France.[141]

Organizing and leading a small band of expatriate zealots into Rupert's Land proved to be as difficult as invading the Ridgeway peninsula and southern Quebec. Rail service only reached the western Minnesota border at the time. Fargo did not yet exist, and prairie fires were burning throughout the northeastern reaches of the Dakota Territory. Traveling sixty miles into Canada and capturing Fort Gary, as O'Neill and O'Donoghue hoped, could only be attempted after a long journey by wagon train on a well-defined but unimproved trail. O'Neill also had to recruit all his own men without Brotherhood support. Recognizing that few East Coast expatriates would venture so far from home, he thus attempted to raise an army of Irishmen as he traveled west. Twin Cities Fenians had remained largely loyal to O'Mahony, however, when the Brotherhood split in 1865. O'Neill's optimistic hope that two thousand expatriate navies would join him once the onset of cooler weather suspended construction of the Northern Pacific railroad for the winter was also farfetched. Rather than remain in rural northern Minnesota, most seasonally employed railmen migrated in search of other work as soon as they were furloughed. He or one of his associates did, however, enlist the support of twenty-eight sawmill workers from the tiny village of Macaulayville. At most, O'Neill only had forty-one men in his company at any one time.

When he departed a railhead in the small village of Morris with two wagons at the end of September, he also had no more than two barrels of pork, three barrels of hardtack, a handful of weapons that had been expropriated from a secret Fenian arsenal in Port Huron, Michigan, and some miscellaneous supplies.[142] An equally significant problem was increasing Canadian government alleviation of Métis grievances. Contrary to O'Donoghue's reports, the fourteen-month-old Manitoba Act had insured that many indigenous socioeconomic interests would be protected upon formal Canadian annexation. An open-minded government official who was sympathetic to the Métis had also been recently appointed to serve as the Royal lieutenant governor of the newly established province.

The fifteen-man Fenian detachment that attacked a Hudson Bay Company trading post a half-mile north of the American border on the morning of October 4 was hardly formidable. In the brief raid, O'Neill captured several prisoners, and then instructed his men to requisition supplies that were to be placed on board a boat that the Fenian leader supposedly hoped to float down the northward-flowing Red River to Fort Garry. The plan never materialized, however, because a person released from the compound rushed to the United States Army stockade in Pembina and informed Captain Lloyd Wheaton that O'Neill had seized the nearby trading post. Adopting a diplomatic approach—even though he had previously received Canadian authorization to use force on Manitoba soil in the event of a Fenian attack—Wheaton thereafter dispatched an intermediary to the Fenian insurgents, but the Fenians immediately detained the man as a hostage.

Direct United States Army intervention led to the prompt conclusion of the Fenian Red River raid. O'Neill, Utica native J. J. Donnelly, and nine other filibusters were easily arrested when Wheaton and his men arrived at the besieged trading post. A fleeing O'Donoghue was captured by several Métis and handed over to American authorities a few hours later, allegedly because Riel had learned that the Fenian Brotherhood was a Catholic Church–censured secret society. In truth, the Métis had likely betrayed O'Donoghue because Riel believed that the ex-priest was an emerging rival.[143] Expatriate filibusters reportedly spotted in a nearby village were never apprehended. O'Neill's time behind bars was once again brief and, by his own admission, relatively pleasant.[144] Tried and acquitted in both Pembina and Saint Paul for yet again violating American neutrality laws, he remained wistfully committed to another Canadian foray even though Department of Justice officials repeatedly attempted to re-indict him up until the spring of 1872. As during the two previous Fenian invasions, Canadian citizens had rallied to defend their nation. Volunteer regiments from Ontario and Quebec had mobilized and started traveling west as soon as they received word of O'Neill's latest attack.[145] After the spy Thomas Beech confirmed that O'Neill was indeed approaching the border, Manitoba governor A. G. Archibald rousted a militia of one thousand Anglo-Canadians and secured the support of the Métis by offering temporary immunity to any fugitive in their community.[146] His only questionable action was the arbitrary arrest of several loyal Fort Garry residents who were placed under government suspicion because they were Roman Catholics with Irish surnames.

The failed Manitoba campaign and increased Fenian involvement in American politics demonstrated how insignificant the transatlantic Irish republican movement had become by the early 1870s. Jeremiah O'Donovan Rossa received thousands of votes when he ran for a New York senate seat against long-time Irish patron Boss Tweed in the November election that followed O'Neill's Red River imbroglio. Yet such ballot box support was largely attributable to Rossa's status as a former prisoner. His continued advocacy of Irish rebellion was, if anything, a liability. Such insistence on violence undermined Rossa's long-shot run for president without major party endorsement when federal elections were held a year later. Other Fenian candidates were more successful. County Clare native and one-time Springfield, Massachusetts circle leader, William Hynes, became a one-term Republican carpetbagger congressman from Arkansas the same year that William Roberts was re-elected by a four-to-one margin over his nearest opponent.[147] As a second-term representative who had survived the *New York Times*–orchestrated demise of his ally Boss Tweed, Roberts was reassigned to the more influential Claims Committee and continued to be an ardent critic of British foreign policy on the House floor. Consistently against Radical Reconstruction, he also opposed continued suspension of *habeas corpus* protections in the South as a means to contain the Ku Klux Klan.[148] He was, however, one of the few Democratic supporters of black suffrage on Capitol Hill. In private life, his second term was marred by the loss of his private fortune after a September 19, 1873, stock market crash precipitated a protracted national recession. To economize, he relocated his Washington residence from the comforts of the prestigious Willard Hotel to a residence on New York Avenue.[149]

John Warren's unsuccessful bid for public office during the Panic of 1873 showed that new expatriate organizations had eclipsed the Fenian Brotherhood. Having served as a leader of the Officer's Irish Brigade Association and as a chairman of a Fenian prisoners relief fund, Warren had little success as the Republican Party nominee for New York City registrar. Many men who would have been his constituents a few years earlier were no doubt among the twenty thousand expatriate members of the four-year-old, 103-chapter strong Irish Catholic Benevolent Union (ICBU).[150] Other Irishmen became actively involved in the rising union movement. Founded in the same year as the ICBU, the Knights of Labor would be led by first generation Irish American and one-time Fenian supporter Terence Powderly within a decade of its establishment.[151]

Whether in political victory or defeat, the career swing many Fenian leaders underwent a similar trend within the larger expatriate community. A standard monthly report form that each O'Mahony faction circle submitted to national headquarters in the early 1870s included no space to inscribe the names of new members. The bottom third of each sheet was reserved, however, for listing "Expulsions and Desertions," presumably because from 1869 to 1874 attendance records show that roughly 50 percent of Massachusetts circle members routinely skipped weekly meetings.[152] Along these lines, a central New England Irish nationalist leader had written to a Boston colleague in July 1871 that "Fenianism is gone down in Worcester though we manage to keep up some semblance of an organization."[153] As another indication of ongoing expatriate nationalist assimilation into mainstream American society, none of the suspected Milford Fenians became charter members of a local AOH chapter when it was established in March 1873.[154]

William Gladstone continued his efforts to prevent any resurgent Fenian activity in Ireland at the same time that John Warren unsuccessfully ran for political office. Mindful that several previous prime ministers had failed in their attempts to reform British higher education, Gladstone personally devoted months of his own time to drafting a cutting-edge proposal that would have secularized all Irish colleges. In exchange for guaranteed state funding and a one-time lump sum financial grant, the Catholic seminary at Maynooth would have been incorporated into an ecumenical university system that precluded the teaching of theology, moral philosophy, and history to decrease religious tension among students. In Gladstone's estimation, dialogue between Catholic and Protestant collegians might have weakened the most rigid social division in Irish society. Cullen summarily rejected revamping Irish higher education, however, because he shared the concern of his 1840s predecessors that "godless colleges" would threaten the role of the Catholic Church in Ireland and compromise the faith of young Catholics. Gladstone thus fell three votes short of enacting the 1873 University Bill because twenty-five Cullen-abiding Irish Catholics were among the forty-three members of his party who opposed the legislation.[155] In a defeat that normally would have triggered his resignation, Gladstone had the consolation of remaining in office because Benjamin Disraeli refused to form a minority Tory government. Lay Catholic students, as a consequence, were denied access to public degrees until the Royal University of Ireland was chartered six years later.[156]

How much of an impact these efforts actually had on the global Irish nationalist movement is uncertain. Political disturbances decreased throughout the

North Atlantic world during the devastating Panic of 1873. Rising unemployment in American and Irish urban centers dampened expatriate interest in republican activities. Higher Irish agricultural commodity prices, conversely, encouraged a spirit of contentment in the Hibernian countryside. As Irish immigration to America temporarily declined, the theatre became a nexus of Fenian expression. Two hundred thousand Dublin, London, and New York patrons flocked to see Dion Boucicault's nationalist-tinged production, *The Shaughraun* in 1874. In his first political melodrama since *Arrah-na-Pogue,* the famed Irish writer initially cast himself in the leading role of Conn, the friend of a former Fenian convict who has returned to Ireland only to be persecuted by a nefarious landlord and an English officer of Norman heritage.

It is ironic that militant Irish nationalists successfully organized a dramatic rescue of Fenian prisoners from a convict settlement in western Australia during a period when noticeable demonstrations of patriotic expression were largely limited to electing former Fenians to political office, attending theater, and participating in occasional leisure activities. As a former IRB recruiter of enlisted men stationed in Ireland, John Devoy believed he had a personal responsibility to assist Fenian prisoners who had served in the British Army. He, accordingly, had long pondered how he could extricate some of his comrades on the other side of the globe from a life of hard labor. Fundraising and logistical problems prohibited Devoy from actually launching a mission, until his fellow members of the *Clan na Gael* voted to underwrite the expedition during their 1875 national convention in Baltimore. Assisted by the ubiquitous Michael Kerwin, a future member of the New York State Supreme Court, and a few other coconspirators, Devoy brokered an ambitious deal with a New Bedford, Massachusetts commercial agent and his ship captain son-in-law. While en route to Fremantle, twenty-nine-year-old George S. Anthony and his mixed race crew of Malay, Portuguese, and African seamen would hunt for whales in the Atlantic and Indian Oceans. When assured that they had obtained enough oil to secure a profit for his father-in-law, Anthony and his men would rendezvous with five Fenian prisoners and their rescue party and then sail for home. The voyage was expected to last eighteen months to two years. If successful, the operation would easily surpass the more improvisational escapes of Mitchel, Meagher, MacManus, and Boyle O'Reilly.

Devoy's plan to convey his five convict compatriots from Fremantle to Anthony's 202.5-ton whaler was particularly ambitious. Posing as wealthy mining investors, John J. Breslin and Thomas Desmond departed San Francisco for Perth four months after Anthony sailed the *Catalpa* out of New Bedford on April 29. Opting to establish a temporary residence in nearby Fremantle when he reached his destination the following November, Breslin contacted the Fenian prisoners through the intercession of a sympathetic Catholic priest and plotted an ambitious escape. On Easter Monday 1876, Breslin and Desmond obtained a cart and two aged horses, collected the six prisoners while they were working unguarded on a road building detail, and raced for the coast. A fifteen-hour row in a whaleboat and the brief harassment from a Royal Navy gunship ensued, but the escapees reached the *Catalpa*.[157] Having previously helped rescue James Stephens from Richmond Bridewell, Breslin solidified his reputation as one of the most resourceful Irish nationalists during the Fenian period. Welcomed back to New York in August with parades and banquets, the *Catalpa* mission operatives and the fugitive Fenian prisoners received tremendous public attention. An anticipated Clan na Gael resurgence never occurred, however. Belatedly, the expedition had demonstrated that one of the most productive methods of tapping limited expatriate support for nationalist endeavors was for expatriates to underwrite guerilla initiatives led by talented men like Breslin. Men who had the capability to circumnavigate the planet and rescue Irish nationalist prisoners were more effective than the vainglorious expatriate leaders who had been responsible for the Fenian invasions of Canada.

The anemic state of both the Fenian Brotherhood and the Clan na Gael prompted Boston Irish nationalists to unite the local affiliates of their two organizations when expatriate support for an independent Ireland remained listless in the wake of the *Catalpa* rescue.[158] The failure of this merger was evident in 1876, however, when a group of Fenians unsuccessfully attempted to suppress expatriate support for gubernatorial candidate Charles Francis Adams. Ironically, the former Fenian nemesis had tried to keep his name off the ballot and had made no serious effort to win the election, yet he won the Boston Irish vote. An ever-optimistic circular issued to former members also did little to boost statewide recruitment. A local Fenian leader, who was the Charlestown owner of a company that produced waterproof leather preservative, thus decided to preside over circle meetings in his own home. Renting a hall, in his estimation, had become prohibitively expensive.[159]

Such economizing was understandable, as some New England Fenian notables had abandoned the organization. The former convict Denis Cashman, for instance, distanced himself from nationalist activity when he became the Boston superintendent of waste water in 1876 and thereafter continued to work intermittently as a journalist.[160] Former IRB leader Thomas Kelly was among a dwindling number of expatriates whose sociopolitical views were conducive to long-standing Fenian objectives. Although a March 1876 letter to his mother mentioned that he had developed a renewed sense of spirituality after not having practiced his Catholic faith for nearly twenty-five years, Kelly still sounded like an ideal Fenian operative when he wrote that he was very leery about the merits of Irish immigration to America. Aspiring migrants were better off at home, in his opinion, since working-class employment was scarce and wages were low.[161]

Expatriate political and financial power was increasingly used to support rising Irish American powerbrokers, such as Patrick A. Collins, after the Fenian Brotherhood became an insignificant expatriate organization. First- and second-generation Irish immigrants widely admired the County Cork native. Arriving in America when he was four, the thirty-two-year-old had parlayed an early life as an Ohio coalminer into a Harvard education and a promising political career.[162] Having left the Brotherhood in 1866 to protest Sweeny's intended plan to invade Canada, Collins had already served as a Massachusetts state senator when he and William Roberts served as delegates at the June 1876 Democratic National Convention in Saint Louis. Campaigning later that same year, Collins summarized a personal platform that would later secure him a seat in the United States Senate and his election as mayor of Boston: "I love the land of my birth, but in American politics I know neither race, nor color, nor creed. Let me say that there are no Irish votes among us. There are Irish-born citizens . . . but the moment the seal of the court was impressed on our papers, we ceased to be foreigners and became Americans."[163]

Jeremiah O'Donovan Rossa primarily led the ever-dwindling pool of militant nationalist supporters in Ireland and America after Patrick Collins became a conventional politician in 1876. Foreshadowing a decade of orchestrating terrorist attacks in England and Scotland, the veteran nationalist gave sixty thousand dollars to the brother of a New York City Fenian who developed the first steam-powered submarine. A marvel of ingenuity even though it was impaired by many mechanical problems, the so-called *Fenian Ram* was originally commissioned to harass British shipping. Instead, the thirty-one-foot-long vessel eventually revolutionized global naval warfare by resolving the prototypical flaws of the Confederate navy submersibles. It is thus plausible that an increasingly small group of Irish American nationalists continued to channel sizable amounts of money into a costly project, because the invention of a vessel that could travel sixty feet underwater for up to an hour further undermined lingering notions of Anglo-Saxon intellectual and physical superiority over the Celtic race. Conversely, the initiative could be viewed as a futile exercise that Rossa supported, because he would (as he said twelve years later) do anything but follow John Mitchel's advice to patiently wait for the next time "England's difficulty would be Ireland's opportunity."[164]

The death of John O'Mahony when the *Fenian Ram* was in preproduction definitively marked the demise of the mid-nineteenth century Irish republican movement. Far from the public spotlight at the time of his demise, O'Mahony succumbed to a severe lung ailment on February 6, 1877. Through the intercession of former colleagues who had made an unexpected visit to his tawdry New York tenement accommodations shortly before his death, O'Mahony was able to receive absolution on condition that he renounce his affiliation with the Fenian Brotherhood. Three priests served as celebrants when his funeral was held in a Manhattan Jesuit church.[165] As a final tribute, twenty thousand mourners accompanied a 69th Regiment cortege through the streets of lower Manhattan on the day that Rossa, Thomas Francis Bourke, Warren, Costello, and other veteran Fenian pallbearers conveyed his body to the Queenstown-bound steamer *Dakota*.[166] As in the MacManus funeral procession, O'Mahony's remains were welcomed into the Cloyne Cathedral by large crowds and by Bishop William Keane's successor, John MacCarthy. Cardinal Cullen would allow the body of the Brotherhood leader to be buried at Glasnevin Cemetery, however, only if no nationalist addresses were made at his graveside. Subsequently, the IRB once again placed one of its deceased heroes in the Mechanics' Institute, where myriads of reportedly grubby-looking nationalist sympathizers paid their respects over the course of a week to a corpse that was rapidly decomposing. Charles Kickham concluded the extended O'Mahony tribute by eulogizing his former comrade before a sizable number of men and women outside the gates to Glasnevin on March 4.[167] In hindsight, many Fenian veterans concluded that O'Mahony had had a good heart, but had been incapable of leading a large nationalist movement. Devoy revealed his mixed feelings toward his former colleague years later by writing that O'Mahony "lacked some of the essential qualities of leadership" but "was one of the most interesting characters in Irish history."[168] Richard O'Flynn of Worcester was more sympathetic in a *fin de siècle* retrospective:

> For myself, after a lapse of twenty years, I have the same profound love and admiration for the man who in manhood, early years, and to his melancholy death, was so true and faithful, to his brave hearts idol-Dear Old Erin. Who bore persecution, exile, obloquy, reproach, age, and hunger for his love__ As I write the tears well up to my eyes at the recollection of his sad death—Cold, hungry, deserted, in a New York tenement attic. I do firmly believe__ that God could not create a truer, nobler, honester, or more patriotic man than John O'Mahony.[169]

Complementing this paean was the anonymously penned "Lament of John O'Mahony." With lyrics written in the Fenian leader's own voice, the ballad offers no apologies for past personal shortcomings. Instead, the aged revolutionary claims that his personal reputation remains intact despite the failure of the

Brotherhood: "I have rescued naught but my honour only." His only punishment, he proceeds to say, is his obligation to live in continued exile in American lands that "hold naught" for him. Disregarding all their past differences, Stephens paid homage to his former comrade in a published tribute. "In his grave today," the IRB founder wrote, "John O'Mahony is dearer to me than any other man, dead or alive."[170]

John O'Neill was enjoying a degree of professional success at the time of O'Mahony's death. As a private citizen, O'Neill had become a salaried land speculator. A number of power-conscious Irish politicians and Catholic Church leaders selfishly resisted westward expatriate migration after the Civil War, but O'Neill established three rural communities in eastern Nebraska during the mid-1870s. Discounting the initial instability of these settlements—several original homesteaders returned home five months after they arrived in the Great Plains—O'Neill fulfilled O'Mahony's pre-Fenian Brotherhood dream of chartering an Irish colony in the Midwest. Formerly known as Rockford, the town that became known as O'Neill eventually attracted several expatriate miners from Pennsylvania to modern-day Holt County. Ever the Irish nationalist, O'Neill contemplated plotting a new town to the south along the Platte River in 1876 for personal gain and to raise money for "the cause of Irish freedom." Omaha bishop James O'Connor, however, endorsed an alternative O'Neill proposal to resell land purchased from either the Union Pacific or the Burlington and Missouri railroad companies at a modest and innocuous profit.[171]

O'Neill died before he acquired as much social influence as the many Fenian veterans who entered American politics. If blessed with better health, he might have fulfilled his expressed December 1876 desire to lead yet another foray into Canada.[172] More likely, he would have followed some of his Fenian colleagues by running for public office. Fellow Ridgeway veteran John Egan would become the speaker of the New Jersey Assembly, while Victor Vifquain had returned to his adopted Nebraska hometown in Saline County and was starting to become an influential Democratic Party leader.[173] O'Neill, however, suffered a stroke shortly before Christmas 1877 and died from injuries when he fell out of an Omaha hospital bed two weeks later.[174] As O'Neill was long remembered for his victory at Ridgeway, the future Irish Taoiseach Eamon DeValera dedicated a monument over O'Neill's grave shortly after he had escaped from an English prison in 1919 and traveled throughout the United States to raise money for Sinn Féin.

Subdued funeral services for O'Neill paled in comparison to a massive January 1878 memorial tribute in Dublin for a just-released rank-and-file IRB prisoner who died shortly before he was to have had breakfast with Charles Stewart Parnell. The death of Charles McCarthy elicited a powerful response throughout

Ireland because the former color guard sergeant suffered a fatal heart attack while en route home to be reunited with his wife. Thousands of mourners joined what some journalists described as the largest funeral procession to Glasnevin Cemetery since the legendary Daniel O'Connell had been laid to rest there three decades earlier.[175] As had been evident on many occasions since the 1798 United Irish rebellion, most Irish men and women had been reluctant to take arms, but had been willing to support a nationalist movement that combined veiled antigovernment threats with nonviolent demonstrations. The funeral of Charles McCarthy thus served as another reminder that the now-defeated Fenian movement would likely have been more effectual if its leaders understood the collective psychology of the Irish people. Most Hibernians in the North Atlantic world were constitutional nationalists: law-abiding protestors with strong political convictions rather than antigovernment soldiers willing to risk arrest and incarceration.

Similar Irish eagerness to support licit protest initiatives was evident in the subsequent formation of the Land League. Originally established as a grassroots movement in County Mayo, the League blossomed into a powerful organization with a substantial presence in every section of the island, except predominately Protestant Ulster, within a year of its founding in October 1878. The adoption of passive resistance techniques, such as the newly coined "boycott," was remarkably effective. Formerly apolitical tenant farmers allied themselves with reindoctrinated Fenians who had come to recognize that independence could not be achieved without the participation of Irish men and women from home and abroad. The one-armed Michael Davitt became the leader of a movement that included Patrick Collins, an estimated twenty-five MPs who backed Parnell in the British Parliament, and John Devoy.[176] One of the principal explanations for the success of the Land League was the New Departure, a strategic agreement among various Irish nationalists. In accordance with the pact, Collins raised money while serving as the president of the Irish Land League of America, while the members of the Clan na Gael and the crippled IRB agreed to temporarily refrain from militant activity. Half the remaining Worcester "Last Call" fund was accordingly forwarded to the Land League. The other five hundred dollars in the fifteen-year-old fund was allocated to a local parish building project in further demonstration of expatriate assimilation into American society; however, expatriates donated money to the League because they wanted to help fellow countrymen who were being evicted at a time when Irish agricultural production had reached a thirty-year low.[177] James Stephens likewise endorsed Davitt's efforts in 1879 after briefly resuming titular control of the Fenian Brotherhood. Further demonstrating that the League represented a new era in Irish nationalist expression, only three of sixty people suspected of Fenian activity in rural County Mayo had been employed in the agricultural sector between 1866 and 1871.[178] The League, however, would have never existed without active peasant participation.

Irish nationalists who were wary of the Land League disparately reacted to Davitt's attempt to link real estate redistribution and independence in the tradition of the deceased James Finton Lalor. Expatriate zealots affiliated either with O'Donovan Rossa or with a breakaway group of Clan na Gael members who continued to support violent initiatives in their quest for an independent Ireland. An IRB assassin murdered former British informant Pierce Nagle by stabbing him through the heart with a cheese knife on the streets of London in 1879.[179] More sensational, however, was the introduction of an indiscriminate bombing campaign in January 1881. Having established a so-called Skirmishing Fund five years earlier, Rossa was able to underwrite successive bombing strikes on the Salford Military barracks, a London government building, and the Liverpool Town Hall within the span of five months. All but the first attack were thwarted and total casualties amounted to the killing of a seven-year-old boy and the wounding of three adults. Yet more devastating operations would follow in the coming years.[180] Romantic Fenian notions of fighting with honor vanished, in sum, once Davitt undermined the militant republican movement by emerging as a powerful social agitator.

The deaths of other prominent Fenians further showed that a new era of Irish nationalist agitation had begun with the advent of the Land League. John Kavanagh succumbed to series of maladies on June 10, 1880 that had plagued him ever since contracting malaria while serving onboard the *San Jacinto* before the Civil War. Only forty at the time of his death, he had once unsuccessfully run as the Republican Party candidate for the coroner's office and had last worked as a watchman at the New York Customs House.[181] Fenian-escapee-turned-politician Timothy Deasy died six months later in his native Lawrence, Massachusetts. Deasy's memorial service resembled many other Fenian funerals that had drawn large crowds of mourners.[182]

Incessant political agitation in the midst of random terrorist attacks led to the passage of the 1881 Irish Land Act. Under legislative provisions established by Gladstone, Hibernian peasants could submit grievances against their landlords to a court of arbitration that would regulate rents and award compensation if tenants improved the value of their fields. This act did not protect families whose leases were in arrears, however, and did not address rising Land League demands for the re-establishment of a semi-autonomous Irish parliament. Parnell, who now used more extreme rhetoric in his speeches to voice opposition to the Land Act and support for a rent strike, was arrested under the Coercion Acts and detained in Kilmainhaim Gaol for six months. Contingent to his release in May

1882, the Irish nationalist leader abolished both the League and a women's affili-ate organization that had eclipsed the Fenian Sisterhood. A new National League was formed shortly thereafter to coordinate political action between Irish subjects and MPs who belonged to Parnell's Irish Parliamentary Party. Yet the spirit of empowerment that had originally surfaced in County Mayo never rematerialized. Grassroots agitation, like militant republicanism, had succeeded as a mechanism to secure concessions from open-minded English politicians such as Gladstone, but it did not lead to Irish independence.

Another brief period of sporadic murders and bombings preceded a lull in Irish nationalist agitation that continued until a new generation of republi-cans emerged on the eve of World War I. A Fenian spin-off group called the Irish National Invincibles appealed to people such as a Clermont, Iowa native who, in a letter to the *United Irishman* the previous January, espoused bombing, burning, shooting, and poisoning "famine-making [British] tyrants." The John McCafferty–led organization achieved its only success, however, through seren-dipity.[183] On May 6, 1882, recently appointed Irish chief secretary Lord Frederick Cavendish and Irish permanent secretary Thomas Burke were fatally slashed in Phoenix Park by two knife-wielding assailants after the bureaucrats had encoun-tered one another in the midst of unscheduled evening strolls. Cavendish, of al-most equal significance, had only arrived in Ireland to assume his new duties on the morning of his death.[184] Unsubstantiated rumors quickly linked Parnell to the crime because he had been released from prison two days earlier. Renewed anti-Irish sentiment in light of the killings was fueled by a common mid-nineteenth century consensus that the use of knives was cowardly even in self-defense.[185] As-sassinations, moreover, were widely perceived at the time to be the method only of "immature" nations, such as Russia and an American republic, where the legacy of violent Irish vigilantism was perpetuated by secret organizations such as the Molly Maguires. Unlike tepid Fenian supporters who only attended picnics and lectures, the Mollys became known in the mid-nineteenth century for murdering private detectives and mine owners who offered low wages and few benefits to expatriate coalminers in the anthracite region of eastern Pennsylvania.[186]

The ever-militant O'Donovan Rossa ensured that British subjects would obstinately oppose Irish independence for decades after the Phoenix Park mur-ders by orchestrating a large-scale bombing campaign in 1883. Three attacks in Glasgow at the beginning of the year drew widespread condemnation through-out the transatlantic world. More significantly, few militant republicans endorsed what is today known as asymmetrical warfare. Thomas O'Neill of Monroesville, Ohio spoke for a distinct minority within the expatriate community when he remitted a subscription fee for Rossa's newspaper and an additional donation to the Rossa Skirmishing Fund on February 24, writing, "Dear Sir, Inclosed find $3; $2 for my yearly subscription for the 'United Irishman', and $1 dollar for dynamite. I think it the most consistent remedy for old tyrant England."[187] Skirmishing Fund leaders justified such brutal tactics by stating in their printed fundraising materials that it enabled "Brave Irishmen [to] MAKE Ireland's opportunity instead of waiting for it." They also defended eye-for-an-eye operations by stating, "England employed Red Indians in America to scalp American men, women, and children, and England burned American cities to the ground. Fight England with England's own weapons."[188]

Such espousals of terrorist activity may have been encouraged by lingering instances of anti-Irish discrimination in the United States. Irish American veterans who lived in the vicinity of Fitchburg, Massachusetts were denied admission into a local Grand Army of the Republic auxiliary during the Gilded Era, while only one Milford, Massachusetts Irishman was selected to serve on a ten-member town committee planning the construction of a veteran's memorial hall in 1884.[189] During the same year, Irish Union army veteran James Sullivan was harassed about the status of his father's citizenship when he applied to unsettled homestead land in his native Wisconsin.[190] Yet terrorist activity only incensed English government officials who rightfully believed that attempts to destroy a London Underground station and other public places in the name of Irish independence were barbaric. Canadian aversion to Irish republicanism continued, moreover, as lingering memories of three John O'Neill–led invasions of their nation were compounded by the 1885 appointment of a former Fenian as American consul in Fort Erie, Ontario.[191]

The repercussions of Irish terrorist attacks against the British people demonstrated the failure of the 1880s neo-Fenian movement, just as much as expatriate assimilation had done so a decade before. During a period when the British nation was under psychological siege, a convicted Fenian murderer had little chance of receiving any clemency for fatally wounding a former IRB informant. Forty-three-year-old American citizen Patrick O'Donnell was hanged (despite the intercession of Patrick Collins and several other Irish American politicians) in December 1883 for killing James Carey while both men were traveling aboard a Cape Colony–bound steamship the previous July.[192] Parnell thereafter had minimal chance of securing Irish independence when an 1867 rebellion leader, William Mackey Lomasney, accidentally killed himself, his brother-in-law, and another man while the three operatives attempted to blow-up London Bridge on the seventeenth anniversary of the Clerkenwell explosion. By the time the bombing campaign ended and Rossa had survived an attempt on his life in 1885, Scotland Yard, a handful of British rail stations, the Tower of London, and the House of Commons had all been targeted. Most Fenians, in the contemporary words of a Boston Irish nationalist, had become "discouraged and dropped out of the fight."[193] Ireland, moreover, remained an integral part of the United Kingdom.

8

LAST HURRAHS

Although "Fenian" became an enduring and often derogatory synonym for Irish militants, few Civil War–era nationalists were still devoted to their republican cause by the close of the nineteenth century. Some former Brotherhood and IRB members, like Roberts and others, were able to parlay their global notoriety into respectable political and professional careers during the Gilded Age. Most rank-and-file nationalists, however, experienced more modest social mobility within an expatriate community that in the 1890s was comprised mostly of manual laborers.[1] As higher living standards became increasingly appreciated among an aging segment of the transatlantic Irish population, the legacy of the mid-nineteenth century Fenian movement was largely reduced to innocuous commemorative balls and nostalgic obituaries. A minuscule remnant of the IRB briefly endured after the conclusion of the Irish Civil War in May 1923, but Stephens and O'Mahony were never revered as great statesmen. Fenianism thus collapsed for a variety of reasons, among them Stephens and O'Mahony's inability to prevent opportunistic expatriates from exploiting the IRB and the stateside Brotherhood for their own benefit.

Irish immigrant assimilation into American society greatly compromised the IRB and the Fenian Brotherhood after the Civil War. Expatriate resentment of lingering nativist discrimination and exploitation diminished during the last third of the mid-nineteenth century. Outside of low per-capita military enlistment, significant participation in the 1863 Draft Riots, and Reconstruction-era Orange riots, Irish Americans generally eschewed anticivic behavior as they struggled to gain greater social respectability. Civil War journalist George Alfred

Townsend accurately noted in a published memoir "when anything absurd, forlorn, or desperate was to be attempted, the Irish Brigade was called upon."[2] Nevertheless, Peter Welsh had astutely predicted progressive Americanization of Hibernian immigrants in a letter to his wife written shortly after the Irish Brigade was decimated at the 1862 Battle of Fredericksburg:

> Ireland is bound to this country by the strongest types of blood and
> sympathy Her sons have penetrated to the remotest parts of the
> union they are interwoven like a network over the whole face of the
> country Their influence is felt in every section and it is increasing
> and will continue until at no very distant day the Irish element will
> be the most powerfull and influential in the land.[3]

Just as Welsh's wife incorrectly assumed that her husband served in a "foreign" army, expatriate consumer behavior reflected Irish integration into a Protestant-dominated culture. Currier and Ives lithographs of Irish American Civil War heroes sold remarkably well after peace was restored in the United States. Conversely, pastoral etchings of Ireland that the company also marketed sold poorly.[4] Contrary to the post-1867 rebellion views of Cluseret, most expatriates who had fought in both combatant armies during the Civil War and, to a lesser per-capita degree, had been ardent nationalists for ideological reasons rather than "for the pleasure" of fighting.[5]

Former Irish militants who became politicians had the most noteworthy personal success after the decline of the mid-nineteenth century Fenian movement. Roberts resigned from the United States House of Representatives after four years on Capitol Hill and successfully ran for a seat on the historically corrupt New York City Board of Aldermen. Whether Roberts accepted kickbacks in this capacity is unknown. Upon later losing an 1879 bid for Manhattan borough sheriff, Roberts defected from Tammany Hall by supporting Grover Cleveland for governor of New York in 1882, and for president two years later. In gratitude, the Buffalo native later appointed Roberts as United States ambassador to Chile. By the time Roberts was en route to Santiago, Galway native John F. Finerty had completed his one-term tenure as an Independent Democrat in Congress. More a journalist than a politician, Finerty had traveled throughout the Great Plains in the 1870s and later wrote anti–Native American books and news articles that focused on the many Indian wars that arose in the 1870s.[6] The thirty-six-year-old had also started a weekly Chicago Irish newspaper before representing a Chicago constituency in the House of Representatives.[7]

Many former Fenians besides Roberts received federal political appointments or were elected to state and local office during the Gilded Age. President

Cleveland struck a balance between veteran members of both erstwhile Fenian Brotherhood factions by providing O'Mahony wing mercenary Victor Vifquain with United States consular appointments to Barranquila and Colon. Among the many Fenians who were elected to lower-ranking political positions, Tipperary native and one-time commission house bookkeeper John Breen became the first Irish Catholic mayor in New England fourteen years after he had returned home from the 1867 IRB rebellion at the age of twenty-five.[8] Meanwhile, one of the organizers of the *Catalpa* rescue was elected New York state recorder, while one of the prisoners he had helped extricate became a San Francisco sheriff. Michael Kerwin's Civil War cavalry service under General Phil Sheridan and his political affiliation with the Stalwart faction of the Republican Party helped the former Fenian become New York City police commissioner in July 1894.[9] Conversely, only two erstwhile IRB members were able to secure significant political office in the latter half of the nineteenth century. The 1874 parliamentary election of IRB Supreme Council member, John O'Connor Power, rekindled long-dormant nationalist expression in his County Mayo constituency and encouraged another former Fenian named Matthew Harris to establish the Ballinasloe Tenants' Defense Association.[10] Francis Xavier O'Brien parlayed his Irish nationalist notoriety into a successful run for Parliament when he stood for a Connaught constituency in 1885. O'Brien represented South Mayo for ten years and then served as an anti-Parnellite backbencher for Cork City until his death a decade later.[11]

John Boyle O'Reilly was one of several lapsed Fenians who became successful writers at the same time many other one-time Irish militants were gaining influence in the American and British governments. As a Boston-based journalist and orator, O'Reilly increasingly bore less resemblance to his younger militant self. In addition to once saying that he hated the word "Fenian," he had written to Rossa on March 1872, "[I] think Fenianism is as big a humbug as Mormonism."[12] An undated request to reschedule a public speaking engagement because it would have conflicted with a Forty Hours' Devotion in a nearby parish church was further reflection of his conservative allegiance to a religious authority that most other Fenian leaders had resisted.[13] Unlike most other Irish Americans, O'Reilly was also an advocate of African American civil rights and a great admirer of the Pilgrims. His 1889 keynote address at the dedication of a Plymouth Rock monument juxtaposed a prewar editorial comment by Thomas Francis Meagher that Massachusetts Puritanism had been the root of contemporary Irish American grievances. In addition, the speech symbolized rising expatriate political power and increasing ecumenical affinity among American Christians.[14] Recalcitrant republican militants had disapproved of O'Reilly's metamorphosis from an escaped Fenian prisoner and *Catalpa* rescue mission supporter into a critic of relentlessly new Irish rebellion schemes.[15] The ardent nationalist-turned-poet became a posthumous romantic hero, however, after he died from an apparent overdose of his wife's sleeping medication in August 1890.[16] Despite having increasingly shared the nonviolent political views of Daniel O'Connell, O'Reilly was often most remembered as a man who, like Rossa, believed Anglophobia was an intrinsic Irish trait.

Augustine Costello remained considerably more nationalistic than O'Reilly after he, too, became a successful author. Upon resigning from the New York City Police Department, the well-known *Erin's Hope* filibusterer started writing a series of books about metropolitan law enforcement and municipal service organizations. Beginning with his former employer in 1885, he eventually wrote eight profiles of police and fire brigades in several cities, including Chicago and Minneapolis. Proceeds for his work were usually used for employee pensions and disability entitlements. His ability to publish all these highly detailed manuscripts in a seven-year span is remarkable, even though he had been described as a man "of literary habits and literary experience" at the time he was on trial for treason in Dublin.[17] In an 1891 letter that concluded with the words "God Save Ireland," the forty-six-year-old lamented to a presumably younger cousin that he should have become a lawyer or some other type of professional. Nevertheless, he was proud of his "profitable and congenial" career as a journalist, given his limited hedge school education in County Galway.[18] Similar to John Finerty's speeches against increasing Anglo-American diplomatic cooperation, Costello's frequent anti-British oratories garnered routine attention in the New York press throughout the 1890s.[19] While criticizing President William McKinley during an 1898 IRB banquet, Costello summed up the views of unrepentant Fenians by stating, "those who were imbued with the principles of 1865 and 1867 are still rebels at heart."[20]

Several other veteran Fenian militants shared Costello's enduring desire to witness the establishment of an Irish republic. Patrick Kain served as an AOH chapter president in northern California before he returned to the East Coast and became a Methodist minister who preached at a small rural church outside Stroudsburg, Pennsylvania.[21] Their fellow *Erin's Hope* crewman Andrew Leonard also served as an Organization of Saint Patrick community leader. William Roberts's former Buffalo point man, Patrick O'Day, continued to display his Irish fealty by sporting an embroidered green harp on the left sleeve of his jackets long after the 1866 Niagara Peninsula campaign had failed.[22] Yet increasing professional and private responsibilities led to even greater Fenian emphasis on recreational rather than militant activities. Fenian dinner-dances became regular events in East Coast metropolitan areas in the 1870s. "Ladies," as an extant imprinted ticket shows, were especially encouraged to attend the eighteenth annual

Fenian Ball in Boston.[23] By 1904, John Devoy and his colleagues would stage a commemorative Brotherhood celebration, which featured a contest between the reigning world shot put champion and a competitor dubbed "Ireland's Greatest Athlete." Similar Fenian activities, which largely dissipated after Devoy's death on September 29, 1928, appealed to a small portion of the expatriate population that included the father of early-twentieth-century American labor crusader Elizabeth Gurley Flynn. A descendent of a United Irishman as well as the granddaughter of a man who had participated in the 1866 Fenian invasion of Canada, Flynn wrote on the first page of her autobiography "until my father died at over eighty, he never said *England* without adding the phrase, "God Damn her!"[24]

Lingering nationalist expression was also evident in the 1887 establishment of the IRB Veterans Mutual Aid Association. Founded three years before a final Fenian convention was held in Paterson, New Jersey, the organization provided unemployment assistance and burial funds to a generation of expatriates that was reaching its sunset years.[25] Most mid-nineteenth century Fenians had advanced out of the lower-middle class by the Gilded Age but never became affluent. Longtime spy Thomas Billis Beech was one of the few people who truly profited from the emergence of a transatlantic republican movement during the Victorian period. Having infiltrated the Clan na Gael after the almost-total demise of the Fenian Brotherhood, Beech did not reveal his true identity until he was called to testify before a British government commission that was investigating an 1889 charge of treason against Parnell. The man formerly known as Henri LeCaron subsequently lived comfortably in London for the remaining five years of his life.[26] Other spies were not as fortunate. Fenians routinely denounced Red Jim McDermott in the press during the latter half of the nineteenth century, and one of Michael Doheny's three sons murdered *Erin's Hope* informer William F. Million.[27]

The creation of a Fenian benevolent society appeared practical, as many prominent nationalist leaders either died or needed financial assistance in the 1890s. William Sweeny enjoyed a long, comfortable retirement before he died in April 1892, because he had returned to active duty after the second Fenian foray into Canada and consequently received an ample government pension. James Stephens, on the other hand, could not afford to buy a home when Parnell arranged for him to return to Ireland. In exchange for agreeing not to participate actively in Irish politics after he had chaired a Rossa lecture and attended Parnell's October 1891 funeral, Stephens was provided a small cottage in Sutton, which admirers had purchased by raising funds through a public subscription. Stephens died a decade later on March 29, 1901.[28] Bridget Warren's unsuccessful efforts to secure a United States Army widow's pension during the months after her husband's death in September 1895 additionally indicate that past prominence within the Fenian Brotherhood did not guarantee personal financial security. A fifty-six-year-old in good health when a piece of stonework came loose from the Boston Masonic Temple and fatally struck him in the head, Warren had been twice married but had never become a parent.[29] When he died at Massachusetts General Hospital, the former *Erin's Hope* celebrity was remembered for having had a workingman's association named after him and for his political and business activities.[30]

The fleeting legacy of the transatlantic Fenian movement was acutely evident when only four people attended William Roberts's 1897 funeral. A victim of a paralytic stroke while in Chile, the one-time charismatic Fenian President had been forced to resign his diplomatic post and return to New York, where he remained a hospitalized invalid for the final eight years of his life. The one-time millionaire was unostentatiously buried in even more obscurity than the less-well-known Warren.[31] The passing of James Kerrigan two years later occurred shortly after the former Nicaragua filibusterer returned from a private expedition to Alaska. In addition to having made an unsuccessful 1876 bid to return to Congress by running as a Greenbacker against the nearly executed IRB leader Thomas Bourke and three other candidates, Kerrigan had helped establish many benevolent organizations while remaining a proponent of Irish independence.

The deaths of five other well-known Fenians occurred at the same time that a handful of longstanding Irish militants had joined foreign armies or organized independent initiatives to continue their armed struggle against the British government at the beginning of the twentieth century. When Gustave Cluseret died of pneumonia near the Mediterranean port of Toulon on August 22, 1900, former IRB prisoner Alfred Aylward was serving in an Irish Brigade unit that had traveled to South Africa to assist Boer insurgents. By the time Michael Davitt served as a pallbearer at the funeral of James Stephens seven months later, a band of expatriates had unsuccessfully attempted to sabotage a Welland Canal lock so that it would be more difficult to convey Canadian goods to British regiments under arms in the Cape Colony.[32] While the convicted bombers were in prison, Stephens's early IRB colleague Thomas Clark Luby died in Jersey City as an American citizen. Victor Vifquain was eulogized at his funeral in Lincoln, Nebraska two years later for a lifetime of military service, which some Irish Americans questioned. Contrary to the views of expatriates who believed that American military action against Spain in 1898 was reminiscent of British imperialism, Vifquain had raised a volunteer regiment that saw no action, but would have been led by William Jennings Bryan if it had reached Cuba before an armistice was signed.[33]

Given that the transatlantic Fenian movement was widely derided after its apex, it is no surprise that the deaths of some Brotherhood members were overshadowed by other events. Having been listed as a Fenian in bad standing twenty-six years earlier, former Boston policeman, GAR member, and *Erin's Hope* filibusterer, William C. Nugent, abandoned his wife in 1900 and died in a Los Angeles Old Soldiers home nine years later. William Hynes (who had practiced law in Chicago and retired to Los Angeles after failing to win a second term in Congress) died three years after the Canadian government issued a one hundred dollar payment in 1912 to every man or his widow who had mustered against the Fenians in 1866 and 1870. During the same summer, future Irish nationalist martyr Padraig Pearse praised all deceased Fenians when he offered a now-famous eulogy to Jeremiah O'Donovan Rossa in Glasnevin cemetery.[34]

The legacy of the Fenians remained strong in certain immigrant communities. One group of indefatigable nationalists proposed yet another Irish American invasion of Canada during World War I. Maurice Dalton, one of the last known 1867 rebels, also remained active in an Irish republican military operation. At the time of the Easter Rebellion, the aging veteran of the Ballyhurst skirmish swore almost sixty Irish Australians into Sydney-, Melbourne-, and Brisbane-based circles of an organization he called the Irish Republican Brotherhood Australia Division. The IRB(A), as it was more commonly known, trained briefly in the Blue Mountains without weapons, in hope that American Clan na Gael leaders would eventually provide them with enough money to purchase firearms and travel to Ireland. Instead, Dalton and several of his men were eventually arrested and detained for various durations.[35] By the time they were released, thousands of Irishmen had actually died fighting for, rather than against, Great Britain in France, Belgium, and Turkey.

The closing chapter of the Fenian movement was fittingly hallmarked by a final series of funerals. Although the title of his May 1922 obituary in John Devoy's newspaper *The Gaelic American* read, "P.N. Kennedy died a Fenian," the relatively unknown Ridgeway veteran was actually described as an assimilated expatriate, "whose love for the motherland was only surpassed by his love for God and America."[36] Richard O'Sullivan Burke garnered similar sympathy when he succumbed to the lingering effects of a stroke in Chicago several days later. As Burke had faithfully served in the IRB and the Union army, his coffin was, appropriately, draped with Irish and American flags during his memorial service. More significantly, a posthumous public subscription to help Burke's widow pay a ten thousand dollar home mortgage was remarkably successful. Socially mobile expatriates were generally willing to aid the survivors of deceased patriots at a time when Irish nationalist sentiment was heightened by the controversial establishment of a semiautonomous Irish state that excluded six Ulster counties.[37] The still-unsolved assassination of IRB leader and 1921 Anglo-Irish Peace Treaty negotiator, Michael Collins, three months later hastened the dissolution of the sixty-four-year-old IRB. The demise of Stephens and O'Mahony's brainchild presumably elicited no mourning among aging Canadian veterans of the 1870 Fenian invasion. Between 1915 and 1930, several obituaries published in the *Huntingdon Gleaner* commended deceased local residents who had rallied in defense of their newly formed nation a half-century earlier.[38]

Thus, laudatory historical references to Fenianism might have been more common from the beginning of the twentieth century onward if transatlantic Irish republicanism had not been compromised by many factors during the mid-Victorian period. Among the most obvious impediments to Fenian success was organizational mismanagement. A specific Fenian political agenda was never circulated in the same manner as the American Declaration of Independence or the French Rights of Man. The editors of the Dublin-based *Irish People* were known to be in favor of secularized government, but how minority Protestants would have been treated in a hypothetically independent Ireland was never clearly enunciated. How land reform would have been implemented was equally nebulous. Country estates and church property were supposedly to have been subdivided, but no specific plan was ever openly promulgated. Without reason to do otherwise, the majority of the global Irish population respected the anti-Fenian admonitions of Catholic priests, and either remained politically apathetic or supported associations that emulated the constitutional nationalism of the legendary Daniel O'Connell. As William D'Arcy notes, the Fenians made the natural mistake of misconstruing the Anglophobia of generally passive Irish peasants as pro-Republican sentiment.[39] Greater success might also have been insured if the Fenian hierarchy had not allowed many of its supporters to manipulate the militant Irish nationalist cause for their own selfish purposes. Benevolent projects and frivolous social activities similarly drained the Brotherhood's fighting capability, but not as much as widespread financial mismanagement.

The ineptitude of James Stephens and John O'Mahony was particularly detrimental to the success of the Fenian movement. Both men were intelligent, well-read people with sincere republican beliefs; however, they lacked the capability to lead a revolutionary crusade. Daniel O'Connell was a charismatic man who sincerely espoused his political agendas. Stephens and O'Mahony, in contrast, were passable orators who frequently lied to the public. Stephens had once unabashedly announced to his colleagues that he was destined for greatness, but his efforts to achieve fame on behalf of fellow Irishmen were inconsistent. Stephens was also a man who loathed admitting mistakes or commending colleagues who abetted the Fenian cause without his guidance or assistance.[40] Stephens had also hypocritically castigated William Smith O'Brien as a political lightweight. While the chivalrous Young Ireland leader had led a rebellion in 1848 that lasted several days, Stephens had been too timid to mobilize his forces at two opportune moments in late 1865.[41] O'Mahony's downfall was his illogical decision making and his reputation for deceit. Why he kept men like Red Jim McDermott on the Brotherhood staff and authorized the Campobello invasion is truly puzzling. In sum, the two founders of Fenianism failed in the same manner as the mythical Fionn macCumhaill—the leader of the legendary army after which the Fenian Brotherhood was named lost his *geis,* or honor, after drinking a forbidden horn of wine. Stephens and O'Mahony compromised their reputations by placing their own self-interests above their supporters in an often mutually competitive quest for fame. Other Fenian leaders, including Roberts and O'Neill, could be faulted for similar personal shortcomings.

The continued geo-political supremacy of Great Britain strongly suggests that the IRB and its stateside auxiliaries would have still been contained if a considerably larger nationalist organization had been led by more competent men, like John Devoy and Richard O'Sullivan Burke. British military officials always would have been able to tap the resources of a global empire. Ireland had a relatively miniscule industrial infrastructure that was largely concentrated in loyalist sections of east Ulster. Long-hoped-for Fenian alliances with France and the United States would not have guaranteed Irish independence. Prior French invasions of Ireland had failed and only a token American expeditionary army would have ever been able to land on Irish soil. If British forces had been preoccupied by rival combatants in a distant military theatre (as John Mitchel had always said was essential for an Irish rebellion to succeed), Fenian warriors would have still had to confront several regiments of veteran soldiers. Magyar revolutionaries had been able to secure the establishment of a quasi-independent Hungarian kingdom under Habsburg control in 1867, but Irish nationalists would have been hard-pressed to attain even the restoration of a largely autonomous parliament in Dublin. At best, a few Fenian guerillas could have endured by receiving limited matériel support from America. Yet, repeated *Erin's Hope* expeditions would have had to have been successfully organized and executed to truly test British resolve to maintain control over Ireland.

Even if Great Britain had been a second- or third-rate political power during the mid-nineteenth century, any Irish nationalist movement would have likely failed because of insufficient expatriate support. Famine-era immigrants, who otherwise would have been ideal Irish rebels, had become progressively more American as they re-acclimated to a post–Civil War peacetime economy at the same time that longstanding anti-Irish Catholic sentiments abated in the United States. Xenophobic Protestants who had once vehemently opposed the proliferation

of the American Catholic population increasingly distanced themselves from racist anti-immigrant organizations after the Confederate attack on Fort Sumter.
Rumors that nativists would retaliate against brutish Irish behavior during the
1863 Draft Riots failed to materialize. The last Know-Nothing national convention, moreover, was held at the same time that hundreds of expatriates were
slaughtered during the Battle of Fredericksburg.[42] The anti-Catholic American
Protective Association also declined, as many Irish Union army veterans respected
the contemporary Republican Party mantra to "vote as they had shot" rather than
support the once proslavery, and still predominately pro-Irish, Democratic Party.[43]
Thus while interconfessional violence was sporadically precipitated during the
Gilded Age by rumors of papal plots to overthrow the United States government
and other catalysts, the Irish American community became an increasingly powerful constituency that, as Peter Welsh predicted, could determine the outcome
of national political campaigns. A presidential candidate in 1884, James Blaine
was a former house speaker and secretary of state who received the endorsement
of many expatriates—including Irish Brigade veterans and Richard O'Sullivan
Burke—because he had previously supported the establishment of an independent Ireland. Blaine was also of Irish and Catholic descent, but his own bid for
the White House was undermined a week before election day, when a Protestant minister endorsed him at a New York City rally and identified Democrats as
members of a party that espoused "Rum, Romanism, and Rebellion."[44]

As Irish Americans improved their social status and anti–Irish Catholic
sentiments declined, Famine-era immigrants had less incentive to actively support Irish independence initiatives. Rising Irish American prosperity had initially
bolstered the Fenian movement. With modest disposable income, thousands of
predominately young working-class men and women attended Fenian picnics and
demonstrations in the mid-1860s. Upon acquiring even greater financial resources,
however, would-be Irish rebels became progressively more interested in American
domestic politics; an expatriate propensity to participate in Irish nationalist activities or violent altercations with African Americans declined in tandem. At a
time when a series of Republican presidents doled many political favors to Protestant allies, Irish Americans maintained a foothold in national affairs by electing
Patrick Collins and other former Fenians whose appeal extended to expatriates
residing outside their own constituencies.[45] O'Mahony himself had indirectly expedited émigré assimilation by advertising the sale of Staten Island residential lots
in his revamped post–Civil War newspaper, *Irish People*. The first streetcar suburbs
did not resemble the bucolic, culturally homogenous Irish countryside that many
Famine-era immigrants had long idealized, but it was an acceptable alternative to

grim urban enclaves that once had been seedbeds of Irish nationalist discontent in the United States and Great Britain.

The history of the mid-nineteenth century Fenian movement can be ultimately encapsulated in the words of a Confederate general who was related to both antebellum United States president Zachary Taylor and Jefferson Davis. In a published memoir that detailed his military career, Richard Taylor wrote, "Strange People, these Irish. Fighting everyone's battles and cheerfully taking the hot end of the poker, they are only found wanting when engaged in what they believe to be their national cause."[46] Mid-nineteenth century Irish valor on the battlefield had indeed been more apparent in America than in Ireland for a variety of reasons, including ineffectual Fenian leadership and the dramatic assimilation of Famine-era immigrants into a once inhospitable New World society. In subsequent decades, the partial link between nationalist expression and social diversion continued, as with one expatriate woman who recounted in an early twentieth-century oral history project that she had joined the Friends of Irish Freedom to meet men.[47] Yet, members of the IRB and the stateside Brotherhood did inspire generations of latter-day Irish nationalists.

The Fenian ideal inspired cultural and constitutional nationalists as well as republicans. The Gaelic League, an organization established in 1893 by Eoin MacNeill and other Irish language advocates to promote the mother tongue, implemented the fiery language of the IRB to inspire the Irish people. Douglas Hyde, the League's first president, asserted "every speech we make throughout this country makes bullets to fire at the enemy." According to R. R. Foster, Hyde also commended James Stephens for his capability to infuse a "breathing national spirit back into the land." Early twentieth-century constitutional nationalists, like John Redmond, leader of the Irish Parliamentary Party, and Arthur Griffith, founder of Sinn Féin, used Fenian connections to expand their respective political bases, demonstrating the importance of bridging the gap between moderate and radical nationalists. The IRB would eventually infiltrate constitutional nationalist organizations to imbue amenable Irishmen with their physical-force ideals.[48]

Early twentieth-century IRB men ultimately formented a revolution that resulted in the creation of the Irish Free State. While Great Britain was distracted on the European continent with World War I, Padraig Pearse, Joseph Plunkett, Thomas MacDonagh, and other IRB men drafted certain members of the Irish Volunteers to create a free Ireland. In 1916, they declared an Irish republic and commenced rebellion on Easter Monday. Although the rebellion failed, it led to a more successful rebellion in 1919 fought by the Irish Republican Army, which resulted in the creation of a semi-autonomous Irish state.

As the IRB evolved into the modern-day IRA, republican polemicists often cited Ridgeway and other Fenian successes as evidence that an independent Ireland was destined to be established. During the Anglo-Irish War, Michael Collins, a high-ranking member of the IRB and director of intelligence for the IRA, utilized guerilla tactics to eradicate British officials from Ireland. Throughout the twentieth century, the IRA implemented the guerilla tactics of earlier Fenian bombers and dynamiters, like Donovan O'Rossa, to terrorize British officials and the public with the hope that the government would vacate Northern Ireland. The IRA continued to garner assistance from Irish America throughout the twentieth century. The Clan na Gael, although a shadow of its former self, still exists today and provides some financial backing for the republican movement in Northern Ireland. The Irish Northern Aid Committee, informally known as Noraid, was formed to financially assist the Provisional IRA (or at least the families of republican prisionsers) during the Troubles of the late twentieth century. The September 2001 attack on the World Trade Center in Manhattan by radical Islamists dampened western support for terrorist organizations like the IRA, but the transatlantic nationalist ideals for a united Ireland still remain apparent. As in Ireland during the 1860s, and more famously during World War I, young working-class Irish men and women continued to smuggle arms into Ireland from places as diverse as Libya and Florida with the same determination of the *Erin's Hope* filibusterers.[49]

Today, the former leaders of the IRA are involved in the peace process in Northern Ireland, but the Provisional IRA, itself an offshoot of the original IRA, has also experienced schisms in the last couple of decades, resulting in the creation of the Continuity IRA and the Real IRA. Both organizations consider themselves the true heirs of the republican movement, as they continue to flail against British involvement in the North. Others have accepted the tenets of the Good Friday Agreement (1998). Martin McGuinness, the current deputy first minister of Northern Ireland, once headed the Provisional IRA. Gerry Adams, also a former IRA member, was recently elected to the Dáil Éireann in the Irish Republic. Reminiscent of the many Fenians who became politicians, Sinn Féin candidate Martin Ferris won a seat in the Dáil Éireann eighteen years after being arrested and imprisoned for a 1984 attempt to help unload six tons of American weapons from a converted trawler that had embarked from Boston to awaiting IRA operatives in County Kerry.[50] Nevertheless, ardent militants within a once-again fractured nationalist movement have recently orchestrated atrocious bombing attacks that most Fenians would have openly scorned. The Fenian legacy thus endures to the present, as militant Irish republicans opposed to the 1998 Good Friday Accords confirm the concern of certain California Fenians who wrote in 1864 "Irishmen fight everywhere well but at home."[51]

NOTES

INTRODUCTION

1. Sean Cronin, *Irish Nationalism: A History of Its Roots and Ideology* (Dublin: Academy Press, 1980), 86–89.

2. Matthew Frye Jacobson, *Special Sorrows: The Diasporic Imagination of Irish, Polish, and Jewish Immigrants in the United States* (Cambridge, MA: Harvard University Press, 1995), 2, 10.

3. See Thomas Brown, *Irish-American Nationalism* (Philadelphia, PA: Lippincott Co., 1866).

4. *New York Times*, May 23, 1866; Anonymous, *James Stephens, Chief Organizer of the Irish Republic* (New York: Carleton, 1866), 27.

1. THE FOUNDATIONS OF FENIANISM

1. Peter Gray, *Famine, Land and Politics: British Government and Irish Society* (Portland, OR: Irish Academic Press, 1999), 293–94.

2. Pauline Millward, "The Stockport Riots of 1852: A Study of Anti-Catholic and Anti-Irish Sentiment," in *The Irish in the Victorian City*, ed. Roger Swift and Sheridan Gilley (Dover, NH: Croom Helm, 1985), 208–9.

3. Kevin O'Connor, *The Irish in Britain* (London: Sedgewick and Jackson, 1972), 25.

4. J. Matthew Gallman, *Receiving Erin's Children: Philadelphia, Liverpool, and the Irish Famine Migration, 1845-1855* (Chapel Hill: The University of North Carolina Press, 2000), 125–26, 144.

5. Padraic Cummins Kennedy, "Political Policing in a Liberal Age: Britain's Response to the Fenian Movement, 1858-1868" (PhD diss., Washington University, 1996), 392.

6. W. J. Lowe, *The Irish in Mid-Victorian Lancashire: The Shaping of a Working-Class Community* (New York: Peter Lang, 1989), 194.

7. Christine Kinealy, *This Great Calamity: The Irish Famine 1845-1852* (Boulder, CO: Roberts Rinehart Publishers, 1995), 314.

8. Kerby Miller, *Emigrants and Exiles: Ireland and the Irish Exodus to North America* (New York: Oxford University Press, 1985), 291; Oscar Handlin, *The Uprooted: The Epic Story of the Great Migrations That Made the American People* (Boston: Little, Brown and Company, 1951), 51.

9. John J. Kane, "Irish Immigrants in Philadelphia: A Study in Conflict and Accommodation, 1840-1880" (PhD diss., University of Pennsylvania, 1950), 12.

10. John Belcham, "Republican Spirit and Military Science: The 'Irish Brigade' and Irish-American Nationalism in 1848," *Irish Historical Studies* XXXIX (May 1994): 57.

11. Gary Owens, "Popular Mobilization and the Rising of 1848," in *Rebellion and Remembrance in Modern Ireland,* ed. Lawrence Geary (Dublin: Four Courts Press, 2001), 56.

12. Jonathan Sperber, *The European Revolutions, 1848-1851* (New York: Cambridge University Press, 1994), 242.

13. Richard Davis, *The Young Ireland Movement* (Totowa, NJ: Barnes and Noble, 1987), 161–62.

14. Ibid., 258–59.

15. Bryan P. McGovern, *John Mitchel: Irish Nationalist and Southern Secessionist* (Knoxville: University of Tennessee Press, 2009), 77–85.

16. David T. Gleeson, "Parallel Struggles: Irish Republicanism in the American South, 1798-1876," *Eire-Ireland* 34, no. 2 (Summer 1999): 105.

17. *Ottumwa Weekly Democrat*, February 15, 1877.

18. Anonymous, *James Stephens, Chief Organizer of the Irish Republic* (New York: Carleton, 1866), 34.

19. Henry A. Brann, *Most Reverend John Hughes* (New York: 1912), 105.

20. Desmond Ryan, *The Fenian Chief: A Biography of James Stephens* (Dublin: Sydney, Gill and Son, 1967), 35, 38, 47.

21. John Mitchel, *The Last Conquest of Ireland (Perhaps)* (New York, 1873), 218–42.

22. Marianne Elliot, *Partners in Revolution: The United Irishmen and France* (New Haven: Yale University Press, 1982), xvii.

23. Patrick D. O'Flaherty, "The History of the Sixty-Ninth Regiment in the Irish Brigade, 1861-1865" (PhD diss., Fordham University, 1963), 92.

24. Hereward Senior, *The Last Invasion of Canada: The Fenian Raids, 1866-1870* (Toronto: Dundurn Press, 1991), 16–17.

25. John Mitchel to James Cantwell (March 1, 1855) in Thomas G. Connors, "Letters of John Mitchel, 1848-1869," *Analecta Hibernica* 37 (1998): 298.

26. Norman Ware, *The Industrial Worker* (Chicago: Quadrangle Books, 1964), 6, 37.

27. Oscar Handlin, *Boston's Immigrants: A Study in Acculturation* (Cambridge, MA: Harvard University Press, 1979), 109.

28. Dennis Clark, *The Irish in Philadelphia: Ten Generations of Urban Experience* (Philadelphia, PA: Temple University Press, 1973), 40.

29. Edwin G. Burrows and Mike Wallace, *Gotham: A History of New York City to 1898* (New York: Oxford University Press, 1999), 747.

30. Theodore Maynard, *The Story of American Catholicism* (New York: MacMillan 1941), i; Handlin, *Boston's Immigrants*, 114–15.

31. D. Clark, *Irish in Philadelphia*, 49; Burrows and Wallace, *Gotham*, 779.

32. Kane, "Irish Immigrants," 85–86.

33. Kane, "Irish Immigrants," 23, 78, 80–81.

34. Dale Knobel, *Paddy and the Republic Ethnicity and Nationality in Antebellum America* (Middleton, CT: Wesleyan University Press, 1986), 132; O'Flaherty, "The History of the Sixty-Ninth Regiment," 114, 139.

35. Michael Feldberg, *The Philadelphia Riots of 1844: A Study of Ethnic Conflict* (Westport, CT: Greenwood Press, 1975), 99, 143; Gilbert Osofsky, "Abolitionists, Irish Immigrants, and the Dilemmas of Romantic Nationalism," *American Historical Review* 80 (October, 1975): 900.

36. Jay P. Dolan, *The Immigrant Church: New York's Irish and German Catholics, 1815-1865* (Baltimore: Johns Hopkins University Press, 1975), 89–90.

37. Folio II, 469–72. Richard O'Flynn Papers. Holy Cross College, Worcester, Massachusetts.

38. Tyler Anbinder, *Nativism and Slavery: The Northern Know-Nothings and the Politics of the 1850s* (New York: Oxford University Press, 1992), 248; John Mulkern, *The Know-Nothing Party in Massachusetts* (Boston: Northeastern University Press, 1990), 103.

39. Michael F. Funchion, *Chicago's Irish Nationalists, 1881-1890* (New York: Arno Press, 1976), 19.

40. David Roediger, *The Wages of Whiteness: Race and the Making of the American Working Class* (New York: Verso Books, 1999), 133–34.

41. Lee Soltow, *Men and Wealth in the United States, 1850-1870* (New Haven, CT: Yale University Press, 1975), 149; Roediger, *The Wages of Whiteness*, 81.

42. Burrows and Wallace, *Gotham*, 556.

43. Burrows and Wallace, *Gotham*, 478, 743–744.

44. Johan Galtung, *A Structural Theory of Revolutions* (Rotterdam: Rotterdam University Press, 1974), 40.

45. Donald M. Fisher, "Born in Ireland, Killed at Gettysburg: The Life, Death, and Legacy of Patrick Henry O'Rorke," *Civil War History* 49, no. 3 (1993): 227.

46. Stephan Thernstrom, *Poverty and Progress: Social Mobility in a Nineteenth Century City* (Cambridge, MA: Harvard University Press, 1964), 107–8; Arnold Schrier, *Ireland and the American Emigration, 1850-1900* (Minneapolis: University of Minnesota Press, 1958), 3, 22.

47. Michael C. O'Laughlin, *Irish Settlers on the American Frontier* (Kansas City, MO: Irish Genealogical Foundation, 1984), 97.

48. John Bodnar, *The Transplanted: A History of Immigrants in Urban America* (Bloomington: Indiana University Press, 1985), 76.

49. Kane, "Irish Immigrants," 171; Dennis J. Clark, "The Philadelphia Irish: Persistent Presence," in *The Peoples of Philadelphia: A History of Ethnic Groups and Lower Class Life, 1790-1940,* ed. Alan F. Davis and Mark H. Haller (Philadelphia, PA: Temple University Press, 1973), 137.

50. Burrows and Wallace, *Gotham*, 750.

51. Charles E. Rosenburg, *The Cholera Years: The United States in 1832, 1849, and 1866* (Chicago, IL: University of Chicago Press, 1987), 139–40; J. Matthew Gallman, *Mastering Wartime: A Social History of Philadelphia during the Civil War* (New York: Cambridge University Press, 1990), 71.

52. Robert Kee, *The Green Flag: The Turbulent History of the Irish Nationalist Movement* (New York: Delacorte Press, 1972), 306; James Fitzgerald to William Sullivan, 7 January 1857). William Sullivan Papers, Western Reserve Historical Society, Cleveland, Ohio; hereafter, WSP/WRHS.

53. William D'Arcy, *The Fenian Movement in the United States, 1858-1886* (Washington, DC: Catholic University of America Press, 1947), 10.

54. Michael F. Funchion, ed., *Irish American Voluntary Organizations* (Westport, CT: Greenwood Press, 1983), 102.

55. Kevin O'Rourke, *Currier and Ives: The Irish in America* (New York: H. N. Abrams, 1995), 91.

56. Edward K. Spann, "Union Green, The Irish Community and the Civil War," in *The New York Irish*, ed., Ronald H. Bayor and Timothy J. Meagher (Baltimore, MD: The Johns Hopkins University Press, 1996), 194.

57. Anonymous, *James Stephens*, 27.

58. Tom Garvin, *The Evolution of Irish Nationalist Politics* (New York: Holmes and Meier Publishers, 1981), 16–17.

59. Michael Doheny, *The Felon's Track: A Narrative of '48* (New York: Farrell and Son, 1867), 140.

60. Anonymous, *James Stephens*, 27.

61. Oliver Rafferty, "Cardinal Cullen, Early Fenianism, and the MacManus Funeral Affair," *Recusant History* 22, no. 4 (October, 1995): 554.

62. John Rutherford, *The Secret History of the Fenian Conspiracy*, vol. I. (London: C.K. Paul and Company, 1877), 60; S. J. Connolly ed., *The Oxford Companion to Irish History* (New York: Oxford University Press, 1998), 482.

63. Des. Ryan, *Fenian Chief*, 74.

64. Desmond Ryan, "O'Mahony," in *The Fenian Movement*, ed. T. W. Moody (Cork: Mercier Press, 1978), 70.

65. Rutherford, *Secret History*, 15.

66. H. A. Crosby Forbes and Henry Lee, *Massachusetts Help to Ireland during the Great Famine* (Milton, MA: Captain Robert Bennet Forbes House, 1967), 17–18, 23, 58.

67. Gallman, *Receiving Erin's Children*, 27–28.

68. Kee, *The Green Flag*, 306–8; Joseph Denieffe, *A Personal Narrative of the Irish Republican Brotherhood* (Dublin: Irish University Press, 1969), 159–60.

69. Des. Ryan, *Fenian Chief*, 94.

70. Anonymous, *James Stephens*, 52.

71. Garvin, *Evolution of Irish Nationalist Politics*, 60.

72. Rafferty, "Cardinal Cullen," 549.

73. Denieffe, *A Personal Narrative*, 39.

74. Oliver MacDonagh, "Ambiguities in Nationalism," in *Interpreting Irish History: The Debate on Historical Revisionism*, ed. Ciaran Brady (Blackrock: Irish Academic Press, 1994), 113.

75. R. V. Comerford, *The Fenians in Context: Irish Politics and Society, 1848-82* (Atlantic Highlands, NJ: Wolfhound Press, 1985), 63.

76. Thomas N. Brown, "Nationalism and the Irish Peasant, 1800-1848," *The Review of Politics* 15 (1953): 442.

77. Brian Jenkins, *The Fenians and Anglo-American Relations During Reconstruction* (Ithaca, NY: Cornell University Press, 1969), 26–27.

78. Des. Ryan, *Fenian Chief,* 153.

79. Ibid., 154–55.

80. John O'Leary, *Recollections of Fenians and Fenianism,* vol. 1 (London 1896), 95–96.

81. David George Boyce, *Nationalism in Ireland* (New York: Routledge, 1995), 176.

82. Robert Anderson, *A Great Conspiracy* (London: John Murray, 1910), 24.

83. *Irish People* (Dublin), April 1, 1865.

84. Patrick Quinliven, "Hunting the Fenians, Problems in the Historiography of a Secret Organization," in *The Creative Immigrant* vol. III, ed. Patrick O'Sullivan (Leicester: Leicester University Press, 1994), 139–40.

85. James MacKillop, *Fionn mac Cumhaill: Celtic Myth in English Literature* (Syracuse: Syracuse University Press, 1986), 5–7, 43; Seumus MacManus, *The Story of the Irish Race* (Old Greenwich, Connecticut: The Devin-Adair Company, 1992), 64–69.

86. Quoted in Patrick Quinliven and Paul Rose, *The Fenians in England: A Sense of Insecurity* (New York: Riverrun Press, 1982), 2.

87. Kenneth E. Nilsen, "The Irish Language in New York," in *The New York Irish,* ed. Bayor and Meagher (Baltimore, MD: The Johns Hopkins University Press, 1996), 264.

88. Sean Cronin, *Irish Nationalism: A History of its Roots and Ideology* (Dublin: The Academy Press, 1980), 68.

89. Adrian Hastings, *The Construction of Nationhood: Ethnicity, Religion, and Nationalism* (New York: Cambridge University Press, 1997), 3.

90. *The Phoenix,* March 24, 1860.

91. *The Phoenix*, December, 10, 1859.

92. *The Phoenix*, June 4, 1859.

93. R. A. Burchell, *The San Francisco Irish* (Berkeley: University of California Press, 1980), 100.

94. Oliver Rafferty, "Fenianism in North America in the 1860s: The Problems for Church and State," *History* 84, no. 274 (April 1999): 259.

95. Kevin Thaddeus Brady, "Fenians and the Faithful: Philadelphia's Irish Republican Brotherhood and the Diocese of Philadelphia, 1859-1870," (PhD diss., Temple University, 1998), 260.

96. Adin Ballou, *History of Milford* (Boston: Franklin Press, 1882), 110; Patrick Cuddihy, *Short History of the Irish Catholics in Milford* (Milford, MA: Times Publishing Company, 1894), 63; Folio II. O'Flynn Papers.

97. Folio II. O'Flynn Papers.

98. Marcus Bourke, *John O'Leary: A Study in Irish Separatism* (Tralee: Anvil Books Limited, 1967), 38.

99. Folio II, 485. Folio V, 133. O'Flynn Papers,

100. *Milford Journal*, July 3, 1859.

101. *Milford Journal*, August 13 and September 3, 1859.

2. THE FIGHTING IRISH

1. Philip Shaw Paludin, *A People's Contest: The Union and Civil War* (New York: Harper and Row, 1988), 282.

2. Ella Lonn, *Foreigners in the Union Army and Navy* (Baton Rouge: Louisiana State University Press, 1952), 74–75.

3. *The Phoenix*, June 1, 1861.

4. John Cornelius O'Callaghan, *History of the Irish Brigades in the Service of France* (Shannon: Irish University Press, 1968), vii–ix; Francis Henry Skine, *Fontenoy and Great Britain's Share in the War of the Austrian Succession, 1741-1748* (London: William Blackwood and Sons, 1906), 181, 184, 288.

5. George Fitz-H. Berkeley, *The Irish Battalion in the Papal Army of 1860* (Dublin: Talbot Press, 1929), 220.

6. Paul Jones, *The Irish Brigade* (London: New English Library, 1971), 16.

7. Joseph M. Hernon, "The Irish Nationalists and Southern Secession," *Civil War History* 12, no. 1 (March 1966): 46.

8. James McPherson, *Ordeal by Fire: The Civil War and Reconstruction* (New York: Alfred A. Knopf, 1982), 22.

9. *Irish People* (Dublin), May 6, 1865.

10. Frederic von Allendorfer, "The Western Irish Brigade: 23rd Illinois Infantry Regiment," *Irish Sword* 2, no. 7 (Winter 1955): 177.

11. Anonymous, *James Stephens*, 47.

12. Phyllis Lane, "Colonel Michael Corcoran, Fighting Irishman of the Irish Brigade," in *The History of the Irish Brigade: A Collection of Historical Essays*, ed. Pia Seija Seagrave (Fredericksburg, VA: Sergeant Kirkland's Museum and Historical Society, 1997), 72.

13. Brian Kelly, "Ambiguous Loyalties: The Boston Irish, Slavery, and the Civil War," *Historical Journal of Massachusetts* 24, no. 2 (Summer 1996): 105.

14. Ernest A. McKay, *The Civil War and New York City* (Syracuse: Syracuse University Press, 1990), 57; O'Flaherty, "The History of the Sixty-Ninth Regiment," 224.

15. Edward K. Spann, *Gotham at War: New York City, 1860-1865* (Wilmington, DE: Scholarly Resources, 2002), 115.

16. William L. Burton, *Melting Pot Soldiers: The Union's Ethnic Regiments* (Ames: Iowa State University Press, 1988), 113, 245.

17. Michael Cavanagh, *Memoirs of Thomas Francis Meagher* (Worcester, MA: The Messenger Press, 1892), 359–60.

18. John O'Mahony to William Sullivan, 28 June 1860. WSP/WRHS.

19. Cavanagh, *Memoirs,* 359–60.

20. Ballou, *History of Milford,* 122–88; Rutherford, *Secret History,* 231; *Official Roster of Soldiers of the State of Ohio in the War of Rebellion, 1861-1866* (Akron, The Werner Company, 1893), 209–33.

21. James Rorty to father, 15 November 1861, James M. Rorty Pension Application. National Archives, Washington, DC.

22. McPherson, *Ordeal by Fire,* viii.

23. James McPherson, *For Cause and Comrades: Why Men Fought in the Civil War* (New York: Oxford University Press, 1997), viii.

24. John Brooke, *The Heart of the Commonwealth: Society and Political Culture in Worcester County, Massachusetts, 1713-1861* (New York: Cambridge University Press, 1989), 396; Jason H. Silverman, "Stars, Bars, and Foreigners: The Immigrant and the Making of the Confederacy," *Journal of Confederate History* 1, no. 2 (Fall 1988): 281.

25. Burrows and Wallace, *Gotham,* 882.

26. Kenneth M. Stamp, *The Imperiled Union Essays on the Background of the Civil War* (New York: Oxford University Press, 1980), 106–7; Paludin, *A People's Contest,* 283; Benjamin J. Blied, *Catholics and the Civil War* (Milwaukee, WI: 1945), 64.

27. Eric Foner, *Free Soil, Free Labor, Free Men: The Ideology of the Republican Party before the Civil War* (New York: Oxford University Press, 1970), 227–31; McKay, *The Civil War,* 20.

28. Maurice Sexton to siblings, 24 November 24, 1861. Arnold Schrier Collection, University of Cincinnati.

29. Richard E. Beringer, Herman Hattaway, Archer Jones, and William N. Still, *The Elements of Confederate Defeat* (Athens: The University of Georgia Press, 1988), 23–32.

30. David T. Gleeson, *The Irish in the South, 1815-1877* (Chapel Hill: University of North Carolina Press, 2001), 137.

31. Ibid., 143–44, 161.

32. Silverman, "Stars, Bars, and Foreigners," 283.

33. Elizabeth and Howell Purdue, *Pat Cleburne, Confederate General* (Hillsboro TX: Hill Junior College Press, 1973), 74.

34. Gleeson, "Parallel Struggles," 111.

35. Margaret E. Fitzgerald and Joseph King, *The Uncounted Irish in Canada and the United States* (Toronto: P. D. Meany Publishers, 1990), 208.

36. *Southern Citizen*, March 18, 1858.

37. Ed Gleeson, *Rebel Sons of Erin: A Civil War Unit History of the Tenth Tennessee Infantry Regiment (Irish) Confederate States Volunteers* (Indianapolis, IN: Guild Press, 1993), 10–11.

38. Gleeson, *Irish in the South*, 190.

39. Silverman, "Stars, Bars, and Foreigners," 282.

40. Christopher-Michael Garcia, "The 'Fighting' Sixty-Ninth New York State Militia at Bull Run," in *The History of the Irish Brigade: A Collection of Historical Essays*, ed. Pia Seija Seagrave (Fredericksburg, VA: Sergeant Kirkland's Museum and Historical Society, 1997), 38; O'Flaherty, "The History of the Sixty-Ninth Regiment," 230.

41. Harold F. Smith, "Mulligan and the Irish Brigade," *Journal of the Illinois State Historical Society* 56 (Summer 1963): 166; *Western Banner*, December, 29, 1860.

42. Benedict Anderson, *Imagined Communities: Reflections on the Origins and Spread of Nationalism* (New York: Verso Books, 1991), 37–46, 141.

43. William L. Burton, "Irish Regiments in the Union Army: The Massachusetts Experience," *Historical Journal of Massachusetts* 11 (June 1983): 105.

44. Burton, *Melting Pot Soldiers*, 181.

45. Burton, "Irish Regiments," 108.

46. Thomas O'Connor, *Civil War Boston: Homefront and Battlefield* (Boston: Northeastern University Press, 1997), 75.

47. Burrows and Wallace, *Gotham*, 871–872.

48. Burton, "Irish Regiments," 114–15.

49. Christian G. Samito, ed., *Commanding Boston's Irish Ninth: The Civil War Letters of Colonel Patrick R. Guiney* (New York: Fordham University Press, 1998), 67–68; Burton, "Irish Regiments," 107.

50. Terry L. Jones, *Lee's Tigers: The Louisiana Infantry in the Army of Northern Virginia* (Baton Rouge: Louisiana State University Press, 1987), 6, 238–41.

51. Minetta Altgelt Goyne, ed. *Lone Star and Double Eagle: Civil War Letters of a German-Texas Family* (Fort Worth: Texas Christian University Press, 1982), 22,

52. Seagrave, *History of the Irish Brigade*, 44.

53. *New York Times*, June 5, 1861.

54. Gleeson, "Parallel Struggles," 112.

55. O'Flaherty, "The History of the Sixty-Ninth Regiment," 300-302; Seagrave, *History of the Irish Brigade*, 66.

56. Seagrave, *History of the Irish Brigade*, 54.

57. Robert G. Athearn, "Thomas Francis Meagher: An Irish Revolutionary in America," *University of Colorado Studies* I (December 1949): 98.

58. Timothy J. Sarbaugh, "Post-Civil War Fever and Adjustment: Fenianism in the California Context 1858-1872," *Working Papers in Irish History* (Boston: Northeastern University Irish Studies Program, 1992), 8.

59. *New York Times*, September 15, 1861.

60. Des. Ryan, *Fenian Chief*, 174.

61. Mary Kelly, "'Forty Shades of Green': Conflict over Community among New York's Irish, 1860-1920" (PhD diss., Syracuse University, 1997), 275.

62. Tomas Ó Fiaich, "The Clergy and Fenianism, 1860-1870," *The Irish Ecclesiastical Record* 5, no. 109 (1968): 82.

63. John Newsinger, *Fenianism in Mid-Victorian Britain* (Boulder, CO: Pluto Press, 1994), 33.

64. Des. Ryan, *Fenian Chief*, 175–76.

65. Breandán Mac Giolla Choille, "Fenian Documents in the State Paper Office," *Irish Historical Studies* 15, no. 63 (March 1969): 264.

66. Tomas Ó Fiaich, "'The Patriot Priest of Partry,' Patrick Lavelle: 1825-1886," *Journal of the Galway Archaeological and Historical Society* 35 (1976): 137, 140. Brady, "Fenians and the Faithful," 97, 101; Rafferty, "Cardinal Cullen," 551, 555, 557.

67. *Irish-American*, February 15, 1862.

68. Richard Shaw, *Dagger John: The Unquiet Life and Times of Archbishop Hughes of New York* (New York: Paulist Press, 1977), 15; Joseph Hernon, "Irish Sympathy for the Southern Confederacy," *Eire-Ireland* 2, no. 3 (Autumn 1967):

69. Norman B. Ferris, *The Trent Affair: A Diplomatic Crisis* (Knoxville: University of Tennessee Press, 1977), 19, 25.

70. Glyndon G. Van Deusen, *William Henry Seward* (New York: Oxford University Press, 1967), 311.

71. Stanley Weintraub, *Disraeli: A Biography* (New York: Truman Tally, 1993), 392.

72. Richard, J. Purcell, "Ireland and the American Civil War," *The Catholic World* 115, no. 685 (April 1922): 81.

73. Maurice Sexton to siblings, 24 November 1861. Schrier Collection.

74. Quoted in Joseph M. Hernon, *Celts, Catholics and Copperheads: Ireland Views the American Civil War* (Columbus: Ohio State University Press, 1968), 49.

75. Joseph M. Hernon, "Irish Sympathy for the Southern Confederacy," *Eire-Ireland* 2, no. 3 (Autumn 1967): 74. Mabel Gregory Walker, *The Fenian Movement* (Colorado Springs, CO: R. Myles, 1969), 13; Purcell, "Ireland and the American Civil War," 82.

76. Gordon H. Warren, *Fountain of Discontent: The Trent Affair and Freedom of the Seas* (Boston: Northeastern University Press, 1981), 47, 220; Robert W. Young, *James Murray Mason: Defender of the Old South* (Knoxville: The University of Tennessee Press, 1998), 112–14.

77. Hernon, "Irish Nationalists and Southern Secession," 44, 49.

3. GREEN AMERICAN

1. R. T. Farrell to James A. Mulligan, 28 December 28 1861. James A. Mulligan Papers, Chicago Historical Society.

2. T. C. Fitzgibbon to James A. Mulligan, 10 February 1862. James A. Mulligan Papers, Chicago Historical Society.

3. Christopher L. Williamson, transcriber, *The Journals of Daniel Finn* (1992), 12.

4. Blied, *Catholics and the Civil War,* 64.

5. Russell Duncan, ed., *The Blue-Eyed Child of Fortune, The Civil War Letters of Robert Gould Shaw* (Athens: The University of Georgia Press, 1992), 17, 104, 182.

6. Randall M. Miller, Harry S. Stout, and Charles Reagan Wilson eds., *Religion and the American Civil War* (New York: Oxford University Press, 1998), 265, 267.

7. Spann, *Gotham at War,* 169.

8. Hubert H. Wubben, *Civil War Iowa and the Copperhead Movement* (Ames: Iowa State University Press, 1980), 62–63.

9. W. J. Rorabaugh, "Who Fought for the North in the Civil War? Concord, Massachusetts, Enlistments," *Journal of American History* 73, no. 3 (December 1986): 696.

10. William T. Pippey to Benjamin Pippey, 31 July 1862. Miller Collection.

11. Thomas Keneally, *The Great Shame: A Story of the Irish in the Old World and the New* (London: Chatto and Windus, 1998), 379.

12. Gallman, *Mastering Wartime*, 106.

13. Gordon A. Craig, *Europe Since 1815* (Hinsdale, IL: The Dryden Press, 1972), 224.

14. Joseph T. Durkin, *John Dooley, Confederate Soldier* (Washington, DC: Georgetown University Press, 1945), 116–17.

15. Barney Kelly, "The Green Flags of the Irish Brigade," in Seagrave, *The History of the Irish Brigade*, 203.

16. John F. Finerty, "Thirty Years of Ireland's Battle," *Donahoe's Magazine* 30 (1893): 66.

17. Kevin Stanton, "Green Tint on Gold Bars: Irish Officers in the United States Army, 1865-1898" (PhD diss., University of Colorado, 2001), 82.

18. Spann, *Gotham at War*, 116.

19. Cited in Kevin O'Brien, "Blaze away and stand to it, boys': Captain Jack Donovan and the Irish Brigade at Fredericksburg," *Irish Sword* 20, no. 80 (1996): 123, 126–27, 130.

20. Steven E. Woodworth, ed., *The Loyal. True, and Brave: America's Civil War Soldiers* (Wilmington, DE: SR Books, 2002), 152.

21. James McPherson, ed., *The American Heritage New History of the Civil War* (New York: Viking, 1996), 256.

22. William McSparron to niece Margaret Ann, January, 1863. Public Record Office, Northern Ireland; hereafter, PRONI.

23. Spann, *Gotham at War*, 118.

24. Maurice Woulfe to uncle, 25 September 1863; Caoimhín Ó Danachair, "A Soldier's Letters Home, 1863-74," *Irish Sword* 3-4 (Summer 1957): 57.

25. C. Williamson, *The Journals of Daniel Finn*, 66.

26. Cited in Brian Kelly, "Ambiguous Loyalties," 184, 195.

27. Andrew Sproule to Frances Sproule, 26 January1863. Southern Historical Collection, University of North Carolina.

28. Lawrence Frederick Kohl, ed., *Irish Green and Union Blue: The Civil War Letters of Peter Welsh* (New York: Fordham University Press, 1986), 62.

29. Cited in T. O'Connor, *Civil War Boston*, 73.

30. Cited in B. Kelly, "Ambiguous Loyalties," 196.

31. Blied, *Catholics and the Civil War*, 98.

32. Burton, "Irish Regiments," 111.

33. B. Kelly, "Ambiguous Loyalties," 192.

34. Goyne, *Lone Star and Double Eagle*, 77–78.

35. Burton, "Irish Regiments," 108, 113.

36. Ibid., 109. Quoted in Bell Irwin Wiley, *The Common Soldier in the Civil War* (New York: Grosset and Dunlap, 1952), 106.

37. Thomas Francis Galwey, *The Valiant Hours* (Harrisburg, PA: The Stackpole Company, 1961), 74–75.

38. Warren Wilkenson, *Mother, May You Never See the Sights I Have Seen: The Fifty-Seventh Massachusetts Veteran Volunteers in the Army of the Potomac* (New York: Harper and Row, 1990), 3, 6; K. Miller, *Emigrants and Exiles,* 361; United States Consular Reports, Dublin T-570.

39. David P. Conyngham, *The Irish Brigade and its Campaigns* (New York: William McSorley and Company, 1867), 87; Seagrave, *The History of the Irish Brigade* 59.

40. Gleeson, *Irish in the South,* 143.

41. William J. K. Beaudot and Lance J. Herdegen, *An Irishman in the Iron Brigade* (New York: Fordham University Press, 1993), 2, 51.

42. Durkin, *John Dooley,* 115.

43. Samito, *Commanding Boston's Irish Ninth,* 91.

44. Bell Irwin Wiley, *The Life of Billy Yank: The Common Soldier of the Union* (New York: Bobbs-Merrill, 1952), 308–9.

45. Beaudot and Herdegen, *An Irishman,* 1.

46. Quoted in Wiley, *Common Soldier of the Civil War*, 102.

47. Burton, "Irish Regiments," 114–15.

48. C. Vann Woodward, ed., *Mary Chestnut's Civil War* (New Haven, CT: Yale University Press, 1981), 820.

49. D. Clark, "The Philadelphia Irish," 114, 116; Albon P. Man, "The Irish in New York City in the 1860s," *Irish Historical Studies* 7, no. 26 (March 1950): 94; K. Brady, "Fenians and Faithful," 261; Bruce Laurie, "Fire Companies and Gangs in Southwark: The 1840s," in *The Peoples of Philadelphia: A History of Ethnic Groups and Lower Class Life, 1790-1940*, ed. Davis Alan F. and Mark H. Haller (Philadelphia, PA: Temple University Press, 1973), 78, 80.

50. McPherson, *Ordeal by Fire,* 360. William Shannon, 57.

51. McKay, *The Civil War,* 160.

52. Burrows and Wallace, *Gotham,* 890; R. Miller et al., *Religion and the American Civil War,* 282; Adrain Cook, *The Armies of the Streets: The New York City Draft Riots of 1863* (Lexington: The University of Kentucky Press, 1974), 78–79; Paludin, *A People's Contest,* 194; Spann, *Gotham at War,* 100.

53. R. Miller et al., *Religion and the American Civil War*, 282.

54. Man, "The Irish in New York City in the 1860s," 94.

55. Shaw, *Dagger John*, 341, 368–69.

56. Dennis P. Ryan, *Beyond the Ballot Box* (Amherst: University of Massachusetts Press, 1983), 132.

57. McKay, *The Civil War*, 206, 209.

58. Rafferty, "Cardinal Cullen," 553.

59. Mark Mulligan to William West, 19 May 1863. United States Consular Dispatches. National Archives Annex, College Park, Maryland, T-570.

60. Thomas Conroy to William West, 28 August 1863. United States Consular Dispatches, T-570.

61. Charles P. Cullop, "An Unequal Duel: Union Recruiting in Ireland, 1863-1864," *Civil War History* 13 (June 1967): 107, 109–10; Hernon, *Celts, Catholics, and Copperheads*," 30–31; Philip Thomas Tucker, *The Confederacy's Fighting Chaplain: Father John B. Bannon* (Tuscaloosa: University of Alabama Press, 1992), 169, 172.

62. Toby Boyce, "The American Civil War and Irish Nationalism," *History Ireland* 4, no. 2 (Summer 1996): 37.

63. R. Anderson, *A Great Conspiracy*, 25.

64. Kevin Quigley, "American Financing of Fenianism in Ireland, 1858-67" (master's thesis, NUI-Maynooth, 1983), 77.

65. "Second Circular Report of the Central Corresponding Society, Fenian Brotherhood, HQ," WSP/WRHS.

66. *Irish People* (Dublin), December 26, 1863.

67. D'Arcy, *The Fenian Movement,* 39; León Ó Brion, *Fenian Fever: An Anglo-American Dilemma* (New York: New York University Press, 1971), 5.

68. Feldberg, *The Philadelphia Riots*, 28–29.

69. *Chicago Tribune*, November 6 and 7, 1863.

70. *Freeman's Journal*, November 21, 1863.

71. *Chicago Tribune*, February 17, 1864.

72. *Richmond Enquirer*, November 21, 1863.

73. William Hanchett, *Irish: Charles G. Halpine in Civil War America* (Syracuse: Syracuse University Press, 1970), 153.

74. *Proceedings of the First National Convention of the Fenian Brotherhood. Irish People* (Dublin: December 5, 1863); *Irish-American*, September 13, 1861.

75. Walker, *The Fenian Movement*, 27.

76. *Irish People*, Dublin: January 9, 1864; John O'Mahony to William Sullivan, 20 June 1861. WSP/WRHS.

77. Bourke, *John O'Leary*, 46.

78. *Irish People* (Dublin), December 19, 1863.

79. DeeGee Lester, "Tennessee's Bold Fenian Men," *Tennessee Historical Quarterly* 56 (Winter 1997): 265.

80. *Irish People* (Dublin), January, 16, 1864.

81. Lane, *Colonel Michael Corcoran*, 72.

82. Open Letter from James Frederick Wood, 17 January 1864. University of Notre Dame Archives. Notre Dame, Indiana; K. Brady, *Fenians and the Faithful*, 174.

83. Brian P. Clarke, *Piety and Nationalism: Lay Voluntary Associations and the Creation of an Irish Catholic Community in Toronto* (Montreal: McGill University Press, 1993), 185, 191; Hereward Senior, *The Fenians and Canada* (Toronto: MacMillan of Canada, 1978), 60; *New York Times*, March 11, 1866; John O'Mahony to William Sullivan, 26 May 1863. WSP/WRHS.

84. Lawrence J. McCaffrey, Ellen Skerret, Michael F. Funchion, and Charles Fanning, *The Irish in Chicago* (Chicago: University of Illinois Press, 1987), 36. Walker, *The Fenian Movement*, 25.

85. D. Clark, *Irish in Philadelphia*, 20–21; Joesph George, "Very Reverend Patrick E. Moriarty, OSA Philadelphia's Fenian Spokesman," *Pennsylvania History* 48, no. 3 (July, 1981): 223, 226–31; James F. Wood to Francis P. McFarland, 8 December 1864. University of Notre Dame Archives.

86. Amadeus Rappe to John Baptist Purcell, 13 September 1865. University of Notre Dame Archives.

87. Donal McCartney, "The Church and Fenianism," *Fenians and Fenianism: Centenary Essays*, ed. Maurice Harmon (Seattle: University of Washington Press, 1970), 14–17.

88. Oliver P. Rafferty, *The Church, the State, and the Fenian Threat, 1861-75* (New York: Saint Martin's Press, 1999), 72; Rafferty, "Fenianism in North America," 259.

89. H. D. Juncker to John Baptist Purcell, 3 April 1864. University of Notre Dame Archives.

90. Burrows and Wallace, *Gotham*, 748.

91. Hernon, "Irish Nationalism and Southern Secession," 43: *Irish People* (Dublin), August 6, 1864.

92. Thomas McManus to Francis McManus, 17 March 1864. Consular Dispatches, Dublin.

93. Hernon, *Celts, Catholics, and Copperheads,* 31–33.

94. *Irish People* (Dublin), May 21, 1864.

95. Quigley, "American Financing of Fenianism in Ireland," 78. *Irish People* (Dublin), April 2, 1864.

96. *Irish People* (Dublin), April 23, 1864.

97. Michael P. Mallaney, "The Fenian Movement in Illinois during the Civil War Period, 1861-1868" (master's thesis, Eastern Illinois University, 1975), 94–96.

98. Quigley, "American Financing of Fenianism in Ireland," 46–50, 114; Newsinger, *Fenianism in Mid-Victorian Britain,* 36; Walker, *The Fenian Movement,* 29, 31.

99. Finerty, "Thirty Years of Ireland's Battle," 65.

100. *Proceedings of the First General Convention of the Fenian Brotherhood on the Pacific Coast* (San Francisco, 1864), 8.

101. Rutherford, *Secret History,* 24.

102. Ella Lonn, *Foreigners in the Confederacy* (Chapel Hill: University of North Carolina Press, 1940), 155.

103. Craig, L. Symonds, *Stonewall Jackson of the West: Patrick Cleburne and the Civil War* (Lawrence: University Press of Kansas, 1997), 245, 255, 259; Irving A. Buck, *Cleburne and his Command* (Wilmington, NC: Broadfoot Publishers, 1995), 73.

104. Woodworth, *The Loyal, True, and Brave,* 70; Ballou, *History of Milford,* 122–88

105. David Herbert Donald, *Lincoln* (New York: Touchstone, 1995), 544; Charles J. Quinn to cousin Eliza, 14 October 1864. FP/CUA.

106. Spann, *Gotham at War,* 59.

107. Ballou, *History of Milford,* 122–88.

108. Seagrave, *The History of the Irish Brigade,* 92.

109. Eric R. Wolf, "On Peasant Rebellions," in *The Sociology of Revolution: Readings on Political Upheaval and Popular Unrest,* ed. Ronald Ye-Lin Cheng (Chicago: Henry Regnery Company, 1973), 157–58.

110. Brian Griffin, "The I. R. B. in Connacht and Leinster, 1858-1878" (master's thesis, NUI-Maynooth, 1983), 65.

111. Charles T. Rice, *A Phase of Fenianism in Ireland: The Movement in Monaghan* (Monaghan: R. & S. Printers, 1956), 4; John O'Mahony to William Sullivan 2 June 1863. WSP/WRHS.

112. Gerard Moran, "The National Brotherhood of St Patrick in Britain in the 1860s," *Irish Studies Review* 7, no. 3 (1999): 332.

113. John O'Leary, *Recollections of Fenians and Fenianism*, vol. 2 (New York: Barnes and Noble, 1969), 239.

114. Connolly, *The Oxford Companion to Irish History*, 159, 184, 186.

115. Brian Griffin, "Social Aspects of Fenianism in Connacht and Leinster, 1858-1870," *Eire-Ireland* 21, no. 1 (Spring,1986): 18–19, 23–24, 28, 38.

116. Mary C. Lynch and Seamus O'Donoghue, *O'Sullivan Burke, Fenian* (Carrigadrohid, County Cork: Ebony Jane Press, 1999), 231; D'Arcy, *The Fenian Movement*, 61; *Irish People* (Dublin), May 6, 1865.

117. Matthew Frye Jacobson, *Whiteness of a Different Color: European Immigrants and the Alchemy of Race* (Cambridge, MA: Harvard University Press, 1999), 55.

118. Eric Lott, *Love and Theft: Blackface Minstrelsy and the American Working Class* (New York: Oxford University Press, 1993), 237.

119. Kevin J. Weddle, "Ethnic Discrimination in Minnesota Volunteer Regiments during the Civil War," *Civil War History* 35, no. 3 (September 1989): 256.

120. Miles O'Reilly, *Baked Meats of the Funeral* (New York: Carleton, 1866), 213.

4. FENIAN RENAISSANCE

1. David Marshall, "The Fenians after Seventy-Five Years," *Catholic World* CLVI, no. 933 (December 1942): 276.

2. O'Leary, *Recollections of Fenians and Fenianism*, vol. 2, 239.

3. Kennedy, "Political Policing in a Liberal Age," 178–79.

4. *San Francisco Daily Dramatic Chronicle*, April 7, 1866.

5. Kennedy, "Political Policing in a Liberal Age," 97.

6. James Stephens to John O'Mahony, 20 May 20 1864. FP/CUA. *The Gaelic American*, June 10, 1922.

7. P. A. Sillard, *The Life and Letters of John Martin* (Dublin: James Duffy and Company, 1901), 178; Hernon, *Celts, Catholics, and Copperheads*, 36.

8. James Bayley to John Martin Spalding, 1 March 1865. John Martin Spalding Papers. Baltimore Cathedral Archives, Baltimore, Maryland.

9. John Devoy, *Recollections of an Irish Rebel* (Shannon: Irish University Press, 1969), 133, 139; Malcolm Brown, *The Politics of Irish Literature: From Thomas Davis to W. B. Yeats* (London: Allen and Unwin, 1972), 158; *Irish Citizen*, February 25, 1871.

10. John O'Mahony, "Final Call of the Fenian Brotherhood," 10 August 1865. WSP/WRHS.

11. Open Letter from Thomas Lavin, 24 August 1862. WSP/WRHS.

12. Edward R. Norman, *The Catholic Church and Ireland in the Age of Rebellion, 1859-1873* (Ithaca, NY: Cornell University Press, 1965), 90.

13. Feargus MacDonald, *The Catholic Church and The Secret Societies in the United States* (New York: United States Catholic Historical Society, 1946), 42.

14. K. Brady, "Fenians and the Faithful," 263.

15. Frank Roney, *Irish Rebel and California Labor Leader* (New York: AMS Press, 1977), 74–75.

16. *New York Times*, February 10, 1866.

17. "Official Monthly Circular, Financial Statement No. 6." FP/CUA.

18. O'Reilly, *Baked Meats of the Funeral*, 226-227.

19. John Finerty to John O'Mahony, 23 May 1865. FP/CUA.

20. Rafferty, "Fenianism in North America," 260.

21. John O'Mahony to William Sullivan, 31 May 1865. WSP/WRHS.

22. "Military Roster." FP/CUA.

23. Arthur H. DeRosier, Jr. "Importance in Failure: The Fenian Raids of 1866-1871," *Southern Quarterly* 3, no. 3 (April 1965): 192.

24. Rice, *A Phase of Fenianism in Ireland*, 45; Stephen Ambrose, *Nothing Like it in the World: The Men who Built the Transcontinental Railroad, 1863-1869* (New York: Simon and Schuster, 2000), 21, 118–19.

25. Sarbaugh, "Post-Civil War Fever and Adjustment," 14.

26. *Irish Canadian*, August 9, 1865.

27. Patrick Hasson to John O'Mahony, 22 July 1865. FP/CUA.

28. Kennedy, "Political Policing in a Liberal Age," 182.

29. Kee, *The Green Flag*, 319; *London Times*, March 7, 1867.

30. Devoy, *Recollections of an Irish Rebel*, 191–92; Kennedy, "Political Policing in a Liberal Age," 199.

31. Michael O'Regan to John O'Mahony, 1 June1865. FP/CUA.

32. *Irish People* (Dublin), August 26, 1865.

33. *Irish People* (Dublin), August 12, 1865.

34. "Report of the Central Corresponding Secretary, Fenian Brotherhood HQ," February 25, 1865 to September 23, 1865. WSP/WRHS.

35. D'Arcy, *The Fenian Movement*, 74–75.

36. *Irish People* (Dublin), September 9, 1865.

37. Folio V, 487. O'Flynn Papers.

38. Rutherford, *Secret* History, vol. I., 308. 39. Ó Brion, *Fenian Fever*, 9; Quigley, "American Financing of Fenianism in Ireland," 77.

40. Patrick Sarsfield O'Hegarty, *Ireland under the Union, 1801-1922* (London: Methuen and Company, 1952), 442.

41. Jane McL Côté, *Fanny and Anna Parnell: Ireland's Patriot Sisters* (New York: St. Martin's Press, 1991), 58–62.

42. G. Boyce, *Nationalism in Ireland*, 179; *Irish People* (Dublin) July 30, 1864.

43. Kee, *The Green Flag*, 303; Des. Ryan, *Fenian Chief*, 64.

44. R. V. Comerford, *Charles J Kickham: A Study in Irish Nationalism and Literature* (Portmarnock, Ireland, Wolfhound Press, 1979), 146–50.

45. David Montgomery, *Beyond Equality: Labor and the Radical Republicans 1862-1872* (New York: Alfred A. Knopf, 1967), 128.

46. Walter McGrath, *A Cork Felon (The Life and Death of Brian Dillon)* (Cork: Brian Dillon Commemoration Committee, 1952), 12,14,126–27.

47. Ó Brion, *Fenian Fever*, 13.

48. *Irish People* (Dublin), September 9, 1865.

49. Amadeus Rappe to John Purcell, 26 October 26, 1865. University of Notre Dame Archives.

50. Sillard, *The Life and Letters of John Martin*, 179.

51. Terry Golway, *Irish Rebel: John Devoy and America's Fight for Ireland's Freedom* (New York: Saint Martin's Press, 1998), 13, 39–40, 49–50; James Reidy, "John Devoy," *Journal of the American Irish Historical Society* 27 (1928): 413.

52. Crane Brinton, "Radicalization of Revolutionary Government," in *The Sociology of Revolution: Readings on Political Upheaval and Popular Unrest*, ed. Ronald Ye-Lin Cheng (Chicago: Henry Regnery Company, 1973), 232.

53. Devoy, *Recollections of an Irish Rebel*, 128.

54. Mark Wyman, *Round Trip to America: The Immigrants Return to Europe, 1880-1930* (Ithaca, NY: Cornell University Press, 1993), 165; Archbishop Paul Cullen to Archbishop Martin John Spalding, 2 February 1865; cited in Rafferty, "Fenian Threat," 70; Bourke, *John O'Leary*, 76.

55. Bourke, *John O'Leary*, 74.

56. Clarke, *Piety and Nationalism*, 170; D'Arcy, *The Fenian Movement*, 126.

57. John M. Taylor, *William Henry Seward: Lincoln's Right Hand Man* (New York: HarperCollins, 1991), 66, 69.

58. Jenkins, *The Fenians and Anglo-American Relations*, 56.

59. *Irish Citizen*, February 29, 1868.

60. K. Brady, "Fenians and the Faithful," 277.

61. *Constitution of the Fenian Brotherhood*, adopted October 21, 1865 at the General Convention of the Fenian Brotherhood held in Philadelphia.

62. Michael Cavenagh to William Sullivan, 25 June 1863. WSP/WHRS.

63. Ó Brion, *Fenian Fever*, 20; Jane Mitchel to Mary, 20 April 1854. Melony-Mitchel Papers, Columbia University; *The Gaelic American*, June 10, 1922. F. S. L. Lyons, *Ireland Since the Famine* (New York: Charles Scribner's Sons, 1971), 113.

64. Wilfried Neidhardt, *Fenianism in North America* (University Park: Pennsylvania State University Press, 1975), 30.

65. *New Orleans Daily Southern Star*, November 12, 1865.

66. *LaCrosse Daily Democrat*, October 26, 1865.

67. Ó Brion, *Fenian Fever*, 17; Des. Ryan, *Fenian Chief*, 213; Anonymous, *James Stephens*, 71–72.

68. Desmond Ryan, *The Phoenix Flame: A Study of Fenianism and John Devoy* (London: A. Barker Limited, 1937), 101; Devoy, *Recollections of an Irish Rebel*, 72.

69. *The Irish Times*, November 13, 1865.

70. Ó Brion, *Fenian Fever*, 24.

71. *New York Times*, December 14, 1885; Anonymous, *James Stephens*, 82.

72. Denieffe, *A Personal Narrative*, 126.

73. Ryan, *Beyond the Ballot Box*, 200; M. Brown, *The Politics of Irish Literature*, 155, 185, 195, 197, 198.

74. M. J. Curran, "Cardinal Cullen: Biographical Materials," *Reportorium Novum* 1, no. 1 (1955), 214; Archbishop Paul Cullen to Bishop John Baptist Purcell, 2 December 1865. University of Notre Dame Archives; F. MacDonald, *The Catholic Church*, 44.

75. R. V. Comerford, "Comprehending the Fenians," *Saothar* 17 (1990–91), 55.

76. Fenian Circular, December 7, 1865. WSP/WRHS.

77. Ezra Henry Pieper, "The Fenian Movement, An Abstract of a Thesis" (PhD diss., University of Illinois, 1931), 5; McKay, *The Civil War*, 94–95; Ellis Paxson Oberholtzer, *Jay Cooke, Financier of the Civil War*, vol. 1 (Philadelphia, PA: George W. Jacobs, 1907), 257.

78. Fenian Circular, December, 6, 1865. WSP/WRHS.

79. *New York Times*, December 10, 1865.

80. Open Letter from John O'Mahony, December 7, 1865. WSP/WRHS.

81. *Irish People* (New York), April 20, 1867.

82. John O'Mahony to William Sullivan, May 31, 1865. WSP/WRHS.

83. Paul Thomas Rubery, "The Fenian Movement in the United States" (master's thesis, Saint Bonaventure University, 1951), 21.

84. Harold A. Davis, "The Fenian Raid on New Brunswick," *Canadian Historical Review* 36, no. 4 (December 1955): 321.

85. *LaCrosse Daily Democrat*, December 8, 1865.

86. B. Jenkins, *The Fenians and Anglo-American Relations*, 30.

87. Stanton, "Green Tint on Gold Bars," 84.

88. *New York Times*, December 13, 1865.

89. *Pawtucket Gazette and Chronicle*, January 5, 1866.

90. Quoted in DeRosier, "Importance in Failure," 184.

91. Jack Morgan, "The Dust of Maynooth:' Fenian Funeral as Political Theatre," *New Hibernia Review* 2, no. 4 (Winter, 1998): 36.

92. "Resolutions Adopted at a Meeting of the Fenian Brotherhood, Buffalo, November 24th, 1865." WSP/WRHS.

93. John Timon to P.P. Lefevere, 8 December 1865. University of Notre Dame Archives.

94. Spann, *Gotham at War*, 119.

95. *Hansard's* vol. 181, 673.

96. R. W. Kostal, "Rebels in the Dock: The Prosecution of the Dublin Fenians, 1865-6," *Eire-Ireland* 34, no. 2 (Summer 2000): 88.

97. Maria Luddy, *Women and Philanthropy in Nineteenth Century Ireland* (New York: Cambridge University Press, 1995), 1–2.

98. Kennedy, "Political Policing in a Liberal Age," 365.

99. Jenkins, *The Fenians and Anglo-American Relations*, 84.

100. Kennedy, "Political Policing in a Liberal Age," 181; Rafferty, "Fenian Threat," 51; Fenian Papers, 3 October 1865. National Archives Ireland; hereafter NAI.

101. A. J. Semple, "The Fenian Infiltration of the British Army," *Journal of the Society for Army Historical Research* 52 (1974):133; Richard Joseph Coyer, "Hero of the Armless

Sleeve: The Military Career of Thomas W. Sweeny" (PhD diss., University of San Diego, 1978), 306; Ó Brion, *Fenian Fever*, 36; Newsinger, "Old Chartists, Fenians, and New Socialists," 41, 45.

102. John Fleming to Robert Humphreys, 28 January 1866. National Library of Ireland; hereafter, NLI.

103. *New York Herald*, March 27, 1866.

104. Denieffe, *A Personal Narrative*, 266; Senior, *Last Invasion*, 60.

105. John Looby to John O'Mahony, 22 January 1866. FP/CUA.

106. Thomas Siske to B. D. Killian, 20 February 20 1866. FP/CUA.

107. John Mitchel to James Mitchel, 7 April 1866. Malony-Mitchel Papers; Rafferty, "Fenian Threat," 78.

108. *Hansard's* vol. 181, 724.

109. Robert Kee, *The Laurel and the Ivy: The Story of Charles Stewart Parnell and Irish Nationalism* (New York: Penguin Books, 1994), 33–35.

110. Carolyn A. Conley, *Melancholy Accidents: The Meaning of Violence in Post-Famine Ireland* (New York: Lexington Books, 1999), 175.

111. Kennedy, "Political Policing in a Liberal Age," 191.

112. *Lowell Daily Courier*, March 2, 1866.

113. *New York Times*, March 11, 1866.

114. *San Francisco Daily Dramatic Chronicle*, April 23, 1866.

115. Sister M. Justille McDonald, *History of the Irish in Wisconsin in the Nineteenth Century* (Washington, DC: The Catholic University of America Press, 1954), 143.

116. Jerome Mushkat, *Fernando Wood: A Political Biography* (Kent, OH: The Kent State University Press, 1990), 159; Copperheads were Northern Democrats who typically opposed the Civil War or, at the very least, Lincoln's handling of the war.

117. *Lawrence Sentinel*, March 3, 1866; *Lawrence American and Andover Advertiser*, March 2, 1866; Robert J. Bateman, *Captain Timothy Deasy: Patriot—Irish American*, Lawrence, MA: Ancient Order of the Hibernians, Division 8 (November 22, 1992), 9.

118. Artemus Ward, "Among the Fenians," in *A 3rd Supply of Yankee Drolleries* (London: John Camden Hotten, 1866).

119. Godfrey Massey to P. J. Downing, 25 February 1866. FP/CUA.

120. Joseph Witherow to Rev. John Witherow, 3 December 1867. PRONI.

121. Godfrey Massey to John O'Mahony, 25 February 1866. FP/CUA.

122. *New Orleans Daily True Delta*, March 4 and March 8, 1866.

123. *Matamoros Daily Ranchero*, March 13, 1866; *Galveston Daily News*, April 21, 1866.

124. *San Francisco Daily Dramatic Chronicle*, April, 12, 1866.

125. Rafferty, "Fenian Threat," 58–60, 66–67.

126. K. Brady, "Fenians and the Faithful," 314.

127. Quoted in Neidhardt, *Fenianism in North America*, 37. *New York Times*, March 5, 1866.

128. James W. O'Brien to H. O'C. MacCarthy, 5 November 1864. FP/CUA.

129. Michael Anciello, "Patrick A. Collins: Bibliographical Note," *Patrick A. Collins Collection Index* Boston College (1996), 3; "Report of the Central Corresponding Secretary, Fenian Brotherhood Headquarters," 25 February 1865 to 28 May 1865. WSP/WRHS.

130. Ann Regan, *Irish in Minnesota* (Saint Paul: Minnesota Historical Society Press, 2002), 44.

131. *Peoria Daily Transcript*, March 13, 1866.

132. *Peoria National Democrat*, March 21, 1866.

133. *Lawrence American and Andover Advertiser*, March 2, 1866; *Peoria National Democrat*, March 18, 1866.

134. *Winona Daily Republican*, March 17, 1866; *San Francisco Daily Dramatic Chronicle*, May 24, 1866.

135. *Winona Daily Republican*, March 17, 1866.

136. *Lowell Daily Courier*, March 10, 1866.

137. *Lawrence Sentinel*, March 17, 1866; *Lawrence American and Andover Advertiser*, April 13, 1866.

138. John C. O'Brien to J. A. McMaster, 5 February 1865. University of Notre Dame Archives; *New York Times*, March 11, 1866.

139. Public Record Office, (United Kingdom); hereafter PRO, FO 5/1341.

140. Coyer, "Hero of the Armless Sleeve," 324.

141. *Matamoros Daily Ranchero*, April 10, 1866.

142. Anonymous, *James Stephens*, 89.

143. Kee, *Green Flag*, 322; Gustave Paul Cluseret, "My Connection with Fenianism," *Littell's; Living Age* CXIV (August 1872): 356; Des. Ryan, *Fenian Chief*, 229–30; Anonymous, *James Stephens*, 90.

144. Denieffe, *A Personal Narrative*, 153, 155.

145. K. Miller, *Emigrants and Exiles*, 582.

146. *Irish People* (Dublin), February 25, May 20, and June 24, 1865.

147. K. Brady, "Fenians and the Faithful," 348.

148. *Winona Daily Republican*, May 29, 1866.

149. Kelly, "Forty Shades of Green," 81–82.

150. Gisela Kaplan, "Feminism and Nationalism: The European Case," in *Feminist Nationalism*, ed. Lois A. West (New York: Routledge, 1997), 25.

151. Sperber, *The European Revolutions*, 175–76. Rutherford, *Secret History* vol. I., 256.

152. D'Arcy, *The Fenian Movement*, 109–10; *Lawrence American and Andover Advertiser*, March 9 and April 13, 1866; *Lowell Daily Courier*, March 21, 1866.

153. *The Gaelic American*, June 10, 1922.

154. Walker, *The Fenian Movement*, 63.

155. *Lawrence American*, April 13, 1866.

156. *Peoria Daily Transcript*, March 22, 1866.

5. FENIAN FIZZLE

1. H. Davis, "The Fenian Raid," 319.

2. Nathaniel Carrothers to "Brother," 29 January 1866. Miller Collection.

3. *Waterloo Courier*, March 29, 1866; K. Brady, "Fenians and the Faithful," 329–30.

4. Coyer, "Hero of the Armless Sleeve," 307.

5. Neidhardt, *Fenianism in North America*, 38.

6. James Cameron, "Fenian Times in Nova Scotia," *Collection of the Nova Scotia Historical Society* 37 (1980): 122.

7. John A. MacDonald, *Troublous Times in Canada: A History of the Fenian Raids of 1866 and 1870* (Toronto: W.S. Johnson and Company, 1910), 19–20, 23; Barlow Cumberland, "The Fenian Raids of 1866 and Events on the Frontier," *Proceedings and Transactions of the Royal Society of Canada*, 3rd series, vol. 10 (1910), 86, 88.

8. William Hodgson Ellis, "The Adventures of a Prisoner of War," *The Canadian Magazine of Politics, Science, Art and Literature* 13, no. 3 (July 1899): 199.

9. William O'Brien to cousin, 6 April 1866. Canadian National Archives.

10. Neidhardt, *Fenianism in North America*, 56; C. P Stacey, "Fenianism and the Rise of National Feeling in Canada at the Time of Confederation," *Canadian Historical*

Review 12, no. 2 (June 1931): 243–44; C. P. Stacey, "A Fenian Interlude: The Story of Michael Murphy," *Canadian Historical Review* 15, no. 2 (June 1934): 144.

11. Daniel McGruar Fonds. Canadian National Archives.

12. Warren F. Spencer, *The Confederate Navy in Europe* (Tuscaloosa: University of Alabama Press, 1983), 80–81, 110.

13. Maurice Woulfe to uncle, 25 September 1863. Kerby Miller Collection.

14. Mark E. Reynolds, "The Only Civil War Battle Fought on New England Soil," *Yankee Magazine* (January 1998): 38.

15. Neidhardt, *Fenianism in North America,* 21.

16. House of Representatives Executive Document, 1 (39:2): 1285.

17. John O'Mahony to John Mitchell, 10 November 1865. FP/CUA.

18. *New Orleans Daily Crescent*, April 2, 1866.

19. Maxwell Vesey, "When New Brunswick Suffered Invasion," *Dalhousie Review* 19, no. 2 (1939): 199.

20. Coyer, "Hero of the Armless Sleeve," 326.

21. Vesey, "When New Brunswick Suffered Invasion," 197.

22. Hereward Senior, *Fenians and Canada*, 37, 51; Breandán Ó Cathaoir, "American Fenianism and Canada, 1865-1871," *Irish Sword* 8, no. 31 (Winter 1967): 78.

23. Thomas D'Arcy McGee, *An Account of the Attempts to Establish Fenianism in Montreal* (Montreal: Post Publishing and Printing Company, 1882), 11.

24. E. A. Cruikshank, "The Fenian Raid of 1866," *Welland County Historical Society Papers and Reports* 2 (1926): 12; D'Arcy, *The Fenian Movement*, 202; Clarke, *Piety and Nationalism,* 171, 176.

25. James Mahoney, "The Influence of Irish-Americans upon the Foreign Policy of the United States, 1865-1872" (PhD diss., Worcester, MA: Clark University, 1959), 104.

26. *New York Times*, April 15, 1866; Stacey, "Fenian Interlude," 141, 145.

27. Stacey, "Fenian Interlude," 153.

28. Cameron, "Fenian Times in Nova Scotia," 124.

29. *New York Times*, May 5, 1866.

30. H. Davis, "The Fenian Raid," 323; Daniel C. Williamson, "American Press Views of Fenianism, 1860-1870" (master's thesis, Villanova University, 1990), 33.

31. J. Vroom, "The Fenians on the Saint Croix," *The Canadian Magazine of Politics, Science, Art and Literature* 10, no. 5 (March 1898): 412; *Winona Daily Republican*, April 19, 1866.

32. *The American Annual Cyclopedia and Register of Important Events*, vol. VI (New York: D. Appleton and Company, 1866), 286.

33. D'Arcy, *The Fenian Movement*, 143; Denieffe, *Personal Narrative*, 231.

34. Vesey, "When New Brunswick Suffered Invasion," 203; Joseph S. Brusher, *The Fenian Invasions of Canada* (St. Louis: St. Louis University Press, 1943), 65.

35. *Lowell Daily Courier*, April 26, 1866.

36. H. Davis, "The Fenian Raid," 330–31; Senior, "Quebec and the Fenians," *Canadian Historical Review* 48, no. 1 (March 1967): 56–57.

37. *Winona Daily Republican*, May 8, 1866.

38. George Gordon Meade, *The Life and Letters of George Meade* (New York: Charles Scribner's Sons, 1913), 285.

39. John O'Mahony, "Letter to the Officers and Members of the Fenian Brotherhood," *Boston Pilot* (May 4, 1866).

40. *Lowell Daily Courier*, March 13, 1866.

41. *Lawrence American and Andover Advertiser*, March 16, 1866.

42. K. Brady, "Fenians and the Faithful," 315.

43. Walker, *Fenian Movement*, 84.

44. *New York World*, May 2, 1866.

45. *Lowell Daily Courier*, May 8, 1866.

46. Thomas W. Sweeny, "Official Report of Thomas W. Sweeny, Secretary of War, Fenian Brotherhood, and Commander-in-Chief of the Irish Republican Army," *Journal of the American Irish Historical Society* 23 (1924): 195.

47. Ibid., 200.

48. Jack Morgan, *Whistle up the Marching Tune: The Life and Times of Thomas W. Sweeny* (Fort Lauderdale, FL: Nova University Press, 1994): 9.

49. William Sweeny, "Thomas Sweeny," *American Irish Historical Journal* 27 (1928): 267.

50. *Hansard's*, vol. 181, 1030; *Woonsocket Patriot and Rhode Island Register,* May 4, 1866.

51. J. MacDonald, *Troublous Times in Canada,* 12; Robert Alan Doan, "Green Gold to the Emerald Shores: Irish Immigration to the United States and Transatlantic Monetary Aid, 1854-1923" (PhD diss., Temple University, 1999), 345.

52. Neidhardt, *Fenianism in North America,* 55; T. Sweeny, "Official Report," 195.

53. Van Deusen, *William Henry Seward*, 502.

54. D. Williamson, "American Press Views of Fenianism," 66.

55. Allan Greer, *The Patriots and the People: The Rebellion of 1837 in Rural Lower Canada* (Toronto: University of Toronto Press, 1993), 341.

56. Patrick Foley to James Sheehan, 20 April 1866. Kerby Miller Collection, University of Missouri.

57. K. Brady, "Fenians and the Faithful," 291.

58. *Woonsocket Patriot and Rhode Island Register*, April 20, 1866.

59. K. Brady, "Fenians and the Faithful," 376; *Woonsocket Patriot and Rhode Island Register*, May 18, 1866.

60. *New York Times*, May 13, 1866.

61. *New Orleans Times Picayune*, May 13, 1866 and May 15, 1866.

62. Brusher, 66.

63. Ibid., 117.

64. K. Brady, "Fenians and the Faithful," 394; Hanchett, *Irish,* 155.

65. *Winona Daily Republican*, May 18, 1866.

66. *Waterbury Daily American*, May 23, 1866.

67. *San Francisco Daily Dramatic Chronicle*, May 22, 1866.

68. *New York Herald*, May 18, 1866.

69. Sarbaugh, "Post-Civil War Fever and Adjustment," 17.

70. John Patrick, "The Cleveland Fenians: A Study in Ethnic Leadership," *The Old Northwest* 9, no. 4 (1985): 312; Carl Wittke, *The Irish in America* (Baton Rouge: Louisiana State University Press, 1956), 154; Frank Hayward Severance, "The Fenian Raid of '66," *Publications of the Buffalo Historical Society* 25 (1921): 263; *Waterbury Daily American*, June 6, 1866.

71. Open Letter from Patrick Meehan, 24 May 1866. WSP/WRHS.

72. Rafferty, "Fenianism in North America," 260.

73. T. Sweeny, "Official Report," 201.

74. Philias S. Garand, *The History of the City of Ogdensburg* (Ogdensburg, NY: Rev. Manuel J. Belleville, 1927), 220

75. *Galveston Daily News*, June 13, 1866.

76. Joe Patterson Smith, "The Republican Expansionists of the Early Reconstruction Era" (PhD diss., University of Chicago, 1930), 78.

77. Mallaney, "The Fenian Movement," 138, 140, 143. 144.

78. Severance, "Fenian Raid," 267.

79. Lester, "Tennessee's Bold Fenian Men," 268–69; P. G. Smith, "Fenian Invasions of Canada," *Military History* 16, no. 6 (February, 2000): 51; Senior, *Last Invasion*, 66.

80. Brusher, 75.

81. Rubery, "The Fenian Movement," 29, 32.

82. F. M. Quealy, "The Fenian Invasion of Canada West," *Ontario History* 53 (1961): 45.

83. *Montreal Herald,* June 2, 1866.

84. Thomas Sweeny, *Proclamation to the People of British North America* (May, 1866).

85. Fred H. McCallum, "Experiences of a Queen's Own Rifleman at Ridgeway, *Annual Report of the Waterloo Historical Society* 3 (1915): 24; Neidhardt, *Fenianism in North America,* 64; Mahoney, 141.

86. Isaac P. Wilson, *Welland Township Committee of Safety Minutes* (Fort Erie, Ontario: June 1 and June 2, 1866).

87. Bradley Alan Rogers, "Guardian of the Great Lakes: The U.S. Paddle Frigate Michigan, an Iron Archetype on the Inland Seas" (PhD diss., The Union Institute, 1994), 239.

88. Cumberland, "Fenian Raids," 98; Colin K. Duquemin, "Banditti and Finnegans: The Niagara Invasions of '38 and '66," *The Military in the Niagara Peninsula* (Saint Catherine's, Ontario: Vanwell Publishing Limited, 1990), 99.

89. Quealy, 48.

90. P. G. Smith, "Fenian Invasions," 53.

91. David Owen, *The Year of the Fenians* (Buffalo: Western New York Heritage Institute, 1990), 68; D'Arcy, *The Fenian Movement,* 118; Brusher, 78.

92. Cruishank, "The Fenian Raid," 19.

93. George R. Gregg and E. P. Roden, *Trials of the Fenian Prisoners at Toronto* (Toronto: Leader Steam Press, 1867), 43.

94. David Meyler, "To the Glory of Our Country, The Fenian Invasion of Canada, 1866," *Command* (March–April, 1992): 65.

95. Brusher, 96.

96. J. F. Dunn, "Recollections of the Battle of Ridgeway," *Welland County Historical Society Papers and Proceedings* 2 (1926): 52.

97. McCallum, "Experiences," 26; Nathaniel Brewster, "Recollections of the Fenian Raid, *Welland County Historical Society Papers and Records* 2 (1926): 75–76.

98. Owen, 74, 79.

99. P. G. Smith, "Fenian Invasions," 54–55.

100. T. McGee, *The Fenian Raids*, 28.

101. John M. Taylor, "Fenian Raids against Canada," *American History Illustrated* 13, no. 5 (August 1978): 33; Severance, *The Fenian Raid*, 268; *Waterbury Daily American*, June 2, 1866; Brewster, "Recollections," 77.

102. Owen, 81.

103. *Buffalo Advertiser*, June 1, 1866.

104. Andrew McIntosh fonds. Archives Canada.

105. G. C. Duggan, "The Fenians in Canada: A British Officer's Impressions," *Irish Sword* 8, no. 31 (Winter 1967): 89, 91.

106. Cumberland, "The Fenian Raids," 92.

107. E. Ascher, "Number One Company, Niagara," *Niagara Historical Society* 27 (1915): 67.

108. Robert Larmour, "With Booker's Column," *Canadian Magazine* 10, no. 3 (January 1898): 231.

109. J. MacDonald, *Troublous Times*, 89.

110. *Philadelphia North American and United States Gazette*, June 6, 1866.

111. Neidhardt, *Fenianism in North America*, 70.

112. *New York Times*, June 9, 1866.

113. Blied, *Catholics and the Civil War*, 136–37.

114. *New York Times*, June 14, 1866.

115. *Davenport Daily Gazette*, April 14 and June 8, 1866; *Davenport Daily Democrat*, June 8, 1866.

116. *Peoria National Democrat*, June 6, 1866.

117. *Lawrence American and Andover Advertiser*, June 8, 1866.

118. W. Ellis, "The Adventures," 202.

119. Ibid., 203.

120. Dunn, "Recollections," 51.

121. J. Douglas Borthwick, *History of the Montreal Prison from A.D. 1784 to A.D. 1886* (Montreal: A. Periard, 1886), 217.

122. *Toronto Leader*, June 5, 1866.

123. Cumberland, "The Fenian Raids," 106.

124. Alyn Brodsky, *Grover Cleveland: A Study in Character* (New York: Saint Martin's Press, 2000), 29–30.

125. Senior, *Last Invasion*, 97; O'Rourke, *Currier and Ives*, 93.

126. Neidhardt, "The Fenian Trials," 60–61, 65, 143–44; J. MacDonald, *Troublous Times*, 95.

127. Stacey, "Fenianism and the Rise of National Feeling," 251.

128. Clarke, *Piety and Nationalism*, 197.

129. D'Arcy, *The Fenian Movement*, 174–75.

130. *Lawrence American and Andover Advertiser*, June 8, 1866.

131. Thomas Hamilton Murray, *History of the Ninth Regiment, Connecticut Volunteer Infantry* (New Haven, CT: Price, Lee, and Adkins Company, 1903), 325, 338, 342, 347.

132. *Irish People* (Dublin) January 21, 1865.

133. *Lowell Daily Courier*, June 6, 1866.

134. *Waterbury Daily American*, June 5, June 7, June 9, 1866.

135. *San Francisco Daily Dramatic Chronicle*, June 8, 1866.

136. *Lowell Daily Courier*, June 4 and June 9, 1866. Lester, "Tennessee's Bold Fenian Men," 271; *Waterbury Daily American*, June 5, June 7, June 9, 1866; *Winona Daily Republican*, May 31, 1866.

137. June 6, 1866. Andrew Johnson Papers;. Quealy, 61–62.

138. *Davenport Daily Gazette*, June 8, 1866.

139. Rubery, "The Fenian Movement," 52; *Lowell Daily Courier*, June 8, 1866; *New York Times*, June 9, 1866.

140. P. G. Smith, "Fenian Invasions," 54; Stacey, "Fenianism and the Rise of National Feeling," 246.

141. *San Francisco Daily Dramatic Chronicle*, June 7, 1866.

142. *Waterbury Daily American*, June 15, 1866.

143. Dispatch to Colonel John Mechan from Samuel P. Spear, 8 June 1866 in Denieffe, *A Personal Narrative*, 253.

144. Homer Calkin, "St. Alban's in Reverse: the Fenian Raid of 1866," *Vermont History* 35, no. 1 (1967): 33.

145. *Waterbury Daily American*, June 15, 1866.

146. J. MacDonald, *Troublous Times*, 120–21; Neidhardt, *Fenianism in North America*, 71.

147. National Archives Congressional Documents: House Executive Document, 1 (39:2) 1285.

148. Francis Wayland Campbell, *The Fenian Invasions of Canada of 1866 and 1870* (Montreal: John Lovell and Son, 1904), 25.

149. *Lawrence American*, June 15, 1866.

150. General William F. Barry, *District of Ontario Proclamation* (June 12, 1866).

151. Walker, *The Fenian Movement*, 104; J. MacDonald, *Troublous Times*, 93.

152. J. MacDonald, *Troublous Times*, 93; Severance, "Fenian Raid," 279.

153. Cumberland, "Fenian Raids," 99.

154. *New Orleans Daily Crescent*, June 7, 1866.

155. J. F. Delury, "Irish Nationalism in the Sacramento Region," *Eire-Ireland* 21, no. 3 (1986): 43.

156. Brusher, 16.

157. J. A. Cole, *Prince of Spies: Henri Le Caron* (Boston: Faber and Faber, 1984), 17.

158. *Atlantic Monthly*, vol. xvii, May 1866, no. CIII, 574.

159. J. F. Delury, "Irish Nationalism," 43.

160. *Congressional Globe, Thirty-Ninth Congress*, First Session (July 2nd, 1866), 3548.

161. Robert Lewis Teela, "Fenianism and Canada: A Contrast Between the Fenian Policies of the Johnson and Grant Administrations" (master's thesis, Roosevelt University, 1970), 68, 90; Walker, *The Fenian Movement*, 122; Anonymous, "Fenianism—By One who Knows, Part I," *Contemporary Review* XIX (1871–1872): 314–15.

162. Neidhardt, "The Fenian Trials," 87; *New York Times*, June 25, 1866.

163. *New York Times*, July 12, 1866.

164. Margaret O'Connell to Thomas Kelly, 31 August 1866. FP/CUA.

165. William Barry to Parents, 2 September 1866. Miller Collection.

166. Walker, *The Fenian Movement*, ix, 105, 113; Severance, "The Fenian Raid 274–75"; Mahoney, "The Influence of Irish-Americans," 164, 184–85.

167. James Fitzgerald to William Sullivan, 29 July 1866. WSP/WRHS.

168. Phillip E. Myers, "The Fenians in Iowa," *The Palimpsest* 62 (1981): 57.

169. Stanton, "Green Tint on Gold Bars," 90–91.

170. Walker, *The Fenian Movement*, 108; Stacey, "Fenianism and the Rise of National Feeling," 260.

171. Neidhardt, *Fenianism in North America*, 22.

172. McDonald, *History of the Irish*, 145; Hans Louis Trefousse, *Andrew Johnson: A Biography* (New York: Norton, 1989), 266.

173. Johnson Papers (June 6, 1866); D'Arcy, *The Fenian Movement*, 197.

174. Coyer, "Hero of the Armless Sleeve," 350, 353.

175. Anonymous, "Fenianism—By One Who Knows, Part II," *Contemporary Review* XIX (1871–1872): 641.

176. Coyer, "Hero of the Armless Sleeve," 351.

177. Stacey, "Fenianism and the Rise of National Feeling," 257; Arthur C. Phillips, *Fort Erie: An Historical Romance of the Fenian Invasion of Canada* (Buffalo: McCarroll and Company, 1868), 247.

178. *New York Times*, October 16, 1866.

179. Severance, "The Fenian Raid," 281.

180. Dale Baum, *The Civil War Party System: The Case of Massachusetts, 1848-1876* (Chapel Hill: University of North Carolina Press, 1984), 112.

181. B. Doran Killian to Andrew Johnson, 19 September 1866. *Andrew Johnson Papers*.

182. R. Anderson, *A Great Conspiracy*, 31.

183. *Missouri Democrat*, November 28, 1866.

184. Maurice Wolfe to uncle, 12 May 1867. Miller Collection; Anonymous, *James Stephens*, 95.

185. *Constitution and By-Laws of the Fenian Brotherhood of Colorado Territory* (Denver: Byers and Dailey, Printers, 1866).

186. A. W. Reaverley, "Personal Experiences in the Fenian Raid," *Welland Papers and Proceedings* 2 (1926): 73.

187. Neidhardt, "The Fenian Trials," 99–100.

188. J. MacDonald, *Troublous Times*, 124.

189. Walker, *The Fenian Movement*, 122.

190. Rubery, "The Fenian Movement," 47.

191. Joseph A. King, "The Fenian Invasion of Canada and John MacMahon: Priest, Saint, or Charlatan?" *Eire-Ireland* 23, no. 4 (1988): 42; Walker, *The Fenian Movement*, 123.

192. King, "The Fenian Invasion," 46.

193. Quoted in K. Brady, "Fenians and the Faithful," 422.

194. D. Williamson, "American Press Views of Fenianism," 54.

195. Walker, *The Fenian Movement*, 130.

196. Wilfrid Neidhardt, "The Fenian Trials in the Province of Canada, 1866-1867: A Case Study of Law and Politics in Action," *Ontario History* 66 (1974): 34.

197. *New York Herald*, November 1, 1866.

198. Neidhardt, "The Fenian Trials," 23, 34.

199. James Fitzgerald to William Sullivan, 19 November 1866. WSP/WRHS.

200. Ó Brion, *Fenian Fever*, 81.

201. *New York Times*, December 7, 1866.

202. Ibid.

203. James Stephens to unidentified recipient, January, 1867. New York Public Library; Cluseret, "My Connection with Fenianism," 357; Neidhardt, "The Fenian Trials," 54.

204. W. J. Lowe, "The Irish in Lancashire" (PhD diss., Trinity College Dublin, 1974), 516.

205. Ó Brion, *Fenian Fever*, 122.

206. Denis Arthur Rayner and Alan Wykes, *The Great Yacht Race* (London, Peter Davies Ltd. 1966), 15.

207. Ó Brion, *Fenian Fever*, 121–22.

208. P. G. Smith, "Fenian Invasions," 58; J. MacDonald, *Troublous Times,* 102–5; Teela, "Fenianism and Canada," 52.

209. H. Davis, "The Fenian Raid," 333; Meade, *The Life and Letters of George Meade,* 289.

210. Neidhardt, "The Fenian Trials," 74; Cumberland, "The Fenian Raids," 99.

6. "No Event of Any Importance"

1. Kee, *Green Flag,* 327; Ó Βριον, *Fenian Fever,* 67.

2. Kee, *Green Flag,* 327.

3. Kane, "Irish Immigrants in Philadelphia," 148–49.

4. Howard Evans, *Sir Randal Cremer: His Life and Work* (New York: Garland Publishing, 1973), 46.

5. John Newsinger, "Old Chartists, Fenians, and New Socialists," *Eire-Ireland* 17 (1982): 34–36; *Contemporary Review* XIX, 632.

6. Cluseret, "My Connection with Fenianism," 359.

7. Lynn Hollen Lees, *Exiles of Erin: Irish Migrants in Victorian London* (Ithaca, NY: Cornell University Press, 1979), 104; O'Connor, *The Irish in Britain,* 25.

8. L. Perry Curtis, *Anglo-Saxons and Celts: A Study of Anti-Irish Prejudice in Victorian England* (New York: New York University Press, 1968), 61.

9. Lees, *Exiles of Erin,* 104.

10. Kennedy, "Political Policing in a Liberal Age," 291; Kee, *Green Flag,* 331; W. J. Lowe, "Lancashire Fenianism, 1864-1871," *Transactions of the Historic Society of Lancashire and Cheshire* 126, no. CXXVI (1997): 173.

11. Seán ó Súilleabhán, "The Iveragh Fenians in Oral Tradition," in *Fenians and Fenianism,* ed. Maurice Harmon (Seattle: University of Washington Press, 1970), 36.

12. Devoy, *Recollections of an Irish Rebel,* 189–91; *Contemporary Review* XIX, 627.

13. D'Arcy, *The Fenian Movement,* 231–32.

14. Maurice Woulfe to uncle, 12 May 1867. Miller Collection.

15. D'Arcy, *The Fenian Movement,* 233.

16. Newsinger, *Fenianism in Mid-Victorian Britain,* 56; Peter Nolan, "Fariola, Massey, and the Fenian Uprising," *Cork Historical and Archaeological Society* 221, no. 75 (1970): 5; *Contemporary Review* XIX, 627–628.

17. Ó Brion, *Fenian Fever,* 89–90.

18. Ibid., 145; John Burk to John O'Mahony, 20 October 1866. FP/CUA.

19. Cluseret, "My Connection with Fenianism," 360–61.

20. Shin-Ichi Takagami, "The Fenian Rising in Dublin, March 1867," *Irish Historical Studies* 29, no. 115 (May 1995): 346.

21. R. Anderson, *A Great Conspiracy,* 33.

22. Michael Kenny, *The Fenians: Photographs and Memorabilia from the National Museum of Ireland* (Dublin: Town House and Country House, 1994), 18.

23. Takagami, "The Fenian Rising in Dublin," 357–59.

24. Ibid., 352–55; Ó Βριον, *Fenian Fever,* 150–51.

25. Takagami, 357–59

26. Ibid., 351.

27. William Rutherford, *'67 Retrospection: A Concise History of the Fenian Rising at Ballyhurst Fort, Tipperary* (Dublin: O'Loughlin, Shields, and Boland, 1903), 11, 15–16.

28. R. Anderson, *A Great Conspiracy,* 34.

29. *Contemporary Review XIX,* 627; *Cork Examiner,* March 7, 1867.

30. Victor Vifquain to Octave Fariola, 5 June 1867. FP/CUA.

31. *Hansard's* vol. 185 (March 6, 1867): 1419, (March 7, 1867): 1427, (March 11, 1867): 1648.

32. *Cork Examiner,* March 13, 1867.

33. Kennedy, "Political Policing in a Liberal Age," 296.

34. Griffin, "The IRB in Connacht and Leinster," 60.

35. Mahoney, "The Influence of Irish-Americans," 235; Jenkins, *The Fenians and Anglo-American Relations,* 224; PRO, FO 5/1341. 40. House Executive Document, 7 (40:2) 1357.

36. Kelly to John Gleeson, 15 March 1867. FP/CUA. Rutherford, *Secret History,* 60.

37. William Barry to parents, 2 September 1866. Miller Collection,

38. Semple, "The Fenian Infiltration of the British Army," 158–59.

39. Ó Brion, *Fenian Fever,* 170.

40. Bryson Edward Clevenger, "Ireland and the Ultraradicals" A Rhetoric of Engagement and Detachment in British Working-Class Ideology" (PhD diss., University of Virginia, 2000), 323.

41. *Cork Examiner,* March 7 and 13, 1867.

42. Keith Amos, *The Fenians in Australia* (Kensington: New South Wales University Press, 1988), 87–88.

43. Tom Nairn, *The Break-Up of Britain: Crisis and Neo-Nationalism* (London, NLB, 1981), 41.

44. Walter McGrath, "The Fenian Rising in Cork," *Irish Sword,* 8, no. 33 (1968): 253.

45. Ó Brion, *Fenian Fever,* 174.

46. *Irish People* (New York), November 30, 1867.

47. R. Anderson, *A Great Conspiracy,* 37–38.

48. Ó Brion, *Fenian Fever,* 174; Kee, *Green Flag,* 332.

49. Kennedy, "Political Policing in a Liberal Age," 312.

50. Rutherford, *'67 Retrospection,* 14.

51. Patrick O'Brien to R.M. Hodgsden, 12 March 1866. FP/CUA.

52. John C. Kavanagh Pension Application. National Archives, Washington, D.C.

53. *New York Times,* October 16, 1875.

54. William O. Scroggs, *Filibusters and Financiers: The Story of William Walker and his Associates* (New York: The MacMillan Company, 1916), 141–44; *New York Times*, December 15, 1860.

55. *Biographical Directory of the United States Congress*. http://bioguide.congress.gov.

56. *New York Times*, October 21, 1874.

57. Captain W. J. Nagle to D. M. Nagle, 14 December 1862. Fredericksburg and Spotsylvania National Military Park, Irish Brigade Collection, Fredericksburg, Virginia.

58. *Irish People* (New York) August 17, 1869; William J. Nagle to E. Murray, 2 February 1866. FP/CUA; *Irish People* (Dublin), August 26, 1865.

59. John Warren Pension Application. National Archives, Washington, DC.

60. J. MacDonald, *Troublous Times*, 13.

61. Fenian Papers R Series. NAI.

62. M. J. O'Mullane, *The Cruise of the Erin's Hope: or, "Gun-running in '67"* (Dublin: Catholic Truth Society of Ireland, 1916), 7–8.

63. Kennedy, "Political Policing in a Liberal Age," 335.

64. *Irish Citizen*, March 28, 1868.

65. John Kavanagh, *Official Report of John Kavanagh*.

66. William C. Nugent Pension Application. National Archives, Washington, DC.

67. *Irish People* (New York) February 12, 1870; O'Mullane, *The Cruise of the Erin's Hope*, 9.

68. *Irish People* (New York), November, 23, 1867.

69. Kennedy, "Political Policing in a Liberal Age," 157.

70. O'Mullane, *The Cruise of the Erin's Hope*, 12.

71. Mahoney, 253–54.

72. Kavanagh, *Official Report of John Kavanagh*; O'Mullane, *The Cruise of the Erin's Hope*, 16; *Dublin Express*, May 28, 1867; Mac Giolla Chiolle, "Fenian Documents in the State Paper Office," 273.

73. O'Mullane, *The Cruise of the Erin's Hope*, 20.

74. *Irish People* (New York), June 22, 1867.

75. O'Mullane, *The Cruise of the Erin's Hope*, 13.

76. *Irish Citizen*, March 28, 1868.

77. O'Mullane, *Cruise of the Erin's Hope*, 24.

78. Newsinger, *Fenianism in Mid-Victorian Britain*, 59.

79. Kee, *Green Flag,* 337; Rutherford, *'67 Retrospection,* 14.

80. Patrick Quinlivan and Paul Rose, *The Fenians in England: A Sense of Insecurity* (New York: Riverrun Press, 1982), 168.

81. O'Mullane, *Cruise of the Erin's Hope,* 25.

82. T. D. Sullivan, *The Dock and the Scaffold: The Manchester Tragedy and the Cruise of the Jacknell* (Dublin: A. M. Sullivan, 1868), 296.

83. Warren Pension Application. National Archives, Washington, DC; *Irish People* (New York) April 1, 1871.

84. *Irish People* (New York); July 6, 1867.

85. *Irish People* (New York); April 1, 1871.

86. *Waterford and County Weekly* 53, April 21, 2000; *The Gaelic American*, June 17, 1922.

87. *Irish People* (New York) June 29, 1867.

88. Kennedy, "Political Policing in a Liberal Age," 336.

89. Lynch and O'Donoghue, *O'Sullivan Burke*, 116.

90. Kee, *Green Flag,* 340; *The Nation*, August 24, 1867.

91. Ó Brion, *Fenian Fever,* 185.

92. *Boston Herald*, November 2, 1890.

93. *Irish People* (New York) November 23, 1867.

94. Des. Ryan, *Phoenix Flame,* 181; T. D. Sullivan, *The Dock and the Scaffold,* 300.

95. John de Courcy Ireland, "A Preliminary Study of Fenians and the Sea," *Eire-Ireland* 47 (Summer 1967): 47; *Boston Herald*, November 2, 1890.

96. PRO, FO 5/1341.

97. D'Arcy, *The Fenian Movement,* 260.

98. Walker, *The Fenian Movement,* 148.

99. D'Arcy, *The Fenian Movement,* 145.

100. House Executive Document, 157 (40:2) 1339.

101. *The Nation*, August 24, 1867.

102. House Executive Document, 157 (40:2) 1339.

103. Dennis O'Connor to George Francis Train, 29 May 1868, reprinted in the *Cork Herald*, May, 1868; *Irish Citizen*, June 27, 1868; Dennis O'Connor Military Record. National Archives, Washington, DC.

104. Mary Buckley to William West, 27 August 1867; House Executive Document, 157 (40:2) 1339.

105. *The Irish Citizen,* June 20, 1868.

106. United States Consular Dispatches, T-570.

107. Fenian Papers, NAI.

108. *The Irish Citizen,* January 25 and February 29, 1868; McGrath, "Fenian Rising in Cork," 246–47.

109. Patrick Hasson to William Seward, 6 September 1866; House Executive Document, 157 (40:2) 1339; Stanton, "Green Tint on Gold Bars," 86.

110. E. D. Steele, "Cardinal Cullen and Irish Nationality," *Irish Historical Studies* XIX, no. 75 (March 1975): 257.

111. Sillard, *The Life and Letters of John Martin,* 182–83.

7. Fenianism on the Defensive

1. Quinliven and Rose, *The Fenians in England,* 46.

2. Kennedy, "Political Policing in a Liberal Age," 351.

3. W. J. Lowe, "Lancashire Fenianism," 177.

4. Rutherford, *Secret History,* vol. II., 60.

5. Bateman, *Captain Timothy Deasy,* 7, 9.

6. Theodore Koditschek, *Class Formation and Urban-Industrial Society: Bradford, 1750-1850* (New York: Cambridge University Press, 1990), 490.

7. *London Times,* October 1, 1867.

8. *Punch,* October 12, 1867.

9. West to Seward, 26 October 1867. United States Consular Dispatches, T-570.

10. Jenkins, *The Fenians and Anglo-American Relations,* 268.

11. Patsy Davis, "Fenian Commemoration in Birmingham," *Irish News Round-Up* Irnet.com (November 15, 2000).

12. Karl Marx and Friedrich Engels, *Ireland and the Irish Question* (New York: International Publishers, 1972), 145.

13. *London Times,* November 15, 1867.

14. Quinliven and Rose, *The Fenians in England,* 62–63.

15. Paul Rose, *The Manchester Martyrs: The Story of a Fenian Tragedy* (London: Lawrence and Wishart, 1970), 104.

16. Ibid. 10. PRO, HO 457799.

17. *Irish Citizen*, December 14, 1867.

18. Rose, *The Manchester Martyrs,* 95–99.

19. PRO, HO 457799/2024, HO 457799/2029.

20. Rose, *The Manchester Martyrs,* 118.

21. Ó Brion, *Fenian Fever,* 205; Comerford, *Fenians in Context,* 149.

22. James Godkin, "Fenianism and the Irish Church," *Fortnightly Review* 10 (February 1868): 194; Sillard, *The Life and Letters of John Martin,* 189.

23. Ó Fiaich, "Clergy and Fenianism," 93–94.

24. Comerford, *Fenians in Context,* 149; Alvin Jackson, *Ireland: 1798-1998, Politics and War* (Malden, MA: Blackwell Publishers Inc., 1999), 104.

25. Amos, *The Fenians in Australia,* 66.

26. Dennis Clark, "Militants of the 1860s, The Philadelphia Fenians," *Pennsylvania Magazine of History and Biography* XCV, no. I (January 1971): 106; K. Brady, "Fenians and the Faithful," 439–441; *The Irish Citizen,* January 8, 1868; *New York Times,* January 9, 1868.

27. Ó Danachair, "A Soldier's Letters Home," 57.

28. Lynch and O'Donoghue, *O'Sullivan Burke,* 137; Kennedy, "Political Policing in a Liberal Age," 388; *Irish Citizen,* January 11, 1868.

29. Quinliven and Rose, *The Fenians in England,* 77–87.

30. Marx and Engels, *Ireland and the Irish Question,* 149; Clevenger, "Ireland and the Ultraradicals," 327, 336–40, 346–47.

31. K. R. M. Short, *The Dynamite War: Irish-American Bombers in Victorian Britain* (Atlantic Highlands, NJ: Humanities Press, 1979), 15.

32. R. Anderson, *A Great Conspiracy,* 40.

33. Quinliven and Rose, *The Fenians in England,* 96.

34. Simon Winchester, *The Professor and the Madman* (New York: HarperCollins Publishers, 1998), 60–64, 116.

35. Quinliven and Rose, *The Fenians in England,* 95–96

36. Kennedy, "Political Policing in a Liberal Age," 394, 396.

37. *London Times,* January 8, 1868.

38. Rutherford, *Secret History,* vol. II, 299.

39. Fenian Papers, R Series NAI; *Irishman,* January 4, 1868.

40. Ó Brion, *Fenian Fever,* 186; House Executive Document, 157 (40:2) 1339.

41. *Irish Citizen*, February 1, 1868.

42. Lynn Bridgers, *Death's Deceiver: The Life of Joseph P. Machebeuf* (Albuquerque: University of New Mexico Press, 1997), 174, 180.

43. *Irish Citizen*, February 1, 1868.

44. D'Arcy, *The Fenian Movement,* 294.

45. Rising Lake Morrow, "The Negotiation of the Anglo-American Treaty of 1870," *American Historical Review* XXXIX (July 1934): 675, 679; House Executive Document, 312 (40:2) 1346.

46. Amos, *The Fenians in Australia,* 71.

47. Hereward Senior, "Quebec and the Fenians," 39, 42; *The Irish Citizen*, September 26, 1868.

48. Quoted in Donald C. Richter, *Riotous Victorians* (Athens: Ohio University Press, 1981), 32.

49. Steven R. Knowlton, "John Mitchel in America: The Desperate Protest of an Irish Exile" (master's thesis, University of Missouri, Saint Louis, 1981), 68.

50. *Irish People* (New York) July 6, 1867; *Irish Citizen*, May 9, 1868.

51. *New York Times*, May 9, 1868.

52. *Irish Citizen*, June 27, 1868. Dennis O'Connor Military Record. National Archives Washington, DC.

53. Lynch and O'Donoghue, *O'Sullivan Burke,* 145.

54. *The Irish Citizen*, August 8, 1868.

55. *Proceedings of the Seventh National Congress, Fenian Brotherhood* (New York: D. W. Lee, 1868), 16.

56. *Milford, Massachusetts City Directory*, 1869, 1872.

57. W. E. Hamilton to Paul Askin, 16 July 1868. NLI.

58. *New York Times*, July 6, 1868.

59. John O'Brien to Frank Gallagher (1862-1870). Fenian Papers, Saint Charles Seminary. Overbrook, Pennsylvania; hereafter FP/SCS.

60. *Irish People* (New York), January 16, 1869; D'Arcy, *The Fenian Movement,* 309; *Irish Citizen*, November 14, 1868.

61. Open Letter from the Fenian War Department, 2 November, 1868. FP/SCS.

62. *The Fenian Volunteer*, November, 1868; Phillips, *Fort Erie,* 253–54.

63. R. V. Comerford, "Patriotism as Pastime: The Appeal of Fenianism in the Mid-1860s," *Irish Historical Studies* 22, no. 87 (March 1981): 241.

64. *Dublin Irishman*, June 2, 1860; Devoy, *Recollections of an Irish Rebel,* 26; *London Times*, March 7, 1867; Ó Brion, *Fenian Fever* 155–56. Quinliven and Rose, *The Fenians in England,* 109.

65. Rutherford, *Secret History,* vol. I. 199; Kennedy, "Political Policing in a Liberal Age," 296–97.

66. Samuel Clark and James S. Donnelly, eds., *Irish Peasants: Violence and Political Unrest, 1780-1914* (Madison: University of Wisconsin Press, 1983), 274.

67. Comerford, *Context*, 99, 115; Comerford, "Patriotism as Pastime," 240–41; Rafferty, "Fenian Threat," 21.

68. Comerford, "Patriotism as Pastime," 240–41; Takagami, "The Fenian Rising in Dublin," 362.

69. Nairn, *The Break-Up of Britain,* 41.

70. David Thornley, *Isaac Butt and Home Rule* (London: MacGibbon and Kee, 1964), 66; D'Arcy, *The Fenian Movement*, 267; *The Irish Citizen*, August 29, 1868.

71. Ó Fiaich, "The Clergy and Fenianism," 95.

72. *Irish Citizen*, February 20, 1869.

73. Knowlton, "John Mitchel in America," 68.

74. Fenian Papers, R Series, NAI.

75. D'Arcy, *The Fenian Movement*, 273, 309–13; Walker, *The Fenian Movement*, 154, 179.

76. *Irish Citizen*, August 14, 1869.

77. *Irish Citizen*, August 28, 1869; *New York Times,* August 16, 1869.

78. *Irish People* (New York) August 17, 1869; *Contemporary Review*, XIX, 636.

79. Quoted in Rafferty, "Fenianism in North America," 269.

80. Rafferty, "Fenianism in North America," 275.

81. King, "The Fenian Invasion ," 32–33. Neidhardt, "The Fenian Trials," 34.

82. C. W. Sullivan III, ed. *Fenian Diary, Denis B. Cashman on Board the Hougoumont* (Dublin: Wolfhound Press, 2001), 26–27.

83. Angela Clifford, translator, "The Fenians and Karl Marx," Irish Communist Organization, 1967.

84. Rafferty, "Fenianism in North America," 263.

85. F. MacDonald, *The Catholic Church*, 47.

86. John O'Neill, "Fenian Circular," 21 January 1870. O'Keefe Papers, Missouri Historical Society.

87. Letter to P. Meehan, 21 February 1870. FP/SC.

88. James Yates Egan Fonds. Canadian National Archives.

89. Box 3, File 10. George Cahill Papers. Boston College.

90. Dennis Clark, "Letters from the Underground: The Fenian Correspondence of James Gibbons," *Records of the American Catholic Historical Society* 81 (1970): 87; D'Arcy, *The Fenian Movement*, 347.

91. James Yates Egan Fonds. Canadian National Archives.

92. *Irish People* (New York), May 21, 1870.

93. Senior, *Last Invasion*, 147; Francis Wayland Campbell, *The Fenian Invasions of Canada of 1866 and 1870* (Montreal: John Lovell and Son, 1904), 39.

94. DeRosier, "Importance in Failure," 191.

95. Anonymous, *The Fenian Raid of 1870, by Reporters Present at the Scene* (Montreal 1871), 7; hereafter, *FR 1870*; Robert Franklin McGee, *The Fenian Raids on the Huntingdon Frontier, 1866 and 1870* (Author: 1967), 12.

96. J. MacDonald, *Troublous Times*, 177–78.

97. Herbert Donovan, "Fenian Memories in Northern New York," *American-Irish Historical Journal* 28 (1929): 149–50.

98. Ibid., 149–50.

99. R. McGee, *The Fenian Raids*, 25–27.

100. Bartholomew Wolfe to Maurice Wolfe, 24 January and 9 June 1870. Miller Collection.

101. *Irish Citizen*, March 12, 1870.

102. D'Arcy, *The Fenian Movement*, 352.

103. DeRosier, "Importance in Failure," 192.

104. Cole, *Prince of Spies*, 64; *Official Report of General John O'Neill*.

105. Neidhardt, "The Fenian Trials," 121.

106. D'Arcy, *The Fenian Movement*, 346.

107. A. G. Evans, *Fanatic Heart: A Life of John Boyle O'Reilly, 1844-1890* (Boston: Northeastern University Press, 1999), 180; Reidy, "John Devoy," 416; *FR 1870*, 23.

108. Cole, *Prince of Spies,* 82.

109. Brusher, 191.

110. *New York Times,* July 30, 1870.

111. DeRosier, "Importance in Failure," 190.

112. *Woonsocket Patriot and Rhode Island Register,* May 27, 1870.

113. R. McGee, *The Fenian Raids,* 34.

114. Brusher, 189.

115. R. McGee, *The Fenian Raids,* 40–42; Campbell, *The Fenian Invasions,* 50.

116. King, "The Fenian Invasion of Canada and John MacMahon," 47–48.

117. Brodsky, *Grover Cleveland,* 30.

118. Campbell, *The Fenian Invasions,* 43.

119. R. McGee, *The Fenian Raids,* 52; *Irish Citizen,* June 4, 1870.

120. Allan Nevins, *Hamilton Fish: The Inner History of the Grant Administration* (New York: F. Ungar Publishing, 1957), 394.

121. D'Arcy, *The Fenian Movement,* 356.

122. Michael A. Gordon, *The Orange Riots: Irish Political Violence in New York City* (Ithaca, NY: Cornell University Press, 1993), 34.

123. R. McGee, *The Fenian Raids,* 30–31.

124. Senior, "Quebec and the Fenians," 43.

125. Richard Shannon, *Gladstone,* vol. 2 (Chapel Hill: University of North Carolina Press, 1999), 83-85.

126. Des. Ryan, *Fenian Chief,* 269–70.

127. *Congressional Directory Forty-Second Congress* (Washington, DC: Government Printing Office, 1872), 64–65.

128. *Irish Citizen,* March 16, 1872.

129. *Irish Citizen,* May 21, 1870.

130. John O'Connor, *Letters of John O'Connor, MP on Fenianism addressed to his Excellency* (Toronto: Hunter Rose and Company, 1870), v–vi.

131. Box Five, Files 37, 46, and 47. Cahill Papers.

132. *Irish Citizen,* February 4, 1871.

133. PRO, HO 45/9331/19461C.

134. *Irish People* (New York) April 8, 1871; Des. Ryan, *Fenian Chief,* 200.

135. Pieper, "The Fenian Movement," 9.

136. Mahoney, "The Influence of Irish-Americans," 367.

137. Brian Jenkins, "The British Government, John A. MacDonald and the Fenian Claims," *Canadian Historical Review* XLIX, no. 2 (April 1968): 143, 158.

138. Gordon, *The Orange Riots,* 62.

139. Alvin C. Gluck, Jr., "The Riel Rebellion and Canadian-American Relations," *Canadian Historical Review* 36, no. 3 (September 1955): 207.

140. PRO, HO 45/9331/19461D.

141. Ryan, *Fenian Chief,* 277, 280.

142. Gilbert McMicken, *An Abortive Raid: An Irish Republic in Manitoba Planned but Crushed Early* (Winnipeg: Manitoba Free Press Print, 1888), 1, 3.

143. Senior, *Last Invasion,* 183–84; DeRosier, "Importance in Failure," 197; A. G. Morice, *The Catholic Church in Western Canada* (Toronto: The Musson Book Company, 1910), 70.

144. *New York Times,* October 22, 1871.

145. Alexander Whyte Wright Fonds. Canadian National Archives.

146. Cole, *Prince of Spies,* 87; McMicken, *An Abortive Raid,* 9.

147. *Biographical Directory of the United States Congress.*

148. William R. Roberts, *Enforcement of the Fourteenth Amendment-Ku Klux Legislation-Bayonets vs. Freedom* (Washington: F & J Rivas and George A. Bailey, 1871), 3–7.

149. *Irish Citizen,* April 22, 1871; *Congressional Directory, Forty-Third Congress, First Session, Third Edition* (Washington, DC: Government Printing Office, 1874), 75, 147; *Dictionary of American Biography* vol. 35. (New York: Charles Scribner and Sons, 1935), 20–21.

150. Kane, "Irish Immigrants in Philadelphia," 107–8. Joan Marie Donohoe, "The Irish Catholic Benevolent Union" (PhD diss., Catholic University, 1953), 32.

151. Terence V. Powderly, *The Path I Trod* (New York: Ames Press, 1968), 175.

152. Box 1, File 78. Cahill Papers.

153. Jeremiah Murphy to George Cahill, 19 July 1871; Box 5, File 82. Cahill Papers.

154. *Milford Daily News,* March 23, 1979.

155. J. L. Hammond, *Gladstone and the Irish Nation* (Hamdon, CT: Archon Books, 1964), 124–25; Roy Jenkins, *Gladstone: A Biography* (New York: Random House, 1997), 362–65.

156. T. W. Moody, "Fenianism, Home Rule, and the Land War (1850-1891) in *The Course of Irish History,* ed. T.W. Moody and F.X. Martin (Niwot, CO: Roberts Rinehart Publishers, 1995), 281.

157. Zephaniah Walt Pease, *The Catalpa Expedition* (New Bedford, MA: George S. Anthony, 1897), 113–61.

158. Box 3, File 31. Cahill Papers.

159. Box 3, File 38-39. Cahill Papers.

160. C. W. Sullivan, *Fenian Diary,* 28.

161. Thomas Kelly to "Mother," 24 March 1876. National Library of Ireland.

162. Anciello, "Patrick A. Collins," 3.

163. Jack Beatty, *The Rascal King: The Life and Times of James Michael Curley* (Reading, MA: Addison-Wesley Publishing Company, 1992), 7; D'Arcy, *The Fenian Movement,* 51.

164. *New York Times,* June 25, 1886.

165. K. Brady, *Fenians and the Faithful,* 175; *New York Times,* February 26, 1877.

166. *New York Times,* February 12, 1877.

167. *New York Times,* February 26, March 9, March 19, 1877.

168. Devoy, *Recollections of an Irish Rebel,* 266; *The Gaelic American,* June 10, 1922.

169. Folio V. O'Flynn Papers.

170. Des. Ryan, in Moody, *The Fenian Movement,* 63.

171. Mary Evangela Henthorne, *The Irish Catholic Colonization Association of the United States* (Champaign, IL: The Twin City Printing Company, 1932), 139–40.

172. "Fenians in Dakota," *South Dakota Historical Collections* vol. VI (1912): 130.

173. *New York Times,* June 27, 1894.

174. D'Arcy, *The Fenian Movement,* 346; Langan, 23, 26–28, 34, 38; *Irish-American,* January 19, 1878; Jeffrey H. Smith, *A Frenchman Fights for the Union: Victor Vifquain and the 97th Illinois* (Varna, IL: Patrick Publishing, 1992), 10.

175. *Irish-American,* January 26 and February 9, 1878.

176. John Bew, *The Glory of Being Britons: Civic Unionism in Nineteenth-Century Belfast* (Portland, OR: Irish Academic Press, 2009), 229.

177. Folio V, 487. O'Flynn Papers.

178. Donald Jordan, *Land and Popular Politics in Ireland* (New York: Cambridge University Press, 1994), 322.

179. M. Brown, *The Politics of Irish Literature,* 186.

180. Short, *The Dynamite War,* 50, 55, 65.

181. Kavanagh Pension Record; *New York Times,* June 11, 1880.

182. *Boston Globe,* February 25, 2001.

183. Myers, "The Fenians in Iowa," 60.

184. Thomas Corfe, *The Phoenix Park Murders: Conflict, Compromise and Tragedy in Ireland, 1879-1882* (London: Hodder and Stoughton, 1968), 15, 27–28.

185. Conley, *Melancholy Accidents*, 33–35.

186. Kevin Kenny, *Making Sense of the Molly Maguires* (New York: Oxford University Press, 1997), 79–80.

187. Short, *The Dynamite War*, 104.

188. Box 1, File 82. Cahill Papers.

189. Gordon Hopper, "Milford's Memorial Building: A Tribute to Civil War Soldiers," *Milford Daily News* (March 18, 1995).

190. Beaudot and Herdegen, *An Irishman*, 4.

191. *New York Times*, August 13, 1885.

192. *New York Herald*, December 9, 1883.

193. Box 1 File 24. Cahill Papers.

8. Last Hurrahs

1. Stephan Thernstrom, *The Other Bostonians* (Cambridge, MA: Harvard University Press, 1973), 186.

2. George Alfred Townsend, *Rustics in Rebellion: A Yankee Reporter on the Road to Richmond* (Chapel Hill: University of North Carolina Press, 1950), 107.

3. Kohl, *Irish Green and Union Blue*, 102.

4. O'Rourke, *Currier and Ives*, 131.

5. Cluseret, "My Connection with Fenianism," 354.

6. Matthew Frye Jacobson, *Special Sorrows*, 184.

7. *Biographical Directory of the United States Congress.*

8. Ancient Order of Hibernians, Lawrence, Massachusetts, "Patriot, Fenian, Statesman, Tribute to John Breen" (November 26th, 1994); *Lawrence Evening Tribune*, December 22, 1910.

9. *New York Times*, July 17, 1894.

10. Clark and Donnelly, *Irish Peasants*, 274–75.

11. Brian M. Walker, ed., *Parliamentary Election Results in Ireland, 1801-1922* (Dublin: Royal Irish Academy, 1978), 134, 152.

12. Box 1, Series 1. John Boyle O'Reilly Papers, Boston College.

13. Ibid.; Box 1, File 1, Subseries A, no. 42.

14. John Wertheimer, "The Green and the Black: Irish Nationalism and the Dilemma of Abolitionism," *New York Irish History* 5, no. 1 (1990–1991): 9. *Boston Irish Reporter*, November, 1999.

15. Box 4, File 6. Cahill Papers.

16. A. G. Evans, *Fanatic Heart,* 248.

17. *Irish Citizen*, November 16, 1867.

18. Augustine E. Costello to cousin "Charles," 9 July 1891. Patrick Sarsfield O'Hegarty Collection. University of Kansas, Lawrence, Kansas. Costello's *Our Firemen: A History of the New York Fire Departments*, which was redistributed to booksellers in the aftermath of the 2001 World Trade Center disaster, is just shy of 1,100 pages.

19. *New York Times*, March 5, 1894; Jacobson, *Special Sorrows,* 188.

20. *New York Times*, March 6, 1900.

21. Patrick J. Kain Pension Application. National Archives, Washington, DC. William O'Brien and Desmond Ryan, *Devoy's Post-Bag, 1871-1928* (Dublin: C.J. Fallon Limited, 1948), 154; P. J. Kain to Jeremiah O'Donovan Rossa, 20 November, 1909. FP/CUA.

22. Dunn, "Recollections," 50.

23. Box 2, File 41. Cahill Papers.

24. Elizabeth Gurley Flynn, *The Rebel Girl: An Autobiography* (New York: International Publishers, 1955), 23, 25–26.

25. *New York Times*, October 22, 1890.

26. Cole, *Prince of Spies,* 204–5.

27. Ó Brion, *Fenian Fever,* 185.

28. *New York Times*, October 11, 1891.

29. Warren Pension Application. National Archives, Washington, DC.

30. *Irish People* (New York) May 21, 1870, October 21, 1871; *Irish Citizen*, December 4, 1869.

31. *New York Times*, August 13, 1897.

32. *New York Times*, May 1, 1900 and April 1, 1901.

33. J. Smith, *A Frenchman Fights for the Union,* 44–45; Jacobson, *Special Sorrows,* 205, 213.

34. Box 2, File 31. Cahill Papers. Nugent Pension Application, National Archives (Washington, DC). Cameron, "Fenian Times in Nova Scotia," 140–14; *Biographical Directory of the United States Congress.*

35. Garrath O'Keeffe, "Australia's Irish Republican Brotherhood," *Journal of the Royal Australian Historical Society* 83, no. 2 (December, 1997): 137–41; Patrick O'Farrell, "The Irish Republican Brotherhood in Australia, the 1918 Internments" *Irish Culture and Nationalism, 1750-1950,* ed. in Oliver MacDonagh, W. F. Mandle, and Pauric Travers (New York: Saint Martin's Press, 1983), 192.

36. *Gaelic-American*, May 20, 1922.

37. *Gaelic-American*, May 27, 1922, August 12, 1922; Lynch and O'Donoghue, *O'Sullivan Burke*, 235.

38. *Huntingdon Gleaner*, February 2, 1915, December 27, 1922, October 6, 1924, March 27, 1926, February 7, 1930.

39. D'Arcy, *The Fenian Movement*, 64.

40. John O'Leary, *Recollections of Fenians and Fenianism* (Shannon: Irish University Press, 1969), 65–66.

41. M. Brown, *The Politics of Irish Literature,* 204.

42. Anbinder, *Nativism and Slavery,* 271.

43. Knobel, *Paddy and the Republic,* 181.

44. *New York Times,* July 29, 1884.

45. Fisher, "Born in Ireland, Killed at Gettysburg," 235.

46. Richard Taylor, *Destruction and Reconstruction: Personal Experiences of the Late War* (Waltham, MA: Blaisdell Publishing Company, 1968), 69.

47. Kathy Lee Peiss, *Cheap Amusements: Working Women and Leisure in Turn-of-the-Century New York* (Philadelphia: Temple University Press, 1986), 61.

48. R. R. Foster, *Modern Ireland: 1600-1972* (New York: Penguin Putnam, 1990), 454.

49. *Boston Globe,* June 14, 2000.

50. *New York Times,* May 16 and 19, 2002.

51. *Proceedings of the First General Convention of the Fenian Brotherhood on the Pacific Coast* (San Francisco, 1864).

BIBLIOGRAPHY

PRIMARY SOURCES

Government Documents

Archives Canada, Ottawa. Various Collections.

Fredericksburg and Spotsylvania National Military Park. Irish Brigade Collection.

Hansard's Parliamentary Debates, London.

National Archives Annex. College Park, Maryland. United States Consular Reports.

National Archives Ireland, Dublin. Various Collections.

National Archives Washington, DC. Pension Application Files and Military Records. United States House of Representatives Executive Documents.

National Library of Ireland, Dublin. Various Letters and Papers.

Public Record Office, Belfast. Various Collections.

Public Record Office, London, United Kingdom. Various Collections.

Public and Private Collections

Andrew Johnson Papers. University of Tennessee Special Collections Library.

Arnold Schrier Collection. University of Cincinnati.

Fenian Papers. Catholic University of America. Washington, DC.

Fenian Papers. Saint Charles Seminary. Overbrook, Pennsylvania.

George Cahill Papers. Boston College.

James A. Mulligan Papers. Chicago Historical Society. Chicago, Illinois.

James Stephens Papers. New York City Public Library.

John Boyle O'Reilly Papers. Boston College. Chestnut Hill, Massachusetts.

Kerby Miller Collection. University of Missouri.

Martin John Spalding Papers. Baltimore Cathedral Archives. Baltimore, Maryland.

Melony-Mitchel Papers. Columbia University.

O'Keefe Papers. Missouri Historical Society. Saint Louis, Missouri.

Patrick A. Collins Papers. Boston College. Chestnut Hill, Massachusetts.

Patrick Sarsfield O'Hegarty Collection. University of Kansas. Lawrence, Kansas.

Richard O'Flynn Papers. Holy Cross College. Worcester, Massachusetts.

Southern Historical Collection. University of North Carolina, Chapel Hill.

University of Notre Dame Archives. Notre Dame, Indiana.

William Sullivan Papers. Western Reserve Historical Society. Cleveland, Ohio.

Miscellaneous Documents

Constitution and By-Laws of the Fenian Brotherhood of Colorado Territory (Denver, 1866).

Constitution of the Fenian Brotherhood, adopted October 21, 1865 at the General Convention of the Fenian Brotherhood held in Philadelphia.

Milford, Massachusetts City Directory (1869).

Official Roster of Soldiers of the State of Ohio in the War of Rebellion, 1861–1866.

Official Report of General John O'Neill.

Proceedings of the First General Convention of the Fenian Brotherhood on the Pacific Coast (San Francisco, 1864).

Proceedings of the First National Convention of the Fenian Brotherhood.

Proceedings of the Seventh National Congress. Fenian Brotherhood (New York, 1868).

Proclamation to the People of British North America (May, 1866).

Welland Township Committee of Safety Minutes (Fort Erie, Ontario: June 1 and June 2, 1866).

Newspapers and Periodicals

Atlantic Monthly

Boston Globe

Boston Herald

Boston Irish Reporter

Boston Pilot

Buffalo Advertiser

Chicago Tribune

Cork Examiner

Davenport Daily Democrat

Davenport Daily Gazette

Dublin Express

Freeman's Journal (New York)

Fortnightly Review

The Gaelic American (New York)

Galveston Daily News

Huntingdon Gleaner

Irish-American

Irish Canadian (Toronto)

Irish Citizen

Irish People (Dublin)

Irish People (New York)

Irish Times (Dublin)

LaCrosse Daily Democrat

Lawrence American and Andover Advertiser

Lawrence Evening Tribune

Lawrence Sentinel

London Times

Lowell Daily Courier

Matamoros Daily Ranchero

Milford Daily News

Milford Journal

Missouri Democrat

Montreal Herald

Nation (Dublin)

New Orleans Daily Crescent

New Orleans Daily Southern Star

New Orleans Daily True Delta

New Orleans Times Picayune

New York Herald

New York Times

New York World

Ottumwa Weekly Democrat

Pawtucket Gazette and Chronicle

Peoria Daily Transcript

Peoria National Democrat

Philadelphia North American and United States Gazette

The Phoenix (New York)

Punch (London)

Richmond Enquirer

San Francisco Daily Dramatic Chronicle

Toronto Leader

Waterbury Daily American

Waterford and County Weekly

Waterloo Courier

Western Banner

Winona Daily Republican

Woonsocket Patriot and Rhode Island Register

Books

Mitchel, John. *The Last Conquest of Ireland (Perhaps)*. New York: Lynch, Cole, and Meehan, 1873.

O'Leary, John. *Recollections of Fenians and Fenianism*. New York: Barnes and Noble, 1969.

O'Reilly, Miles [Charles Halpine]. *Baked Meats of the Funeral*. New York: Carleton, 1866.

Rutherford, John. *'67 Retrospection: A Concise History of the Fenian Rising at Ballyhurst Fort, Tipperary*. Dublin: O'Loughlin, Shields, and Bolan, 1903.

———. *The Secret History of the Fenian Conspiracy*. London: C. K. Paul and Company, 1877.

Secondary Sources

Articles

Anonymous [Robert Anderson]. "Fenianism—By One who Knows." *Contemporary Review* XIX (1871–1872).

Anciello, Michael. "Patrick A. Collins: Bibliographical Note." *Patrick A. Collins Collection Index.* Boston College (1996).

Ascher, E. "Number One Company, Niagara." *Niagara Historical Society* 27 (1915).

Athearn, Robert G. "Thomas Francis Meagher: An Irish Revolutionary in America." *University of Colorado Studies* I (December 1949).

Bateman, Robert J. *Captain Timothy Deasy: Patriot—Irish American.* Lawrence, MA: Ancient Order of the Hibernians, Division 8 (November 22, 1992).

Belcham, John. "Republican Spirit and Military Science: The 'Irish Brigade' and Irish American Nationalism in 1848." *Irish Historical Studies* XXXIX (May 1994).

Boyce, Toby. "The American Civil War and Irish Nationalism." *History Ireland* 4, no. 2 (Summer 1996).

Brewster, Nathaniel. "Recollections of the Fenian Raid." *Welland County Historical Society Papers and Records* 2 (1926).

Brown, Thomas N. "Nationalism and the Irish Peasant, 1800–1848." *The Review of Politics* 15 (1953).

Burton, William L. "Irish Regiments in the Union Army: The Massachusetts Experience." *Historical Journal of Massachusetts* 11 (June 1983).

Calkin, Homer. "St. Alban's in Reverse: the Fenian Raid of 1866." *Vermont History* 35, no. 1 (1967).

Cameron, James. "Fenian Times in Nova Scotia." *Collection of the Nova Scotia Historical Society* 37 (1980).

Chesson, Michael. "Harlots or Heroines? A New Look at the Richmond Bread Riots." *The Virginia Magazine of History and Biography* 92, no. 2 (April 1984).

Clark, Dennis. "Letters from the Underground: The Fenian Correspondence of James Gibbons." *Records of the American Catholic Historical Society* 81 (1970).

———. "Militants of the 1860s, The Philadelphia Fenians." *Pennsylvania Magazine of History and Biography* XCV, no. I (January 1971).

Clifford, Angela. "The Fenians and Karl Marx." Irish Communist Organization (1967).

Cluseret, Gustave Paul. "My Connection with Fenianism." *Littell's; Living Age* CXIV (August 1872).

Comerford, R. V. "Comprehending the Fenians." *Saothar* 17 (1990–1991).

———. "Patriotism as Pastime: The Appeal of Fenianism in the Mid-1860s." *Irish Historical Studies* 22, no. 87 (March 1981).

Connors, Thomas G. "Letters of John Mitchel, 1848–1869." *Analecta Hibernica* 37 (1998).

Cruikshank, E. A. "The Fenian Raid of 1866." *Welland County Historical Society Papers and Reports* 2 (1926).

Cullop, Charles P. "An Unequal Duel: Union Recruiting in Ireland, 1863–1864." *Civil War History* 13 (June 1967).

Cumberland, Barlow. "The Fenian Raids of 1866 and Events on the Frontier." *Proceedings and Transactions of the Royal Society of Canada* Third Series 10 (1910).

Curran, M. J. "Cardinal Cullen: Biographical Materials." *Reportorium Novum* 11 (1955).

Davis, Harold A. "The Fenian Raid on New Brunswick." *Canadian Historical Review* 36, no. 4 (December 1955).

Davis, Patsy. "Fenian Commemoration in Birmingham." *Irish News Round-Up* (November 15, 2000) Irnet.com

Delury, J. F. "Irish Nationalism in the Sacramento Region." *Eire-Ireland* 21, no. 3 (1986).

DeRosier, Arthur H., Jr. "Importance in Failure: The Fenian Raids of 1866–1871." *Southern Quarterly* 3, no. 3 (April 1965).

Donovan, Herbert. "Fenian Memories in Northern New York." *American-Irish Historical Journal* 28 (1929).

Duggan, G. C. "The Fenians in Canada: A British Officer's Impressions." *Irish Sword* 8, no. 31 (Winter 1967).

Dunn, J. F. "Recollections of the Battle of Ridgeway." *Welland County Historical Society Papers and Proceedings* (1926).

Ellis, William Hodgson. "The Adventures of a Prisoner of War." *The Canadian Magazine of Politics, Science, Art and Literature* 13, no. 3 (July 1899).

Finerty, John F. "Thirty Years of Ireland's Battle." *Donahoe's Magazine* 30 (1893).

Fisher, Donald M. "Born in Ireland, Killed at Gettysburg: The Life, Death, and Legacy of Patrick Henry O'Rorke." *Civil War History* 49, no. 3 (1993).

George, Joseph. "Very Reverend Patrick E. Moriarty, OSA Philadelphia's Fenian Spokesman." *Pennsylvania History* 48, no. 3 (July 1981).

Gleeson, David. "Parallel Struggles: Irish Republicanism in the American South, 1798–1876." *Eire-Ireland* (Summer 1999).

Gluck, Alvin C., Jr. "The Riel Rebellion and Canadian-American Relations." *Canadian Historical Review* 36, no. 3 (September 1955).

Griffin, Brian. "Social Aspects of Fenianism in Connacht and Leinster, 1858–1870." *Eire-Ireland* 21, no. 1 (Spring, 1986).

Hernon, Joseph M. "Irish Sympathy for the Southern Confederacy." *Eire-Ireland* 2, no. 3 (Autumn 1967).

———. "The Irish Nationalists and Southern Secession." *Civil War History* 12, no. 1 (March 1966).

Ireland, John de Courcy. "A Preliminary Study of Fenians and the Sea." *Eire-Ireland* 47 (Summer 1967).

Jenkins, Brian. "The British Government, Sir John A. MacDonald, and the Fenian Claims." *Canadian Historical Review* XLIX, no. 2 (April 1968).

Kelly, Brian. "Ambiguous Loyalties: The Boston Irish, Slavery, and the Civil War." *Historical Journal of Massachusetts* 24, no. 2 (Summer 1996).

King, Joseph A. "The Fenian Invasion of Canada and John MacMahon: Priest, Saint, or Charlatan?" *Eire-Ireland* 23, no. 4 (1988).

Kostal, R. W. "Rebels in the Dock: The Prosecution of the Dublin Fenians, 1865–6." *Eire Ireland* 34, no. 2 (Summer 2000).

Larmour, Robert. "With Booker's Column." *Canadian Magazine* 10, no. 3 (January 1898).

Lester, DeeGee. "Tennessee's Bold Fenian Men." *Tennessee Historical Quarterly* 56 (Winter 1997).

Lowe, W. J. "Lancashire Fenianism, 1864–1871." *Transactions of the Historic Society of Lancashire and Cheshire* 126, no. CXXVI (1997).

Mac Giolla Choille, Breandán. "Fenian Documents in the State Paper Office." *Irish Historical Studies* 15, no. 63 (March 1969).

McCallum, Fred H. "Experiences of a Queen's Own Rifleman at Ridgeway." *Annual Report of the Waterloo Historical Society* 3 (1915).

McCartney, Donal. "The Church and Fenianism," *Fenians and Fenianism: Centenary Essays,* ed. Maurice Harmon, pp. Seattle: University of Washington Press, 1970.

McGrath, Walter. "The Fenian Rising in Cork," *Irish Sword*, 8, no. 33 (1968).

Man, Albon P. "The Irish in New York City in the 1860s." *Irish Historical Studies* 7, no. 26 (March 1950).

Marshall, David. "The Fenians after Seventy-Five Years." *Catholic World* CLVI, no. 933 (December 1942).

Meyler, David. "To the Glory of Our Country, The Fenian Invasion of Canada, 1866." *Command* (March–April 1992).

Moran, Gerald. "The National Brotherhood of St Patrick in Britain in the 1860s." *Irish Studies Review* 7, no. 3 (1999).

Morgan, Jack. "'The Dust of Maynooth:' Fenian Funeral as Political Theatre." *New Hibernia Review* 2, no. 4 (Winter 1998).

Morrow, Rising Lake. "The Negotiation of the Anglo-American Treaty of 1870." *American Historical Review* XXXIX (July 1934).

Myers, Phillip E. "The Fenians in Iowa." *The Palimpsest* 62 (1981).

Neidhardt, Wilfried. "The Fenian Trials in the Province of Canada, 1866–1867: A Case Study of Law and Politics in Action." *Ontario History* 66 (1974).

Newsinger, John. "Old Chartists, Fenians, and New Socialists." *Eire-Ireland* 17 (1982).

Nolan, Peter. "Fariola, Massey, and the Fenian Uprising." *Cork Historical and Archaeological Society* 221, no. 75 (1970).

O'Brien, Kevin. "'Blaze away and stand to it, boys': Captain Jack Donovan and the Irish Brigade at Fredericksburg." *Irish Sword* 20, no. 80 (1996).

Ó Cathaoir, Breandán. "American Fenianism and Canada, 1865–1871." *Irish Sword* 8, no. 31 (Winter 1967).

Ó Danachair, Caoimhín. "A Soldier's Letters Home, 1863–74." *Irish Sword* 3-4 (Summer 1957).

O'Keeffe, Garrath. "Australia's Irish Republican Brotherhood." *Journal of the Royal Australian Historical Society* 83, no. 2 (December 1997).

Ó Fiaich, Tomas. "The Clergy and Fenianism, 1860–1870." *The Irish Ecclesiastical Record* 5, no. 109 (1968).

———. "The Patriot Priest of Partry," Patrick Lavelle: 1825–1886." *Journal of the Galway Archaeological and Historical Society* 35 (1976).

O'Mullane, M. J. *The Cruise of the Erin's Hope: or, "Gun-running in '67."* Dublin: Catholic Truth Society of Ireland (1916).

Patrick, John. "The Cleveland Fenians: A Study in Ethnic Leadership." *The Old Northwest* 9, no. 4 (1985).

Purcell, Richard J. "Ireland and the American Civil War." *The Catholic World* 115, no. 685 (April 1922).

Quealy, F. M. "The Fenian Invasion of Canada West." *Ontario History* 53 (1961).

Rafferty, Oliver. "Cardinal Cullen, Early Fenianism, and the MacManus Funeral Affair." *Recusant History* 22, no. 4 (October 1995).

———. "Fenianism in North America in the 1860s: The Problems for Church and State." *History* 84, no. 274 (April 1999).

Reidy, James. "John Devoy." *Journal of the American Irish Historical Society* 27 (1928).

Reaverley, A. W. "Personal Experiences in the Fenian Raid." *Welland Papers and Proceedings* 2 (1926).

Reynolds, Mark E. "The Only Civil War Battle Fought on New England Soil." *Yankee Magazine* (January 1998).

Rorabaugh, W. J. "Who Fought for the North in the Civil War? Concord, Massachusetts, Enlistments." *Journal of American History* 73, no. 3 (December 1986).

Sarbaugh, Timothy J. "Post-Civil War Fever and Adjustment Fenianism in the California Context 1858–1872." *Working Papers in Irish History*. Boston: Northeastern University Irish Studies Program (1992).

Semple, A. J. "The Fenian Infiltration of the British Army." *Journal of the Society for Army Historical Research* 52 (1974).

Senior, Hereward. "Quebec and the Fenians." *Canadian Historical Review* 48, no. 1 (March 1967).

Severance, Frank Hayward. "The Fenian Raid of '66." *Publications of the Buffalo Historical Society* 25 (1921).

Silverman, Jason H. "Stars, Bars, and Foreigners: The Immigrant and the Making of the Confederacy." *Journal of Confederate History* 1, no. 2 (Fall 1988).

Smith, Harold F. "Mulligan and the Irish Brigade." *Journal of the Illinois State Historical Society* 56 (Summer 1963).

Smith, P. G. "Fenian Invasions of Canada." *Military History* 16, no. 6 (February 2000).

Stacey, C. P. "A Fenian Interlude: The Story of Michael Murphy." *Canadian Historical Review* 15, no. 2 (June 1934).

———. "Fenianism and the Rise of National Feeling in Canada at the Time Confederation." *Canadian Historical Review* 12, no. 2 (June 1931).

Steele, E. D. "Cardinal Cullen and Irish Nationality." *Irish Historical Studies* XIX, no.75 (March 1975).

Sweeny, Thomas W. "Official Report of Thomas W. Sweeny, Secretary of War, Fenian Brotherhood, and Commander-in-Chief of the Irish Republican Army." *Journal of the American Irish Historical Society* 23 (1924).

Sweeny, William. "Thomas Sweeny." *American Irish Historical Journal* 27 (1928).

Takagami, Shin-Ichi. "The Fenian Rising in Dublin, March 1867." *Irish Historical Studies* 29, no. 115 (May 1995).

Taylor, John M. "Fenian Raids against Canada." *American History Illustrated* 13, no. 5 (August 1978).

Vesey, Maxwell. "When New Brunswick Suffered Invasion." *Dalhousie Review* 19, no. 2 (1939).

Von Allendorfer, Frederic. "The Western Irish Brigade: 23rd Illinois Infantry Regiment." *Irish Sword* 2, no. 7 (Winter 1955).

Vroom, J. "The Fenians on the Saint Croix." *The Canadian Magazine of Politics, Science, Art and Literature* 10, no. 5 (March 1898).

Weddle, Kevin J. "Ethnic Discrimination in Minnesota Volunteer Regiments during the Civil War." *Civil War History* 35, no. 3 (September 1989).

Wertheimer, John. "The Green and the Black: Irish Nationalism and the Dilemma of Abolitionism." *New York Irish History* 5, no. 1 (1990–1991).

Theses and Dissertations

Brady, Kevin Thaddeus. "Fenians and the Faithful: Philadelphia's Irish Republican Brotherhood and the Diocese of Philadelphia, 1859–1870." PhD diss., Temple University, 1998.

Clevenger, Bryson Edward. "'Ireland and the Ultraradicals'" A Rhetoric of Engagement and Detachment in British Working-Class Ideology." PhD diss., University of Virginia, 2000.

Coyer, Richard Joseph. "Hero of the Armless Sleeve: The Military Career of Thomas W. Sweeny." PhD diss., University of San Diego, 1978.

Doan, Robert Alan. "Green Gold to the Emerald Shores: Irish Immigration to the United States and Transatlantic Monetary Aid, 1854–1923." PhD diss., Temple University, 1999.

Donohoe, Joan Marie. "The Irish Catholic Benevolent Union." PhD diss., Catholic University, 1953.

Griffin, Brian. "The I.R.B. in Connacht and Leinster, 1858–1878." Master's thesis, NUI Maynooth, 1983.

Kane, John J. "Irish Immigrants in Philadelphia: A Study in Conflict and Accommodation, 1840–1880." PhD diss., University of Pennsylvania, 1950.

Kelly, Mary C. "'Forty Shades of Green': Conflict over Community among New York's Irish, 1860–1920." PhD diss., Syracuse University, 1997.

Kennedy, Padraic Cummins. "Political Policing in a Liberal Age: Britain's Response to the Fenian Movement, 1858–1868." PhD diss., Washington University, 1996.

Knowlton, Steven R. "John Mitchel in America: The Desperate Protest of an Irish Exile." Master's thesis, University of Missouri Saint Louis, 1981.

Lowe, William J. "The Irish in Lancashire," PhD diss., Trinity College, Dublin, 1974.

Mahoney, James. "The Influence of Irish-Americans upon the Foreign Policy of the United States, 1865–1872." PhD diss., Worcester, Massachusetts: Clark University, 1959.

Mallaney, Michael P. "The Fenian Movement in Illinois during the Civil War Period, 1861–1868." Master's thesis, Eastern Illinois University, 1975.

O'Flaherty, Patrick D. "The History of the Sixty-Ninth Regiment in the Irish Brigade, 1861–1865." PhD diss., Fordham University, 1963.

Pieper, Ezra Henry. "The Fenian Movement." Thesis abstract, Urbana, Illinois, University of Illinois, 1931.

Quigley, Kevin. "American Financing of Fenianism in Ireland, 1858–67." Master's thesis, NUI-Maynooth, 1983.

Rogers, Bradley Alan. "Guardian of the Great Lakes: The U.S. Paddle Frigate Michigan, an Iron Archetype on the Inland Seas." PhD diss., The Union Institute, 1994.

Rubery, Paul Thomas. "The Fenian Movement in the United States." Master's thesis, Saint Bonaventure University, 1951.

Smith, Joe Patterson. "The Republican Expansionists of the Early Reconstruction Era." PhD diss., University of Chicago, 1930.

Stanton, Kevin. "Green Tint on Gold Bars: Irish Officers in the United States Army, 1865–1898." PhD diss., University of Colorado, 2001.

Teela, Robert Lewis. "Fenianism and Canada: A Contrast between the Fenian Policies of the Johnson and Grant Administrations." Master's thesis, Roosevelt University, 1970.

Williamson, Daniel C. "American Press Views of Fenianism, 1860–1870." Master's thesis, Villanova University, 1990.

Books

Ambrose, Stephen. *Nothing Like it in the World: The Men Who Built the Transcontinental Railroad, 1863–1869.* New York: Simon & Schuster, 2000.

Amos, Keith. *The Fenians in Australia: 1865–1880.* Kensington: New South Wales University Press, 1988.

Anbinder, Tyler. *Nativism and Slavery: The Northern Know-Nothings and the Politics of the 1850s.* New York: Oxford University Press, 1992.

Anderson, Benedict. *Imagined Communities: Reflections on the Origins and Spread of Nationalism.* New York: Verso Books, 1991.

Anderson, Robert. *A Great Conspiracy.* London: John Murray, 1910.

Beatty, Jack. *The Rascal King: The Life and Times of James Michael Curley.* Reading, MA: Addison-Wesley Publishing Company, 1992.

Bodnar, John. *The Transplanted: A History of Immigrants in Urban America*. Bloomington: Indiana University Press, 1985.

Ballou, Adin. *History of Milford*. Boston: Franklin Press, 1882.

Bauder, Roger. *The Catholic Church in Louisiana*. New Orleans: 1939.

Baum, Dale. *The Civil War Party System: The Case of Massachusetts, 1848–1876*. Chapel Hill: University of North Carolina Press, 1984.

Bayor, Ronald H., and Timothy J. Meagher eds. *The New York Irish*. Baltimore, MD: The Johns Hopkins University Press, 1996.

Beaudot William J. K., and Lance J. Herdegen. *An Irishman in the Iron Brigade*. New York: Fordham University Press, 1993.

Beringer, Richard E., Herman Hattaway, Archer Jones, and William N. Still. *The Elements of Confederate Defeat*. Athens: The University of Georgia Press, 1988.

Berkeley, George F.-H. *The Irish Battalion in the Papal Army of 1860*. Dublin: Talbot Press, 1929.

Bew, John, *The Glory of Being Britons: Civic Unionism in Nineteenth-Century Belfast*. Portland, OR: Irish Academic Press, 2009.

Blied, Benjamin J. *Catholics and the Civil War*. Milwaukee, WI: 1945.

Borthwick, J. Douglas. *History of the Montreal Prison from A.D. 1784 to A.D. 1886*. Montreal: A. Periard, 1886.

Bourke, Marcus. *John O'Leary: A Study in Irish Separatism*. Tralee: Anvil Books Limited, 1967.

Boyce, David George. *Nationalism in Ireland*. New York: Routledge, 1995.

Brady, Ciaran, ed. *Interpreting Irish History: The Debate on Historical Revisionism*. Blackrock: Irish Academic Press, 1994.

Brann, Henry A. *Most Reverend John Hughes*. New York: 1912.

Bridgers, Lynn. *Death's Deceiver: The Life of Joseph P. Machebeuf*. Albuquerque: University of New Mexico Press, 1997.

Brodsky, Alyn. *Grover Cleveland: A Study in Character*. New York: Saint Martin's Press, 2000.

Brooke, John. *The Heart of the Commonwealth: Society and Political Culture in Worcester County, Massachusetts, 1713–1861*. New York: Cambridge University Press, 1989.

Brown, Malcolm. *The Politics of Irish Literature: From Thomas Davis to W. B. Yeats*. London: Allen and Unwin, 1972.

Brown, Thomas. *Irish-American Nationalism, 1870–1890*. Philadelphia, PA: Lippincott Co., 1866.

Brusher, Joseph S. *The Fenian Invasions of Canada*. St. Louis: St. Louis University Press, 1943.

Buck, Irving A. *Cleburne and His Command*. Wilmington, NC: Broadfoot Publishers, 1995.

Burchell, R. A. *The San Francisco Irish*. Berkeley: University of California Press, 1980.

Burrows, Edwin G., and Mike Wallace. *Gotham: A History of New York City to 1898*. New York: Oxford University Press, 1999.

Burton, William L. *Melting Pot Soldiers: The Union's Ethnic Regiments*. Ames: Iowa State University Press, 1988.

Campbell, Francis Wayland. *The Fenian Invasions of Canada of 1866 and 1870*. Montreal: John Lovell and Son, 1904.

Cavanagh, Michael. *Memoirs of Thomas Francis Meagher*. Worcester, MA: The Messenger Press, 1892.

Cheng, Ronald Ye-Lin. *The Sociology of Revolution: Readings on Political Upheaval and Popular Unrest*. Chicago: Henry Regnery Company, 1973.

Clark, Dennis. *The Irish in Philadelphia Ten Generations of Urban Experience*. Philadelphia, PA: Temple University Press, 1973.

Clark, Samuel, and James S. Donnelly, eds. *Irish Peasants: Violence and Political Unrest, 1780–1914*. Madison: University of Wisconsin Press, 1983.

Clarke, Brian P. *Piety and Nationalism: Lay Voluntary Associations and the Creation of an Irish Catholic Community in Toronto*. Montreal: McGill University Press, 1993.

Cole, J. A. *Prince of Spies: Henri Le Caron*. Boston: Faber and Faber, 1984.

Comerford, R. V. *Charles J. Kickham: A Study in Irish Nationalism and Literature*. Portmarnock, Ireland: Wolfhound Press, 1979.

———. *The Fenians in Context: Irish Politics and Society, 1848–82*. Atlantic Highlands, NJ: Wolfhound Press, 1985.

Conley, Carolyn A. *Melancholy Accidents: The Meaning of Violence in Post-Famine Ireland*. New York: Lexington Books, 1999.

Conyngham, David P. *The Irish Brigade and its Campaigns*. New York: William McSorley and Company, 1867.

Cook, Adrain. *The Armies of the Streets: The New York City Draft Riots of 1863*. Lexington: The University of Kentucky Press, 1974.

Corfe, Thomas. *The Phoenix Park Murders: Conflict, Compromise and Tragedy in Ireland, 1879–1882*. London: Hodder and Stoughton, 1968.

Craig, Gordon A. *Europe Since 1815*. Hinsdale, IL: The Dryden Press, 1972.

Cronin, Sean. *Irish Nationalism: A History of its Roots and Ideology*. Dublin: The Academy Press, 1980.

Cuddihy, Patrick. *Short History of the Irish Catholics in Milford*. Milford, MA: Times Publishing Company, 1894.

Curtis, L. Perry. *Anglo-Saxons and Celts: A Study of Anti-Irish Prejudice in Victorian England*. New York: New York University Press, 1968.

D'Arcy, William. *The Fenian Movement in the United States, 1858–1886*. Washington, DC: Catholic University of America Press, 1947.

Davis Alan F., and Mark H. Haller, eds. *The Peoples of Philadelphia: A History of Ethnic Groups and Lower Class Life, 1790–1940*. Philadelphia, PA: Temple University Press, 1973.

Davis, Richard. *The Young Ireland Movement*. Totowa, NJ: Barnes and Noble, 1987.

Denieffe, Joseph. *A Personal Narrative of the Irish Republican Brotherhood*. Dublin: Irish University Press, 1969.

Devoy, John. *Recollections of an Irish Rebel*. Shannon: Irish University Press, 1969.

Dickson, R. J. *Ulster Emigration to Colonial America, 1718–1775*. London: Routledge and Kegan Paul, 1966.

Dolan, Jay P. *The Immigrant Church: New York's Irish and German Catholics, 1815–1865*. Baltimore, MD: Johns Hopkins University Press, 1975.

Donald, David Herbert. *Lincoln*. New York: Touchstone, 1995.

Doheny, Michael. *The Felon's Track: A Narrative of '48*. New York: Farrell and Son, 1867.

Doyle, David Noel. *Ireland, Irishmen, and Revolutionary America*. Dublin: The Mercier Press, 1981.

Dublin, Thomas. *Women at Work: The Transformation of Work and Community in Lowell, Massachusetts*. New York: Columbia University Press, 1979.

Duquemin, Colin K. "Banditti and Finnegans: The Niagara Invasions of '38 and '66." In *The Military in the Niagara Peninsula*, edited by Wesley B. Turner, 95–132. Saint Catherine's, Ontario: Vanwell Publishing Limited, 1990.

Dunaway, Wayland. *The Scotch Irish in Pennsylvania*. London: Archon Books, 1962.

Duncan, Russell, ed. *The Blue-Eyed Child of Fortune, The Civil War Letters of Robert Gould Shaw*. Athens: The University of Georgia Press, 1992.

Durkin, Joseph T. *John Dooley, Confederate Soldier*. Washington, DC: Georgetown University Press, 1945.

Elliot, Marianne. *Partners in Revolution: The United Irishmen and France*. New Haven, CT: Yale University Press, 1982.

Emery, Helen Fitch. *The Puritan Village Evolves: A History of Wayland Massachusetts*. Canaan, NH: Phoenix Publishing, 1981.

Evans, A. G. *Fanatic Heart: A Life of John Boyle O'Reilly, 1844–1890*. Boston: Northeastern University Press, 1999.

Evans, Howard. *Sir Randal Cremer: His Life and Work*. New York: Garland Publishing, 1973.

Feldberg, Michael. *The Philadelphia Riots of 1844: A Study of Ethnic Conflict*. Westport,Connecticut, Greenwood Press, 1975.

The Fenian Raid of 1870, by Reporters Present at the Scene. Montreal: 1871.

Ferris, Norman B. *The Trent Affair: A Diplomatic Crisis*. Knoxville: University of Tennessee Press, 1977.

Fitzgerald Margaret E., and Joseph King. *The Uncounted Irish in Canada and the United States*. Toronto: P.D. Meany Publishers, 1990.

Flynn, Elizabeth Gurley. *The Rebel Girl: An Autobiography*. New York: International Publishers, 1955.

Foner, Eric. *Free Soil, Free Labor, Free Men: The Ideology of the Republican Party Before the Civil War*. New York: Oxford University Press, 1970.

Forbes H. A. Crosby, and Henry Lee. *Massachusetts Help to Ireland during the Great Famine*. Milton, MA: Captain Robert Bennet Forbes House, 1967.

Ford, Henry Jones. *The Scotch Irish in America*. Hamden, CT: Archon Books, 1915.

Foster, R. R. *Modern Ireland, 1600–1972*. New York: Penguin Putnam, 1990.

Funchion, Michael F. *Chicago's Irish Nationalists, 1881–1890*. New York: Arno Press, 1976.

Funchion, Michael F., ed. *Irish American Voluntary Organizations*. Westport, CT: Greenwood Press, 1983.

Galtung, Johan. *A Structural Theory of Revolutions*. Rotterdam: Rotterdam University Press, 1974.

Galwey, Thomas Francis. *The Valiant Hours*. Harrisburg, PA: The Stackpole Company, 1961.

Garand, Philias. *The History of the City of Ogdensburg*. Ogdensburg, NY: Rev. Manuel J. Belleville, 1927.

Garvin, Tom. *The Evolution of Irish Nationalist Politics*. New York: Holmes and Meier Publishers, 1981.

Geary, Lawrence, ed., *Rebellion and Remembrance in Modern Ireland*. Dublin: Four Courts Press, 2001.

Gallman, J. Matthew. *Mastering Wartime: A Social History of Philadelphia during the Civil War*. New York: Cambridge University Press, 1990.

Gallman, J. Matthew. *Receiving Erin's Children: Philadelphia, Liverpool, and the Irish Famine Migration. 1845–1855*. Chapel Hill: University of North Carolina Press, 2000.

Gleeson, David Thomas. *The Irish in the South, 1815–1877*. Chapel Hill: University of North Carolina Press, 2001.

Gleeson, Ed. *Rebel Sons of Erin: A Civil War Unit History of the Tenth Tennessee Infantry Regiment (Irish) Confederate States Volunteers*. Indianapolis, IN: Guild Press, 1993.

Golway, Terry. *Irish Rebel: John Devoy and America's Fight for Ireland's Freedom*. New York: Saint Martin's Press, 1998.

Gordon, Michael A. *The Orange Riots: Irish Political Violence in New York City*. Ithaca, NY: Cornell University Press, 1993.

Goyne, Minetta Altgelt, ed. *Lone Star and Double Eagle: Civil War Letters of a German Texas Family*. Fort Worth: Texas Christian University Press, 1982.

Gray, Peter. *Famine, Land and Politics: British Government and Irish Society*. Portland, OR: Irish Academic Press, 1999.

Gregg George R., and E. P. Roden, *Trials of the Fenian Prisoners at Toronto*. Toronto: Leader Steam Press, 1867.

Greer, Allan. *The Patriots and the People: The Rebellion of 1837 in Rural Lower Canada*. Toronto: University of Toronto Press, 1993.

Hammond, J. L. *Gladstone and the Irish Nation*. Hamdon, CT: Archon Books, 1964.

Hanchett, William. *Irish: Charles G. Halpine in Civil War America*. Syracuse: Syracuse University Press, 1970.

Handlin, Oscar. *Boston's Immigrants: A Study in Acculturation*. Cambridge, MA: Harvard University Press, 1979.

———. *The Uprooted: The Epic Story of the Great Migrations that made the American People*. Boston: Little, Brown and Company, 1951.

Hastings, Adrian. *The Construction of Nationhood: Ethnicity, Religion, and Nationalism*. New York: Cambridge University Press, 1997.

Henthorne, Mary Evangela. *The Irish Catholic Colonization Association of the United States*. Champaign, IL: The Twin City Printing Company, 1932.

Hernon, Joseph M. *Celts, Catholics and Copperheads: Ireland Views the American Civil War*. Columbus, OH: Ohio State University Press, 1968.

Ignatiev, Noel. *How the Irish Became White*. New York: Routledge, 1995.

Jackson, Alvin. *Ireland: 1798–1998, Politics and War*. Malden, MA: Blackwell Publishers Inc., 1999.

Jackson, Carlton. *A Social History of the Scots-Irish*. New York: Madison Books, 1993.

Jacobson, Matthew Frye. *Special Sorrows: The Diasporic Imagination of Irish, Polish, and Jewish Immigrants in the United States*. Cambridge, MA: Harvard University Press, 1995.

———. *Whiteness of a Different Color: European Immigrants and the Alchemy of Race*. Cambridge, MA: Harvard University Press, 1999.

James Stephens, Chief Organizer of the Irish Republic. New York: Carleton, 1866.

Jenkins, Brian. *The Fenians and Anglo-American Relations During Reconstruction*. Ithaca, NY: Cornell University Press, 1969.

Jenkins, Roy. *Gladstone: A Biography*. New York: Random House, 1997.

Jones, Terry L. *Lee's Tigers: The Louisiana Infantry in the Army of Northern Virginia*. Baton Rouge: Louisiana State University Press, 1987.

Jones, Paul. *The Irish Brigade*. London: New English Library, 1971.

Jordan, Donald. *Land and Popular Politics in Ireland*. New York: Cambridge University Press, 1994.

Kee, Robert. *The Green Flag: The Turbulent History of the Irish Nationalist Movement*. New York: Delacorte Press, 1972.

———. *The Laurel and the Ivy: The Story of Charles Stewart Parnell and Irish Nationalism*. New York: Penguin Books, 1994.

Keneally, Thomas. *The Great Shame: A Story of the Irish in the Old World and the New*. London: Chatto and Windus, 1998.

Kenny, Kevin. *Making Sense of the Molly Maguires*. New York: Oxford University Press, 1997.

Kenny, Michael. *The Fenians: Photographs and Memorabilia from the National Museum of Ireland*. Dublin: Town House and Country House, 1994.

Kinealy, Christine. *This Great Calamity: The Irish Famine 1845–1852*. Boulder, CO: Roberts Rinehart Publishers, 1995.

Knobel, Dale. *Paddy and the Republic Ethnicity and Nationality in Antebellum America*. Middleton, CT: Wesleyan University Press, 1986.

Koditschek, Theodore. *Class Formation and Urban-Industrial Society: Bradford, 1750–1850*. New York: Cambridge University Press, 1990.

Kohl, Lawrence Frederick, ed. *Irish Green and Union Blue: The Civil War Letters of Peter Welsh*. New York: Fordham University Press, 1986.

Lees, Lynn Hollen. *Exiles of Erin: Irish Migrants in Victorian London*. Ithaca, New York: Cornell University Press, 1979.

Lonn, Ella. *Foreigners in the Confederacy*. Chapel Hill: University of North Carolina Press, 1940.

———. *Foreigners in the Union Army and Navy*. Baton Rouge: Louisiana State University Press, 1952.

Lott, Eric. *Love and Theft: Blackface Minstrelsy and the American Working Class*. New York: Oxford University Press, 1993.

Lowe, W. J. *The Irish in Mid-Victorian Lancashire: The Shaping of a Working-Class Community*. New York: Peter Lang, 1989.

Luddy, Maria. *Women and Philanthropy in Nineteenth Century Ireland*. New York: Cambridge University Press, 1995.

Lynch, Mary C., and Seamus O'Donoghue, *O'Sullivan Burke, Fenian*. Carrigadrohid, County Cork: Ebony Jane Press, 1999.

Lyons, F. S. L. *Ireland Since the Famine*. New York: Charles Scribner's Sons, 1971.

MacDonagh, Oliver. W. F. Mandle, and Pauric Travers, eds. *Irish Culture and Nationalism, 1750–1950*. New York: Saint Martin's Press, 1983.

MacDonald, Feargus. *The Catholic Church and The Secret Societies in the United States*. New York: United States Catholic Historical Society, 1946.

MacDonald, John A. *Troublous Times in Canada: A History of the Fenian Raids of 1866 and 1870*. Toronto: W.S. Johnson and Company, 1910.

MacKillop, James. *Fionn mac Cumhaill: Celtic Myth in English Literature*. Syracuse: Syracuse University Press, 1986.

MacLean, John C. *A Rich Harvest: The History, Buildings, and People of Lincoln, Massachusetts*. Lincoln, MT: Lincoln Historical Society, 1987.

MacManus, Seumas. *The Story of the Irish Race*. Old Greenwich, CT: The Devin-Adair Company, 1992

Marx, Karl, and Friedrich Engels. *Ireland and the Irish Question*. New York: International Publishers, 1972.

Maynard, Theodore. *The Story of American Catholicism*. New York: MacMillan 1941.

McCaffrey, Lawrence J., Ellen Skerret, Michael F. Funchion, and Charles Fanning, *The Irish in Chicago*. Chicago: University of Illinois Press, 1987.

McDonald, M. Justille. *History of the Irish in Wisconsin in the Nineteenth Century*. Washington, DC: The Catholic University of America Press, 1954.

McGee, Robert Franklin. *The Fenian Raids on the Huntingdon Frontier, 1866 and 1870*. Author. 1967.

McGee, Thomas D'Arcy. *An Account of the Attempts to Establish Fenianism in Montreal*. Montreal: Post Publishing and Printing Company, 1882.

McGovern, Bryan P. *John Mitchel: Irish Nationalist and Southern Secessionist.* Knoxville: University of Tennessee Press, 2009.

McGrath, Walter. *A Cork Felon (The Life and Death of Brian Dillon).* Cork: Brian Dillon Commemoration Committee, 1952.

McKay, Ernest A. *The Civil War and New York City.* Syracuse: Syracuse University Press, 1990.

McL Côté, Jane. *Fanny and Anna Parnell: Ireland's Patriot Sisters.* New York: St. Martin's Press, 1991.

McMicken, Gilbert. *An Abortive Raid: An Irish Republic in Manitoba Planned but Crushed Early.* Winnipeg: Manitoba Free Press Print, 1888.

McPherson James, ed. *The American Heritage New History of the Civil War.* New York: Viking, 1996.

McPherson, James. *For Cause and Comrades: Why Men Fought in the Civil War.* New York: Oxford University Press, 1997.

——. *Ordeal by Fire: The Civil War and Reconstruction.* New York: Alfred A. Knopf, 1982.

Meade, George Gordon. *The Life and Letters of George Meade.* New York: Charles Scribner's Sons, 1913.

Miller, Kerby. *Emigrants and Exiles: Ireland and the Irish Exodus to North America.* New York: Oxford University Press, 1985.

Miller, Randall M., Harry S. Stout, and Charles Reagan Wilson, eds. *Religion and the American Civil War.* New York: Oxford University Press, 1998.

Montgomery, David. *Beyond Equality: Labor and the Radical Republicans, 1862–1872.* New York: Alfred A. Knopf, 1967.

Moody T. W., ed. *The Fenian Movement.* Cork: Mercier Press, 1978.

Moody T. W., and F. X. Martin, eds. *The Course of Irish History.* Niwot, CO: Roberts Rinehart Publishers, 1995.

Morgan, Jack. *Whistle up the Marching Tune: The Life and Times of Thomas W. Sweeny.* Fort Lauderdale, FL: Nova University Press, 1994.

Morice, A. G. *The Catholic Church in Western Canada.* Toronto: The Musson Book Company, 1910.

Mulkern, John. *The Know-Nothing Party in Massachusetts.* Boston: Northeastern University Press, 1990.

Murray, Thomas Hamilton. *History of the Ninth Regiment, Connecticut Volunteer Infantry.* New Haven: Price, Lee, and Adkins Company, 1903.

Mushkat, Jerome. *Fernando Wood: A Political Biography*. Kent, OH: The Kent University Press, 1990.

Nairn, Tom. *The Break-Up of Britain: Crisis and Neo-Nationalism*. London, NLB, 1981.

Neidhardt, Wilfried. *Fenianism in North America*. University Park: Pennsylvania State University Press, 1975.

Nevins, Allan. *Hamilton Fish: The Inner History of the Grant Administration*. New York: F. Ungar Publishing, 1957.

Newsinger, John. *Fenianism in Mid-Victorian Britain*. Boulder, CO: Pluto Press, 1994.

Norman, Edward. R. *The Catholic Church and Ireland in the Age of Rebellion, 1859–1873*. Ithaca, NY: Cornell University Press, 1965.

Oberholtzer, Ellis Paxson. *Jay Cooke, Financier of the Civil War*, Vol 1. Philadelphia, PA: George W. Jacobs, 1907.

O'Brien William, and Desmond Ryan. *Devoy's Post-Bag, 1871–1928*. Dublin: C.J. Fallon Limited, 1948.

ÓBrion, León. *Fenian Fever: An Anglo-American* Dilemma. New York: New York University Press, 1971.

O'Callaghan, John Cornelius. *History of the Irish Brigades in the Service of France*. Shannon: Irish University Press, 1968.

O'Conner, Thomas. *Civil War Boston: Homefront and Battlefield*. Boston: Northeastern University Press, 1997.

O'Connor, John. *Letters of John O'Connor, MP on Fenianism Addressed to his Excellency*. Toronto: Hunter Rose and Company, 1870.

O'Connor, Kevin. *The Irish in Britain*. London: Sedgewick and Jackson, 1972.

O'Hegarty, Patrick Sarsfield. *Ireland Under the Union, 1801–1922*. London: Methuen and Company, 1952.

O'Laughlin, Michael C. *Irish Settlers on the American Frontier*. Kansas City, MO: Irish Genealogical Foundation, 1984.

O'Rourke, Kevin. *Currier and Ives: The Irish in America*. New York: H. N. Abrams, 1995.

O'Sullivan, Patrick, ed. *The Creative Immigrant*. Vol. 3. Leicester: Leicester University Press, 1994.

Owen, David. *The Year of the Fenians*. Buffalo: Western New York Heritage Institute, 1990.

Paludin, Philip Shaw. *A People's Contest: The Union and Civil War*. New York: Harper and Row, 1988.

Pease, Zephaniah Walt. *The Catalpa Expedition*. New Bedford, MA: George S. Anthony, 1897.

Peiss, Kathy Lee. *Cheap Amusements: Working Women and Leisure in Turn-of-the-Century New York*. Philadelphia, PA: Temple University Press, 1986.

Phillips, Arthur C. *Fort Erie: An Historical Romance of the Fenian Invasion of Canada*. Buffalo, NY: McCarroll and Company, 1868.

Powderly, Terence V. *The Path I Trod*. New York: Ames Press, 1968.

Purdue, Elizabeth, and Howell Purdue. *Pat Cleburne, Confederate General*. Hillsboro, TX: Hill Junior College Press, 1973.

Quinliven, Patrick, and Paul Rose. *The Fenians in England: A Sense of Insecurity*. New York: Riverrun Press, 1982.

Rafferty, Oliver P. *The Church, the State, and the Fenian Threat, 1861–75*. New York: Saint Martin's Press, 1999.

Rayner, Denis Arthur, and Alan Wykes. *The Great Yacht Race*. London: Peter Davies Limited, 1966.

Regan, Ann. *Irish in Minnesota*. Saint Paul: Minnesota Historical Society Press, 2002.

Reedy, George. *From the Ward to the White House: The Irish in American Politics*. New York: Charles Scribner's Sons, 1991.

Rice, Charles T. *A Phase of Fenianism in Ireland: The Movement in Monaghan*. Monaghan: R. & S. Printers, 1956.

Richter, Donald C. *Riotous Victorians*. Athens: Ohio University Press, 1981.

Roberts, William R. *Enforcement of the Fourteenth Amendment-Ku Klux Legislation Bayonets vs. Freedom*. Washington, DC: F & J Rives and George A. Bailey, 1871.

Roediger, David. *The Wages of Whiteness: Race and the Making of the American Working Class*. New York: Verso Books, 1999.

Roney, Frank. *Irish Rebel and California Labor Leader*. New York: AMS Press, 1977.

Rose, Paul. *The Manchester Martyrs: The Story of a Fenian Tragedy*. London: Lawrence and Wishart, 1970.

Rosenburg, Charles E. *The Cholera Years: The United States in 1832, 1849, and 1866*. Chicago, IL: University of Chicago Press, 1987.

Ryan, Dennis P. *Beyond the Ballot Box*. Amherst: University of Massachusetts Press, 1983.

Ryan, Desmond. *The Fenian Chief: A Biography of James Stephens*. Dublin: Sydney, Gill and Son, 1967.

———. *The Phoenix Flame: A Study of Fenianism and John Devoy*. London: A. Barker Limited, 1937.

Samito, Christian G., ed. *Commanding Boston's Irish Ninth: The Civil War Letters of Colonel Patrick R, Guiney*. New York: Fordham University Press, 1998.

Schrier, Arnold. *Ireland and the American Emigration, 1850–1900*. Minneapolis: University of Minnesota Press, 1958.

Scroggs, William O. *Filibusterers and Financiers: The Story of William Walker and his Associates*. New York: The MacMillan Company, 1916.

Seagrave, Pia Seija, ed. *The History of the Irish Brigade: A Collection of Historical Essays*. Fredericksburg, VA: Sergeant Kirkland's Museum and Historical Society, 1997.

Senior, Hereward. *The Fenians and Canada*. Toronto: MacMillan of Canada, 1978.

———. *The Last Invasion of Canada: The Fenian Raids, 1866-1870*. Toronto: Dundurn Press, 1991.

Shannon, Richard. *Gladstone*, Vol. 2. Chapel Hill: University of North Carolina Press, 1999.

Shannon, William V. *The American Irish*. New York: MacMillan, 1963.

Shaw, Richard. *Dagger John: The Unquiet Life and Times of Archbishop Hughes of New York*. New York: Paulist Press, 1977.

Short, K. R. M. *The Dynamite War: Irish-American Bombers in Victorian Britain*. Atlantic Highlands, NJ: Humanities Press, 1979.

Sillard, P. A. *The Life and Letters of John Martin*. Dublin: James Duffy and Company, 1901.

Skine, Francis Henry. *Fontenoy and Great Britain's Share in the War of the Austrian Succession, 1741–1748*. London: William Blackwood and Sons, 1906.

Smith, Jeffrey H. *A Frenchman Fights for the Union: Victor Vifquain and the 97th Illinois*. Varna, IL: Patrick Publishing, 1992.

Soltow, Lee. *Men and Wealth in the United States, 1850–1870*. New Haven, CT: Yale University Press, 1975.

Spann, Edward K. *Gotham at War: New York City, 1860–1865*. Wilmington, DE: Scholarly Resources, 2002.

Spencer, Warren F. *The Confederate Navy in Europe*. Tuscaloosa: University of Alabama Press, 1983.

Sperber, Jonathan. *The European Revolutions, 1848–1851*. New York: Cambridge University Press, 1994.

Stampp, Kenneth M. *The Imperiled Union Essays on the Background of the Civil War*. New York: Oxford University Press, 1980.

Sullivan, C. W. III, ed. *Fenian Diary: Denis B. Cashman on Board* The Hougoumont. Dublin: Wolfhound Press, 2001.

Sullivan, T. D. *The Dock and the scaffold: the Manchester tragedy and the Cruise of the Jacknell.* Dublin: A. M. Sullivan, 1868.

Swift, Roger, and Sheridan Gilley, eds. *The Irish in the Victorian City.* Dover, New Hampshire: Croom Helm, 1985.

Symonds, Craig, L. *Stonewall Jackson of the West: Patrick Cleburne and the Civil War.* Lawrence: University Press of Kansas, 1997.

Taylor, John M. *William Henry Seward: Lincoln's Right Hand Man.* New York: HarperCollins, 1991.

Taylor, Richard. *Destruction and Reconstruction: Personal Experiences of the Late War.* Waltham, MA: Blaisdell Publishing Company, 1968.

Thernstrom, Stephan. *The Other Bostonians.* Cambridge, MA: Harvard University Press, 1973.

———. *Poverty and Progress: Social Mobility in a Nineteenth Century City.* Cambridge, MA: Harvard University Press, 1964.

A Third Supply of Yankee Drolleries. London: John Camden Hotten, 1866.

Thornley, David. *Isaac Butt and Home Rule.* London: MacGibbon and Kee, 1964.

Townsend, George Alfred. *Rustics in Rebellion: A Yankee Reporter on the Road to Richmond.* Chapel Hill: University of North Carolina Press, 1950.

Trefousse, Hans Louis, *Andrew Johnson: A Biography.* New York: Norton, 1989.

Tucker, Philip Thomas. *The Confederacy's Fighting Chaplain: Father John B. Bannon.* Tuscaloosa: University of Alabama Press, 1992.

Van Deusen, Glyndon G. *William Henry Seward.* New York: Oxford University Press, 1967.

Wakin, Edward. *Enter the Irish-American.* New York: Crowell, 1976.

Walker, Brian M., ed. *Parliamentary Election Results in Ireland, 1801–1922.* Dublin: Royal Irish Academy, 1978.

Walker, Mabel Gregory. *The Fenian Movement.* Colorado Springs, CO: R. Myles, 1969.

Ware, Norman. *The Industrial Worker.* Chicago, IL: Quadrangle Books, 1964.

Warren, Gordon H. *Fountain of Discontent: The Trent Affair and Freedom of the Seas.* Boston: Northeastern University Press, 1981.

Weintraub, Stanley. *Disraeli: A Biography.* New York: Truman Tally, 1993.

West, Lois A., ed., *Feminist Nationalism.* New York: Routledge, 1997.

Wiley, Bell Irwin. *The Common Soldier in the Civil War.* New York: Grosset and Dunlap, 1952.

———. *The Life of Billy Yank: The Common Soldier of the Union*. New York: Bobbs-Merrill, 1952.

Williamson, Christopher L., transcriber, *The Journals of Daniel Finn*. 1992.

Wilkenson, Warren. *Mother, May You Never See the Sights I have Seen: The Fifty Seventh Massachusetts Veteran Volunteers in the Army of the Potomac*. New York: Harper and Row, 1990.

Winchester, Simon. *The Professor and the Madman*. New York: HarperCollins Publishers, 1998.

Wittke, Carl. *The Irish in America*. Baton Rouge: Louisiana State University Press, 1956.

Woodward C. Vann, ed., *Mary Chestnut's Civil War*. New Haven, CT: Yale University Press, 1981.

Woodworth, Steven E. *The Loyal. True, and Brave: America's Civil War Soldiers*. Wilmington, DE: SR Books, 2002.

Wubben, Hubert H. *Civil War Iowa and the Copperhead Movement*. Ames: Iowa State University Press, 1980.

Wyman, Mark. *Round Trip to America: The Immigrants Return to Europe, 1880–1930*. Ithaca, NY: Cornell University Press, 1993.

Young, Robert W. *James Murray Mason: Defender of the Old South*. Knoxville, TN: The University of Tennessee Press, 1998.

Reference Materials

Biographical Directory of the United States Congress

Congressional Directory, 42nd Congress Second Edition

Congressional Directory, 43rd Congress Second Edition

Congressional Globe, Thirty-Ninth Congress

Dictionary of American Biography. New York: Charles Scribner's Sons, 1946.

The American Annual Cyclopedia and Register of Important Events. New York: D. Appleton and Company, 1866.

INDEX

Wilkes, Charles, 45–46
Wilson, Henry, 110
Winooski, 114–15
Wisconsin, 98, 122, 130, 221
Witherow, Joseph, 99
Wolfe, Bartholomew, 202
Wolfe, General James, 119
Wood, Fernando, 98

Wood, James Frederick, 66–67, 78, 187
Wordsworth, William, 17
World War I, 220, 229, 233–34
Woulfe, Maurice, 54–55, 110, 141, 159, 187

Young Ireland, xii–xiv, 1–10, 17–24, 44, 54, 58,
    90–93, 112, 144, 173, 231